The civil service and the revolution in Ireland, 1912–38

MANCHESTER
1824

Manchester University Press

The civil service and the revolution in Ireland, 1912–38

'Shaking the blood-stained hand of Mr Collins'

Martin Maguire

Manchester University Press
Manchester and New York
Distributed exclusively in the USA by Palgrave

Published by Manchester University Press
Oxford Road, Manchester M13 9NR, UK
and Room 400, 175 Fifth Avenue, New York, NY 10010, USA
www.manchesteruniversitypress.co.uk

Distributed exclusively in the USA by
Palgrave, 175 Fifth Avenue, New York,
NY 10010, USA

Distributed exclusively in Canada by
UBC Press, University of British Columbia, 2029 West Mall,
Vancouver, BC, Canada V6T 1Z2

British Library Cataloguing-in-Publication Data
A catalogue record for this book is available from the British Library

Library of Congress Cataloging-in-Publication Data applied for

ISBN   978 0 7190 7740 1 *hardback*

First published 2008

17 16 15 14 13 12 11 10 09 08   10 9 8 7 6 5 4 3 2 1

Typeset in Minion 10.5/12.5pt
by Servis Filmsetting Ltd, Manchester
Printed in Great Britain
by CPI Antony Rowe Ltd, Chippenham, Wiltshire

Contents

Acknowledgements

This book and the original Ph.D. thesis on which it is based have been shaped through discussion with my supervisor Professor Eunan O'Halpin and with my colleagues in the Contemporary Irish History seminar at Trinity College Dublin; my first debt of gratitude is to them. I would like to record my thanks to the archivists of the National Archives Ireland, especially Tom Quinlan and Mary Markey; the staff of the National Library Ireland in both the reading room and the manuscripts room; of Trinity College Library; Séamus Helferty and the staff of the University College Dublin Archives Department; Theresa Moriarity of the Irish Labour History Archive and Museum; Christine Woodland in the Modern Records Centre at the University of Warwick; the staff at National Archives in London; the British Library; the Bodleian Library at Oxford; the Wiltshire and Swindon Record Office and the Public Record Office Northern Ireland. I would also wish to thank Mr James McGuire for facilitating access to the database under preparation for the Royal Irish Academy Dictionary of Irish Biography.

For granting access to sources in private collections I record my thanks to Mary Murphy for the records of the Civil Service Clerical Association held by the Civil and Public Services Union; to Shay Cody for the records of the Institution of Professional Civil Servants, held by IMPACT Union; to Dan Murphy for the records of the Customs and Excise Federation held by the Public Services Executive Union; and for access to the memoir of Michael Gallagher I thank his son Fr Colm Gallagher, Arklow, Co. Wicklow.

Individuals who have offered critical responses to the work and to whom I offer my thanks are Professor Michael Laffan, Professor W.E. Vaughan, Professor David Fitzpatrick, Dr Deirdre McMahon and Dr Daithí Ó'Corráin.

I would like to record my gratitude to the management of Dundalk Institute of Technology and especially to all my colleagues in the Department of Humanities for their support and encouragement. My thanks also to the editorial staff at Manchester University Press for their guidance in seeing the book to print.

This research was funded by an Irish Research Council for the Humanities and Social Sciences (IRCHSS) Senior Research Scholarship. I would like to record my thanks to the IRCHSS for the award without which the research would not have been possible.

My final and most profound debt of gratitude is to Celia and it is to her and to Nora and Betty that the work is dedicated.

Abbreviations

ACA	Assistant Clerks' Association
AEO	Association of Executive Officers
ASCOCS	Association of Staff Clerks and Other Civil Servants
CDB	Congested Districts Board
CEA	Customs and Excise Association
COA	Clerical Officers' Association
CPSU	Civil and Public Services Union
CSA	Civil Service Alliance
CSCA	Civil Service Clerical Association
CSF	Civil Service Federation
CSO	Chief Secretary's Office
CSRC	Civil Service Representative Council
DATI	Department of Agriculture and Technical Instruction
DMOA	Dublin Municipal Officers' Association
DMP	Dublin Metropolitan Police
GAA	Gaelic Athletic Association
GCICS	General Committee of Irish Civil Servants
GVO	General Valuation Office
HLRO	House of Lords Record Office
ILC	Irish Land Commission
ILGOU	Irish Local Government Officers' Trade Union
ILPTUC	Irish Labour Party and Trade Union Congress
IPCS	Institute of Professional Civil Servants (Ireland)
IRB	Irish Republican Brotherhood
LGB	Local Government Board
NA	National Archives, London
NAI	National Archives Ireland
NEB	National Education Board
NHIC	National Health Insurance Commission
NLI	National Library of Ireland
OPW	Office of Public Works

POCA   Post Office Clerks' Association
POWU   Post Office Workers' Union
PRONI   Public Record Office Northern Ireland
RIC   Royal Irish Constabulary
TCD   Trinity College Dublin
TD   Teachta Dála
TOPA   Transferred Officers' Protection Association
UCDAD   University College Dublin Archives Department
UVF   Ulster Volunteer Force
WSRO   Wiltshire and Swindon Record Office
WUMRC   Warwick University Modern Records Centre

Note: Nationalist and Unionist is used to denote members of political parties, nationalist and unionist is used to denote supporters and sympathisers.

Introduction

THIS BOOK BEGAN AS research into two contradictory accounts of the process by which an Irish State replaced the British State in Ireland. On the one hand there is Kevin O'Higgins, a minister in the Provisional Government, describing Ireland in 1922 thus:

> there was no State and no organized forces. The Provisional Government was simply eight young men in the City Hall standing amidst the ruins of one administration with the foundations of another not yet laid, and with wild men screaming through the keyhole. No police force was functioning through the country, no system of justice was operating, the wheels of administration hung idle battered out of recognition by the clash of rival jurisdictions.[1]

On the other hand there is the magisterial calm of Joseph Brennan, who had been a senior civil servant in Dublin at the handover. In 1936, in remembering the transfer of power, he wrote:

> The passing of the State services into the control of a native Government, however revolutionary it may have been as a step in the political development of the nation, entailed, broadly speaking, no immediate disturbance of any fundamental kind in the daily work of the average Civil Servant. Under changed masters the main tasks of administration continued to be performed by the same staffs on the same general line of organisation and procedure.[2]

O'Higgins described a failed State collapsing into ruin. Brennan, on the other hand, described a smoothly running State machine handed over intact into new hands. Can both these contradictory accounts be both correct and accurate? Which is closer to the truth?

Traditional nationalist interpretations of the process of State-building tended toward the O'Higgins view of smoking ruins and revolutionary violence. The modern Irish State emerged out of revolution and State-building in independent Ireland was from the ground up, starting anew. Depending on how the Treaty is interpreted this process is seen as being either ultimately successful or ultimately thwarted. Revisionist interpretations of the process give considerable significance to the Brennan view of essential continuity. According to this view the independent State ensured its stability by abandoning the chimera of revolution and merely assuming control of the levers of power of the existing regime. Thus it is argued that what happened was hardly in fact a revolution at all, merely the transfer of the existing State from one political authority to another; very much a case of business as usual.

This book sets out to answer these questions of revolution or continuity through a close examination of the role and fate of the civil service in the process of State-building. It questions whether the new government did simply retain the same civil service, given that every other institution of the British State in Ireland was abolished – parliament, executive, judiciary, police and the military. If that was the case, as many historians argue, then why did the new Irish government readily accept what was described as an anti-Irish, extravagant, corrupt and rundown apparatus? Had the civil service that was condemned in May 1920 as unworkable been successfully rebuilt into a modern and efficient machine in a mere eighteen months? That transformation would in itself be remarkable. If so, how was it achieved? What sort of relationship bound the civil service firstly to the British State and then to the new Irish State which replaced it? What did the civil service of the Dublin Castle regime itself think of the new government and what was its relationship with the infant civil service of the underground counter-State of the revolutionaries? Finally and simply, what was it like for the civil service to be embroiled in a revolution, or even a counter-revolution?

The rhetoric of the Irish revolutionaries of this period was focused on the 'nation', an appealing trope that was modern, vague and abstract. The Irish State, unlike the nation, was a concrete, ancient and visible institution.[3] The Irish State, which had its beginning in the twelfth-century lordship of Ireland, was centralised in the sixteenth-century Kingdom of Ireland. The 1801 Union of Great Britain and Ireland incorporated the Irish State into the new United Kingdom under the sovereignty of Westminster. However, the continuance of a separate Irish executive and administration quickly emerged as an anomaly. Despite the legislative Union and the presence of Irish MPs at Westminster, the administration of Ireland was 'distinctly colonial in form and function'.[4] In fact the truly anomalous element in the relationship between Ireland and Great Britain became the presence of Irish MPs at Westminster. Strip away this redundancy and the unequal and colonial nature of the relationship is clear. Typical of a colonial administration, control relied more on coercion than on consent.[5]

In Ireland, physically and metaphorically, the State was identified with its location, Dublin Castle. In Ireland the representative of the Crown lived in a lodge, bishops lived in a palace, and the State resided in a Castle. At the head of the Irish administration was the Lord Lieutenant, representing the Crown.

The Lord Lieutenant had all the trappings of a monarch with a court and gentlemen-in-waiting, but he did not preside over a parliament. Unlike the Crown the Lord Lieutenant was a political appointment, taken up and vacated with the ruling political party at Westminster. Again, unlike the non-political Crown, the Lord Lieutenant occupied several politically powerful posts as head of the government boards, he exercised independent political judgement and he gave an account of his ministry to parliament. The Chief Secretary Ireland was also a political office and one whose authority overlapped with that of the Lord Lieutenant in the government of Ireland. He was, however, secretary to the Lord Lieutenant and did not function with the authority of the Scottish Secretary, created in 1885. Usually but not invariably the Chief Secretary Ireland, and not the Lord Lieutenant, sat at the cabinet. The actual running of the Irish administration was split between Dublin Castle and the Irish Office in Whitehall.

Reform of the Irish administration was taken by some to mean the abolition of the lord lieutenancy, regarded as an obsolete 'Irish Court', and its substitution by promoting the Chief Secretary to the cabinet as a powerful Secretary of State for Ireland. The abolition of the Irish lord lieutenancy achieved the status of a hardy perennial regularly proposed in parliament.[6] The posts of Under-Secretary and Assistant Under-Secretary were developed as essentially civil service posts where the Assistant Under-Secretary in particular was to be thoroughly acquainted with the whole of the detailed arrangements of the administration of Ireland office. The Under-Secretary was considered head of the Irish civil service.[7]

'Castle Government', the generally used metaphor for British administration in Ireland since at least the time of Edmund Burke, suggested medievalism, secretiveness, a fortress of tyrannical and unaccountable power exercising a malevolent influence from within its labyrinthine corridors. Political discourse on Castle government was consistently critical. Whitehall was the butt of good-natured satire, the Castle of bitter invective. For all shades of political opinion the Castle symbolised everything that was wrong with Irish government.

Administrative reforms that imposed examination entry, formal qualifications, promotion by merit and hierarchies of responsibility had transformed the British civil service into a discipline of non-political bureaucratic practices available equally to whatever party happened to be in power. The State became an organised machinery of policy-making in response to demands in society, which was the role of elected politicians, and policy-enactment, which was the role of properly appointed civil servants. By impartially applying policies determined by their political masters the civil service negotiated the complex interaction between State and society and legitimised the exercise of power by elected politicians. The civil service was bound to the State as a discipline of policy advice and policy execution. In return the State granted permanent and secure status for its civil servants with a pension at retirement. A professional, non-political civil service drawn from the best in the British education system and available to the government in power regardless of its political complexion became a British national institution.

In contrast, the space between the civil servant and the politician, and between the State and society, remained ill-defined in Ireland. Under the Union Ireland had developed a strong bureaucracy that acted as the conduit for British influences and ideas. Though increasingly complex, the civil service in Dublin Castle remained highly politicised by the sectarian divisions in Irish society and by the political divisions on the Home Rule question. It was also distant from the source of its authority in London. Though Ireland had all the apparatus that signalled a powerful State – a militarised police force, a legal-judicial system and an administrative complex of government departments run by a civil service housed in Dublin Castle – the State as representing the whole of civil society, the community, was weak. The British State in Ireland received only the tacit consent of most Irish opinion. The Irish civil service could successfully deliver all that was demanded of it in applying policies on land transfers, regional development in the impoverished west, local government and public health reform, educational development and all the other tasks set by an interventionist British State. What it could not do was make that State accepted as the legitimate government in Ireland.

This book, therefore, is a history of the relationship that bound the civil service and the State in Ireland to each other in the period from the beginning of the third Home Rule crisis in 1912, through the years of revolution and partition and the establishment of the Irish Free State under the 1921 Anglo-Irish Treaty, to the enactment in 1937 of *Bunreacht na hÉireann*, the constitution of the independent State of Ireland and the 1938 Anglo-Irish agreement. The book examines the relationship between the State in Ireland and the civil service under, first, British rule, then under the Provisional Government that took control within the terms of the 1921 Anglo-Irish Treaty and defended its authority in the Civil War, then under the Cumann na nGaedheal and the Fianna Fáil governments of an independent State. Each chapter maps out the organisational response of the civil service to each of these changes in the State and how the civil servants succeeded or failed in shaping the changes in the State. The book sets out to explain how the civil service responded to, and was able to influence, the process by which the British State withdrew from Ireland and two Irish States came into being.

The State is usually treated as the empty stage on which the struggle for power is enacted. This leads to the assumption that the civil service was an automaton, a machine waiting passively while others decided its fate. But the civil service had interests of its own and had developed the organisation and the ability to control its own destiny at least in some degree. In a revolution every interest that has a stake in the existing structures and is identified with the existing State is under threat. But revolution also offers new opportunities to organised interests that, by acting quickly, can enhance their prospects. The Irish civil servants, embodying the State, were able to identify, articulate and defend their own interests. The Irish revolutionaries took control of the civil service, not on the terms that they had wished, nor on terms dictated by the British, but rather on terms that the civil service itself had shaped. By reconstructing the experience of civil servants in the period of State-collapse, revolution and State-building the work seeks to locate them as active agents in those processes of change.

Much of this book is taken up with details of discussions on pay and conditions for civil servants. This is because these issues were the language in which deeper issues of good faith and loyalty were negotiated. In order to facilitate Home Rule the British government proposed to empower the Irish government to dismiss the entire civil service in Ireland and appoint a new one. Civil service traditions gave it as understood that so long as they faithfully served the State, even if they disagreed with government policy, civil servants would have secure employment, would receive sufficient salary to maintain a middle-class standard of living, be offered promotional opportunities and retire with a decent pension. Thus Home Rule, so far as it provided for the civil service, represented a profound breach of the good faith that had bound the civil service to the British State. While negotiating with skill and considerable endurance the terms on which the civil service would be treated, the objective ultimately was to establish a contractual relationship to bind the new State more firmly to its civil service. Although some within the civil service continued to be attached to the idea of a relationship of trust binding it to the State, especially in the independent State, for most it was understood that good faith was no longer good enough.

R.B. McDowell, Ronan Fanning, John McColgan, Eunan O'Halpin and Lawrence McBride have previously examined the administrative system in Ireland and its fate in the revolutionary period.[8] McDowell's is a descriptive history of the array of government departments in Dublin Castle from the Union to 1914. McColgan analyses the administrative history of partition between 1920 and 1922, including a chapter on the civil service. However, McColgan does not fully recognise the extent to which the Irish civil service was already different to the rest of the UK service. Nor was it as resigned to accepting whatever decision the British government made as he suggests. O'Halpin details the actual working of the Castle system, noting the links between failed administrative reform and failed political reform. His work is at the level of high administrative politics, dealing with the senior officials and not the lower ranks. McBride looks at the changing policy of recruitment to the Irish bureaucracy, from one dominated by Protestant unionists to one dominated by Catholic nationalists. He suggests that this change gave the stability necessary to found the new State out of civil war. Only Fanning deals with the civil service of the independent State. However, Fanning accepts the view that for the civil service it was business as usual. This is a view that this book challenges. Arthur Mitchell has written on the revolutionary government of Dáil Éireann with great detail and insight.[9] But he concentrated on the elite of that administration. This book seeks to add to his work by reconstructing the experience of the ordinary men and women who found themselves acting as the civil service of the revolutionary government.

This book seeks to build on what has been done already, by utilising new sources and advancing new interpretations. Firstly, most of these histories have stopped at the moment of the creation of the two new States in Ireland. This book takes the history forward to the de Valera government and the 1937 constitution. Secondly, these histories have generally viewed the Irish administration from a 'top-down' perspective. By looking at the experience of the civil servants themselves this analysis offers a 'bottom-up' perspective. The emphasis will therefore be on the previously under-used records generated by the civil servants themselves. It also uses the records of the Irish government made available by the opening in 1986 of the National Archives Ireland, which were unavailable to the previous historians of the subject. The records of the British State in Ireland held in London and those of the Northern Ireland government held in Belfast are used. The civil service sources that are utilised are the records of early Irish organisations still retained by their later descendants, the civil service trade unions. Also used are the records of the Irish branches of the British civil service associations held at the Modern Records Centre at Warwick University. A new source is an uncatalogued collection of early establishment material of the Irish Free State amounting to some thirty boxes and covering the period 1922–25. This includes the records of the Wylie committee on the discharged and retiring civil servants of the former British regime. Personal records include not only the papers of government ministers and civil servants, but also the recently released witness statements of the Bureau of Military History, which offer many insights into the everyday working of the revolutionary Dáil administration. The unpublished and witty memoir of Michael J. Gallagher provides an invaluable insight into the response of a key civil service trade unionist to a period of revolutionary State transformation. By investigating in detail the experience of revolution from the perspectives of both the State and the civil service and by treating the revolution as a 'State' rather than 'nation' event, this book offers a fresh perspective on the civil service, the State and the Irish revolution.

Notes

1 Terence de Vere White, *Kevin O'Higgins* (Tralee, 1966), pp. 83–4.
2 Saorstát Éireann R.54/3, *The Commission of Inquiry Into the Civil Service* (3 vols, 1932–35), vol. 1, paras 8–12 (Brennan Commission).
3 R.V. Comerford, *Inventing the Nation: Ireland* (London, 2003), pp. 7–8.
4 David Fitzpatrick, 'Ireland and the Empire' in Andrew Porter (ed.) *The Oxford History of the British Empire Volume III, The Nineteenth Century* (Oxford, 1999), pp. 494–521, 495.
5 Ibid., pp. 516–17.
6 *Parliamentary Debates* (Commons), Third Series, XXXII, col. 277, 25 Jan. 1886.
7 Virginia Crossman, *Politics, Law and Order in Nineteenth-Century Ireland* (Dublin, 1996), p. 69.
8 R.B. McDowell, *The Irish Administration 1801–1914* (London, 1964); Ronan Fanning, *The Irish Department of Finance 1922–58* (Dublin, 1978); John McColgan, *British Policy and the Irish Administration 1920–22* (London, 1983); Eunan O'Halpin, *The Decline of the Union: British Government in Ireland 1892–1920* (Dublin, 1987); Laurence W. McBride, *The Greening of Dublin Castle: The Transformation of Bureaucratic and Judicial Personnel in Ireland 1892–1922* (Washington D.C., 1991).
9 Arthur Mitchell, *Revolutionary Government in Ireland: Dáil Éireann 1919–22* (Dublin, 1995).

1

The civil service and the State in Ireland, 1912–18

Introduction

For the Irish civil servants Dublin Castle represented dead-end departmentalism. Political influence and personal connections were the avenues to advancement in an administration that was a byword for nepotism. The failure of examination entry to open up the Irish higher posts to genuine competition and the continuance of patronage, whether 'Green' or 'Orange', in the elite division of the Castle became a major source of dissatisfaction. Even nationalist and Catholic civil servants preferred a meritocratic system to the corruption of preferential patronage.[1] Frustrated by the narrow field of opportunity offered in the Castle, the Irish civil service sense of corporate identity was based on a general and widespread feeling of shared grievance and disappointment.

Although presented primarily as political reforms, the Irish Home Rule bills introduced by Gladstone in 1886 and 1893 were also shaped to deliver administrative reform. The separate Irish executive in Dublin Castle was, in Gladstone's view, operating without the restraint of a popularly elected assembly. The result was an inexorable growth in the size and cost of the Irish administration, a cost that was borne by the British Treasury. Home Rule proposed to address this by cutting the bonds that attached the civil service to the British State and by transferring it to the authority of an Irish assembly which, it was implied, would have to make drastic cuts. The Irish civil service was unprepared for the 1886 bill and failed to act. But it responded to the introduction of the 1893 bill by organising under a single all-service committee to agitate and lobby for the security of their positions, salaries and pensions under a future Home Rule assembly. This committee, led by the senior members of the Irish civil service, represents the most significant mobilisation of the entire Irish civil service. The committee adopted public and political tactics that ordinarily would have been treated as rank insubordination or even subversion of the established relationship between parliament and the civil service. Both bills failed but the question of Irish Home Rule was now embedded in both Irish and British party politics and in the consciousness of the Irish civil service.

The Home Rule Bill, 1912

Though Ulster Unionist resistance eventually overwhelmed the third Home Rule Bill, it was the financial question that initially dominated the debate. In 1912 government spending in Ireland, boosted by enormously expensive developments in national insurance, land transfers, congested districts relief, regional development and an old-age pension, had exceeded Irish revenues by £2 million and was continuing to grow. The immediate and, it seemed, insurmountable problem was how to grant executive and financial autonomy to an Ireland that was technically bankrupt.[2] Herbert Samuel, the Postmaster-General, was given the task of drawing up the financial aspects of the Home Rule Bill, thus separating the financial from the constitutional aspects of Irish self-government. His financial proposals were so complex that it was said that only he himself could understand them fully. What he proposed was that Ireland should be given a grant of £6 million to meet national expenditure, including administrative costs, and would be then expected to live within that budget. The Liberal government thus hoped to use the financial provisions of the bill to encourage the Irish to stop looking to London for money and learn to govern themselves cheaply.[3] It was therefore generally accepted that a Home Rule government would be compelled to reduce its administrative costs by reducing its civil service. The Castle civil servants had no involvement in drawing up the 1912 bill nor did Francis Greer, the parliamentary draftsman for Ireland, prepare it.[4] Home Rule as shaped by the 1912 bill was a system of indirect rule with local administrative responsibility. Initial Ulster Unionist opposition to what constitutionally speaking was a very modest proposal concentrated on objecting to the control of the Irish civil service being handed over to the Irish government. Fears were expressed about the future of Protestant civil servants and the potential for administrative rather than legislative discrimination.[5]

However, as Ulster exclusion came to dominate the proceedings the clauses relating to the civil service in the 1912 bill generated little debate in a 'sparsely filled and languid house'.[6] The assumptions that underlay the contributions to the debate by Augustine Birrell, the Chief Secretary Ireland, and John Redmond, the leader of the Irish Parliamentary Party and probable prime minister of an Irish Home Rule assembly, were of broad continuity in the civil service allied with necessary reductions in its size and cost. The reason that the civil service clauses generated so little debate was the Irish civil service had not waited for the Home Rule proposals but had itself seized the initiative at the earliest opportunity. In May 1911, when it was clear that the Liberal government was committed to bringing in a Home Rule Bill, three senior civil servants – A.R. Barlas, secretary to the Local Government Board (LGB), P.E. Lemass, secretary to the National Education Board (NEB) and Alfred Beckett, chief clerk to the General Valuation Office (GVO) – circularised the staff of the government departments with a proposal that the Irish civil service should immediately organise in readiness for the Home Rule Bill. In the circular these civil servants explained how they had attempted to meet with Birrell to discuss the implications of any Home Rule legislation for existing officers, but that he had refused on the grounds that a meeting would be premature in advance of a definite bill. Nonetheless, rather than wait for the Home Rule Bill to emerge they had decided to press ahead with the formation of a general committee representative of the government departments. This general committee would draw up an authoritative statement of the views of the officers as to the safeguards they considered necessary in the event of a Home Rule Bill being submitted to parliament.[7]

This was a revival of the strategy adopted by the civil service during the debate on the 1893 Home Rule proposal. The civil service had formulated a united response and used vigorous political and public agitation to win guarantees for their security under a Home Rule executive. Both Barlas and Beckett had been active on the 1893 committee so it might be supposed that the 1911 initiative represented simply the reactivation of that committee. However, the new committee was in several respects different to that of 1893 and represented an innovation in strategy in three areas: its representative nature, its eschewal of political lobbying at parliament in favour of influencing the key administrative and political figures, and in setting the terms of the civil service clauses of the 1912 bill at the drafting stage.

The initial circular emphasised that any committee must have the authority to represent the views of the entire service. It therefore suggested, as a preliminary, the formation of a 'provisional committee consisting of one delegate from each department to determine the proportion in which the several classes of civil servant in each office should be represented'. The provisional committee, made up of a representative delegate from each department, then decided the number of delegates that each department and class should return to the general committee. Although the Irish administration defied any attempt at precise analysis, the 1911 committee had close to full saturation with representatives from all departments.[8] The only substantial section of the civil service not represented on the committee were the postal workers; however, as they had their own organisation, and previous Home Rule bills excluded the postal service as an imperial service from the authority of the Irish executive, their absence was not significant. The committee did have representatives from the GPO, the administrative core of the postal system in Ireland.

The general committee was also carefully constructed so as to represent not only each government department but also all grades within each department. The intent was not that it should be strictly proportionate to the relative size of each department, but that it should be fully representative of each grade within each department. The number of representatives for each department reflected the complexity of the grades within the department rather than simply its size. This was innovative inasmuch as civil service organisations usually confined membership to particular grades. The 1911 committee was simultaneously a vertical and a horizontal organisation. The land commission was represented by its professional, higher grade, second division and clerical officers, all sitting around the same table. At the same time the professional officers of the land commission were working with the professional officers of the other government departments. For many civil servants the 1911 committee was an introduction to later civil service trade union organisation. The committee was financed by a levy of 6d (2.5p) for every £50 of annual income of each civil servant member to create a fighting fund. An executive committee of the General Committee of Irish Civil Servants (GCICS) was then formed. The executive committee drew from all the civil service grades, preserving the cross-class nature of the general committee. The single representative of the lady clerks marks the hesitant emergence of women civil servants' organisation.

Perhaps the most remarkable aspect of the 1911 GCICS committee was that across a wide spectrum of grades and departments it succeeded in securing agreement on a response to the implications of Home Rule for the civil service. The explanation for this emphasis on cross-service, representative mobilisation lies not only in the previous mobilisation of 1893, but also in the growth of trade union or quasi-trade union organisation and consciousness within the civil service. That the committee could demonstrate its representative base proved vital in the committee stage of the debate on the civil service clauses. Just a week before the debate a section of Belfast-based civil servants denied that the Dublin committee was in any sense representative of Irish civil servants. Barlas, who suspected that this was a 'mud-slinging operation' inspired by elements in the Orange Order, was able to detail to Francis Greer the fully representative membership of the committee and to underline the considerable financial outlay made by each civil servant's donation as illustrative of the commitment of the vast majority to its success.[9]

In assessing the innovatory aspects of the 1911 GCICS, we may turn next to the method of agitation. In contrast to the public agitation adopted in 1893, the 1911 committee preferred to exercise influence within the administrative system to make their views known and win concessions. Birrell placed a lot of emphasis on the many meetings he had held with the Irish civil service committee and the extent to which he had endeavoured to meet their fears.[10] The 'Preliminary Statement' of the civil servants, initially sent to Birrell, found its way to Greer and the legislation was generally shaped to meet their points. Barlas kept Greer informed of civil service sentiment at each key stage. His letters suggest a frank relationship in which Barlas felt that Greer could be trusted with confidential disclosures. In December 1912, when the key civil service clauses were coming up for debate in the committee stage at the House of Commons, Barlas wrote to Greer to assure him (and Birrell) that though 'a lot of stupid amendments have been put on the order paper . . . they merely expressed the views of individual civil servants in very small sections'.[11] During the debate the committee of the Irish civil service met to pass a motion expressing support for the government on the clauses in the Home Rule Bill touching on the civil service, support which Birrell used to good effect.[12]

The civil service clauses of the Home Rule Bill

The final innovatory aspect to the 1911 committee was its decision not to wait for the legislation and then react to it, but instead to shape it before it emerged into the political arena. In November 1911 the committee was ready to issue a preliminary statement of their position and demands. This statement began by setting down a clear and unambiguous commitment; the Irish civil servants wanted it to be clearly understood that as a body they 'were anxious to continue to work under the new Government of Ireland to be established under the Bill, provided that their interests are safeguarded as regards tenure of office, remuneration, prospects of promotion, and pension rights'. What the civil servants wanted was assurance that the *status quo* would be preserved and that civil servants would be 'liable to perform the same duties as heretofore or duties analogous thereto, and should continue to receive the same salaries, gratuities and pensions, paid out of the Exchequer of the United Kingdom'. Having established that the civil service would wish to continue to serve so long as it was bound to the Irish State under the same terms as before, the committee statement then concentrated on securing the best terms for those civil servants either compelled to retire by the new Irish government, or who chose to retire voluntarily. The usual protest that what induced civil servants to enter State service was security and the promise of a pension, was made more firmly contractual rather than moral by extensive quotations from the official Civil Service Commissioners' circulars. These circulars promised to successful candidates for civil service posts secure salaries starting at specific amounts, rising to certain *maxima* by definite yearly amounts and with rights to standard pensions on retirement. Many of the Irish civil servants would regard these as definite promises contingent only on good behaviour. The breach of such promises deserved better than usual compensation.

The position of professional civil servants also demanded better compensation than the usual abolition of office terms. These were men that had entered the service of the Crown late in life and, in some cases, after abandoning private practice in favour of what they had been assured was a secure civil service position. Other professional and permanent officers serving in Dublin were there simply because it happened that they had been assigned to Ireland though recruited to the United Kingdom civil service. These officers (mostly Englishmen), the statement argued, should in fairness be offered the opportunity to transfer to Great Britain and be compensated for the expenses connected with removal. The claims of the temporary civil servants were pressed with high moral outrage. Many of them were too old to secure other employment, they had served the State well and faithfully in poorly paid posts in the belief that so long as there was government work to be done, and they did it well, they would continue to be employed despite their temporary status. It should be borne in mind that the key practical difference between temporary and established civil servants was that the latter were entitled to a pension and the former were not. The case that the committee was making was that temporary civil servants not retained by the Irish government ought in fairness to be offered a pension, even though in strict regulation they were not entitled to one. Compulsory retirement would also mean that civil servants who, by implication, had been promised annual increments would suffer the loss of those increases and also the increases that would have followed any promotion. The committee wanted compensation not only for loss of salary but also for loss of prospective increases and promotions.

Just as it is an article of faith in common law jurisprudence, precedence is a fetish in the civil service. Conflating these, and no doubt drawing from its own reserves of legal expertise, the committee statement detailed the many precedents where far higher than statutory compensation had been conceded on abolition of offices. These ranged from the obscure to the obvious but the most telling precedent cited was the Act of Union itself. Under the Act of Union all displaced officers were pensioned on full pay. These precedents supported the civil service case that those compelled to retire should not suffer 'undue loss'. It then remained to set out what the civil service committee regarded as undue loss. Having set out their case that the Irish civil servants had an implied contract with the 'imperial' government and that in order to facilitate a constitutional change those contracts were to broken, the committee then devoted the remainder of the statement to suggestions for better than usual compensation for those civil servants either compelled to retire, or who volunteered to retire, in order to facilitate the constitutional change. The structure of the suggestions in the 1911 statement supposed that the 1893 bill would provide the model for the anticipated legislation. The statement listed what were in effect fourteen suggested changes to the scheme of the 1893 bill with alterations made necessary by the intervening 1909 Superannuation Act. The 1909 Act offered civil servants the option of accepting a reduced final rate of pension in exchange for a payment of one year's salary to his representatives if he died in service, or a lump sum payment on ordinary retirement. The rate of pension under the 1859 Act was one-sixtieth, under the 1909 Act one-eightieth, of final salary, multiplied by the number of years of service. Most of the Irish civil servants had opted to change over to the 1909 Act in the belief that they would be working to the normal retirement age and that the new scheme offered some security to their families. However, if the civil servants were to be compelled to retire at an earlier age they would suffer a loss by being on the lower rate of pension. The civil service committee wanted any officer compelled to retire to have the option of reverting to the terms of the 1859 Act. Other suggested changes were added years for professional officers in recognition of qualifications; facilities for exchange between Great Britain and Ireland; that the vague term 'officers in the service of the Crown' should be clarified so as to offer temporary officers the same pensions as 'officers in the permanent civil service of the Crown'; that commutation terms based on the Irish Church Disestablishment Act, which were more generous than the usual Treasury commutation terms, be allowed; and that a committee should be established to settle the retiring allowance rather than leave it to the tender mercies of the Treasury.[13]

In summary, the 'Preliminary Statement' of the Irish civil service staff representatives offered to transfer allegiance to the new State provided that those civil servants continuing service with the new Irish government 'should be in no worse position as respects tenure of office, terms of service, salary, or pension'. As some civil servants may be dismissed to facilitate constitutional changes, and not because of any failure or incompetence on their own part, the statement argued that they were entitled to expect more generous compensation than the usual abolition of office terms. Based on a presumption that the 1912 bill would follow the terms of the 1893 bill, the statement suggested what those more generous terms ought to be.

The Irish civil servants could not have been unaware of the example and precedent of the treatment of the civil servants in the Transvaal in the aftermath of the Boer War. The Liberal government elected in 1906 inherited a defeated and abysmally administered Transvaal and Orange River Colony, the former Boer republics.[14] The Liberal government's Transvaal Bill established a self-governing Transvaal with a government responsible to a parliament and assisted by a permanent civil service. So successful were the Liberals in reconciling the former Boer republicans that in 1910 all four South African provinces were able to come together in the Union of South Africa, apparently uniting English and Boer while securing British imperial interests. For the Milnerite imperialists this was a brilliant achievement, which no doubt also provided a practical example of the reconciliation of imperial and local interests that could be applied to Ireland.[15] However, for the Irish civil service the Transvaal example, far from being exciting, was deeply depressing. Within a year of the granting of self-government the defeated Afrikaners dominated the Transvaal parliament. Legislation was passed making Dutch of equal status to the English language and, most significantly to the Irish civil service, securing control of the Transvaal civil servants. Under the guise of retrenchment there followed a purge of English civil servants and their replacement by Boers.[16] Most alarming to the Irish civil servants was that the British government accepted without question the Transvaal government's bland assurance that the retrenchment was necessary and that there was no victimisation of British civil servants. A few of the retrenched officers, 'Milner's Kindergarten', managed to secure employment in the other colonies. Lionel Curtis found himself within a few years at the centre of what must have seemed oddly familiar negotiations on Ireland. For the remainder there was an inadequate gratuity and some sympathetic noises from London but little else.[17]

In gauging the success of the Irish civil servants' committee in shaping the relevant clauses of the 1912 bill, it must therefore be borne in mind that no civil servant held office by any sort of secure tenure; all were 'during pleasure' and civil servants had no legal rights arguable in courts of law. The demand that the *status quo* be preserved was a demand, in reality, for very little. As Greer reminded the Chief Secretary, the security of the civil service 'merely rests on the good faith and practice of the Government of the United Kingdom'.[18] Nevertheless when the bill was published it was clear that the civil servants had been able to exercise considerable influence on the shape of clauses 33 to 36 on the civil service and the attached schedules. The previous Home Rule bills of 1886 and 1893 had assumed that within a five-year transition period there would be a clean sweep of the entire existing service, with officers either resigning, being compelled to resign, or managing to make a completely new agreement with the Irish government. The civil service in 1886 and in 1893 faced the certainty of dismissal with only a possibility of re-employment. The 1912 bill instead offered the certainty of continued employment with only a possibility of dismissal. The bill, in terms taken from the Irish civil servants' statement, proposed to transfer the existing Irish officers of the civil service to the Irish government with the 'same tenure and upon the same terms and conditions (including conditions as to remuneration and superannuation) as heretofore'.[19] The 1912 bill guaranteed continuity of tenure as to salary, conditions of employment, and pension on like terms as those in existence on the day appointed for the transfer of authority. The third schedule offered compensation for removal from office, or for retirement due to material alteration in the nature of the duties to be discharged. An officer in the Irish civil service retained the right to retire within a five-year period, but only if he could convince a Civil Service Committee that he was retiring because the duties were neither the same as nor analogous to the duties under the old regime, or his conditions had materially altered to his detriment.[20] This Civil Service Committee, consisting of one Treasury representative, one representative of the Irish executive and a chairman appointed by the Lord Chief Justice of England, represented a dilution of Treasury authority, though not necessarily to the advantage of the civil servants. An officer opting for retirement, as opposed to being required to retire, could only expect a pension such as he would get if retiring on medical grounds rather than on the more generous abolition of office terms. These terms could be, and were, interpreted as being formulated to allow the Irish government to economise by driving out expensive senior officials on cheap pensions and filling the vacancies with lower-paid officials, though Redmond denied this. However, the insistence within the bill that the cost of any pension would be deducted from the Irish budget does underline the assumption of continuity in the civil service.

Allied with the assumption of continuity remained an insistence on the need to cut the numbers of civil servants. To take an extreme example, if the Irish government dismissed the entire existing civil service and recruited a new staff on starting salaries, it would immediately reduce its expenditure on administration by about one-third – the difference between the salaries of new officers and the pensions of dismissed officers. The implication persisted that the Irish administration was overstaffed and wasteful and that Home Rule would lead to considerable savings. This was particularly so, according to Birrell, in the case of 'the large number of non-established officers, quite out of proportion to the rest of the United Kingdom' recruited to the new departments 'which had been somewhat hastily created by the House of Commons'.[21]. A great many of these were professional civil servants whose status was sometimes doubtful. To meet their case Birrell proposed an innovation in empowering the three-man Civil Service Committee to define whether any particular officer was or was not a civil servant (a power normally reserved to the Civil Service Commission), what was an 'Irish' as opposed to an 'imperial' officer, and to determine the claims or pension to which such an officer was entitled. The opposition contribution to the debate in the Commons on these clauses lacked focus and was easily dealt with. Clearly the Conservatives were concentrating on Ulster opposition to destroy the bill and had lost interest in the administrative details of Home Rule.

When the Home Rule Bill was published the GCICS committee welcomed it, but suggested a series of amendments that would 'render the terms of compensation satisfactory to the service generally as well as to safeguard interests not covered by the Clauses as they stand'.[22] The most important change the civil servants asked was that the normal age of retirement mentioned in the bill should be sixty-five (as was customary in Ireland) and not sixty as regulated by the Treasury. The reason was to prolong the period of employment of the retained civil servants and therefore increase their final retiring salary.[23] In the case of premature dismissal, which it was anticipated would be the case for a great many officers, the compensation for anticipated loss provided for in the bill would also be greater by the increments of an additional five years of notional service – the so-called 'abolition years'. The Statement also asked that the scale of abolition years should be altered so as to benefit second division officers recruited at age eighteen. This would involve simply tinkering with the age at which abolition years could be added. The bill provided that an officer under thirty-six years of age should get additional seven years and for an officer under thirty the additional years should be five. The civil servants' statement asked that the ages should be reduced slightly to thirty-three and twenty-eight years. This would in effect automatically grant all younger officers recruited at age eighteen ten additional years' compensation on abolition. Greer wrote to Birrell that these changes were reasonable and, if conceded, would give general satisfaction. Greer was content to urge concessions to the persistent though discreet pressure from the Irish officers, so long as the concessions did not offer markedly better conditions to the Irish officers than to British officers. For Greer this was a fundamental principle and one that made sense when it is borne in mind that there would still be in Ireland some sections of an 'Imperial' civil service.[24] A cynic might note in passing that Greer had no difficulty in imposing on the Irish government charges that would never be imposed on a British government.

The implications of Ulster exclusion

In early 1914, as Home Rule was being put through its final passage in the houses of parliament, it became clear that an amendment to deal with Ulster exclusion would be necessary, further confusing an already complicated measure.[25] The GCICS immediately pushed for further concessions. Arguing that the division of the Irish departments, which must follow the amendment, represented a serious and detrimental alteration to their conditions of work, the committee requested that the terms for voluntary as opposed to compulsory retirement should be liberalised and improved. Instead of five years of a transitional period they asked for seven years, along with additional added years in the case of those with long service, which would bring them within the compensation terms attendant on abolition of office. In addition, to compensate for the lack of promotional opportunities in a diminished Irish civil service, they asked for special facilities for exchanges between the imperial and Irish service.[26]

These negotiations and discussions were conducted against a background of political crisis as the Tories and the Ulster Unionists combined to destroy the Home Rule Bill and the Asquith government. With the bitterness of the debate sharply dividing British and Irish society it would have been impossible for the civil service to escape its influence. The British civil service tradition had no difficulty in giving unswerving loyalty to the government in power. In Ireland the third Home Rule debate plumbed deeper loyalties of religion and nationality and the civil service could not but be influenced by the opinions of their own families, relatives and upbringing.[27] The inevitability of Home Rule and the growing threat of civil war over Ulster overcame professional impartiality and, in the general anticipation of the transfer of power, self-interest demanded hard thinking about where personal security lay. George Chester Duggan, a first division clerk in the Chief Secretary's Office (CSO) concluded that he would have to resign if the Ulster crisis 'reached a climax of force'.[28] Maurice Headlam, the Treasury Remembrancer in Dublin Castle, thought the crisis was so grave that he was justified in leaking government memoranda to the opposition.[29] The inability of the government to offer clear direction to the civil service also added to the sense of disarray. The pusillanimous response of the Asquith government to the arming of the loyalist paramilitary force the Ulster Volunteer Force (UVF), which was committed to resisting a Home Rule government by force, followed by the humiliating dismissal of the assistant commissioner of the Dublin Metropolitan Police (DMP), W.V. Harrel, after his heavy-handed response to the landing of arms by the nationalist Irish Volunteers was clear enough warning of the danger of showing initiative.[30]

The MacDonnell Commission on the civil service

The 1912–14 royal commission on the civil service chaired by the former Irish Under-Secretary Sir Antony Patrick MacDonnell provides a last insight into the culture of the Irish civil service before war and rebellion swept over it.[31] MacDonnell had already experience of the Irish civil service and had very strong opinions on the need for reform. When he arrived in Dublin Castle as Under-Secretary in 1902 he arrived with a clear objective to reform the Irish administration.[32] MacDonnell was of the view that Ireland required the discipline of self-management more than it required self-government. The keystone of his policy was not to abolish but rather to strengthen the position of Dublin Castle by giving it real control over the many independent boards and departments. This model of administrative reform had been first circulated by David Harrel, Under-Secretary in 1898.[33] MacDonnell's pursuit of administrative reform was embodied in the 1904 devolution proposal and the even more ambitious Irish Council Bill of 1907. In both cases his model was India, where he had blazed a dazzling trail with the autonomous provincial councils that he had set up there.[34] His ambitious plans for reform of the Irish administration, with a greatly strengthened CSO with financial autonomy, working in co-ordination with locally elected representatives, brought down the two Chief Secretaries Wyndham and Bryce and ended the policy of constructive unionism. Because he thought administrative reform was a non-political question he assumed that everybody else would think the same. In his view the Irish administration system was unco-ordinated, irrational, profligate and inefficient.[35] The Irish Council Bill failed and MacDonnell retired but he never lost faith in his own wisdom and, in his contribution to a series of essays on the 1912 Home

Rule Bill, returned once again to his argument that the problem with the Irish government was the lack of centralised control over the many State agencies working in the country.[36]

MacDonnell's method on the royal commission was to examine the heads of departments first and then to listen to representations from that head's departmental staff. His first witness was his successor as Under-Secretary Sir James Brown Dougherty. The confusion as to the authority exercised by the Lord Lieutenant over the Castle apparatus is evident in the presentation of Dougherty. Their inability to agree on which departments were inside and which outside the control of the Lord Lieutenant underlines the fact that despite the decades of debate the Castle was still a labyrinth of dispersed authority.[37] MacDonnell quickly took up where he had left off on his departure from the Castle and he and Dougherty debated at some length the pros and cons of the diffusion of authority within the Irish government. Dougherty was willing to concede that though the Chief Secretary answered to parliament for most of the Irish departments the Castle actually exercised very little control over the departments; he had responsibility but no authority. The Department of Agriculture and Technical Instruction (DATI) was independent of the Chief Secretary and the Congested Districts Board (CDB), the autonomous western development board, acted as if it was independent of everybody. The LGB answered to the Treasury and was outside the jurisdiction of the Lord Lieutenant, as were the various educational boards, the Commissioners of Public Works, the clerical establishment of the Four Courts and of course all the Whitehall departments which operated in Ireland. These were all government organisations that operated in Ireland but were free of Castle control. However, Dougherty was not prepared to concede to MacDonnell on the implied irrelevance of the Castle. Noting that the 'young gentlemen' of the Treasury (and perhaps by implication MacDonnell) could never grasp that the Irish executive was in fact a 'quasi-separate government' and that 'the people of Ireland look to what they call "The Castle" despised as it is by many, for advice and guidance, and above all, they make it the repository of their complaints', Dougherty emphasised the symbolic importance of the Castle in Irish government.[38] For all its faults it alone embodied the State in Ireland, apart from the army and the paramilitary Royal Irish Constabulary (RIC).

For Dougherty the main problem in the Irish government was not the dispersal of authority but rather the power of a tight-fisted Treasury. He had only five first class clerks to handle the entire judicial, financial and administrative work of the office and two of these were in London during the parliamentary session. Despite repeated appeals to the Treasury for more first class officers it had actually attempted to cut Dublin's higher establishment. The paucity of first class posts meant that ambition was stifled. Dougherty was utterly opposed to the Treasury's preferred option of appointing temporary clerks to deal with extra work but he did agree with MacDonnell that there was no marked line of division between the work of the first and the second division men in his office.

Sir Henry Robinson, head of the LGB, was one of the Castle unionists who ran a frankly sectarian department disguised as a mix of 'sensible' English, 'accurate and cautious' Scottish and 'brilliant and resourceful' Irish. Robinson ignored the Treasury gradations of first and second division clerks, retaining his own upper and lower division and abstractor class. He made no bones about preferring English and Scottish in his upper division, men who 'looked upon our political dissensions with a certain amount of indifference'. [39] His main complaint was against the Treasury attitude that maintained pay scales in the Irish LGB substantially below those in the English LGB, frustrating his desire to see his department as a first division office. Lemass confined himself to answering MacDonnell's queries with points of information on the staff of his office, though he did offer an opinion that the clerks of his department were doing well. On this he was in agreement with Sir John Barton of the Commissioners of Valuation. T.P. Gill represented the DATI, the most modern of the Irish departments. Gill had a strong dislike of the first division civil servants who 'come in with a notion from the manner in which they have been brought in and the privileged position in which they are placed in the service from the first, that they are, so to speak, of superior clay to the men of the other divisions they find in the office'. He preferred a single entry grade with promotion to the top of the service through ability and time. [40] In this he was close to the opinion of the civil service representatives. Gill probably saw himself as embodying the virtues of the self-made man. Energetic, multi-lingual, cosmopolitan, a journalist who had served as a nationalist MP for Louth South until the Parnellite split, Gill had made his mark as assistant to Horace Plunkett in the co-operative movement, on the Recess committee and as secretary to the DATI. [41]

It has been said that it takes three things to fit out a civil servant; a bowler hat, an umbrella and a grievance. [42] The Dublin Castle civil servants who gave evidence to MacDonnell were exceptionally well fitted-out with grievances. These were the lack of promotional opportunities and the related problem of patronage appointments in a Castle rife with sectarianism, lower grades doing work indistinguishable from the higher grades, and the chronic insecurity of the temporary clerks. The memorial from the staff of the Register General's Office complained that the work they were doing was not routine but required highly technical and specialised knowledge that would be more properly described as the work of first division officers. They were also unhappy that posts that formerly were promotional posts open to the second division had been professionalised and turned into patronage appointments in the gift of the departmental head. T.W. Smith, representing the second division officers of the GVO, echoed the complaint of promotional posts being closed off by re-grading them as professional grades. Smith was an Englishman who had been transferred to Dublin and found himself in a promotional dead end. The lack of promotional opportunities was also the complaint of the second division officers of the education boards, the land commission and the DATI. These officers all placed the blame for this at the door of departmental heads exercising patronage by professionalising former promotional posts. The outdoor posts of the LGB were a notorious case of patronage as all were in the gift of Robinson. MacDonnell got quite annoyed at the repeated reference to professional posts as patronage posts and the implication that corruption was at work. In his view the increasing professionalisation of higher posts was exactly the sort of direction he favoured the Castle administration taking. The alternative was an amateur service in which, by merely waiting long enough, the passage of time would deliver the higher posts. The assistant clerks of the LGB also complained that there was no distinction between the work they did and the work of the second division men, that they were all examination entry and therefore there ought not to be any distinction of pay or rank. Another block on promotion alluded to, and one that in some sense contradicted the picture painted by the civil service witnesses, was the popularity of the Castle among the Irish civil servants working in England who all competed for any Dublin posts that came available.[43]

Most of the Irish civil service witnesses represented departments and grades within departments and none claimed to speak on behalf of a permanent organisation. The grades that did make such a claim were the most marginal within the service – the temporary clerks and the women clerks of the Post Office. The temporary clerks occupied a difficult position, and perhaps because of this were the best organised. The Irish Temporary Clerks' Association claimed to represent 250 of the 400–500 temporary clerks in Dublin Castle. Their demand was for permanent status, a demand that was bound to be resisted by both the permanent staff and the Treasury. As temporary clerks they had entered the civil service without any examination. The permanent officers assumed that they had all got their posts either by political influence or through the patronage of the departmental heads and saw them as a further block to promotion. The Treasury reluctantly allowed temporary appointments as a compromise with the demands of the Irish government for increased staff.[44]

Not only was the Association of Post Office Women Clerks the only women's association to represent Irish opinion to the MacDonnell commission, it was also the only British-based one to do so. Women were employed in large numbers by the Post Office. In 1903 the women clerks had responded to a cut in pay by organising the association. The association later amalgamated with the Federation of Women Clerks to form the first women civil servants' trade union, the Federation of Women Civil Servants.

MacDonnell recommended that all of the administrative, formerly first division, class of civil servants should be recruited on common scales of salary with a strict adherence to the principle of open competition and that the Irish administration should have more administrative officers. He also recommended an inquiry into the question of trade union organisation within the civil service with formal machinery for assessing staff grievances on pay and conditions. These recommendations were suppressed with the outbreak of war in August 1914 but they established a benchmark for the civil service organisations.

By a happy coincidence four of the more prominent civil servants in the Castle wrote memoirs of this period.[45] The memoirs of Robinson betray his condescension toward the Irish peasantry whose dependency on his largesse affirmed his own bloated sense of self-importance. His memoirs are a striking contrast to those of W.L. Micks of the CDB, which reveal a passionate advocate of local autonomy who valued local initiative, though he was unpopular with both his staff and the Treasury. Andrew Magill's memoir is relentlessly anecdotal and largely unaware of the larger forces at work within the State administration, a characteristic that he shares with Maurice Headlam. Headlam's reminiscences reveal a functionary for whom the business of administration was an unwelcome interruption to his fishing expeditions. The impression conveyed by these several memoirs is of an administration crumbling under the pressure of sectarian suspicions and the corrosive effect on the State of politicised civil servants. With officials like these Dublin Castle could no longer facilitate political or administrative development, in fact it acted to obstruct it.

The First World War and the civil service

The First World War intensified the presence of the State in British society as it took on the task of mobilising the entire resources of the nation to win the war. This new role dwarfed the previous expansion of the State under the Liberal government of 1906 and the British civil service was tested to near-destruction by the demands of 'total war'. New tasks could not be accomplished by old methods and the Treasury lost control of staffing in the new departments created to fight the war, especially the vast Ministry of Munitions which grew from nothing to a staff of 25,000 by 1918, controlling 250 factories and employing two million workers. Administrative revolution also occurred at the other end of the scale with the creation of the inner cabinet office.

A new British army was quickly recruited, as hundreds of thousands volunteered. By war's end five million men had enlisted. The uncontrolled volunteering of 1914–16 rapidly distorted the labour force and necessitated the industrial employment of young boys, women and temporary and part-time workers. These were rapidly 'skilled-up' as trade unions were forced to relax demarcation boundaries, though these new workers continued to be paid unskilled labourer rates. The long war caused inflation in food prices and rents. Inflation in turn led to wage militancy with waves of strikes in 1917 and 1918. It was apparent to workers that the war was profiting the owners of the war industries with guaranteed prices and markets and a skilled workforce on unskilled wages. The government was forced to intervene by introducing food rationing, price controls, and centralised wage bargaining. These controls led in turn to a further expansion in the size of the civil service. One of the most striking changes in the culture of the civil service due to the war was the growing employment of women in every department as they were substituted for enlisted men. Segregation between men and women broke down and most departments had some women working alongside men by war's end. The rapid and uncontrolled expansion of the service also led to a big influx of temporary civil servants who were far less deferential and respectful of the civil service traditions than those they replaced.[46] For all grades of workers, not least the civil service, the pervasiveness of State control meant that the highest gains were to be made by a closer engagement with the State and a race developed to exert the greater pressure on the government.

The wartime growth in the size and complexity of the State in Great Britain was not matched in Ireland. This was an era of bold experiment in the organisation of the State in Britain, but not in Ireland, where any attempt to improve the administration ran the danger of being interpreted as an attempt to preempt the decisions of the now imminent Home Rule government. The general expectation of Home Rule and the marginal importance of Ireland to the war economy meant that in an era when the strong State emerged, the Irish State atrophied. Many of the professional civil servants in Ireland were transferred to war work. The DATI enjoyed a new status as it led the drive for increased food production.[47] Branches of two new departments were established in Ireland, the Ministry of Food and the Ministry of National Service.[48] At the same time, as expenditure not related to the war effort was severely curtailed, most of the other Irish departments faced paralysing cuts, in particular the CDB land redistribution plans, though the government remained aware of the political dangers of too severe an economy drive.[49] Eventually, even the DATI, which initially was so important in the drive to increase food production, faced cuts in budget and staff.[50]

The most immediate result of the outbreak of war was the passing and then suspension of the Home Rule legislation. John Redmond, anxious to counter the view that Irish nationalism was anti-imperial, urged all Irishmen to enlist and play their role in defending the empire. His support for the war split the nationalist paramilitary force, the Irish Volunteers. The majority joined the newly named National Volunteers and enlisted, leaving only a minority in the now evidently separatist and anti-imperial Irish Volunteers. As the war dragged on and the Ulster Unionists entered the war cabinet in May 1915 the likelihood of Irish self-government diminished. However, that Home Rule was not likely was never admitted and the Castle remained in the limbo of anticipated change that forever receded. As war transformed the British State the Castle became anachronistic because it remained the same.

Sir Matthew Nathan and Dublin Castle

In September 1914 the new Under-Secretary, Sir Matthew Nathan, arrived to a difficult situation. A protégé of Joseph Chamberlain, Nathan had served on the Imperial Defence Committee and arrived in Ireland with a list of steady achievements as a Royal Engineer and administrator in the Sudan, Sierra Leone, the Gold Coast, Hong Kong and Natal Province. Nathan was also Jewish and therefore, being neither Catholic nor Protestant, was an unfamiliar exotic in the sectarian hothouse of Dublin Castle. His new duties in Dublin 'proved more difficult than any he had yet undertaken'.[51]

Although Home Rule had passed into law the outbreak of war had led to its immediate suspension 'for the duration'. From the beginning Nathan was unpopular with the Castle civil servants not only because he was a Liberal Home Ruler among die-hard Tories but also because he brought G.P. Kurten with him from London as his own private secretary, snubbing the established staff in the Under-Secretary's department for whom this was an eagerly sought-after promotional post. In the world of Dublin Castle, with limited opportunities for promotion, civil servants usually distinguished themselves by acting as private secretary to the permanent head of a department, or to a minister, or by acting as secretary to a commission or departmental committee.[52] As soon as he arrived Nathan was the recipient of complaints at the lack of opportunity that Dublin presented and requests to be transferred to London where prospects were better.[53] Brennan, who as first division officer in the CSO was effectively passed over, was warned by J.P. Crowley, a fellow Corkman in the London service, to act with circumspection because a private secretary brought in to the Castle 'is . . . a dangerous person to talk to with any expansiveness'.[54] This advice neatly illustrates the contradictions that were undermining the Castle administration. The fundamental basis of the relationship between the British civil service and the government was that a minister would always be clear as to what his senior civil servants thought on any issue, even if he chose to disregard their views. Walter Long sent Nathan a 'friendly' warning to avoid the fate of Lord MacDonnell who tried and failed to reform the Irish civil service and succeeded only in destroying the confidence of the ordinary civil servant.[55]

Nathan's job as Under-Secretary was twofold; firstly to cut expenditure in the Irish administration and secondly to prepare it for transfer to a future Home

Rule government which would come to power after the war.[56] The former was achieved by delegating the duties of retired officials to lower-ranking civil servants, and by freezing recruitment and promotions. Leave was suppressed to as few days as possible.[57] The Irish Land Commission (ILC) was instructed to end the temporary contracts of barristers working on land transfers as the commission had its moneys for land purchase cut off by the Treasury.[58] But there were some limits to the economies that Nathan could enforce. Sir Henry Robinson reacted with alarm to the news that Nathan claimed only the third class fare for journeys undertaken for official purposes. Robinson nervously queried whether the journey had in fact been in the third class carriage or whether it was only the claim that was made at this rate. He was relieved to be assured that although Nathan himself always travelled third class he was not intending to lay down any rule for the civil service generally in the matter.[59]

To prepare for Home Rule and to brief them on the mechanics of government (on which, to the amusement of Nathan, they were wholly ignorant), the Under-Secretary had a series of meetings from February to September 1915 with John Redmond, John Dillon his second-in-command, and the Irish Party's financial expert J.J. Clancy. For some of the meetings Francis Greer accompanied Nathan.[60] These meetings had to take place in Dillon's own home such was the almost pathological hatred of the Irish nationalist leaders for Dublin Castle.[61]

The discussions were principally concerned with rationalising and reducing the staff in the many and varied departments of the Irish government. Nathan had little interference from Redmond or Dillon as he pushed forward with his own plans for a drastic reduction and reshaping of the Castle. These would have brought the Irish government into line with the evolving British model of each department of State being under a political head answerable to parliament, advised by his permanent officials. David Harrel had suggested these changes earlier to Wyndham when he took up the post of Chief Secretary, so they were well known and uncontroversial.[62] Nathan suggested a government of eight ministries: prime minister, finance, justice, local affairs and public health, lands and agriculture, trade and industry, education, with posts and telegraphs run on an agency basis. The Ministry of Finance was to assume immediate responsibility for civil service pay and conditions and departmental administration.[63] As Francis Greer pointed out the Home Rule Act did not transfer any of the existing departments to the Irish government. Instead it empowered the Lord Lieutenant to establish new departments for the administration of Irish services except those for which the Irish government had no power to make laws. However, as many of the existing Irish departments performed both Irish and imperial services, it would be necessary for the two governments to make agreements to divide up the work hitherto performed by a single Irish department.[64] This would of course be of vital concern to the civil servants in those departments, who could end up working for either government. Would they be allowed choose? The secretary of the Board of Works had already signalled his bafflement as to how he could allocate the work of the board between transferred and reserved services. His best estimate was about one third imperial for the work of the surveyors, the engineers could be taken as wholly Irish as were the land loans staff, but the drainage engineers were wholly imperial. The puzzle was how it could be possible to transfer services without transferring staff.[65] Nathan expected the heads of the departments to co-operate in the transfer of authority and reshaping the administration. He asked the heads to supply him with confidential memorandum on what adaptations would be required in their departments in order to bring them into line with a more streamlined administrative system of seven departments under an Irish prime minister sharing responsibility with the London administration.[66] The CDB refused to co-operate, taking the high view that it had nothing to do with Dublin Castle and should answer only to the imperial parliament.[67]

At these confidential meetings Redmond and Dillon brought no ideas of their own, they simply reacted to those of Nathan. In some respects this was the usual relationship between a political head and his senior civil servant. Redmond had signalled for years that he wanted cheaper and more efficient administration and an end to the 'ridiculously extravagant' Castle system.[68] Nathan as a senior civil servant was bringing forward ideas to accomplish that objective, but Redmond and Dillon had the final determination. However, the suspicion that Nathan's advice may have been shaped by British rather than Irish interests did not seem to have crossed the mind of Redmond or Dillon. The emphasis of Nathan's advice was always on avoiding conflict between the Irish and the British governments and little thought was given to the relationship between the new Home Rule executive and the existing civil service. Even in the case of the completely new finance department Redmond and Dillon were oddly passive, Dillon merely enthusing that they regarded the British system of Treasury control as the 'best in the world'. Nathan advised that the new department be staffed on 'necessarily economical lines rather than on the past extravagances of the Irish administration'. In this he was merely echoing nationalist rhetoric. The only intervention was when Dillon disagreed on the appropriate salary scales for the departmental heads. Dillon interpreted Nathan's suggestion of a rate below that of London as a slight on the status of the Irish government and insisted on London rates of £2,000 for the secretary of the Department of Finance and £1,500 for all other departmental heads.[69] Nathan strongly urged Redmond, who did not demur, not to appoint 'civil service types' to represent Irish interests on the joint British-Irish Treasury board, on which they would have two members, but apart from the permanent head of the Irish Treasury to 'go for someone to speak with authority for the industrial and manufacturing section of the community'.[70] These qualifications would have been taken as spelling out a Protestant Unionist.

Nathan also got Redmond to agree that the Irish government would continue to use the British civil service commissioners for recruiting and examining candidates for employment in the Irish civil service.[71] This would mean perpetuating the stranglehold of the Oxbridge colleges on the elite administrative division and higher posts in the civil service. That Redmond did not demur signals his utter fixation on the representative aspects of Home Rule along with a disregard for the reality of executive authority. The main argument in favour of Home Rule advanced since the days of Isaac Butt, the founder of the Home Rule party, and repeated by Redmond himself when he described the Castle administration as a school of experimentation for English 'shake-beggars', was that Ireland was grossly misgoverned by the very system that he now blithely agreed to perpetuate.[72] This was precisely the response of Maurice Headlam who was hugely amused at being asked by Nathan to suggest suitable staff for an Irish department of finance:

> one of the chief arguments for Home Rule has always been the necessity for governing Ireland according to 'Irish' ideas. The Treasury is regarded here as the embodiment of 'English' ideas. Hence it is not without humour that you should ask a Treasury official for guidance for an Irish Treasury and that the politicians should be unable, or unwilling, or forbidden by the government which has encouraged the 'Irish ideas' theory to evolve any scheme of their own.[73]

In fact Nathan was deeply pessimistic as to the viability of an Irish Treasury. The insurmountable problem for an Irish department of finance was the elaborate safeguards of the Home Rule Act securing the status of the Irish civil servants. The finances of the Home Rule scheme were premised on reducing the size and cost of the administration of Ireland, yet if the Irish government was to observe the safeguards attached to the civil service that guaranteed no worsening of conditions it would be fatal to economies. If the Irish government, in pursuit of economy, violated the conditions of service of the civil servants it would entitle the officers to the 'most liberal compensation payable'.[74] Before it even came into existence the Irish government had lost the battle of the economy because the Irish civil service had already won it. If the 1914 Act had in fact been put into force the British exchequer would have had to come to the immediate rescue of an Irish Treasury.

In November 1915, following the establishment of a similar committee in Britain, an Irish retrenchment committee was established. The function of the committee was to generate savings in the government of Ireland, savings that would go to the war effort.[75] This committee soon proved as much a failure as previous attempts to cut Irish expenditure. When the Irish Party realised that the savings in the Irish administration were not going to be applied in Ireland but were to be transferred to Britain they boycotted the committee. Redmond was also afraid that allowing Whitehall complete freedom of action in Dublin Castle might create difficulties for a future Home Rule administration. The retrenchment committee retreated behind the hope that Dublin Castle would 'carry still further the scrutiny of expenditure which has already taken place'.[76]

Enlistment and the Irish civil service

The British civil service had, like the rest of British society, been swept up in the initial enthusiasm for the war. Departmental heads, fearful of the disruption that would follow a mass exodus of staff into the ranks for a war that 'would be over by Christmas', simply refused permission to enlist on the grounds that the staff member was essential to the war effort. But the failure to win by Christmas and the pressure on recruitment meant that the civil service had to be seen to be carrying its share of the burden. In June 1915 the War Office called on civil servants to enlist, promising they would continue to receive the same salary and that they would not lose out in seniority or years of service. This call was taken up by the heads of the government departments in Dublin Castle who circularised every man of military age on their staff, urging them to join up.[77] The Irish civil service proved reluctant recruits, particularly when compared to the English and Scottish officers. A return of the Irish civil service, prepared but never published, shows that of the 3,004 civil servants of military age in the Irish civil departments at the outbreak of war, excluding the postal and revenue departments, only 823 had enlisted by April 1916. That is, about 27 per cent. In comparison 54 per cent of the English and 62 per cent of the Scottish civil servants had joined up.[78] The only department of the Irish government to show any degree of enthusiasm for volunteering was the Lord Lieutenant's household, made up of military men for the most part.[79]

The Northcliffe newspapers led the campaign on the recruiting question and the alleged cowardice of the civil service. These featured farcical accounts of unlimited numbers of 'young shirkers' hiding in government departments, labelled 'funkholes'. These were to be 'rounded-up' and 'combed out'.[80] Civil servants who had applied to join up in 1914 but were refused permission as 'indispensable' were increasingly resentful at the press campaign, the attitude of the War Office and the failure of their departmental heads to defend them. Denied the privilege of volunteering when they had a choice of units and having endured the white feathers of 'patriotic young misses', they now faced compulsory conscription into the infantry and the certainty of being pushed up to the trenches and the front line.[81]

Nathan was a keen supporter of the drive to recruit civil servants of military age in Ireland. He dismissed their work in Dublin Castle as essentially elementary for the most part and said that they would be of better service to the State enlisting to defend the empire.[82] He put pressure on the temporary second division clerks to enlist by threatening them with discharge at the end of their period of employment. It was implied that should they be lucky enough to survive the trenches they would be certain of a permanent position after the war. Dillon was unhappy at Nathan's bullying offer of enlistment or dismissal, especially as the Castle had not established equivalents to the British military tribunals empowered to determine exemptions to military service.[83] That Nathan was issuing the threat suggests both that the second division men were refusing to enlist and that he regarded the refusal as unacceptable in any servant of the Crown, even a temporary one. Most significantly, it signals the extent to which the lower-ranking Irish civil servants regarded the British State as simply their employer, to whom they owed no more than the contractual loyalty due to any employer.[84] Most Irish civil servants were of the opinion that the war in France was 'not our war', and, with Home Rule imminent, 'the better part of valour was to stay at home and await developments'.[85]

The 1916 Rising

However, among the Irish civil service there was a minority for whom opposition to enlistment was an expression of deep-seated hostility to the British State. As well as bearing the usual metropolitan scorn for the Dublin Castle administration, Nathan quickly became deeply suspicious of the loyalty of the Irish civil service.[86] Shortly after his arrival he reported that there were 'a good number of the lower officials in this undesirable organisation Sinn Féin . . . and we shall have to put a strong check on their increased Activity'.[87] Sinn Féin was a minor political party formed in 1905 by the nationalist journalist Arthur Griffith. Sinn Féin, meaning 'Ourselves Alone', argued that Irish Nationalist MPs, instead of asking the British parliament to permit Irish self-government, should simply assemble in Dublin and declare themselves the legitimate Irish parliament. The Irish people would recognise and obey the native government and its institutions, making the British State in Ireland an irrelevance. With the passing of the Home Rule Act it seemed that Redmond's strategy of relying on the British parliament had been vindicated. On the outbreak of war, when Redmond had urged Irishmen to enlist in the British army, Sinn Féin had disrupted recruitment platforms and had opposed the war as being of no concern to Ireland. Within Dublin Castle 'Sinn Féin' had become a general term for all anti-war opinions and for Nathan covered all anti-recruitment and nationalist organisations.[88]

During the Hardinge Commission hearings into the Easter Rising of 1916 Nathan suggested that many in the Irish civil service had a 'pious dislike' of England arising from the opinion that England had treated Ireland badly.[89] The move from a dislike of government to actively participating in a revolutionary attempt to overthrow that government does require explanation. Civil servants acquired a deep identification with the State as part of their training and sometimes came to regard themselves as a better guardian of the public interest than their political masters. The motivation of those civil servants who joined a revolutionary movement actively working against the State therefore goes against the grain. For many civil servants their introduction to separatism was initially cultural rather than political. The progress of a section of the civil service from the cultural organisations like the Gaelic League, or sports clubs like the Gaelic Athletic Association (GAA), to the political organisations like Sinn Féin, and ultimately to revolutionary organisations such as the Irish Republican Brotherhood (IRB) and the Irish Volunteers is a barometer of the growing alienation of these Irish civil servants from the British State.

The Gaelic League, organised to revive Gaelic as the spoken language of the Irish people, was formed at a meeting held in Martin Kelly's civil service grind school at 9 Lower Sackville Street. Civil servants dominated the first executive. Eoin MacNeill, founder of the Gaelic League, was a clerk in the Accountant-General's office at the Four Courts, the only Catholic on the permanent staff of the office.[90] The membership of the premier Keating branch of the Gaelic League was mostly civil servants and teachers. The Gaelic League and the GAA were typical of the sort of self-improvement society that always proved attractive to the middle-class ethos of the civil service. Moreover, membership of cultural nationalist movements initially did not mean an automatic sympathy with political nationalism. James Kavanagh, a clerk in the Board of Works in Dublin Castle, 1916 Volunteer and later secretary of the Dáil Éireann Department of Local Government, reckoned that many of the teachers and civil service members of the Keating branch of the Gaelic League were antagonistic to his separatist politics. He recalled that on one occasion the Keating branch was riven by a dispute when a woman member insisted on playing 'God Save the King' on the piano as the king being above politics, it could not be a '"political' song.[91] But for many civil servants these cultural movements were the initial introduction to '"Irish-Ireland' ideas that then led to the more advanced separatist politics of the Irish Volunteers, the IRB and Sinn Féin.[92] Take out the civil servants and the separatist movement looks a lot less formidable: Michael Collins, Richard Mulcahy, Ernest Blythe, Liam Archer, Eamon Broy, Alf Cotton, Con Collins (who was arrested in Tralee trying to make contact with Roger Casement), Patrick J. Daly (who rose to become assistant secretary, Department of Local Government), Hugo Flinn, Diarmuid Lynch, Dr Conn Murphy, Joe O'Reilly (one of 'the Squad' assembled by Collins to assassinate key figures in police and military intelligence in Dublin Castle) and Diarmuid O'Hegarty. The civil service, by separating them from home and community, gave them independence and a cosmopolitan and critical outlook on Irish life.[93] What it did not do was create any identification with the State.

However, if the 'exile' from Irish life was too extended it diminished rather than increased the radicalism of the young civil servant. Michael Gallagher felt that he was well on the way to being 'poured into the mould of an ordinary Englishman' during his service in London, had he not secured a transfer to Dublin.[94] Michael, John and Maurice Moynihan were the sons of a prominent IRB man in Tralee. Michael was successful in the civil service exams in 1910 and joined the Inland Revenue in London. His correspondence with his brother John shows a gradual decline in radicalism and an absorption into the ethos of the British civil service. He eventually joined the Civil Service Rifles and then the King's Liverpool regiment and was killed in June 1918 at the front. His brothers John and Maurice, both republicans, had equally distinguished service in the civil service of the independent Irish State. What made the difference between Michael and his brothers was his years of independent living in London.[95]

When the Irish Volunteer Convention of October 1914 rejected Redmond's call for the Volunteers to enlist in the British army, it also adopted an openly revolutionary policy that included 'the abolition of the system of governing Ireland through Dublin Castle and the British military power and the establishment of a National Government in its place'. Nathan used this declaration to forbid members of the government service 'to belong to an organisation of which the avowed object was to thwart and injure that government'.[96] He prepared a circular to be sent to any civil servant suspected of associating with the Irish Volunteers but there is no evidence that the carefully drafted memorandum was ever actually distributed.[97] Joseph Devlin, MP for West Belfast, cautioned Nathan against suppressing the anti-war press but was prepared to support action against civil servants taking part in 'pro-German' meetings, by which he meant anti-enlistment activity.[98] As late as February 1916 Nathan was assuring the Irish Unionist Lords Midleton and Barrymore that he was taking action against civil servants who were taking part in 'Sinn Féin' activities.[99]

Dismissals occurred in the Inland Revenue, Ordnance Survey and the Post Office. Many of those dismissed were to prove significant revolutionary figures, a confirmation of Nathan's assessment. They included Austin Stack and Robert Monteith. Stack, a significant figure in the Irish revolutionary movement, was dismissed from the Inland Revenue. Monteith, dismissed from the Ordnance Stores, went to America and from there to Germany where he met with Roger Casement whom he secretly returned with to Ireland aboard a German U-boat in advance of the 1916 Rising. Dismissal was one response to civil service disaffection, but deportation under the guise of redeployment was more frequent. Ernest Blythe, a clerk in the DATI, and Liam Mellows, a Post Office engineer, were both deported to England. P.S. O'Hegarty, the postmaster of Queenstown, was deported to Welshpool in Wales.[100] John Cox, an excise-man in the port of Dublin, and P.F. Burke, excise-man in the Monaghan-Louth area and an IRB man, both of whom were to be arrested after the 1916 Rising, were identified as 'active Sinn Féiners' and were pensioned off in order to be rid of them.[101] Other dismissals were petty. The postmistress of Dalkey was deprived of the post because her daughter was active in Cumann na mBan.[102]

In the aftermath of the 1916 Rising Nathan, however, could recollect only eight or nine men being actually dismissed because most civil servants when asked whether they were members of the Volunteers would say 'we do not deny it', which was not quite an affirmation of membership. The Volunteers remained a legal organisation and therefore civil servants who were members were not breaking the law, only regulations. To enforce discipline would require either specific evidence of membership or an admission, and in many cases Nathan had neither. It was believed by Nathan that the Volunteers took especial care to safeguard civil servants from observation by the police while on route marches.[103] Hugh Hehir, a civil servant in the ILC and later registrar of the Dáil Éireann courts in Co. Clare, who had progressed through the usual cultural initiations of the GAA and the Gaelic League to the political circles of Sinn Féin, the IRB and the Volunteers, was ordered by Sean MacDermott to publicly sever connections with the movement after he had been identified by the secretary of the ILC as active in the Irish Volunteers.[104] Mortimer O'Connell, an excise officer and IRB man, was another civil servant directed to withdraw from Volunteer parades. O'Connell believed that Sean MacDermott had several IRB informants among the Castle departments besides O'Connell himself, that kept him informed on government policy changes.[105] Eugene Smith, a Volunteer and civil servant who escaped detection, claimed to have passed many sensitive documents over the years to the Volunteer executive, including plans for conscription, arms raids and the German Plot arrests.[106]

The only senior civil servant prepared to speak in defence of the lower ranks was A.H. Norway, secretary of the Post Office, Ireland. Norway had been alert to the growth of separatist movements within the civil service, but he had been shrugged off by the Castle.[107] Vexed at the prominence given to allegations that the Irish Post Office was a hotbed of Sinn Féin agitation, Norway used the Hardinge Commission to detail the steps that he had taken to forbid civil servants to join or remain in the Volunteers. In the period leading up to the 1916 Rising, as Irish Volunteer activity grew more intense he issued the following letter to every member of the postal staff alleged to be a member of the Irish Volunteers:

> Sir,
> The attention of the Postmaster General has recently been called to the fact that you are a member of the Irish Volunteers under the leadership of a committee presided over by Mr John McNeill. The Postmaster General has also been apprised of the open hostility of this organisation to recruitment in the Forces of the Crown and generally, to the Government under which you are serving. Of this,

the public utterances of the leaders of the organisation and matter contained in the newspaper which purports to be its official organ are sufficient evidence. While it appears to the Postmaster General that an openly hostile attitude towards the Government, such as is indicated by membership of the body referred to, by taking part in its exercises and by association with its leaders in its business would at any time be improper in a member of the Civil Service, such an attitude in the time of war on the part of persons entrusted with business of the State is fraught with risk to the country which no Government is justified in incurring. In those circumstances I am directed to call on you to cease all connection with the Irish Volunteers or any similar organisation or face dismissal.[108]

In the aftermath of the 1916 Rising the loyalty of the Irish civil service to the State while it was at war could not be taken for granted. But what can be done with a disloyal civil servant? At one extreme it could be argued that disloyalty in a servant of the Crown was equivalent to treason, and the penalty for treason is death. In fact disloyalty in the civil service in Ireland was treated with considerable leniency. Every opportunity to retreat from separatist actions was offered. The incorrigible were simply dismissed, facing no other charge.

Nathan called for a full statement from civil servants of their movements including where they stayed each night from noon on Saturday 22 April to noon on Monday 1 May, the period of the Rising. The statements of the staff were corroborated by checking details with the DMP or the military.[109] This may appear particularly pointless as those civil servants who were active in the rebellion were by then in British gaols and the rest had been confined to their homes, but the statements were intended for future use to weed out those that had escaped detection and also the passive sympathisers. Each head of department was directed to ensure that all staff supplied a statement. These were then forwarded to the CSO. Officers missing or failing to provide a detailed statement were pursued. When the two clerks Francis Shouldice and Thomas Cotter of the National Health Insurance Commission (NHIC), both already suspected of involvement in the Volunteers, failed to return to work after the Rising two senior clerks called to their homes where they were fobbed off with vague answers to their queries.[110] DMP detectives came to the offices of the ILC looking for Hugh Hehir. Hehir, who had avoided public associations with the Volunteers after March 1915, remained a member of C Company under Thomas McDonagh. He also successfully resisted efforts to transfer him to London where he would face conscription. Ironically Hehir was in the dark about the Rising and spent Easter 1916 on holiday in Co. Clare. Nevertheless he was arrested on his return and sent to Frongoch.[111] Of course there were also the usual anonymous letters informing the Castle about the suspicious behaviour of certain civil servants: 'I beg to inform you that a young man named John Roche of Seville Place employed in the Land Commission Office is a Sinn Féin Volunteer and was with them during the week of Rising in Dublin but escaped and got home.'[112]

The Sankey committee

A committee was appointed under Mr Justice Sankey to investigate individual cases of the thousand plus persons detained in the post-rebellion attempt to crush Irish separatist organisations.[113] About ninety civil servants were investigated, half of them in the Post Office.[114] The possibility of servants of the Crown being engaged in subversion created more excitement than the absolute numbers involved, which were very small given the size of the Irish civil service. The suspicion was that the few who were revealed to have been actively engaged in 1916 were merely the tip of the iceberg of civil service disaffection and that many more lay concealed below the surface. There were immediate protests, especially from J.A. Pease in the Irish Post Office, at the deportation on the flimsiest evidence of many postal staff.[115] In some civil service cases it is clear that Sankey's inquiries were very brief. James Kenny, a civil servant and member of the 4th battalion of the Volunteers active in the GPO garrison, was simply asked if he had any knowledge beforehand of the Rising and, on denying any such knowledge, was released.[116] Internees who expressed defiance or refused to co-operate were simply continued in detention.[117] Thus, except where there was evidence that the civil servant was in a leadership position, or was defiant, they were soon released. Naturally enough they then returned to their government offices, citing their release as evidence of their innocence of any wrongdoing. T.W. Russell accepted that Sankey's release of John Daly, an assistant agricultural overseer in the DATI, exonerated him. He was reinstated in his post and paid the back money due since his arrest. Home Secretary Samuel immediately ordered his suspension dryly noting that 'it does not necessarily follow that because this man was released from internment in England he is a fit person to be employed by the Crown'.[118] The re-employment of these ex-internees, naturally enough, provoked the Irish Unionist MPs. In July Major Walter Guinness asked the prime minister about the clerks Patrick Kelly, Patrick Sheehan and Robert Rooney of the ILC, who had fought in the rebellion, had been released by Sankey and returned to the land commission, where they were cheered as returning heroes, and were once again put in receipt of government pay. However, the growing sympathy for the rebels was already affecting the interpretation of the Rising and Thomas Lundon, the Nationalist MP for East Limerick, immediately accused Unionists like Major Guinness of using the rebellion to 'drive Catholics out of every government post in Dublin'.[119]

The cases of Sheehan, Kelly and Rooney illustrate the confusion that began to surround the question of disloyalty in the civil service. Patrick Sheehan had been arrested at his home in the immediate aftermath of the Rising by the military when they found ammunition and a uniform at his home. The G Division detectives in the DMP in fact considered Sheehan a member of the Redmondite

National Volunteers. This difference was too subtle for the military authorities and he was sent to Knutsford prison even though he had not participated in the Rising. Patrick Kelly was unknown to the police but had been arrested as part of the Jacob's factory garrison. He maintained that he had simply gone to Jacob's factory out of curiosity and had been ordered inside at gunpoint by the rebels. Rooney had been arrested by the military at his office but he was unknown to the police and no evidence of any wrongdoing had been found. It is possible that he was the victim of a malicious informer.[120] Sheehan became something of a *cause célèbre*. After Major Guinness's parliamentary question he was suspended from his department. Lundon used his case to make the general point that Sinn Féin sympathy was growing in the Irish civil service because they saw 'day after day Protestants and Freemasons being appointed over their heads to the positions which Catholics should enjoy'.[121] Sheehan, he suggested, was 'fingered' by lower-division clerks anxious to fill his position. Sheehan was finally dismissed but found immediate employment as permanent secretary of Sinn Féin. There is no doubt that Sheehan was in fact an active Irish Volunteer.[122] He, however, clearly felt that, although he was sympathetic to its aims, as he was not active in the Rising he was entitled to retain his post. He was exactly the sort of civil servant that Guinness wanted purged because in his view the security of the State depended on having confidence in the unswerving loyalty of its civil service.[123] To Irish nationalist opinion Guinness was simply trying to start a witch-hunt against Catholics in the civil service and was being egged on by malicious informants. This, in their view, had nothing to do with State security and everything to do with sectarian ambitions. By July Laurence Ginnell was asking the prime minister for the names of each civil servant in Ireland dismissed, threatened with dismissal, reduced in rank, denied normal promotion or transferred, due to connection with Irish Volunteers from July 1914 to April 1916 when the Volunteers were not an illegal organisation.[124]

The Wilson and Byrne inquiry

Sankey's inquiry was in fact of the most cursory kind. He did a quick trawl to sort out the 1,841 cases of internees and, having identified the 569 dangerous cases to be kept in internment, allowed the release of the others. He did not in fact attempt to determine guilt or innocence, simply the degree of danger presented to the State.[125] The government therefore established an internal and confidential inquiry to deal with the problem of the civil servants who had been released by Sankey, but now remained suspended. In July Sir Guy Fleetwood Wilson and Sir William Byrne, an English Catholic recently appointed as Assistant Under-Secretary, began a discreet investigation to 'consider the cases of Irish Civil Servants who have been suspended from their duties owing to their suspected complicity with the recent Rebellion and to advise how they should be dealt with'.[126] These were not only those released by Sankey and suspended but also those civil servants who had escaped detention but were suspected by the departmental heads of Sinn Féin sympathies. Civil servants still in detention were taken to have been proved guilty and were not considered. In the growing reaction against the Castle regime and the prevailing spirit of reconciliation, Wilson and Byrne deliberately avoided associating their investigation with the Castle. They dealt directly with the departmental heads, private rooms were secured in Hume Street and secretarial and clerical assistance dispensed with. Working from lists of suspects forwarded by the heads of departments along with departmental, military and police records, and after interviewing fourteen of the departmental heads, the investigation looked at the cases of forty-two men, mostly of the lower ranks. The accused were encouraged to make the best possible case for themselves and were assured that both Wilson and Byrne, as civil servants themselves, would find it 'a genuine pleasure' to recommend reinstatement.[127] The reaction of the accused, however, dismayed their interrogators:

> We had greatly hoped that no cases, or only isolated instances of evident disloyalty would come before us, but we regret to have to state that in a good many cases we have felt it our duty to recommend removal from the service. The confession of faith of the suspect was often tendered freely, frankly and unblushingly. Briefly it amounted in many cases to a declaration that so long as the individual in question discharged his official duties satisfactorily during office hours, he was fully entitled to do as he pleased out of office hours, even if it involved violence which might lead to the killing of troops or police officers. This view was expressed not by the lowest ranks only. In more than one instance the allegation that a man engaged in military operations had not actually fired at a soldier was advanced as sufficient justification for re-instatement. We have been struck by the readiness with which a considerable number of those inculpated air views quite incompatible, in our view, with their position as public servants. In no instance were we altogether satisfied that such Civil Servants as actually took active part in the rebellion, under alleged compulsion, could not have withdrawn at an early stage of it. . . . Owing to the peculiar political situation in Ireland, we did not, broadly speaking, judge men only from the standpoint of their continued connection with the Sinn Fein movement. We were guided by their activities, their explanations thereof, by their mental attitude towards the rebellion, and by their expressed intention in the future to subordinate or otherwise, their loyalty as public servants, to their political creed.[128]

The most senior civil servant dismissed was J.J. McElligott, a first class clerk in the LGB, whose plea that he had been forced at gunpoint into participation in the Rising did not save him, although participation, albeit reluctant, did help to further his later successful career in the Irish Free State civil service.[129] Of the forty-two cases dealt with twenty-three were dismissed, one pensioned, and eighteen reinstated. No notes were kept and there is no evident rationale in the decisions, which probably reflected the demeanour of the accused. It is said that it is easier to sack the Pope than a civil servant, but by any reckoning Wilson and Byrne may be considered very generous in their treatment. However, it was very deliberately noted by them that their investigation found no evidence whatsoever for Nathan's assertion that civil servants had been circularised to withdraw from the Irish Volunteers, nor could any of those interviewed recollect any such circular. Such a circular had indeed been drafted but apparently never actually issued. Arguably therefore simple membership of the Volunteers without active participation in the rebellion was, in their view, excusable.[130]

At a more general level Wilson and Byrne were clearly worried by the evident lack of identification with the State among Irish civil servants and the gulf between the senior and junior ranks. The ethos of non-political bureaucratic service binding the civil service to the State in Britain was non-existent in Dublin. Their report recommended that

> advantage should be taken of the present situation, by serious and combined effort on the part of all concerned, to instil a higher tone in the ranks of the Irish Civil Service and to require a more distinct recognition of the obligation which properly attach to Public Service. We believe that much good would result if increased interest were shown in, and if friendly advice were more freely tendered to, young Civil Servants by their Chiefs.[131]

One idea that Wilson and Byrne advanced as a way to remind civil servants of a sense of duty was that all civil servants throughout the United Kingdom ought to be obliged to take an oath of allegiance to the Crown such as was required of the armed forces. This proposal reappeared much later, in 1918, though now with no reference to Ireland. Some MPs, Col McCalmont the Ulster Unionist was prominent, managed to become convinced that British failures on the western front were due to pro-German elements in the civil service either leaking secrets to the German military command or deliberately sabotaging the British war machine. Viscount Haldane, because of his admiration for German scholarship, was an early casualty of Unionist xenophobia, being dropped from government in May 1915.[132] The solution was an oath of allegiance, which, apparently, would reveal the traitors. In Ireland this demand for an oath was seen as an attempted 'combing out' of nationalists. The oath was avoided where possible, taken with bad grace in most cases, and in a few cases refused outright.[133] Those who refused were F.X. Thunder, David O'Donoghue and E. Cleary in the ILC, Diarmuid O'Hegarty and Michael McDunphy, both second division clerks in the DATI, Tom McArdle, a second division clerk in the LGB, and P. Cremins and Eamon Duggan in the Post Office. A protest meeting of the

'recusants' was organised but they all remained dismissed.[134] The newly organised Assistant Clerks' Association (ACA) took up the case of the oath, which
they regarded as an encroachment on their civil rights, but failed to organise any
significant opposition to it. The ACA continued to financially support dismissed members until they found employment.[135] Dismissal for refusing to take
the oath of allegiance was one of the criteria accepted by the committee for the
reinstatement of civil servants, set up by the Free State government under the
chairmanship of P.S. O'Hegarty. In all fifty-three cases were considered of civil
servants who could establish that they had been dismissed for sympathy with or
participation in the 1916 rebellion; or for refusing the Oath of Allegiance, or for
refusing to join the British armed forces.[136] None of those actually dismissed in
1918 for refusing to take the oath were among those who made an application
to the 1923 P.S. O'Hegarty committee.

As the administration in Dublin Castle returned to what passed for normal-
ity the civil servants noted the few vacant places, none of them a surprise.[137] For
the mass of the Irish civil service, the foot soldiers in the State apparatus, the
Rising had been a brief burst of excitement but apart from the dismissal of a few
colleagues one that brought no significant changes. One cynic described the
Rising as 'the most exciting event in the Irish government since a senior clerk
was promoted, probably mistakenly'.[138] The Irish National Aid Association,
formed by Collins to assist the survivors of the Rising and to re-mobilise the revolutionary movement, which we might assume had the most complete list of
those affected, assisted seventy-two dismissed civil servants.[139] However, as the
government investigation into the Rising deepened, its conclusions indicated
that the problem was more than a very few disaffected civil servants in the minor
grades. The suspicion lingered that the numbers detected concealed a far greater
number that remained hidden.

Dublin Castle after the Rising

Lloyd George reported to the House of Commons in the immediate aftermath
of the Rising that the existing system of government in Ireland had broken
down.[140] The Hardinge inquiry into the Rising utterly damned the entire
Dublin Castle administration as 'anomalous in quiet times, and almost
unworkable in times of crisis'.[141] The most dramatic impact of the Rising was
therefore on the top ranks of the Irish administration.

Wimborne remained as Lord Lieutenant but both Birrell and Nathan
resigned and a military regime was instituted under General Maxwell.
Meanwhile Lloyd George tried and failed to inveigle the Irish Nationalists and
Unionists to accept an immediate implementation of Home Rule for the
twenty-six counties by promising the Nationalists that partition was temporary
while assuring the Unionists it was permanent. Meanwhile the opportunity to

reform the administration, which all admitted was an urgent task, slipped away. In the absence of any initiative the old administrative system reasserted itself as H.E. Duke (a 61-year-old English barrister and Unionist MP with no ministerial experience) was appointed Chief Secretary with Robert Chalmers, famous for being the rudest man in Whitehall whose 'pomposity and cynicism concealed his many benefactions', as Under-Secretary.[142] Chalmers was one of the most brilliant and ruthless officials in the Treasury. A liberal in his politics he played a key role during the 1909 'People's Budget' struggle. Falling out of favour with Lloyd George he was exiled to Ceylon in 1913. His return to Dublin Castle signalled perhaps a step toward full rehabilitation and a return to Whitehall. Duke was lauded by Asquith for bringing to the position a judicial mind, a firm hand, administrative capacity, sympathy with the Irish people and a strong desire to promote an Irish settlement. His first task, according to Asquith, was to undertake a careful survey of the whole administrative situation with all its possibilities.[143] There is no evidence that any such survey was undertaken.

Both Chalmers and Duke made it clear to the staff in the Castle that they had reluctantly agreed to come to Dublin and expected to be bothered as little as possible.[144] Chalmers was not going to waste his time and expertise on reform of the Irish administration and by October had gone back to Whitehall. Castle government returned to Ireland, advised and assisted by a civil service that only some weeks previously had been condemned as useless. In October, after the departure of Chalmers, Magill replied to Duke's complaint that he, Duke, was having to run the office on his own, with a description of the cuts that the war had wrought on his staff. In 1913 the Irish Office in London had a staff of seven: a private secretary, a parliamentary private secretary, an assistant private secretary, one chief clerk, one second division clerk and two typists. It now consisted of Magill himself and two typists, one of whom was about to be called up by the military. Since the outbreak of the war Magill had had one week's leave, had worked on Sundays and holidays and had to constantly divide his time between London and Dublin. Clearly Magill was feeling little sympathy for his Chief Secretary. The only solution he could suggest was that Duke should try and get Duggan and Hamilton, who had gone to the Admiralty, to return. But the derisory salaries offered by the CSO would have to be improved to attract them back. Magill once again struck what was now a familiar note when he underlined the urgency of an inquiry into the staffing of the CSO and the Irish Office.[145]

The overwhelming needs of the war were not only cutting a swathe through the staff in Dublin Castle, they were also constraining the ability of Duke to pursue an imaginative Irish policy. The summer of 1916 saw the disaster of the Somme campaign, the failure of the British navy to win the Battle of Jutland and the death of Kitchener, the symbol of the British war spirit. In comparison

Ireland was parochial. Also, as Duke was reporting to a coalition cabinet divided only by Ireland, it would be foolhardy to invite dissensions. Walter Long revived once again the old idea of abolishing the viceroyalty and strengthening the office of the Chief Secretary to that of a full secretary of state, but Wimborne resisted, determined to be important.[146] The reforms that were introduced were primarily personnel rather than structural. In a process of 'Greening' the administration John J. Taylor was passed over for the post of Under Secretary for William Byrne, a Catholic (though English) and joint investigator of the civil service participants in the 1916 Rising. The new head of the RIC was also Catholic, General Sir Joseph Byrne; so was the new Attorney General, James O'Connor.[147] At a private lunch Duggan told Magill that he was not 'too eager to return to the intricacies of Irish policy and the work of Dublin Castle'.[148]

By year's end it was being complained that the Irish offices were under-manned to the point of crisis and economy was being applied beyond the bounds of common sense, yet the Treasury remained inflexible. The needs of the war demanded that no new posts should be created, no promotions made and that shortfalls would have to be made good by loans of staff from other departments.[149] The DATI was subject to an investigation by Maurice Headlam and Sir John Irwin. Irwin, a minor figure in Dublin Unionist politics, was a paper merchant who appeared regularly in *Stubb's Gazette* as a defaulter. Their investigation showed a complete inability to understand the organisation or function of the DATI and was utterly worthless.[150] The failure to restructure the Castle, along with the failure to rethink Irish policy, was the end of any realistic attempt to engage with the problems of Irish administration.

The Irish Convention

The Irish Convention, which met from July 1917 to April 1918, was an attempt by Lloyd George to rush an Irish settlement, partly in answer to American critics and partly to rescue the Home Rule party, which was clearly losing ground to Sinn Féin. However, even though it was apparent that the Home Rule Bill would be amended, the general expectation was still that in the end Ireland would be governed by some form of Home Rule with the supremacy of Westminster intact. Overall, government policy remained one of Home Rule with provision for Ulster exclusion.

As it became clear that Home Rule was once again subject to amendment the GCICS seized the opportunity to present a position paper to the Irish Convention requesting that any future proposals for an Irish government would address deficiencies in the clauses dealing with civil servants in the 1914 Act.[151] Under the operation of patronage by the Birrell regime in particular and with the advance of competitive entry in general, the lower ranks of the civil service in Ireland, in what has been called the 'Greening of Dublin Castle', were becoming more Catholic and nationalist.[152] The membership of the 1917 GCICS, and the demands put forward in the statement, attest the dominance in Irish civil service organisation that had been achieved by the lower (and therefore Catholic) grades of the second division and clerical staffs since the formation of the original 1911 committee.[153] The continued expansion of the State in Ireland is also reflected in the increase in the number of government departments represented on the committee – thirty-four as opposed to the twenty-nine of 1911. All of the new departments were Irish branches of British departments. The 1917 committee also had delegates from twenty-one civil service associations. The 1911 representative scheme of delegates from the professional, higher, second division and clerical grades had not been sustained. Instead, the 1917 GCICS was composed of quasi-trade union associations representing the clerkdom of the lower grades only, along with representatives of departments. Of the 114 delegates on the general committee, 40 were from civil service associations, many of which were Irish branches of British organisations. In contrast to the general committee, which was still dominated by departmental delegates, association delegates dominated the executive committee.

Not only did the clerical grades, the rank and file of the civil service, dominate the representation on the general committee they also dominated its proposals, and the demands of the professional and higher-grade officers were added on almost as an afterthought. The demands of the civil servants for a better retirement and severance deal would imply either an expectation or intent of leaving the service of a Home Rule executive. Such were the demands of the GCICS in 1912. The 1917 committee, however, while addressing issues of a better severance deal, was primarily focused on security for meritocratic promotion. This implies an expectation and commitment of continuous service to a future Home Rule administration. The former demand for a severance deal is implicitly unionist, the latter demand for security for promotion is implicitly nationalist. By 1917 the Civil Service Committee, as it became dominated by the lower grades and temporary clerks, had become implicitly nationalist. This also reflected a generational difference. Older men were most concerned that the terms for voluntary or compulsory retirement would be sufficient to secure them continuity in the lifestyle to which they had become accustomed. The 1917 committee wanted even better money terms for those compelled to retire (and there was an even greater expectation of compulsion after 1916) as well as better security for those who opted to retire. With the experience of wartime inflation the statement also wanted a provision that pensions should match salary increases in the relevant grade for a period of years.[154]

Loyal to the huge numbers of temporary fellow civil servants the statement demanded recognition of temporary whole-time officers as permanent civil servants, recognition of temporary years for reckoning pension entitlements, and an entitlement to added years in calculating pensions for those officers with a professional qualification in recognition of their years of study. But the key new demand put forward by the 1917 committee was not for better retirement conditions but rather for guarantees for promotional opportunities for the lower grades. The great fear within the civil service was that with the complete disruption of structures and departments imposed by the war, and with the local uncertainties of post-1916 Ireland, the post-war civil service would be used to award the friends of those in power. The immediate demand of the civil servants' committee was for additional security regarding promotion within the Irish service, 'a question which is regarded by all ranks as a vital one'. They asked for a provision in the bill to prevent the appointment of 'outsiders' to posts that could be filled by fully qualified officers already in the service. The committee in their statement did acknowledge that there might be some appointments to posts 'for which certain special technical or professional qualifications are essential' but did anticipate that such cases would be comparatively rare. Clearly the GCICS was very sceptical about the claims of expertise made for the great majority of higher-grade posts and saw these as sinecures and patronage appointments blocking the usual avenues of promotion.[155] The wartime halt to recruitment to the higher grades had created large gaps in government departments that would have to be filled. The fear was that these higher posts would become filled by a recrudescence of patronage under a future Home Rule government.

Recognising that the Irish civil service would in all probability be a much smaller service, with limited promotional opportunities, the 1917 statement wanted legislation to allow for transfers and exchanges between the British and Irish services, and for Irish civil servants to be allowed to continue to compete for promotional posts within the British service. The British service had supplied nearly 90 per cent of the promotional opportunities for Irish civil servants. The loss of that opportunity opened up a depressing prospect of a lifetime of assistant clerkship. This also suggests that the lower ranks of the Irish civil service, though more nationalist, were not necessarily separatist.

In general the statement made it clear that it was expected that what it described as 'the natural channels' of promotion from within the ranks would be clearly laid down in any amended legislation, and followed. The statement also strongly expressed the preference within the Irish civil service for the extension of entry exclusively by open competitive examination. Where a vacancy occurred for a post that required specialist qualifications the vacancy should be publicly advertised with particulars of the qualifications required. These posts could also be filled through promotion from within the service by a limited competition or a qualifying examination. The 1917 committee identified the Civil Service Committee established by the 1914 Act to deal with questions affecting the rights of existing officers as an important strategic advantage, one that diluted Treasury power, and asked for increased representation on, and increased powers for, that committee. They asked that the committee be increased to five members with two members elected by the Irish civil service, and that the quorum of the committee should be three. They also wanted the Civil Service Committee to be empowered to act as a court of appeal for any civil servant unhappy with his retirement terms.[156]

Attitudes toward the Irish civil service were generally less sympathetic with allegations of shirking war service being bandied about. Also the 1916 Rising had revealed that the Irish civil service had within its ranks a lower standard of loyalty than was expected. The report of the Convention contented itself with pious generalities rather than specific measures. The report suggested that an Irish civil service commission, following as closely as possible English practices and with Unionist representation, be established to regulate competitive examinations for admission to the public services, to determine salaries appropriate to Ireland, to decide on promotions and to exercise the patronage of higher appointments.[157]

Walter Long and the Irish civil service

On 9 April 1918 Lloyd George announced that Ireland was to have both conscription and a new measure of self-government. Walter Long was persuaded to act as chairman of the drafting committee on the new Home Rule Bill.[158] The key figure on the GCICS was its chairman, Barlas of the LGB, a veteran of every civil servant Home Rule committee since 1893 and a diligent worker in the corridors of political power. Edward Saunderson, second son of Colonel Saunderson, the first leader of the Ulster Unionist Party, gave Barlas access to the cabinet through his close relationship with Walter Long. Long had been instrumental in getting Saunderson a permanent post at the LGB and then promotion to the coveted and influential post of private secretary to the new Lord Lieutenant French in April 1918. The LGB seems to have been a fertile source for civil servants of impeccable 'die-hard' unionist opinion. From there Sam Watt was parachuted into position as private secretary to the new Chief Secretary Ian Macpherson in early 1919, over the heads of two better-qualified Catholic candidates. Saunderson remained Long's creature and as a unionist 'die-hard' he exercised a malign influence on Lord French.[159]

There was little prospect of a Home Rule measure being actually passed by parliament in 1918 but any bill that was produced would help set out the terms under which any future Irish settlement would be made.[160] It was in that spirit that Barlas immediately wrote a private letter to Saunderson, before a meeting of the Home Rule committee. What Barlas asked was that Saunderson should contact Long 'who has always been sympathetic to the Irish civil servants' and pass on to him a copy of the 1917 statement with an offer to meet with Barlas who could convey the fears of the civil service and the hope that he might address these in the bill.[161]

Long immediately replied to Barlas and, in an exchange of letters, Barlas outlined the principles that ought to guide the civil service clauses. Barlas complained that the Irish Convention had 'contented themselves with a pious expression of opinion that the rights of existing officers should be preserved'. The only practical suggestion that had been made was the establishment of an Irish civil service commission. The position of the Irish civil service would be anything but secure under any Irish government likely to be elected in the circumstances of anti-conscription agitation. Barlas was himself quite fearful, more so probably than the majority of the lower ranks of the service. 'The feeling in the greater part of the country is notoriously anti-British' he told Long, and 'civil servants transferred will be in a much more precarious position now than they would have been in had the 1914 Act come into operation 3 or 4 years ago'. It was his position that the GCICS statement of 1917 was no longer sufficient to protect the interests of the civil service. While mindful of the importance of the difficult question of loss of prospects and security regarding promotion (at the core of the 1917 statement and mainly affecting civil servants determined to stay on) Barlas was of the opinion that 'the whole thing narrows itself down to the financial penalties to be imposed on any new government for removing civil servants without just cause or for alteration of their present rates of remuneration and status'.[162] He wanted the British government to legislate so that any future Home Rule governments would find it not only administratively difficult but also financially crippling to impose cuts on the civil service. Long then forwarded to Sir Robert Chalmers at the Treasury an edited version of Barlas's letter, containing the requested legislative changes, along with a copy of the 1917 statement. The 1918 Home Rule proposal petered out, but Walter Long was now entrenched as the cabinet liaison with the Irish administration and the primary influence on Irish legislation.

Notes

1 Mary E. Daly, 'The formation of an Irish nationalist elite? Recruitment to the Irish civil service in the decades prior to independence 1870–1920', *Paedogogica Historica* (Belgium), 30:1 (1994), pp. 281–301.

2 Patricia Jalland, 'Irish Home Rule finance: a neglected dimension of the Irish question, 1910–14', *Irish Historical Studies*, 23:91 (1983), pp. 233–53.

3 Alan O'Day, *Irish Home Rule 1867–1921* (Manchester, 1998), pp. 243–6.

4 University College Dublin Archives Department (UCDAD), LA24, George Chester Duggan, 'The Life of a Civil Servant', chapter 3.

5 *Parliamentary Debates* (Commons), XXXVIII, col. 121, 11 Apr. 1912.

6 Government of Ireland Act, 1914 [4 & 5 Geo. 5. c. 90] sections 32 to 36, Third Schedule; *Irish Times* 9 Dec. 1912.

7 National Archives, London (NA), TS 18/235, Treasury solicitor's general series papers: civil service provisions under the Government of Ireland Act, 1912, 'Letter 10 May 1911, Barlas et al.'.

8 Ibid., 'Preliminary Statement of Irish civil servants as to their position, having regard to contemplated legislation dealing with the Government of Ireland' (Nov. 1911).

9 Ibid., 'Barlas to Greer, 5 and 30 Dec. 1912'.

10 *Parliamentary Debates* (Commons), XLV, cols 90–6, 9 Dec. 1912.

11 NA, TS 18/235, 'Barlas to Greer, 5 Dec. 1912'.

12 Ibid., Civil service resolutions 19 Dec 1912; *Parliamentary Debates* (Commons), XLV, cols 90–6, 9 Dec. 1912.

13 NA, TS 18/235, 'Preliminary Statement of Irish civil servants as to their position, having regard to contemplated legislation dealing with the Government of Ireland' (Nov. 1911).

14 Donald Denoon, *A Grand Illusion: The Failure of Imperial Policy in the Transvaal Colony During the Period of Reconstruction 1900–1905* (London, 1973).

15 Deirdre McMahon, 'Ireland and the Empire-Commonwealth, 1900–1948' in Judith M. Brown (ed.) *The Oxford History of the British Empire Volume IV, The Twentieth Century* (Oxford, 1999), pp. 138–62, 148.

16 *Parliamentary Debates* (Lords), CLXII, cols 633–66 31, July 1906, (Commons), CLIII, col. 290, 6 Mar. 1906; *The Times*, 19 Aug. 1907.

17 *The Times*, 6 and 9 June, 18 July, 5 and 14 Aug. 1908 for statements, articles and correspondence on the Transvaal retrenched officers.

18 NA, TS 18/235, 'Greer to the Chief Secretary Ireland, 6 Feb. 1912'.

19 Government of Ireland Act, 1914 [4 & 5 Geo.5., c. 90] clause 33.

20 Ibid., Third Schedule.

21 *Parliamentary Debates* (Commons), XLV, col. 29, 9 Dec. 1912.

22 NA, TS 18/235, 'Further Statement of Irish Civil Servants as to their position under the Government of Ireland Bill, 1912' (June 1912), p. 1.

23 NA, Home Office, Northern Ireland files, CJ4/30, 'Spender, Anderson, Waterfield correspondence on article 65 of the Eighth schedule 1920 Act', 1930–31.

24 NA, TS 18/235, 'Memorandum on the proposals of the committee of civil servants', 19 Dec. 1912.

25 National Library of Ireland (NLI) Joseph Brennan Papers, MS 26,149, 'Draft of Government of Ireland (Amendment) Bill Section 5 existing officers'.

26 NA, TS 18/235, 'Further Statement submitted by the General Committee of the Irish Civil Servants as to their position in view of amendments to the Government of Ireland Bill' (May 1914), p. 1.

27 UCDAD, LA24, Duggan, 'Life of a civil servant', p. 3.

28 Ibid.

29 Maurice Headlam, *Irish Reminiscences* (London, 1947), p. 196; O'Halpin, *Decline of the Union*, pp. 139, 177.

30 Charles W. Magill (ed.) *From Dublin Castle to Stormont: the memoirs of Andrew Philip Magill, 1913–1925* (Cork, 2003), p. 24.

31 *Royal commission on the civil service second appendix to the fourth report of the commissioners, minutes of evidence 9 Jan. 1913–20 June 1913 with*

appendices, Parliamentary Papers, HC 1914, XVI [Cd.7340], 363 (MacDonnell Commission).

32 O'Halpin, *Decline of the Union*, pp. 33–6.

33 Trinity College Dublin (TCD), MS 3918A, Sir David Harrel, 'Recollections and reflections', pp. 157–8.

34 Ibid., pp. 44–51.

35 Ibid., pp. 74–6.

36 Lord MacDonnell of Swinford, 'Irish Administration under Home Rule' in J.H. Morgan (ed.) *The New Irish Constitution: an exposition and some arguments* (London, 1912), pp. 50–80.

37 MacDonnell Commission, evidence of Sir James Dougherty.

38 Ibid., evidence of Sir James Dougherty, pp. 547–9.

39 Ibid., evidence of Sir Henry Robinson.

40 Ibid, evidence of T.P. Gill, p. 240.

41 Marie-Louise Legg, 'Gill, Thomas Patrick (1858–1931)', *Oxford Dictionary of National Biography*.

42 M.J. Gallagher, 'Memoirs of a civil servant 1895–1974' (typescript in the possession of his son Rev. Colm Gallagher, Arklow, Co. Wicklow), p. 4

43 MacDonnell Commission, evidence of staff representatives, pp. 602–74.

44 Ibid., evidence of the Irish Temporary Clerks' Association, p. 553.

45 Magill (ed.), *From Dublin Castle to Stormont*; W.L. Micks, *An Account of the Constitution, Administration and Dissolution of the Congested Districts Board for Ireland from 1891 to 1923* (Dublin, 1925); Henry Robinson, *Memories: Wise and Otherwise* (London, 1923); Headlam, *Irish Reminiscences*.

46 B.V. Humphreys, *Clerical Unions in the Civil Service* (Oxford, 1958), p. 78.

47 Mary E. Daly, *The First Department: A History of the Department of Agriculture* (Dublin, 2002), pp. 598–9.

48 R.B. McDowell, 'Administration and the public services' in W.E. Vaughan (ed.) *A New History of Ireland VI, Ireland under the Union, II, 1870–1921* (Oxford, 1996), pp. 571–605, 598.

49 O'Halpin, *Decline of the Union*, pp. 111–12.

50 Daly, *The First Department*, p. 60.

51 Colin Newbury, 'Nathan, Sir Matthew (1862–1939)', *Oxford Dictionary of National Biography*, vol. 40, pp. 268–9.

52 UCDAD, LA24, Duggan, 'Life of a civil servant'; McBride, *The Greening of Dublin Castle*, p. 182.

53 Oxford, Bodleian Library, Nathan Papers, MS 454, fols 4–5.

54 Leon Ó'Broin, *No Man's Man: A Biographical Memoir of Joseph Brennan Civil Servant and First Governor of the Central Bank* (Dublin, 1982), pp. 30–1.

55 Oxford, Bodleian Library, Nathan Papers, MS 455, fol. 222.

56 Ibid., MS 454, fol. 29.

57 UCDAD, LA24, Duggan, 'Life of a civil servant'.

58 NLI, Brennan Papers, MS 26,151, 'Memos of interviews, Nov. 1914–Jan. 1916'.

59 Ibid., 'Interview Sir Henry Robinson 12 Jan. 1916'.

60 TCD, John Dillon Papers, MS 6801/156–82.

61 Leon Ó'Broin, *Dublin Castle and the 1916 Rising* (London, 1966), p. 39.

62 TCD, MS 3918A, Sir David Harrel, 'Recollections and reflections', p. 157.

63 TCD, Dillon Papers, MS 6801/161, 'Meeting 17 Feb. 1915'.

64 Ibid., 'Meeting 24 Feb. 1915, memorandum by Sir Francis Greer'.

65 NLI, Brennan Papers, MS 26,149, 'Letter secretary OPW, 26 Apr. 1913'.

66 TCD, Dillon Papers, MS163, 'Meeting 24 Feb. 1915'.

67 Ibid., MS 167, 'Meeting 11 Mar. 1915'.

68 John Redmond, *Ireland's Financial Relations With England: The Case Stated* (Dublin, 1905), p. 4.

69 NLI, Brennan Papers, MS 26,174, 'Conference 2 July 1915'.

70 TCD, Dillon Papers, MS 6801, 'Meeting 5 Mar. 1915'.

71 Ibid., MSS 6801/167 and 182.

72 Redmond, *Ireland's Financial Relations*, p. 5.

73 NLI, Brennan Papers, MS 26,175, 'Memo prepared by Maurice Headlam 1 April 1915'.

74 Ibid., 'Memorandum on the Irish Dept of Finance'.

75 Oxford, Bodleian Library, Nathan Papers MS 453, fol. 155.

76 *Second report of the committee on retrenchment in the public expenditure,* Parliamentary Papers, HC 1914–16, XXXIII [Cd.8139], 375; Headlam, *Irish Reminiscences*, pp. 69–70; Patrick Maume, *The Long Gestation: Irish Nationalist Life, 1891–1918* (Dublin, 1999), pp. 173–4.

77 Ó'Broin, *No Man's Man*, pp. 37–9.

78 National Archives Ireland (NAI), Chief Secretary's Office Registered Papers (CSORP), 1916/25, 469 and 26,040, 'Notice for parliamentary question, 12 Oct. 1916'.

79 Ibid., 1917/10,637, 'Files relating to civil servants in receipt of army pay'.

80 *Red Tape*, 6:62 (Nov. 1916).

81 Ibid., 6:68 (May 1917).

82 Oxford, Bodleian Library, Nathan Papers, MS 450, fol. 210.

83 NLI, Brennan Papers, MS 26,189, 'Memorandum of interview with Mr John Dillon 16 Mar. 1916'.

84 Ó'Broin, *Dublin Castle and the 1916 Rising*, pp. 37–9, 77.

85 Gallagher, 'Memoirs of a civil servant', pp. 9–11.

86 Robinson, *Memories: Wise and Otherwise*, p. 223.

87 Quoted in Ó'Broin, *Dublin Castle and the 1916 Rising*, p. 32.

88 Oxford, Bodleian Library, Nathan Papers, MS 450, fols 169–70.

89 *Royal commission on the rebellion in Ireland, minutes of evidence and appendix of documents*, Parliamentary Papers, HC 1916, XI, [Cd. 8311], 185, pp. 17–18.

90 Michael Tierney, *Eoin MacNeill Scholar and Man of Action 1867–1945*, ed. F.X. Martin (Dublin, 1980), p. 9.

91 NAI, Bureau of Military History (BMH), witness statement (ws) 889, James Kavanagh.

92 E.g. ibid., ws 804, Mortimer O'Connell (Customs and Excise); 848, Harry C. Phibbs (Cuchullain Clubs); 334, Eugene Smith (Dublin Castle official); 683, Hugh Hehir (Irish Land Commission); 889, James Kavanagh (Post Office).

93   Tom Garvin, *The Evolution of Irish Nationalist Politics* (Dublin, 1981), pp. 100–2.

94   Gallagher, 'Memoirs of a civil servant', p. 6.

95   Deirdre McMahon (ed.), *The Moynihan Brothers in Peace and War 1909–1918: Their New Ireland* (Dublin, 2004).

96   *Royal commission on the rebellion in Ireland*, evidence of Sir Matthew Nathan, pp. 186–204, steps taken to prevent civil servants joining the IV 189–90.

97   Oxford, Bodleian Library, Nathan Papers, MS 454 fols 256–8.

98   NLI, Brennan Papers, MS 26,151 'Interview with Devlin 11 Nov. 1914'.

99   Ibid., MS 26,189, 'Memo of interview 29 Feb. 1916'.

100   Ó'Broin, *Dublin Castle and the 1916 Rising*, pp. 32–7.

101   NLI, Brennan Papers, MSS 25,151 and 26,164.

102   Ibid., MS 26,177, 'Memoranda official interviews by Matthew Nathan, 4 May 1915'.

103   *Royal commission on the rebellion in Ireland*, evidence of Sir Matthew Nathan.

104   NAI, BMH, ws 683, Hugh Hehir.

105   Ibid., ws 804, Mortimer O'Connell.

106   Ibid., ws 334, Eugene Smith.

107   Mary Louise and Arthur Hamilton Norway, 'Irish experiences in war' in *The Sinn Féin Rebellion as they saw it*, ed. Keith Jeffrey (Dublin, 1916, 1999 reprint edition), pp. 87–122.

108   *Royal commission on the rebellion in Ireland*, evidence of Mr A.H. Norway.

109   NAI, CSORP, 1916/7703, 'General prisons board'; /7709, 'RIC office staff'; /7720, 'Customs and Excise Dublin'; /11,391, 'DATI staff'; /11,416, 'Land Registry staff'; /11,495, 'National Education Office staff'; /11,499, 'DMP office staff'.

110   Ibid., 1916/11,492, 'Staff statements NHIC, 10 May 1916'.

111   NAI, BMH, ws 683, Hugh Hehir; CSORP, 1916/11,501, 'Irish Land Commission return of staff'.

112   NAI, CSORP, 1916/11,501, 'Irish Land Commission return of staff'.

113   O'Halpin, *Decline of the Union*, pp. 126–7.

114   NLI, Brennan Papers, MS 26,194, 'Sankey committee May–Aug. 1916'.

115   O'Halpin, *Decline of the Union*, p. 127.

116   NAI, BMH, ws 141, James Kenny.

117   NAI, CSORP, 1916/21,649, 'Joseph Derham, Land Commission'.

118   Ibid., 1916/13,070, 29 July 1916.

119   *Parliamentary Debates* (Commons), LXXXIII, cols 1508–9, 5 July 1916; LXXXIV, col. 658, 17 July 1916.

120   NAI, CSORP, 1916/12,149, 'DMP G Division report on Irish Land Commission clerks'.

121   *Parliamentary Debates* (Commons), LXXXIV, cols 1771–8, 26 July 1916.

122   NAI, BMH, ws 1050, Vera McDonnell; 889, James Kavanagh.

123   *Parliamentary Debates* (Commons), LXXXIV, col. 2159, 31 July 1916.

124   NAI, CSORP, 1916/25,941, 'Return for parliamentary question 5 July 1916'.

125   *Parliamentary Debates* (Commons), LXXXIV, col. 2139, 26 July 1916.

126   NLI Brennan Papers, MS 26,185, 'Report on the cases of Irish civil servants suspended in connection with the recent rebellion by Right Hon. Sir Guy Fleetwood

Wilson, G.C.I.E, K.C.B., K.C.M.G. and Sir William P. Byrne, K.C.V.O., C.B', 16 August 1916, p. 1.

127 Ibid.

128 Ibid., p. 2.

129 O'Halpin, *Decline of the Union*, pp. 127–8.

130 'Report on the cases of Irish civil servants suspended in connection with the recent rebellion', p. 3.

131 Ibid.

132 H.C.G. Matthew, 'Haldane, Richard Burdon (1856–1928)', *Oxford Dictionary of National Biography*; *Parliamentary debates* (Commons), Fifth Series, CVIII, col. 1444, 22 July 1918; CX, col. 432, 21 Oct. 1918.

133 NAI, BMH, ws 462, Seán O'Broin.

134 Ibid., ws 460, Joseph Thunder.

135 *Red Tape*, 8:88 (Jan. 1919), 'AGM of Dublin branch ACA 9 Dec. 1918'.

136 NAI, 'Victimised civil servants files 1923' [a miscellaneous box marked 'shelf 3/717'].

137 Gallagher, 'Memoirs of a civil servant', p. 29.

138 *Red Tape*, 6:64 (Jan. 1917).

139 NLI, MS 24,351, 'Irish National Aid Volunteer Dependents Fund papers'; George Gavan Duffy Papers, MS 24,357, 'Irish National Aid and Volunteer Dependents Fund'.

140 *Parliamentary Debates* (Commons), LXXXII, cols 2309–12, May 1916.

141 *Royal commission on the rebellion in Ireland*, p. 23.

142 G.C. Peden, 'Chalmers, Robert, Baron Chalmers (1858–1938)', *Oxford Dictionary of National Biography*.

143 *Parliamentary Debates* (Commons), LXXXIV, cols 2144–7, 31 July 1916.

144 Robinson, *Memoirs: Wise and Otherwise*, pp. 245–6.

145 NAI, Department of Finance, 'early E files', E1/8, 'CSO staff arrangements, Magill to CS, 10 Oct. 1916'. [The 'early E files' are an unlisted deposit of some thirty boxes from the Department of Finance transferred in 2001 to the NAI. These files relate to the earliest civil service establishment of the 1922–25 period. My thanks to Tom Quinlan and Mary Mackey of the NAI for making these available.]

146 House of Lords Record Office (HLRO), Lloyd George Papers, F/74/1/7, 'Wimborne to PM, 24 Mar. 1918'.

147 O'Halpin, *Decline of the Union*, pp. 118–34; McBride, *The Greening of Dublin Castle*, pp. 214–19.

148 NAI, Department of Finance, 'early E files', E1/8, 'Duggan to Edward O'Farrell, 27 Oct. 1916'.

149 Ibid., 'Memorandum to the Chief Secretary, 2 Jan. 1917'; 'Treasury memorandum, 24 Jan. 1917'.

150 HLRO, Lloyd George Papers, F/74/19/1–2.

151 NLI MS Ir.32341, 'Statement by the General Committee of Irish Civil Servants as to their position in view of further legislation affecting the Government of Ireland' (Dec. 1917). There is a copy of the statement in the Long Papers, Wiltshire and Swindon Record Office 947/147, with correspondence between Barlas and Long.

152 McBride, *The Greening of Dublin Castle*, pp. 187–92.
153 Martin Maguire, 'The civil service, the State and the Irish Revolution, 1886–1938'
     Ph.D University of Dublin, Trinity College, 2005, Appendix, table 4, Members of
     the General Committee of Irish Civil Servants, 1917.
154 NLI, MS Ir.32341, 'Statement by the General Committee of Irish Civil Servants as
     to their position in view of further legislation affecting the Government of Ireland'
     (Dec. 1917), pp. 6–7.
155 Gallagher, 'Memoirs of a civil servant', p. 40.
156 NLI, MS Ir.32341, 'Statement by the General Committee of Irish Civil Servants as
     to their position in view of further legislation affecting the Government of Ireland'
     (Dec. 1917), p. 5.
157 *Report of the proceedings of the Irish Convention*, Parliamentary Papers, HC 1918,
     X [Cd. 9019], 697, pp. 16–17.
158 John Kendle, *Walter Long, Ireland, and the Union, 1905–1920* (Montreal, 1992),
     pp. 148–71.
159 O'Halpin, *Decline of the Union*, pp. 164–6.
160 Turner, *Lloyd George's Secretariat* (London, 1980), p. 85.
161 Wiltshire and Swindon Record Office (WSRO), Walter Hume Long Papers,
     947/412/b, 'Barlas to Saunderson, 16 April 1918'.
162 Ibid., 'Barlas to Long 23, April 1918'.

2

Dublin Castle in crisis, 1918–21

Introduction

THE END OF THE FIRST WORLD WAR created new pressures on the civil service in Britain. The government, alarmed at the rise in numbers of civil servants created by wartime demands on the State, was determined to reduce its size and cost. The civil servants focused on organising to resist the Treasury's attempt to reassert control of numbers and pay. An arbitration system, the Whitley Councils, that acted as a powerful incentive to organisation, was no sooner devised than it came under attack from the Treasury. Meanwhile the demand of demobilised soldiers for State employment created another sort of pressure as the civil service associations identified these men as potential threats to hard won gains. The civil service responded to these pressures by a wave of organisation and consolidation of associations. The Irish civil service joined in this wave, but it also faced its own pressures. First and foremost were the increasingly complex forms of Home Rule being devised by the cabinet Irish situation committee under Walter Long. At the same time, opinion in Whitehall began to find agreement with the long-standing view of nationalists that saw the Castle government as itself an 'Irish problem'. Within the cabinet a consensus emerged on the necessity of administrative reform while disagreement continued on political reform. Administrative reform meant applying to the Castle the sort of reorganisation that was being proposed for the British service. Whether that was what was required is a question that was not asked. A further pressure on the Irish civil service was the victory of Sinn Féin in the December 1918 election. Transformed into a mass party by the entirely erroneous description of the 1916 Rising as a 'Sinn Féin' rebellion, the party now dominated Irish nationalist representation. In January 1919 the Sinn Féin MPs met in Dublin and declared themselves to be, as Dáil Éireann [the Assembly of Ireland], the legitimate government of the Irish republic declared in 1916. On the same day an attack on the RIC by the reorganised Irish Volunteers, now describing itself as the Irish Republican Army (IRA), launched the war against the British State in Ireland.

Post-war civil service organisation

The wartime expansion of government in Britain created both alarm at the growing cost of administration and a consciousness of the defects of the administrative machine.[1] The entire British civil service that had been 73,000 in 1914 had grown to 193,000 by 1919. Of this increase of 120,000 about 72,000 could be laid at the new wartime departments and 48,000 at the older departments. In Whitehall a consensus emerged on the need to reduce the size and cost of government while improving the civil service.[2] The single most important administrative change to emerge out of these enquiries was the formal strengthening of Treasury control of the civil service. In Whitehall the post-war retirement of many senior civil servants created an opportunity to reorganise the Treasury and impose the control of the civil service that had eluded reformers. Between September 1919 and March 1920 the Treasury was reorganised into three divisions of finance, supply and establishment. The status of the permanent secretary to the Treasury as head of the civil service was confirmed, as was the power of the Treasury to regulate and control the departments of government.[3] The collection of loosely connected departments that characterised Whitehall was reorganised into a highly centralised bureaucratic apparatus. The organisation of the civil service was rationalised and restructured. Departmental grades were to be abandoned and the entire civil service was to be assimilated into the new and universal system of administrative, executive and clerical grades. This would facilitate the allocation of staff between the different departments of the government and the most efficient deployment of civil servants.

As the State transformed its own administrative structures that transformation in turn necessitated a change in the way the civil service organised to deal with the State, its employer. These years comprise a period of the most rapid organisation in the history of civil service associations.[4] By 1920 British civil servants were organised in *de facto* trade unions that were using vigorous united action, demanding collective negotiation and affiliating with the broader trade union movement. The inhibiting effect of hierarchical structures, status and competitive promotions evaporated under the pressure of rapid change. The main objective of all civil service associations was to end Treasury dominance and win some control over their conditions, preferably through a permanent parliamentary committee or arbitration system.[5]

In Ireland the civil service joined this mobilisation. Despite the fact that the wartime experience of the two services was so radically different, most civil service organisations in Ireland were offshoots of British organisations. Whereas the British service experienced a huge expansion the Irish service largely atrophied, as Ireland was in many respects marginal to the war effort. A few departments experienced a small growth in the number of temporaries, but these hardly matched the loss of permanent officers on military service. Apart from some shell factories the Ministry of Munitions, the engine of civil service growth in Britain, did not organise in Ireland. The other 'mushroom' ministry, the Ministry of Food, was irrelevant in Ireland where food production and not rationing was the priority.[6] For the Irish civil service there were the added and very local issues of Home Rule, partition and the challenge of the counter-State posed by Dáil Éireann, all problems with which the British service had no concern. But as a result of the war the concerns and interests of civil servants in Ireland on pay and conditions matched those of the British service and, based on that shared concern, the wave of organisation in Britain reached and transformed the Irish service. They shared the view that the main problem facing the civil service was the Treasury with its apparent contempt for all other departments of the State.

The civil service associations and alliances, formed under the pressure of war and post-war conditions, were emphatically fighting organisations. Irish organisation began as local branches of British associations, reflecting not only a general trend in trade union organisation but also the development of general all-service classes across the United Kingdom.[7] A new civil service leadership emerged from this period of organisation. The surge of organisation and the new leadership that emerged reflects the fact that there was a great deal of discontent in the Irish civil service that had nothing to do with Home Rule. In fact among many of the lower-grade Irish civil servants there was an expectation that a national government would provide both better opportunities and better redress for their grievances than the British Treasury.[8]

Irish civil servants participated in the wave of organisation, sent delegates to meetings, joined in demonstrations and negotiated alongside their British colleagues. That the Castle administration in Ireland was a failure was axiomatic for Irish nationalists. By the end of the war this also became the view of a significant section of the British administrative and political elite. This realisation was born not only from the defects of the Castle apparatus but also of the more penetrating scrutiny of the whole civil service as a result of the war.

The first and foremost issue driving organisation in both Britain and Ireland was pay. During the First World War prices rose rapidly, leading to a general agitation among workers for pay increases. In 1915 two million working days were lost in strikes in Britain. Within the civil service the strict Treasury rule that pay claims could only be considered at departmental level was overwhelmed by the rapid inflation. After the Treasury rejected a pay claim by the postal workers the government, fearing a strike, referred the claim to an arbitrator. The reward of the 'war bonus', a variable top-up to basic salaries, by the arbitrator Sir James Woodhouse, announced in July 1915, not only marks the first increase awarded to civil servants in compensation for the increased cost of living, it also marks the wartime marginalisation of the Treasury in these matters. The increase was extended later in 1915 to all civil servants whose basic salary did not exceed fifty shillings per week. The continued rise in prices led to further applications for increases. As the bonus was initially small and inflation continued all civil servants therefore had a common and immediate grievance in the decline in real salaries.

The increased pressure of applications led to the establishment of the civil service conciliation and arbitration board early in 1917, thus taking pay determination entirely out of the hands of the Treasury.[9] The conciliation and arbitration board issued thirteen awards in the period 1917–19, all of which took the form of percentage additions (called war bonuses) to basic salaries in compensation for the rise in the cost of living.[10] Added to the issue of inadequate pay were issues of grading structures and promotional opportunities. The expansion of administration that had begun under the Liberal government and mushroomed in the war had not led to an expansion of opportunity. Many of the senior posts in the new departments were filled by nomination rather than by promotion with patronage taking on new forms.

The establishment of the arbitration board was a tremendous incentive to organisation as it was only through associations or trade unions that representations could be effectively made. With inflation continuing the associations had to return again and again to the arbitrator, using arbitration to perfect organisation. The Treasury began to respond to Irish departmental claims with offers. These offers were calculated to avoid the necessity of an arbitration hearing and perhaps also to avoid revealing the incoherence of the Castle administration.[11] This in turn encouraged organisation. As the arbitration system became established and as inflation surged ahead the number of civil service associations more than doubled from 80 in 1913 to 194 at the war's end.[12]

Whitley Councils in the civil service

As early as 1916 the British government, recognising the changes that the war had brought about in British industry and fearful of the growing militancy of shop stewards, accepted that trade unions and collective bargaining had become a normal feature of the workplace and looked to foster more co-operative industrial relations in the post-war world. A committee of officials from employer bodies and trade unions was appointed, under the chairmanship of the Deputy Speaker of the House of Commons J.H. Whitley, to make proposals for 'securing a permanent improvement in relations between employers and workmen and to recommend ways of systematically reviewing industrial relations in the future'.[13] The Whitley report, as it became known, recommended the creation of joint worker-employer industrial councils. Whitleyism was not intended to extend beyond industrial employment but the civil service associations argued that the government ought to set an example by instituting a Whitley Council for its own employees, the civil service.[14] Sir Thomas Heath, Assistant Secretary to the Treasury, was appointed to chair a sub-committee to draw up a scheme of Whitleyism for administrative staffs. The Heath committee offered crumbs to the civil service associations; consultation and a promise of a 'greater share in and responsibility for the determination and observance' of their conditions of work. But it restated the doctrine of ministerial responsibility, which meant that Whitley Councils could not diminish the right of a minister (read Treasury) to accept or reject the conclusions of any joint council. These councils as envisaged by Heath could never be more than advisory and consultative.[15] More than anything it was the threatened recrudescence of unfettered Treasury control, personified by Heath, that galvanised the civil service associations. At a packed Caxton Hall meeting with Chancellor Austen Chamberlain, a meeting attended by several Irish representatives, the civil service showed a remarkable discipline. Led by the postal workers representative Stuart-Bunning, the meeting unanimously rejected Chamberlain's plea to 'give it a go' and demanded that a provisional joint committee of staff and official sides be directed to draw up a detailed scheme for a Whitley Council in the civil service. The Heath report was consigned to the dustbin and on 3 July 1919, a mass meeting approved the resolutions of the joint conference of official and staff representatives, jointly chaired by Stuart-Bunning and Malcolm Ramsay (first controller of establishments at the Treasury), proposing a two-tier National Whitley Council for the civil service with departmental councils of departmental heads (not politicians as the civil service wanted) representing the official side and representatives of the civil service associations representing the staff side, and with an over-arching national council representing the government and the staff associations.[16] Notwithstanding its many limitations the National Whitley Council was a great advance for civil servants. For the first time the civil service associations now had a determining rather than a mere consultative role in their own work conditions.

The Irish civil servants had asked that the Ramsay and Stuart-Bunning committee establish a separate national council for Ireland. However, the committee concluded that it was not competent to make any definite recommendation and merely expressed an opinion that 'questions exclusively affecting the conditions of service of Irish civil servants must be dealt with by joint bodies on which Irish civil servants have full and direct representation'.[17] The Irish civil service delegates evidently had considerable sympathy among their British colleagues. The only amendment to the report of the provisional committee presented to the mass meeting of civil servants was that moved by the Irish delegates and fully supported by the rest of the service. The amendment asked for a concurrent meeting of Irish staff and official sides to frame proposals for the setting up of separate machinery to safeguard Irish interests. The Chancellor, recognising that some arrangement would be necessary to meet the situation in Ireland, where devolved government was imminent, accepted the Irish amendment.[18] Two weeks later a meeting of the Irish Provisional Joint Council was held in the Privy Council chamber at Dublin Castle.[19] The provisional committee was to 'frame proposals for the setting up of machinery to safeguard Irish interests'.[20] The official side was headed up by the Under-Secretary James MacMahon and included most heads of departments. The staff side represented the civil service grade associations rather than the departmental associations.[21] Most importantly, the Whitley Council staff side was made up of the elected delegates of the associations. Therefore, because the Irish civil service had few in the executive grades, the staff side of the Irish Civil Service Joint Committee was dominated by the clerical grades, representing the masses in the lower class of the service. James MacMahon was appointed chairman with Gerald Mulvin of the Irish Civil Service Alliance as vice-chairman. Patrick Ryan acted as official side and Michael Gallagher as staff side secretaries.[22] James MacMahon, because he was an Irishman who had risen through the ranks from the second division, and also perhaps because he was Catholic and sympathetic to nationalist aspirations for self-rule, was well regarded by the staff side even though he was a wily negotiator who knew every ploy available to the ranks out of which he had risen.[23]

A dispute arose immediately as to the power of the Irish council. Chamberlain had ruled that the subjects that were proper for discussion by the Irish council were those which, *after reference to the National Council, are agreed by that body* [my italics] to be either (a) exclusively Irish questions, or (b) exclusively Irish aspects of general questions. The staff side immediately objected to giving the London-based national council prior authority to determine the issues that would be considered by the Irish committee, thus making the Irish a sub-committee of the British body.[24] The London officials of the associations at the national council gave full support to the Irish demand for an autonomous Irish Whitley Council, attending meetings alongside Michael Gallagher, Gerald Mulvin and Thomas Murphy and reinforcing their arguments.[25] After several meetings through the autumn and winter, when it seemed at times that the Irish committee would never come into real existence, Chamberlain finally agreed to the deletion of the requirement for a prior reference to the national council. In March 1920 the national council delegated power to the Irish committee to *itself* determine what were 'exclusively' Irish questions or aspects of Irish questions, granting *de facto* autonomy to the Irish body.[26]

The success of the staff side in securing autonomy for the Irish led to problems for the official side. In the confusion of authority that characterised the Irish administration it was very difficult to determine which were the Irish departments and therefore the appropriate departmental council to which grievances should be brought. Staff members of the Inland Revenue belonged to an 'imperial' department. Should the officers of that department, who happened to be stationed in Dublin, participate in an Irish committee concerned 'exclusively' with Irish affairs? Should the staff of an imperial department be allowed to bring 'exclusively Irish' problems to the Irish committee or should they be brought to the departmental council in London? Giving the London-based national council the power to determine what were 'exclusively Irish' issues would have secured the necessary control. Now that the Irish committee had thrown over that control there was a real danger that civil servants in the Irish departments would be able to secure double representation on the Whitley Councils of Ireland and of Great Britain and use one to secure gains that had been denied in the other in an administrative version of the 'Midlothian Question'. MacMahon's advice to the official side to use the proviso 'exclusively Irish' to intervene if it was felt that the Irish committee was straying into the territory of the national council was hardly adequate and clearly this was an area ripe for confusion.[27] The staff of the Irish branches of British departments, conscious of the distance from Whitehall and the peculiarities of the Irish situation, were themselves pressing for local departmental councils.[28]

The Irish civil servants now had two effective organisations for the service as a whole: the ad hoc GCICS that had been around since 1893 representing the entire Irish civil service, in the senior grades for the most part, well-connected politically and accepted as competent to negotiate with the government on the conditions attached to Home Rule; and alongside, a representative and formal Irish Whitley Committee to negotiate on general service conditions, made of nominated representatives of the different grades and classes but dominated by the clerical grades and regarded with suspicion by the Treasury. The Whitley Committee was the Irish expression of a British original, dominated like the British organisation by the representatives of the quasi-trade union civil service associations.

Organisation in the Irish civil service

The relationship between the Irish and British organisations was complex. The Irish associations had considerable autonomy and took an independent line on Irish issues. The Irish civil service was more militant than the British; its demands for salary increases were usually set higher and conference speeches were more pugnacious.[29] The April 1920 strike in support of the Irish political prisoners, which was supported by the Irish associations, was regarded with some awe by the British civil service as was the decision by the Irish Civil Service Alliance (CSA) to establish a strike fund. British civil servants hesitated to even contemplate using the strike weapon.[30] However, the Irish organisations tended to look to London for leadership and direction and were quick to criticise that leadership for any tardiness in responding to Irish issues. Even as late as October 1921 the executive officers in the CDB looked to the London leadership to help their claim for reorganisation.[31] On the other hand the London leadership were wary that too much attention to Irish issues would raise the danger of fragmentation of the associations into geographic units with the Scottish members taking their lead from Dublin.[32]

The emphasis on class and grade organisation of the British associations was a break with Irish organisational traditions, which were emphatically departmental and 'all-Irish'. Because the Irish departments had in effect a single political head, the Chief Secretary, the permanent heads had little interference in how they ran their departments and so every civil servant's career depended to an uncomfortable degree on their head of department. The Irish clerical grades generally held the official Treasury representative in the Castle, Maurice Headlam, in contempt.[33] Also, there was little movement of civil servants between the Irish departments.

The movement toward large grade-based organisations was not welcome to one small group, the professional civil servants. These, despite their title, were the only civil servants not trained as civil servants. Rather, they were professionally qualified auditors, surveyors and engineers who happened to work for the State. Discontented with the dominance achieved by the clerical grades, in February 1920 a group of professional civil servants met in Dublin and formed the Institution of Professional Civil Servants (Ireland) (IPCS).[34] The creation of the IPCS and the constitution it adopted closely followed on the foundation of a similar Institution of Professional Civil Servants in England in January 1919. Just like the English institution the IPCS was essentially an alliance of the associations of the professional and technical civil servants in the various government departments.[35] During the summer of 1920 the IPCS canvassed the possibility of affiliating with the English institution, but as the English institution was less than enthusiastic and as the constitutional situation in Ireland became more uncertain the proposal was allowed to lapse.[36] By the time of the annual general meeting of March 1921, the first annual report of the IPCS could record eleven constituent associations, 367 full members and 71 associate members.[37]

The Association of Staff Clerks and Other Civil Servants (ASCOCS) was formed in 1916 to organise a 'war bonus' claim for civil servants with salaries exceeding £300 per annum. The Dublin branch of ASCOCS (organising the senior grades on salaries over £400 per annum) was an affiliate of the British organisation along with Malta and West Africa.[38] The Dublin branch was organised by J.E. Highton who also acted as the staff clerks' delegate on the 1917 Civil Service Committee on the Home Rule Bill. He represented Irish staff clerks at a 'war bonus' appeal in November 1917, but the London organisation seem generally to have had little contact with the Dublin members.[39] By early

1919 the Dublin branch was demanding separate representation at the general meeting of all civil service associations at Caxton Hall, called to co-ordinate a response to the Heath committee report.[40] ASCOCS remained aloof from the movement for cross-service unity. An invitation from the Civil Service Alliance (CSA) to join in a campaign for the abolition of Treasury control and security for promotion, an invitation supported by the Irish staff clerks, was rejected on the grounds that the clerical grades alliance had a membership 'of an essentially different character from that of the Staff Clerks', an example of the inhibiting effect of grade snobbery on civil service organisation.[41] ASCOCS instead joined with the Society of Civil Servants (SCS), which was more a club than a fighting organisation. The Irish membership expressed their dissatisfaction with the SCS, criticised the failure of the London executive to keep the Irish members informed on issues and, in 1920, demanded and got a seat on the executive committee.[42] The Irish chairman was Thomas A. Murphy, the Irish secretary was Mr J. McInerney. The tendency through 1920 was for the Irish branch, under the leadership of Dr. Cornelius (Conn) Murphy, Michael Smithwick, Murphy and McInerney, to take an independent and more militant line on reorganisation and re-grading. The Irish members seem to have been regarded as a welcome ginger group by the London executive and the Irish membership at 490 was not insignificant in comparison with the British figure of 1,249.[43] With the fragmentation of the grade under reorganisation (all staff clerks above £450 were automatically re-graded as higher executive, those in the range £200–400 were to be graded individually) it was decided to amalgamate with the Association of Executive Officers (AEO) and to leave the SCS and join with the CSA. This represents a more militant attitude born of the failure of the association to win better terms in the civil service reorganisation. It was a course fully supported by the Irish members.[44]

The most shadowy group in the civil service were the temporary clerks. Departments could employ temporary clerks to meet pressure of work without bringing it to the notice of the Treasury. Once in a department they tended to become fixtures and, if efficient, ended up doing higher work than they had been originally recruited to do. In Dublin Castle Headlam noted that the assistant clerks were extremely jealous of the temporary clerks, whom they regarded as a patronage class recruited on a sectarian basis, undermining the conditions of their grade and damaging their prospects.[45]

The most numerous civil service class was the assistant clerk, a Treasury grade devised to fill the gap between the first and second divisions and one that constituted a low-paid 'submerged class' of the service.[46] In 1902 the assistant clerks of the government departments in Dublin combined to present a united demand for improved pay directly to the Treasury, bypassing their departmental heads. The example of the Dublin clerks was followed in Edinburgh and London and led to the founding of the Assistant Clerks Association (ACA) in 1904, under the leadership of W.J. Brown, the most militant of all civil service organisers, along with David Milne.[47] The aim of the ACA was to recruit all clerical grade staff in the civil service and to win the right to deal directly with the Treasury. The ACA campaigned for a 'living wage' and better promotional prospects. From 1911 it published the journal *Red Tape*. Dublin assistant clerks joined the ACA from its beginning but through their departmental organisations rather than as specifically Irish clerks.[48] In 1904 the Dublin departments with members in the ACA were the GPO, the ILC and the LGB. Each year a few of the other departments joined in; the Inland Revenue, DATI, the Board of Works and so on. The growth in membership may well have reflected the slow movement of individual assistant clerks through the departments bringing with them the habit of organisation.[49] In 1921 the ACA merged with the Post Office Engineering Clerical Assistants to form the Clerical Officers' Association (COA). In 1921 the COA merged in turn with the lower section of the re-graded ASCOCS members to become the Civil Service Clerical Association (CSCA).[50]

A key figure in the expansion of clerical organisation in Ireland was Michael J. Gallagher. Gallagher entered the civil service through the competitive examinations and worked in London in the GPO engineering section. Through contacts in the Irish Parliamentary Party, the sort of backstairs influence that (rightly) he was later to condemn, he secured a transfer back to the Dublin NHIC office.[51] His London experience, brief though it was, made him more self-conscious of his status as Irish, Catholic and as a 'black-coated worker'. From London he also brought back a conviction of the need for civil service organisation. The fight for a war bonus was the campaign that marked him out as a natural organiser.

Tom Barrington of the DATI statistics section, who later was to exert a profound influence on Irish administrative thought, wrote an analysis of wartime rising prices and their impact on civil service salaries for the Irish CSA.[52] This short pamphlet had a revolutionary impact on civil service thinking on salary claims and led directly to the indexing of the war bonus. Barrington, using the rather homely metaphor of the dairy farmer diluting milk, proved that the government had been 'adulterating' the value of money by 'watering it down' through issuing paper pounds that were not backed up by gold reserves. In effect this was a dilution of the purchasing power of the pound sterling. What civil servants and other workers were demanding therefore was not an increase in salaries but restitution by the government for the adulteration in the value of money. Barrington had in fact produced a short and brilliant analysis of inflation, a phenomenon unfamiliar to a generation used to stable prices. Gallagher was able to use the civil servant's habits of record keeping to substantiate Barrington's argument. By collecting and analysing the grocery bills of many civil servants, which tended to be the same items over the years, he could show that the pound in 1920 bought far fewer items than it had in 1914. The cost of maintaining the same standard of living had increased and therefore the onus lay with the government to either restore the value of the pound or offer a compensatory increase. Civil servants could no longer be apologetic in demanding pay increases, rather the government should be apologetic for causing the need for them.[53]

Whereas most Irish delegates of the other civil service associations seem to have been relatively unknown in the London offices Gallagher was close to W.J. Brown. Gallagher brought Brown to Dublin to ginger up the organisation and assist in a recruitment drive. He attended the annual general meeting of the ACA in London and on one occasion was chosen to second a militant motion brought forward by Brown to the annual conference.[54] Gallagher imbibed some of the ideas of the guild socialists while in London and advocated the 'control of the civil service by civil servants and the abolition of grades'.[55] He affiliated the 450–member Civil Service Assistant Clerks, Dublin branch, into the Irish Labour Party and Trade Union Congress (ILPTUC) in 1920, the only civil service organisation outside the Post Office to do so.[56] He was described as the 'Irish WJB' with the appearance of a 'mild-mannered pedagogue' but 'pugnacious if opposed', whose aggression frequently made enemies but who was also a 'tireless worker for the interests of his class'.[57]

In 1919 the executives of both the Irish and British Second Division Clerks Association (SDA) met, implying their essentially separate existence, and promised a more sympathetic relationship in which the London executive would do all that was necessary to defend the interests of the Irish membership under any Home Rule parliament.[58] In 1920 following the reorganisation of the civil service, the SDA was renamed the Association of Executive Officers (AEO).[59] The AEO was relatively active in pursuing the case of Irish members during the 1920–21 reorganisation of the Irish departments under A.J.P. Waterfield (see pp. 75–86).[60] There was a suggestion that the Irish AEO was not paying its fair share of the overheads of the association, but the resolution of that issue involved an even closer affiliation between the Irish and British organisations. This does suggest that Home Rule was not regarded as a barrier to continuing trade union organisation within the civil service executive grades of a self-governing Ireland.[61] The Irish organisers of the AEO were Mr R. Clarke, Mr Attride and Michael Smithwick (formerly of ASCOCS), after his transfer out of the Staff Clerk grade. The key figure was, however, Sam Sloan of DATI, regarded already as a legend in civil service organisation.[62] Sloan was described as a 'typical Ulsterman'; aggressive and blunt in negotiation. He was exceptionally well-versed in the minutiae of regulations and unequalled in his recall of commission and inquiry reports.[63] He later transferred to Belfast and ended up as establishment officer in the Northern Ireland Department of Finance, a case of poacher turning gamekeeper. Within the broader movement of civil service organisation the AEO and the COA were to the forefront of the movement toward a general organisation of civil servants.[64]

The civil service, while generating grade organisations, was also forming federal organisations. In 1909 the Civil Service Federation (CSF) was formed as a cross-grade movement.[65] It was originally intended that it would act as an all-service organisation to agitate for a standing committee of the House of Commons to form a committee of appeals on civil service grievances. Under the influence of the postal unions, always the most radical, the purpose of the CSF then became explicitly political, demanding the right for civil servants to contest elections. This turn from a campaign on pay and conditions to one on politics, allied with the tendency of the postal unions to go it alone in fighting pay claims, led to the disaffiliation of the clerical and second division associations.[66]

In 1916, building on the success of a joint campaign on hours of work, the ACA, the Second Division Association, the Federation of Women Civil Servants and the Civil Service Typists Association combined in the Civil Service Alliance (CSA) with the objective of promoting the efficiency of the civil service and providing the 'conditions of a good life' for civil servants.[67] As the CSA grew it restricted membership to organisations representing civil servants of clerical associations with similar conditions (and therefore grievances), thus lessening the possibility of the sort of rifts that had weakened the Federation. The CSA represented 15,000 civil servants in the clerical grades of the United Kingdom. In 1921 the CSA and the CSF merged to form the Civil Service Confederation (CSC).

As the larger federal structures emerged the Irish followed the lead of the British movement forming Irish federations with affiliate or branch status to the British organisations. The Irish CSA of thirteen associations totalled 1,500 in comparison with over 24,000 in the British Alliance.[68] The Irish CSA, along with the Irish Association of Post Office Clerks (IAPOC), organised the largest mass meeting ever by the Irish civil service in November 1919. The meeting was called to protest at the recent 10 per cent offer made by the arbitration board. The meeting approved resolutions calling for closer and more effective organisation and greater union with outside workers, along with a readiness to use the strike weapon. Only thus, it was said, could the civil service hope to win justice.[69]

The leadership of the civil service associations

Sloan, along with Gallagher of the assistant clerks, Gerald Mulvin, Michael Smithwick, Conn Murphy, Thomas A. Murphy, and Ronald J.P. Mortished formed the backbone of Irish civil service organisation. What united all these across their several classes and departments was a shared conviction that grade exclusiveness was the weakness of the Irish service. They all voiced at some stage their support for the syndicalist concept of the 'One Big Union' for the entire administrative, executive and clerical grades. Among these activists there were two distinct groups, reflecting two different analyses of the situation they now faced. Some of the civil service leadership, such as Gallagher, saw the function of the Irish organisations as being no more than maximising membership in support of the London leadership. They saw Home Rule as no more and no less an alteration in the conditions of service than reorganisation of departments or recasting grades.[70] Priority had to be given to the struggle for pay and re-grading, a struggle that was shared with the British civil service. Along with Gallagher we could list Sam Sloan of the executive officers, Thomas A. Murphy of the staff clerks, William F. Nally of the postal workers and Gerald Mulvin of the Irish CSA. However, among the activists there were some who pressed for what they saw as the necessity for a consciously nationalist outlook within civil service associations in Ireland. This group would include Mortished, Michael Smithwick and Dr Conn Murphy.

Mortished, while remaining a member of the AEO, was a founder of the Irish Civil Service Union (ICSU), a federal organisation 'open to all civil servants, working to promote complete unity of organisation in the service in Ireland'. He was also editor of its journal the *Irish Civil Servant*.[71] The origins of the ICSU lay in the order in council of 1918 demanding that civil servants take an oath of allegiance to the Crown. As has been noted this arose from a political and newspaper campaign alleging that disloyal civil servants were sabotaging the war effort. The oath was not regarded as controversial among British civil servants but in Ireland it was seen as a manoeuvre by the loyalists in Dublin Castle to get at nationalist-minded civil servants. Mortished was one of those at a meeting in the Forester's Hall called to establish a Society for the Protection of the Rights of Civil Servants 'open to established, unestablished and disestablished civil servants' out of which the ICSU was formed.[72] Mortished had already a reputation within the Treasury and the service for radical labour views. Born in London of Irish parents, he was a graduate of the London School of Economics where he was actively involved in socialist politics and where he joined the Independent Labour Party. In 1909 he entered the civil service and was sent to the Registry of Deeds in Dublin. He joined the Socialist Party of Ireland and was close to Larkin and Connolly at a time of spectacular growth for the syndicalist Irish Transport and General Workers' Union (ITGWU).[73] In 1914 he had been disciplined and forfeited two increments in pay for writing articles in the *Workers' Republic* critical of the war. He was again disciplined during a Dublin dock strike of 1916 after a speech to a Liberty Hall meeting condemning the clerical staff of the Dublin Steampacket Company as 'blacklegs' for continuing to work. He narrowly missed dismissal but did lose another increment in salary. The speech was made in early April but the reaction came in the aftermath to the Easter Rising. The site and the tenor of the speech signalled sympathy, or even prior knowledge, of the Rising. Mortished was eventually able to use his position as vice-chairman of the departmental Whitley Council to win a restoration of his lost increments.[74]

Mortished used his editorship of the *Irish Civil Servant* to criticise the Irish associations for merely imitating the British organisations. While ready to acknowledge the achievements of Gallagher, Sloan, Murphy and Mulvin he maintained that as much could have been achieved through the British associations, implying the redundancy of the Irish organisations. He urged the fusion of all Irish organisations into a single national union, livelier and more aggressive than the single-grade unions in Britain, imbued with class-consciousness rather than grade exclusiveness, and ready to use the strike weapon.[75] In his writings he returned again and again to the theme that the Irish organisations were being smothered by the 'English'; and that an explicitly separatist agenda was needed. By the summer of 1921 as 'Carsonia' (as he termed Northern Ireland) was being established, he was writing that it was positively dangerous for the Irish associations to give the British organisations the right to act on behalf of the Irish civil servants.[76]

Mortished was unusual in that it was his labour activism that brought him into civil service organisation. Other leaders emerged out of the cultural movements. Michael Smithwick's area of activism was the Irish language movement. Both he and Conn Murphy were founder-members of the Gaelic League. Smithwick (who gaelicised his name to Smidic) was close to Douglas Hyde, the president of the League and Gaelic language scholar. Conn Murphy was a link with the revolutionary movement. The first to be awarded a Ph.D from the Royal University, he gave lectures on logic to civil servants, not to introduce them to the beauty of philosophy but to prepare them for negotiation – analysing arguments and spotting flawed logic. He was active in Sinn Féin politics.[77]

For the civil service associations a significant achievement was that the reorganisation of the civil service into the new administrative, executive and clerical grades was to be undertaken by the service itself through the Whitley Councils and not by the Treasury. Whitley Councils of all the various government departments were instructed to work out a departmental reorganisation into the new grades, which was to be then submitted to the Treasury for final approval.

Reorganisation necessarily opened the further question of assimilating civil servants to new grades. The associations wanted 'weight for age' to apply; that is any individual would be assimilated at the point of the new scale that he would have achieved at his present age. The Treasury would only accept assimilation at the same actual monetary point on the scale; that is a civil servant would enjoy at best a modest rise in salary on assimilation even if the point of assimilation represented far fewer years of service than actually served. A related issue was that of inflation continuing to erode wages at a steady rate. The 'cost-of-living committee' established the 1914 cost of living as a baseline and awarded periodic percentage increases to compensate for the rise in the cost of living over that figure since 1914. In 1920 this stood at 130. The war bonus was then calculated at 130 per cent over 1914 salary levels and was to be periodically adjusted by the fall and rise of the prices index. This, it was hoped, would end the perpetual battles with the Treasury followed by rounds of conciliation and arbitration.[78]

The Government of Ireland Act, 1920

In October 1919 Walter Long was asked to chair the cabinet committee on Ireland and to prepare a new Home Rule Bill for Ireland. The 1920 Government of Ireland Act, as shaped by Long, went through increasingly complicated variations of devolution that provided for governments of Southern and Northern Ireland, an Irish Council and a hypothetical future Irish parliament while retaining Westminster sovereignty. Long's proposal for two limited Home Rule assemblies, one based in Belfast for Ulster and one based in Dublin, with an overarching Council of Ireland but reserving some services in Whitehall, necessitated even further administrative confusion as it partitioned sections of the civil service between north and south while retaining an imperial service. Its only virtue was that, as it partitioned Ireland, it held the coalition government together.[79]

The GCICS was reactivated, though the Dublin council of the CSCA now regarded the Whitley committee as the better vehicle for defending the interests of the membership, referring to the GCICS as being no more than 'useful'. It was decided to continue representation on the general committee but there is no record of any active engagement.[80] The committee, based on years of experience, used very different methods to those of the associations to put forward and win its demands. While the associations were energetically using the Whitley Councils to win the best deal on reorganisation and re-grading the GCICS, or more accurately an inner coterie, was busy building up a network of influence in the cabinet and the Treasury.

Barlas was again immediately in contact and supplied Long with a copy of the "Statement by the General Committee of Irish Civil Servants as to their position in view of further legislation affecting the Government of Ireland".[81] The victory of Sinn Féin in the December 1918 general election made Barlas more pessimistic and even a little wistful for the comforts of the lost 1914 Act. It was incontrovertible, he wrote, that

> the position of Irish civil servants, especially those of fairly long service, will be immeasurably more insecure now, having regard to recent developments, than it

would have been if the Government of Ireland Act of 1914 had come into operation in that year. Civil servants not in sympathy with the views of any new government in this country will, almost certainly, have to vacate their positions and
the terms of compensation on retirement (either voluntary or compulsory) provided by the Act of 1914 should, therefore, be substantially improved.

He also feared that the power of the government in the 1914 Act to retain for
up to five years civil servants who might wish to retire would expose them to
intolerable pressures.[82]

Cabinet committee records and the relevant clauses of the 1920
Government of Ireland Act indicate that the GCICS executive committee,
exploiting the political access and status provided by the patronage of Long,
succeeded to a large degree in influencing and shaping the clauses on the civil
service.[83] The 1919 statement asked that the concessions requested in 1917
should be granted along with additional concessions to meet the changed circumstances. The 1917 statement had concentrated on security for promotion
for civil servants continuing in the service of the new government. It had only
incidentally asked for improved terms for civil servants retiring either voluntarily or under compulsion. The 1919 supplementary statement was much
more focused on the terms of retirement, the special classes of civil servant on
the autonomous Irish boards and the consequences of partition. Barlas
wanted increased representation from one to three members for civil servants
on the Civil Service Committee established by the 1914 Act, which had the
authority to permit retirements and award pensions. He asked that the avail-
ability of the special terms of retirement be extended from seven to ten years
after the appointed day. The voluntary retirement terms had been limited in
the 1914 Act to officers under sixty years of age. He wanted the age limit
extended to sixty-five, reflecting the large cohort of senior officers approaching retirement age. Under the 1914 Act the Civil Service Committee had the
power to postpone voluntary retirement indefinitely; Barlas wanted this
limited to two years.

Ian Macpherson, Chief Secretary for Ireland, 1919–20, adopted the cause of
the GCICS and supplied the cabinet committee with a brief in which he
endorsed Barlas's pessimism. He wrote, 'It is contended with some reason that
safeguards as to security of tenure, promotion, prospects and transfers, are
likely to prove of little practical value in the case at least of the South of Ireland
Government, and this consideration strengthens the claim for improvement of
the terms of retirement, whether voluntary, compulsory, or "permissive". This
is the most important question that arises.'[84] Macpherson was in favour of
adding to the power of the Civil Service Committee and of increasing the civil
service representation on it. He was at the same time mindful of the danger of
offering terms for retirement so generous they would strip the new governments of their entire civil service.

Worthington-Evans, Minister for Pensions, was willing to extend the civil servants representation on the statutory Civil Service Committee, though to two members only and not to the three requested by Barlas. On limiting the stay on voluntary retirement to two years, he was agreeable. He also supported extending the upper age limit for the special terms to sixty-five but did not support the extension of the option to retire under special terms to ten years after the appointed day.[85]

The cabinet memoranda plainly stated that 'in deference to representations from the Committee of Irish Civil Servants' the terms of compensation for officers who retired were now more generous than those in the 1914 Act.[86] Hitherto a 'civil servant' had been a person paid out of a fund voted by parliament. The committee proposed to define an 'Irish officer' in terms so broad it included all and every person whether permanent or temporary, in departments of State or autonomous boards, paid by vote, fees or allowances. Pension rights were also to be extended to categories that, up to then, had none, such as the CDB officers, provided the Treasury processed the necessary regulations before the appointed day. It would not do if Home Rule legislation imposed on the Irish governments concessions that had been refused by the British government. Compensation for retirement was, however, the nub of the issue so far as Barlas was concerned. Here the cabinet committee were prepared to meet the civil service without reservation. The transitional period, it was proposed, would be extended from five to seven years. This was not as generous as Barlas's ten years, but it still extended beyond the retiring age of a great number of the senior civil servants. The terms of permissive retirement were equally generous. Under the 1914 Act the Civil Service Committee permitted retirement if a civil servant could show that his position had been altered to his detriment. Under the 1920 bill it was required only that the position had been materially altered. Also, under the 1914 Act the question of permitting retirement arose only after the transitional period of five years. After all, an officer, if he did not like the new conditions but was not compelled to retire, could simply opt for voluntary retirement during the five years. The difficulty for such an officer, however, was that the terms of voluntary retirement were much less generous than those for permissive retirement. The intent of the 1914 Act was to encourage civil servants to stay on for at least five years by offering security that conditions would not get worse and might even get better after the transition. The 1920 Bill, in response to Barlas and the civil service representations, abolished that distinction. An officer retiring without permission could expect the same terms as an officer retiring with permission. By agreeing to extend the normal retirement age from sixty to sixty-five, and by extending the transition period to seven years, the actual sums of compensation (which were based on years to retirement and transitional years) were greatly increased. The compensation scale of the 1914 Act became the minimum of the new scale, with a maximum of two-thirds of retiring salary. The cabinet committee also proposed to allow the civil servants two representatives, rather than one, on the Civil Service Committee. The two representatives would be drawn from north and south and the committee was extended to seven.[87]

Clauses 54–9 with the eighth schedule of the 1920 Government of Ireland Act were the achievement of the GCICS. This achievement was the result of a long campaign that began with the 1911 overtures to the Home Rule Bill of 1912. The achievement was, for a while, overshadowed by the revolutionary changes that swept Castle government into the dustbin of history. However, those achievements were vital in allowing the civil service to negotiate the shifting direction and speed of reform as the Irish administration, now in the hands of an English 'junta' of elite civil servants, turned to face the challenge of partition and a revolutionary State claiming true legitimacy. Since 1911 the committee had succeeded in forging a combination that crossed classes, grades, departments and the political allegiance of nationalist and unionist civil servants. Sharing many of the same activists with the associations and the departmental Whitley Councils it relied exclusively on personal and private contacts and not at all on mass mobilisation or the fraternal support of fellow officials. By persistent but discreet lobbying within the corridors of power it succeeded in shaping and amending legislation so as to win better terms and security for the status, pay and promotions and pensions of the Irish civil service. Most significantly of all it succeeded in winning what was in effect a 'written constitution'. By 1920 the vested interests of Irish civil servants, who previously were employed 'at pleasure', had been transformed into rights that were legal and parliamentary, and therefore defensible at law. The relationship binding the new Irish State and its civil service would be contractual.

Walter Long's Government of Ireland Bill, which would establish a Council of Ireland with two local parliaments in Belfast and Dublin, began to make its passage through parliament. If, as appeared likely, it was accepted by the Ulster Unionists but rejected by Sinn Féin then the government would partition the country and rule the south by military government.[88] A new dual policy emerged of smashing Dáil Éireann while proffering the Government of Ireland Bill as a final settlement. Greenwood's Restoration of Order (Ireland) Act imposed imprisonment without trial and courts martial in designated areas. The 'Black and Tans' and the Auxiliaries bolstered the crumbling RIC as county after county was put under martial law. It was also clear that the police and soldiers enjoyed considerable freedom in interpreting the law. Reprisals were sanctioned and became official policy, destroying any legitimacy that the State might have retained in British and international eyes. The only political policy was the mechanical progress of the 1920 bill through parliament and the partition of the administration.

The 'Junta' in Dublin Castle

Throughout the 1919–21 period, when the State in Ireland teetered on the edge of collapse Sir Warren Fisher, Secretary to the Treasury and head of the civil service, was deeply engaged in the most far-reaching reforms of the British civil service.[89] The entire civil service in Britain, from the senior to the most junior ranks, through the departmental Whitley Councils, was now engaged in thinking about the problems of reorganisation and reform as part of post-war reconstruction. It was inevitable that such thinking would influence policy on Ireland. Since the failure of the 1917 Convention the Castle administration had not come up with any politically creative ideas. The attempt to link Home Rule and conscription in 1918 had proved a disaster and had boosted Sinn Féin. The December 1918 general election results demonstrated that Sinn Féin now represented the majority of the Irish electorate. Concluding that no political solution was possible Dublin Castle turned to imposing coercion, a policy that led increasingly to a militarisation of the administration.[90] As H.A.L. Fisher pointed out to Lloyd George, the strategy being pursued by the Irish government would mean that Irish Home Rule, which was on the statute books, would be accompanied by military law.[91] A Castle clique of the new Chief Secretary Ian Macpherson, the Viceroy Lord French, and the senior civil servants Sir John Taylor, W.P.J. Connolly, Edward Saunderson and Samuel Watt supposed that everyone except 'Ulster', and all opinion that was not 'loyal', was to be subject to indiscriminate coercion. Taylor, identified as the dominant personality in this centre of reaction, was unable to see that Dáil Éireann's claim to be the legitimate State presented a wholly different challenge than the 'rick-burning and cattle drives' of earlier agitation.[92] Under them the RIC was further militarised and Sinn Féin, the political representatives of the majority of the Irish people, was suppressed and its supporters punished. As the failure of militarising the administration to deliver social order became evident, the fault was laid at the door of the civil service administrators and not the policy. The problem, it was alleged, was the unreliability or even incompetence of elements within the civil service. Lord French blamed the failure of his repression on the 'weakness and inefficiency of some officials' and moved to purge the civil service of any officials with Sinn Féin sympathies, which meant all Catholics in the administration came under suspicion.[93] MacMahon, the Catholic Under-Secretary, was marginalised as the ultra-loyalist Sir John Taylor was appointed Assistant Under-Secretary, vaulting over the highly able Joseph Brennan, a Catholic. Headlam was so determined to defend the *status quo* that he secretly kept Unionist critics informed on the Irish policy of the government, which is the most serious possible breach of civil service ethics.[94] The civil servants in the Castle split into two camps, those who backed MacMahon and those who backed Taylor. The deepening politicisation of the bureaucracy in Dublin Castle fatally weakened the State as a culture of militarism expelled anyone counselling dialogue with nationalism.[95] The key role of the modern civil servant, to inform, to advise and to warn, was a nullity. A culture of militaristic machismo, revealed by the frequent accusation of 'cold feet' being hurled against any who counselled caution, prevailed.[96] Duggan remembered this time as the 'unhappiest twelve months of my civil service career'.[97] General Sir Joseph Byrne, the Catholic head of the RIC, was pushed out of office because, Lord French alleged, 'he had lost his nerve' and was too soft on Sinn Féin.[98] Far from losing his nerve, however, he was in fighting form and complained to the cabinet that the problem was the Castle government, which was out of touch with all opinion save its own.[99] As the challenge of the republican forces grew the British government further militarised the administration. Hamar Greenwood, who had no knowledge of Ireland and no cabinet experience, replaced Macpherson as Chief Secretary, now in turn accused by Edward Saunderson of showing 'cold feet'.[100] Sir Nevil Macready was appointed General Officer Commanding.

The soldiers appointed to govern Ireland in early 1920 – Colonel Ormond Winter, chief of intelligence; General Tudor, head of the RIC; General Macready, Commander-in-Chief of the army; General Boyd, head of the DMP; and Brigadier Crozier, head of the Auxiliaries; all sent to Ireland to defeat Sinn Féin by military repression – found themselves filling an administrative vacuum. Macready confessed himself 'fairly astonished' at the chaos and incompetence that prevailed in the Irish administration.[101] Sir Hamar Greenwood, the new Chief Secretary, reported to cabinet in May 1920 that his real difficulty was 'the inadequacy and sloppiness of the instruments of government'.[102] After a blistering attack on the incompetence of the Castle apparatus by Macready, Sir Warren Fisher was sent in May 1920 to Dublin to investigate the Irish administration. Fisher, accompanied by Sir John Anderson from the Inland Revenue board, visited Maurice Headlam. Headlam, after expressing strong suspicions about some Catholic official to his visitors, was rattled to be treated with something very like contempt.[103] Headlam was also puzzled as to the purpose of the visit but, as all heads of departments ought to know well, visitations by the Treasury were always the prelude to great changes. Fisher did not share in the Castle paranoia of Irish Catholics. A supporter of Home Rule for Ireland, he liked the country and the people, besides which his wife was half-Irish and a Catholic.[104]

The British government insisted that Fisher's investigation into Dublin Castle was merely to prepare the ground for implementing in Ireland the recently approved recommendation of the National Whitley Council on reorganisation.[105] However, the signals that something more thorough was being planned were already, in early April, sufficiently strong to thoroughly alarm Robert Lynn a Unionist MP for Belfast. Writing to Bonar Law he implored him to 'refuse to allow the betrayal of the faithful servants by an act of government treachery', or at least, if they were to be 'thrown to the wolves' to ensure that they received adequate pensions.[106] The Fisher report on the Irish administration was unequivocal, direct and plain-speaking in its condemnation:

> The castle administration does not administer. On the mechanical side it can never have been good and is now quite obsolete; in the infinitely more important sphere (a) of informing and advising the Irish government in relation to policy and (b) of practical capacity in the application of policy it simply has no existence . . . The prevailing conception of the post of Under Secretary – who should be the principal permanent adviser to the Irish government in civil affairs – appears to be that he is a routine clerk . . . The position at the present moment is seemingly that no one in the Chief Secretary's Office, from the Under Secretary downwards, regards himself as responsible even for decisions on departmental papers, let alone for a share in the solution of difficulties in the realm either of policy or of execution. The Chief Secretary, for his part, appears to be under the illusion that a Civil Servant – even though he has the position and emoluments of a permanent head of the Irish administration – is entirely unconcerned with the exploration or settlement of the problems which the Irish administration exists to solve.[107]

Warren Fisher's view was that Macready, appointed as GOC, had in fact been playing the role of Under-Secretary and had therefore hidden the fundamental weakness of the administration. He recommended that MacMahon, though inadequate, should be left in the post of Under-Secretary not least because he 'holds views more in keeping with 20th century sentiment than those expressed by the ascendancy party and the supporters of indiscriminate coercion'. But Taylor had to be got rid of and a new team of senior civil servants sent in to thoroughly recast the administration.

In a supplement to the report Warren Fisher concluded that the government of Ireland was 'woodenly stupid' and that the problems in the Castle administration were not simply administrative but were political. The continuance of government by 'folly and brute force' would lead to no alternative but military rule in Ireland. Fisher recommended that any solution would need to be both imaginative and one that showed the government seizing the initiative, offering the maximum of both political and administrative reform. These would include the abolition of the lord lieutenancy, 'a pinchbeck royalty', the abandonment of Walter Long's Government of Ireland Bill, which had no friends in Ireland, and an offer of Dominion Home Rule with safeguards for defence and Ulster.[108] The cabinet rejected out of hand his recommendations on political reform but his recommendations on administrative reform were accepted and a team of civil servants were sent to sort out Dublin Castle.[109]

Fisher executed a coup of the Irish administration. Taylor was ditched. His claim for £11,070 compensation, pursued relentlessly with Walter Long and Austen Chamberlain, was dismissed both by Malcolm Ramsay, who noted that nobody but Sir John Taylor could suppose he was that valuable, and by Warren Fisher, who informed Long that Taylor had enjoyed advancement far beyond anything that a modestly efficient English department would have given a man of similar calibre. Eventually he gratefully settled for £3,000.[110] Connolly, who had moved into the Castle after the killing of Alan Bell, a civil servant too successful in tracking down the hidden funds of Dáil Éireann, ran up a considerable bill at the officer's mess and was moved to Bournemouth.[111] Headlam was moved back to an obscure department in the Treasury in London to serve out his years to retirement.[112] Interestingly, no other senior civil servants were moved, not even Micks the head of the notoriously difficult CDB. Clearly what was at issue was not efficiency but an over-zealous and uncritical identification with reactionary policies which blinded Taylor and his like-minded coterie to the collapse of the State civil machine.

The moment in May 1920 when the reins of the Castle administration passed into the hands of a team of English civil servants is recognised as crucial to the history of the Irish administration in the period of revolution. It is generally argued that this team of non-political experts transformed a demoralised and outmoded administrative machine into an efficient and modernised civil service, just in time for the Treaty settlement.[113] This would be a remarkable achievement and deserves further examination into precisely who they were and what they did to the Irish civil service. It would also bring the civil service and the State to the centre of the revolutionary struggle.

The team of English civil servants sent to Dublin were led by John Anderson, forming a 'junta' in the words of George Chester Duggan, the superintending clerk in the CSO at the time.[114] John Anderson was chairman of the Board of Inland Revenue. During the war he had served as secretary of the Ministry of Shipping. In Dublin Anderson was appointed joint Under-Secretary with the powers of a permanent head of the Treasury and given a free hand; 'no civil servant has ever wielded, or is ever likely to wield, such power as he did during his twenty-one months of tenure of office as Under-Secretary'.[115] Accompanying Anderson were A.W. [Andy] Cope, a customs detective who was to play the decisive role in negotiating the Truce; Mark Sturgis, chairman of the Treasury Selection Board, who left a racy diary of those years; Basil Clarke, former war correspondent of the *Daily Mail*, director of Public Information in the newly created Ministry of Health and seconded to Dublin as head of Publicity (as propagandist he has had greater success with later historians than he had with his contemporaries); Geoffrey Whiskard, of principal officer rank, a crime specialist to co-ordinate civil and military forces; L.N. Blake-Odgers, seconded from the Home Office; T.D. Fairgrieve, seconded from the Scottish Office; Norman Gerald Loughnane, a Treasury principal officer; and Alexander Percival Waterfield who was made Treasury Remembrancer with the power of Assistant Under-Secretary; with William Thomas Matthews and Bernard

Gilbert, both Treasury principal officers, appointed assistants to Waterfield.[116] W.E. Wylie, the legal advisor to the government, was deeply impressed by the group and, as his own analysis and prescription so closely mirrored that of Anderson, he was absorbed into the team.[117] The Anderson team constituted, from the day of their arrival until the Treaty, a 'super bureaucracy' of competent and trustworthy civil servants in Ireland.[118] Their status within the service was signalled by Treasury circulars from Warren Fisher and from Johnson the establishment officer, directing that all papers 'dealing with, bearing on, or arising out of the present abnormal Irish conditions' were to be treated with the 'utmost despatch at every stage'.[119] Anderson brought one immediate advantage to the Irish administration; there were to be no more humiliations at the hands of the Public Accounts Committee for the heads of the Irish civil service. In 1920 MacMahon's mild suggestion that many departments made expenditures in *anticipation* of Treasury sanction flung the committee into a righteous fury. Anderson had no such trouble as extra allowances were nodded through for his English officials living in luxury hotels, travelling first class and enjoying special allowances.[120] As Duggan puts it, Anderson arrived 'drawing forth a well-filled purse'.[121] As the 'economy' frenzy swept through Whitehall, Fairgrieve airily dismissed a Treasury demand for reductions in staff, writing that 'ordinary conditions applicable to Great Britain are not possible as regards Ireland just yet'.[122] These 'suave and sophisticated Englishmen', with neither careers nor commitments in Ireland, cosseted and believed to be receiving huge salaries, aroused deep resentment in the old unionist 'die-hards' of the Castle establishment.[123] The nationalist press, in the hope that it signalled the abolition of the hated Dublin Castle, cheered their arrival.[124]

It is clear that both Warren Fisher and Anderson also interpreted the new regime as signalling a new policy for Ireland. They were also clear what this policy was to be: an immediate offer of Dominion Home Rule for Ireland, with protection for Ulster and British defence interests, allied with unflinching coercion. This was the policy that Macready, Warren Fisher, Anderson and Wylie agreed and brought to the cabinet in July 1920.[125] This was also the policy that Wylie reported to Anderson had brought the southern Unionists, churchmen and 'political' Sinn Féin 'in with us'.[126] However, despite the arguments of the Irish specialists, the cabinet was not convinced and Churchill along with Tudor won support for more coercion. Walter Long rejected the Fisher report and insisted that Home Rule would be accepted; all that was required was for the government to 'stand up to the Irishman' and he assured Lloyd George that 'it is dogged does it'.[127] However, the Anderson team acted as if the cabinet decision not to offer Dominion Home Rule was a delay, rather than a rejection of the policy. Cope continued to develop his own contacts with Sinn Féin, despite the cabinet decision that no authority existed for any person serving the Irish government to contact Sinn Féin except to convey government policy.[128]

As well as referring to the failure of administration Warren Fisher also wrote to Lloyd George on the failure of statecraft in Ireland and on the absence of an understanding of the role of a modern civil servant – 'to inform to advise and to warn'. A civil servant is not a soldier, he may disagree and he should certainly speak with complete frankness. In Dublin Castle none of the civil servants were prepared to do that and all avoided responsibility. Irish government was in danger of being overwhelmed by those who thought there was nothing more to be done than to defeat the gunmen. The ascendancy party in Dublin Castle were actually quite content with the *status quo* accompanied by additional coercion. The Anderson team were sent to Dublin to deal with a technical problem of administration, but also to provide the statecraft that was lacking. The danger was that the Irish government was abdicating to the military and quite unwittingly was creating the conditions in which the State in Ireland would come under a military executive. The mission of the Anderson team was to prevent the eclipse of civil government and to ensure that when the cabinet finally arrived at the correct decision it would be possible to enact it. They understood the enormous difference between civil government and military government and the difficulty of going back to civil government. As Macready put it, enforcing relative peace by military rule was not difficult; it was what was done after that was difficult.[129] What this group also saw clearly was that the key republican force was not the IRA but Dáil Éireann and that the actions of Dáil Éireann and Sinn Féin in establishing the counter-State indicated a desire to maintain social order and the rule of law, and a wise government would have encouraged this desire.

Warren Fisher and Anderson presented the cabinet with a clear choice – to govern Ireland by a civil or a military government. In presenting this clear choice they were not only arguing against the cabinet decision but also displaying a deeper loyalty to the State. As Warren Fisher reminded Lloyd George, 'there is all the difference in the world between a military machine and a civil machine in circumstances such as now obtain in Ireland'.[130] The military has the means to enforce its decisions because it is not dependent on civil society to execute its orders. Civil government requires the consent of society, military government does not. A further difference that Warren Fisher did not draw out was that whereas a soldier obeys an order, a civil servant responds to an order, sometimes critically. That Ireland would eventually have to be given self-government was evident to all except the most hard-bitten, die-hard unionist. The form of the State in Ireland after attaining self-government would be continuous with that of the last British regime, either civil or military. For Warren Fisher in particular, failure to ensure continuity of civil government of the State would be devastating. Hence his veiled threat to withdraw the Anderson team if the policy of coercion was pursued to its logical ends.

Warren Fisher could clearly see the connection between civil service reform, the crisis in Ireland and a threatened failure of the State. Although expressed in purely administrative language, the role of the Anderson team was clearly political in the sense that they responded to the crumbling of British political supremacy in Ireland. As Wylie pointed out, the people were either hostile or neutral 'because they no longer looked upon the government as the government'.[131] Sturgis put the same conclusion more colourfully: 'the Irish may not be fit to govern themselves, but neither were the English, nor the Welsh'.[132] The over-riding objective of the Anderson team was to ensure, first, that the civil government of Ireland would not be swept aside by military government and, second, that the civil government would provide continuity into a new government in Ireland. In pursuing these goals they acted outside the tradition of the civil service, but with the confidence that their political masters simply needed time to agree with the superior insight of their civil servants. Despite the posturing of Greenwood and the generals, the civil service were agreed that it was Anderson who was the 'most powerful force in the British administration in Ireland'.[133] The condition of Ireland and the infestation of the State apparatus by the military justified the exercise of executive power by an objective civil service in order to ensure the survival of the State itself.

The group was selected not on ability alone but also because they largely agreed with Warren Fisher on Ireland. Before transfer to Ireland Sturgis's briefing at the Treasury was a process of acquiring Warren Fisher's views on the failures of the old 'Castle Gang'.[134] Cope, the central figure in the secret contacts and negotiations that led to the Truce and Treaty, was an anti-militarist and a democrat.[135] As civil servants they recognised that there was a lot more to do in Ireland than simply beating an enemy.[136] It was lucky for Dáil Éireann that the cabinet resisted for so long. The IRA guerrilla campaign could ensure its own survival, but it could not topple a State. It was the failure of the British State in Ireland that created the conditions in which what might have been a comic operetta of Dáil Éireann succeeded in taking State power.

Andy Cope, highly strung with a nervous energy, was then and is now recognised as the key figure in securing the Truce and Treaty. For the mass of the Irish civil servants Waterfield was the key figure, one very much less significant in the bigger picture and not mentioned at all by Sturgis. But if the view that an administrative apparatus on the verge of collapse was thoroughly modernised within eighteen months is to be accepted, his achievement deserves recognition.

Treasury (Ireland), 1920–22

The creation of Treasury (Ireland) on 16 June 1920, with responsibility for 'all expenditure of all Irish departments, universities and colleges, including all questions of supply and establishment' with the authority to 'advise and make observations' on the Irish branches of the 'English' departments such as the Admiralty, Air Force, Ministry of Labour, Ministry of Pensions and Revenue

Departments; achieved in an instant the centralised control of the Irish departments that had often been proposed but never achieved.[137] However, that
control now lay with a civil servant, not a politician. Waterfield, as Assistant
Under-Secretary at Treasury (Ireland), was now head of the Irish civil service
answering to Anderson himself.[138]

Some of the pressing administrative problems that Waterfield had to deal
with had nothing to do with the political crisis and were common to both
Britain and Ireland. Most immediate were the demands of the demobilised soldiers and sailors. Across Europe embittered demobilised soldiers, organised in
groups such as the German Freikorps and the Italian Arditi, were becoming a
dangerous and destabilising force in society. In the immediate aftermath of
the Armistice there was a general expectation of improvements in the British
economy. The release of pent-up savings and the backlog of unsatisfied
demands, allied with the end to the slaughter of war, created a public euphoria
encouraged by a government declaration promising a 'land fit for heroes'. It
was anticipated that the post-war economy would easily cope with the discharged soldiers, and that the government would do its bit by giving them jobs.
A committee of inquiry into the employment of ex-servicemen in the civil
service, headed by Lord Lytton, put a lot of pressure on the government departments to employ these men, especially the disabled. Apart from the few with
recognised qualifications most of the ex-soldiers were virtually illiterate and,
by repeatedly failing the qualifying examinations, had proved incapable of
achieving a basic acceptable standard. It became necessary to simply ignore
their failings and admit them on the recommendation of the departmental
heads. In Ireland these men were often rapidly promoted into permanent
posts, by-passing other temporary men who were better qualified but regarded
as less loyal.[139] A particular animus of these veterans was the number of women
employed in civil service posts. The veteran associations were feared and hated
by the established civil servants; when they amalgamated to form the British
Legion and began recruiting ex-servicemen within the civil service W.J. Brown
of the CSCA attacked them as a union-breaking force and as a sinister movement close in spirit to the *fascisti* of Italy.[140]

In Dublin the 4,600 ex-servicemen of the 'Irish Federation of Discharged and
Demobilised Sailors and Soldiers' and 'Comrades of the Great War' were well
organised, bitter, and vocal.[141] The Federation had boycotted the official Peace
Day celebrations of July 1919 in protest at the government's lack of action on
their behalf.[142] The 'Association of Ex-Service Civil Servants' alleged victimisation at the hands of the Irish departments who, they claimed, were ignoring the
claims of those who had risked life and limb. They wanted new posts and promotions reserved for ex-servicemen.[143] They minutely scrutinised the departments for the lists of women employees and bombarded the heads of those
departments with demands for their replacement by veterans.[144] General

Macready was generally sympathetic and a willing conduit to Anderson for their grievances about the Irish departments.[145] John Anderson was anxious that the veterans living in the midst of a hostile population 'whose value to the cause of settled government at the present time is very great' should be have as many positions as possible opened to them.[146] The DATI was particularly anxious to please and Gill assured Anderson that 'where possible all professional and technical staff are ex-servicemen'.[147] The Irish Federation of Discharged and Demobilised Sailors and Soldiers demanded representation on the departmental Whitley Councils of the Irish government. Waterfield was nervous of this group and wanted them excluded despite Anderson's support for them, but he left it to the civil service unions to keep them out.[148] On the other hand Waterfield was quite prepared to put pressure on the heads of departments to dismiss women in temporary posts and employ the ex-servicemen in their place.[149]

The other main task that Waterfield faced was the application of the Whitley report on reorganisation. The sub-committee, formed entirely of former and serving civil servants, including Sir John Anderson, reported in February 1920. The report recommended that the entire civil service, consisting of twelve classes, should be re-graded into just four classes: writing assistants, clerical, executive and administrative; with higher and lower grades where appropriate.

So far as the civil service associations were concerned the gains offered by the reorganisation report were an end to the university monopoly on the administrative posts, a clear pyramid of promotion from the clerical to the administrative class, the retention of the seven-hour day and the improved scales of pay which offered a 'marrying' wage at age twenty-five. The disadvantages were the creation of the new writing assistant class and the formalising of discrimination against women who were doing the same work at the same grade as men but for a lower pay.[150] In Ireland the reorganisation report had been condemned by the ILC assistant clerks because of the discrimination against women and the perpetuation of a dead-end in the writing assistant grade. However, the rest of the service accepted the report by an overwhelming majority.[151]

The civil service associations assumed that assimilation would be a straightforward process whereby the assistant clerks would become clerical officers and the second division clerks would become executive officers. It was also assumed that the transfer would be 'weighted for age', that is to say that a civil servant would enter the new class at an increment corresponding to his age. Instead the Treasury offered transfer at an increment equivalent to a slight increase on the salary actually enjoyed at the moment of transfer. In real terms what that meant was that while an assistant clerk aged forty years, with twenty-two years service, might expect to arrive at a salary for a clerical officer with the same twenty-two years of service, the Treasury might instead offer a salary equivalent to only ten years of clerical officer service. Leading the reaction to reject these terms were the Dublin civil servants. Furious at the chronic delay that accompanied the whole reorganisation process and disillusioned with Whitleyism, large numbers of the Dublin civil servants were prepared to abandon Whitleyism, establish a strike fund and revive the demand for an arbitration board under parliamentary control.[152] The Treasury relented and, by offering a guarantee for a substantial increase in actual salary for all assimilated officers, did secure agreement but at the cost of a great deal of suspicion and bad feeling.

As Waterfield established himself in Dublin Castle as Treasury (Ireland) he faced the task of reorganising departments and assimilating a disgruntled and suspicious Irish civil service to their new classes and grades. The procedure, ideally, was that departmental Whitley Councils would draw up a proposed reorganisation scheme for submission to Waterfield, allocating the work of the department to a number of administrative, executive and clerical officers. He would then evaluate and, if he thought it necessary, modify the scheme, usually by reducing the proposed number of administrative and executive posts. The departmental council could then reconsider the modified scheme, but as was made clear the 'fundamental principle of Whitleyism is that the Whitley Council in no way detracts from the supreme authority of the head of department and the Treasury and no proposal can be acted on without the approval of the Treasury'.[153] What this meant in reality was that the only real reorganisation was the Treasury offer, which the staff was free to accept or reject. The next stage was assimilation. Each individual civil servant's immediate superior would certify that he was fit for allocation to a certain class and grade; higher clerical or lower executive for instance.[154] On a date to be decided by Whitehall the reorganisation would take effect and the entire service would transfer to the new classes.

In doing this Waterfield at all times tried to act according to the principles that were being followed in Whitehall and so had to constantly refer to the Treasury. Waterfield soon found that, not surprisingly, the heads and staff of the Irish departments saw him as an English interloper and tended to combine against him. At the same time the civil service associations remained active on behalf of individual civil servants and certain classes. As a background to all these was the problem posed for civil service organisation by the passing of the Government of Ireland Act, 1920 and the establishment of three or four executive powers of Southern Ireland, Northern Ireland, Council of Ireland and the United Kingdom parliament.

In early October 1920 Waterfield met the heads of the Irish departments to discuss the difficulties that the Whitley reorganisation posed and to set out some general principles. It was an opportunity for the departmental heads to put to him some of the difficulties they had encountered. A Treasury directive had instructed all departments to appoint an establishments officer to deal with all staff matters. These officers formed the official side of the departmental councils. Waterfield, however, dealt with the departmental heads only. This protected him from the rough-and-tumble of negotiation but ensured control of the process.[155]

At this point Waterfield was attempting to board a moving train as several of the Irish departments had already begun negotiations with Whitehall. The staff side on the Whitley Councils interpreted the reorganisation report as setting out a proportion of higher and lower classes and grades in each department such as would offer a reasonable prospect of promotion. This was not an unreasonable interpretation, but the Whitehall view was that such a proportion represented an ideal, rather than a hard and fast rule. It did not follow for instance that all departments must have an administrative class, they might have to be satisfied with an executive class as the highest the department could aspire to. This immediately created the suspicion that the only department that would actually have an administrative class would be the Treasury. The question also arose whether an exceptional civil servant of a clerical class might be promoted to a higher executive class in another department, or were these reserved for the clerical officers of that department.[156]

On all these and other questions Waterfield looked to his colleagues in Whitehall for authoritative guidance before approving Irish reorganisation schemes.[157] Some of the cases were utterly inconsequential and must have tried the patience of the Treasury. A second division clerk in the DATI was clearly shell-shocked in the war and now was 'un-nerved by the sight of figures'. Yet Gill, the head of DATI wanted to promote him to the lower executive class. What Gill most likely had in mind was providing that the unfortunate clerk would be able to retire under the 1920 Act on a significantly improved pension, albeit at the expense of the Irish taxpayer. Waterfield looked to London to see whether there had been a similar case in England.[158] At the same time Waterfield was under pressure not to concede to the Irish service anything that could be cited by the British service as a precedent in their reorganisation. He was also under pressure from London to do no more or less than ensure that each department was ready for handing over to the new governments 'in good working order with neither unfilled obligations nor arrears of maintenance'.[159] Waterfield enjoyed considerable autonomy so long as he was not creating precedents or encouraging civil service expansion, but his constant reference to the Treasury for guidance and the often brusque responses he got suggest that Waterfield felt himself to be on a tight leash held by Whitehall.

In early 1921, confident that he was not deviating from the approved Treasury norms and armed with the Government of Ireland Act, Waterfield grew more assertive in his dealings with the reorganisation committees and the pace of change accelerated. The reorganisation process began with the departments themselves coming up with a proposal. Waterfield would then review and revise the proposal and send it back to the department for agreement.[160] Waterfield's method of officious and minute investigation of departments alienated the departmental heads. Refusing to accept the view of either the establishment officer or the departmental head, Waterfield swept through each department 'looking at the work as it is performed' asking 'how we should grade the department entirely afresh'.[161] It is probable that Waterfield was following through a personal directive from Anderson to use reorganisation as an opportunity to simplify and reduce the cost of the Irish administrative machine, the same task that Warren Fisher was pursuing in Whitehall.[162] It was generally expected that the Irish administration would lose a lot of its civil service after Home Rule through voluntary and compulsory retirement. The last salary scales before retirement would determine pensions, whether they had been enjoyed for one week or one year. A high burden of pensions would allow the Irish governments to negotiate a cut in the £18 million contribution to the British war debt. It was therefore in the interests of the Treasury to ensure that the salary levels in Dublin were as compressed as possible.

It was possible for a department to refuse to play along and attempt to shorten the process by asking Waterfield to come up with a reorganisation scheme, as happened with the always difficult CDB. But Waterfield resolutely refused, insisting that his job was to review, not initiate, schemes. Eventually, as Micks dug in his heels, it fell to the staff associations in the CDB to force a reorganisation scheme through the departmental Whitley Council.[163] Sometimes the staff and official sides on a departmental committee would combine against Waterfield. The staff side would put a proposal on the agenda and send a copy to Waterfield inviting him to the next meeting. At the next meeting, with no objection noted from Treasury (Ireland), agreement by the official and staff sides would be recorded and forwarded to Waterfield, who would promptly reject it. The staff side would then refuse to attend any further meetings until the Treasury made a prior undertaking to accept any agreements reached by departmental Whitley Councils – a 'preposterous manner' of settling reorganisation according to Waterfield.[164] The least troublesome reorganisation was effected where the head of department sounded Waterfield out first, as did Stevenson of the Board of Works. Waterfield soothed Stevenson with assurances that these discussions were not a matter of bargaining but rather of 'each doing what is best for the public service as a whole'.[165]

The area of disagreement was always in the proportion of administrative, executive and clerical posts in the department. Most heads of departments, for reasons of status, wanted the greatest number of higher posts possible. Generally, but not always, this was supported by the staff side. Waterfield, on the other hand, looked to reduce the cost of each department by classifying its work as suitable for the lower class. Where a departmental head proved obdurate Waterfield was unsparing in his contempt. Dilworth of the NEB was told that his superintendents did no actual work, that much of the work of his office could be handled by writing assistants, and that the examiners had no 'professional' qualifications and their position ought to be opened up to the clerical officers as a promotional post.[166] Butler of the Intermediate Education Office was told that the work of his office was inferior and quasi-routine, suitable for writing assistants rather than clerical grades, with overly generous salary scales.[167]

Generally speaking the heads of the Irish departments found reorganisation to be a humiliating experience. Required to act as the bearer of Waterfield's bad tidings they either adopted his schemes as their own, or were exposed to the staff side on their departmental councils as powerless. Atkinson of the Commissioners of Charitable Donations found all his executive posts re-graded as clerical and, correcting the belief that 'a high degree of qualifications in accountancy was necessary for the proper performance of his duties', Waterfield re-graded the accountant as a clerk and a clerk he remained, despite the best efforts of Atkinson and the AEO.[168] In the GVO Beckett, in an attempt perhaps to save face, showed the staff side his correspondence with Waterfield, drawing down the full wrath and majesty of Treasury (Ireland):

> It is an essential part of the civil service constitution that where the head of a department has done his best to get the Treasury to agree to a proposal, and has failed, he must accept the Treasury decision loyally and do his best to carry it out. Whitleyism does not in any way affect this fundamental principle; indeed it is obvious that discipline would be reduced to a farce if it were to do so . . . I should perhaps add that the Treasury do not anticipate or regard it as necessary that there should be agreement between the official and staff sides in proposals of this kind. They would of course prefer it, but they cannot undertake to make concessions, of the necessity of which they are not convinced, merely in order to secure formal agreement.[169]

Even Sir Henry Robinson of the LGB, possessed of a monumental sense of his own importance, was brought to heel. Robinson presented the reorganisation scheme to the departmental Whitley Council as being a 'Treasury' scheme, which he himself had neither accepted nor rejected. Waterfield upbraided him for revealing his disagreement with the Treasury which 'it is of course desirable to conceal as far as possible' from the staff side. The issue on which they disagreed was the fundamental one of whether the LGB department should be re-graded as administrative or executive. This would determine whether it would recruit at a clerical level or at the highest administrative level. Robinson, who was notorious for nepotism, wanted to grade his department as administrative, but Waterfield refused. In this case the staff side generally supported Waterfield rather than Robinson because his scheme offered the best prospects for promotion in the longer term. If Robinson had his way he would simply promote his favourites to the plum posts. In fact he still managed to slip a couple past Waterfield, promoting a Captain Harris to the post of secretary of the Irish Public Health Council and a second division clerk to the post of deputy legal assistant on £500 per annum. Robinson eventually handed over the reorganisation to Barlas who enjoyed a better relationship with Waterfield. In his letter authorising Barlas's scheme Waterfield revealed his own attitude to the staff side and the Whitley Councils. Noting that the LGB process had been irregular and that the staff side would reject the proposed reorganisation, with which they were already familiar, as inadequate, Waterfield suggested that Barlas 'call a special meeting, lay the scheme before them as an official scheme, give them an hour or two to talk, then apply the closure and ask whether you are to record the matter as formally agreed, or not, making it clear on the assumption that nothing new emerges that the scheme will not be modified further whichever line they take'.[170]

Sometimes, however, Waterfield got it wrong. In the land registry the clerical officers regarded the assistant inspectorate as highly desirable promotional posts. Waterfield encouraged this expectation in his reorganisation of the department. The head of the land registry preferred to follow a different Treasury policy of reserving these posts for ex-service temporary officers. With the only avenue of promotion choked off the clerical staff furiously accused the departmental head of a breach of faith. He in turn accused Waterfield of making him look ridiculous in front of his staff.[171] Some departmental heads simply threw in the towel and left it to the staff associations to fight it out themselves with Waterfield.[172] The only departments where reorganisation was uncontroversial were the Castle departments under Andy Cope and the land courts under Wylie.[173] In the reorganisation of the CSO Cope assimilated almost the entire former clerical class into the new executive class.[174]

Waterfield also looked to London for guidance on dealing with the civil service organisations. The most difficult year for the Irish civil service associations was 1920. The increasing violence of the IRA, a curfew, and the activities of the 'Black and Tans' curtailed meetings. The debate on the Government of Ireland Bill generated uncertainty as to their future.[175] In the midst of these difficulties the Irish Whitley Committee seemed to secure some measure of control over their destiny. The civil service had already gathered that Warren Fisher was not an enthusiast for the Whitley Councils and Waterfield, in first meeting with the staff associations, was so frankly dismissive of Whitleyism that the staff associations were taken aback.[176] Determined that the reorganisation would not become a competition between the executive and clerical grades the Irish staff associations agreed that the departmental staff side committees would exchange information on the progress of each scheme. The COA and the AEO, on a joint motion of Mortished and Smithwick, agreed to co-operate on reorganisation.[177] The CSA suggested to Waterfield that they might be brought into negotiations in cases where the departmental Whitley Council would not accept the Treasury reorganisation scheme. The CSA representatives, Duff, Sloan and Mulvin, suggested that they might be able to induce the staff side to accept the Treasury decision. Waterfield was wary of a transparent attempt by the CSA to get involved directly in departmental negotiations but was prepared to be guided by Treasury opinion. He also revealed his impressions of the Irish organisers; Sloan he did not like as too obstinate and a troublemaker, but he thought Mulvin more diplomatic and tactful and willing to see the point of view of the Treasury.[178] The offer was of course refused. Otherwise every department would want to appeal to the CSA.[179] Interestingly, one of those that he consulted in Whitehall was H.P. Boland who was within a few years to become the establishment officer in the Department of Finance of the Irish Free State.[180]

In dealing with the civil service associations Waterfield resorted to the threat of imminent partition under the 1920 Act to force through agreement. Writing to Mulvin (his more favoured association delegate) he noted that 'the passing of the Government of Ireland Act makes it urgent that schemes should be settled as soon as possible. Staff will have sufficient time to consider the official scheme but we cannot be held responsible for the consequences of delay.'[181] The choice offered to the staff associations was to either accept Waterfield's proposals or be handed over to the 'tender mercies of the new governments' without reorganisation.[182] With the 'appointed day' for the transfer to the new governments postponed and with the signing of the Truce with the republican forces in July 1921 this threat lost its potential to frighten. The staff associations had no inducement to reach agreement. The associations argued that until the very day of transfer they remained civil servants of the United Kingdom and therefore entitled to all the benefits and advantages gained by the rest of the service. They argued that there was every possibility that a new government might take a less oppositional line to the Whitley Councils and the staff generally than was being shown by Treasury (Ireland). Furthermore, they had secured a commitment from Waterfield that reorganisation would be completed before partition and transfer of the departments. Therefore the staff side had nothing to lose (as they would transfer with existing rights protected) and the possibility of something to gain by refusing to accept the Treasury schemes, or at least leaving agreement to the last minute. Waterfield could have allowed it to drift but as he admitted 'such a failure is a confession of weakness of administration on our part which we ought to endeavour to overcome if we can'.[183]

Generally it proved to be the case that it was to the advantage of the departments if they could secure an agreed reorganisation sooner rather than later. The NHIC moved very quickly on reorganisation. The staff side, led by Gallagher and Duff, watched the English claim closely and simply demanded the same. They were not able to secure the number of higher posts that they wanted but were relieved to agree to a complete re-grading of the 198 staff by early 1921.[184] This need for haste had little to do with Treasury (Ireland) but arose from the British newspaper campaign demanding economy in the civil service that led to the 'Geddes Axe' and a series of wage cuts beginning in August 1921. As the post-war improvement in the economy petered out, and the scale of the inherited wartime debt became apparent, a relentless pressure from the Treasury for savings soon over-rode all other considerations. The suspicion grew that Waterfield was using the departmental reorganisation schemes submitted for approval as a device to secure reductions in staffing and grades.[185] In March 1921 Waterfield instructed that reorganisation schemes should provide for 'no addition to the established staff of Irish departments except from the ranks of ex-servicemen' and that new grades must be 'on a scale which is lower by not more than ten per cent than the London scale'.[186] The Irish associations complained of the manner in which the duties of the Irish departments were being compressed to the clerical class and of the rapidly growing number of the writing assistant class, which was being imposed in every department.[187] By August a new demand for economy flatly instructed that no vacancies and no promotions were to be filled.[188] It was now clear to the staff associations that the primary purpose of re-grading was not to promote efficiency but to make it easier to control, and therefore reduce, the level of salaries. However, the post-Truce negotiations with the Dáil delegation had begun, with no certainty as to what would emerge, except that it would be more than Home Rule offered. It was now in the interests of the civil service to secure the assurance of an agreement on salaries, even if the agreement was one that would ordinarily be rejected.

By November Waterfield could report that almost all of the Irish departments were organised and either in operation or awaiting enforcement. To complete reorganisation all that was required therefore was that the Irish branches of the British departments should roll out their schemes. However, the Treasury in Whitehall, under pressure to retrench, had abandoned reorganisation though without saying as much.[189] Waterfield therefore secured permission to go ahead himself with the reorganisation of the Irish branches. He was able then to report on the 2 December, four days before the Treaty was signed, that all the Irish departments and the Irish branches of the British departments were ready to go with reorganisation.[190] Was this reorganisation then the transformation of the universally condemned Castle into a modern bureaucratic machine?

Waterfield was of the 'candle-ends' school of administration. His instincts were to see the interests of the State as embodied in the interests of the taxpayer. In his analysis no matter what settlement emerged in Anglo-Irish negotiations, the interests of the Irish taxpayer and the British Treasury were at one.[191] No expenditure was too insignificant, or distasteful, for his attention. After the hanging on 14 March 1921 in Dublin of six republican convicts Waterfield bargained for a cut in the executioner's fee. The executioner demanded the usual fee, multiplied by six, for himself and his assistant. Waterfield, noting that the executions had been on the same day, imposed what was in effect a group discount; sanctioning £15 for the first and £5 for each subsequent hanging for the executioner, with £5 and then £2 10s 0d for his assistant.[192]

The Irish civil service saw Waterfield as a zealous and ruthless guardian of the Treasury interest, fair in so far as his downgrading of departments was seen to be utterly even-handed.[193] So far as the associations were concerned, he was certainly an improvement on Headlam.[194] His instincts in dealing with the Irish civil service were essentially decent. He pushed very hard to ensure that the many temporary civil servants, who would no doubt in time become established, received their certificates before the appointed day under the 1920 Act, just in case the new government might take a different view.[195] On the other hand he was not going to allow the interests of any future Irish State to be compromised. He was committed to handing over the Irish departments in good working order, by which he meant as close to the Treasury norm as possible. In many of the departments, by coincidence, the heads were all due for retirement. The demand to keep the departments in good working order would ordinarily have meant making a new appointment. This would have led to intense lobbying and political pressures from the eligible officials, with the danger that the successful candidates would then promptly retire on a substantial pension having served perhaps only a few weeks. In order to avoid having to make a new appointment Waterfield 'in the public interest', refused to allow these departmental heads to retire leaving the incoming government free to make whatever appointments it saw fit.[196]

Civil service associations were there to voice grievances and it would never do to say there was no grievance. But the reorganisation did, with few exceptions, mean that the Irish civil servant received something like a promotion when assimilated to the new grades and certainly an increase in salary. An assistant clerk on a maximum of £200 became a clerical officer on a maximum of £250; second division clerks on a maximum of £300 became lower executive officers on a maximum of £400. With clear cross-service structures the possibility of promotion to the heights of the administrative class, hitherto closed to all without the right political connections, now opened up. With hindsight, Michael Gallagher acknowledged that the reorganisation and assimilation of the Irish civil service to the new classes was an enormous achievement in which Waterfield succeeded in turning the labyrinthine multiple departmental grades into a coherent service-wide structure. However, Waterfield was pedestrian in his vision of the State and his work at Treasury (Ireland) was simply the financial conclusion of a policy decided elsewhere, it was not a policy in itself. He was often paralysed by the fear of creating a precedent and ultimately was guided by fear of losing contact or influence in Whitehall, his natural home. Reorganisation in administration has never produced economies, it can only produce better management. The Irish civil service in any case had not experienced the phenomenal growth of the British service during the war years. In July 1914 the Irish service was 25,192. In July 1921, at the Truce, it was still only 27,671.[197] That the cost had risen was not due to any increase in numbers but to the war-induced inflation. Nor by any stretch of the imagination could Waterfield's reorganisation of classes and grades be described as the transformation of a decrepit administration into the efficient apparatus of an independent State. Waterfield did not even touch on what all commentators agreed was the main weakness in Irish administration – the quasi-independence of many of the boards and departments and the lack of any clear line of responsibility binding politicians and civil servants. On the other hand the chorus of derision that met the Castle from all sides lacked perspective. In any specific policy that required complex administrative action, such as the transfer of the land to the tenant class, the Irish civil service had demonstrated undoubted ability. The problem in Castle government was its nepotism and the uncritical identification of the State in Ireland with unionist opinion. The Irish civil service also suffered from the assumption that the Whitehall system was administrative perfection and the Irish system with its autonomous boards and lack of clear political control was deficient. Ireland had efficient and able civil servants; what it did not have was a civil service that could make the British government popular or accepted in Ireland. This was equally true before and after the efforts of Waterfield and Treasury (Ireland). The State in Ireland was a political and not an administrative failure.

Notes

1 Kathleen Burk (ed.) *War and the State: The Transformation of British Government, 1914–1919* (London, 1982).
2 Eunan O'Halpin, *The Head of the Civil Service: A Study of Sir Warren Fisher* (London, 1989), pp. 24–5, 55–7.
3 Kathleen Burk, 'The Treasury: from impotence to power' in Burk (ed.) *War and the State*, pp. 84–107.
4 Humphreys, *Clerical Unions*, p. 128.
5 Eric Wigham, *From Humble Petition to Militant Action: A History of the Civil and Public Services Association 1903–1978* (London, 1980), pp. 35–41.
6 McDowell, 'Administration and the public services', pp. 595–600.
7 Gallagher, 'Memoirs of a civil servant', p. 40.
8 Ibid., p. 7.
9 Wigham, *Humble Petition to Militant Action*, pp. 65–6.
10 NAI, Department of Finance, establishment division, E121/12/33, 'Memo by civil service organisations'; Humphreys, *Clerical Unions*, pp. 80–9.
11 NA, T1/12315, 'Conciliation Board, Land Registry Ireland clerical assistants, 2 Apr. 1919'; T1/12345 'Assoc. of second division clerks memorial, Apr.-Mar. 1918'.

12 Garry Sweeney, *In Public Service: A History of the Public Service Executive Union 1890–1990* (Dublin, 1990), p. 17.

13 Quoted in W. Hamish Fraser, *A History of British Trade Unionism 1700–1998* (London, 1999), pp. 141–2.

14 *Second report of the committee of the Ministry of Reconstruction on the relations of employers and employed on Joint Standing Industrial Councils,* Parliamentary Papers, HC 1918, X, [Cd. 9002], 659(Whitley Committee), p. 6.

15 Humphreys, *Clerical Unions,* pp. 109–12, 112.

16 *Interim report of the national provisional joint committee on the application of the Whitley report to the administrative departments of the civil service,* Parliamentary Papers< HC 1919, XI [Cmd. 198], 239 (Ramsay and Stuart-Bunning).

17 Ibid., para. 39.

18 Gallagher, 'Memoirs of a civil servant', pp. 48–9.

19 Ibid., appendix chapter seven.

20 *Red Tape,* 8:95 (Aug. 1919).

21 Maguire, 'The civil service, the State and the Irish Revolution, 1886–1938', appendix, table 5: 'Members of the Irish provisional joint committee, July 1919'.

22 Gallagher, 'Memoirs of a civil servant', pp. 48–55; *Red Tape,* 8:95 (Aug. 1919).

23 *Irish Civil Servant,* 1:1 (Nov. 1920).

24 Gallagher, 'Memoirs of a civil servant', p. 50.

25 Warwick University Modern Records Centre (WUMRC), MSS 415, Association of Assistant and Supervisory Clerks, 'Council meeting, 22 Jan. 1920'.

26 Ibid., MS 296, 'National Whitley Council minutes', 14 Oct. 1919, 19 Mar 1920; MSS 415, Association of Assistant and Supervisory Clerks, 'Council meeting, 22 Jan. 1920'.

27 NA, T158/1, 'S.E. Minnis to the director of establishments', re: proposed Irish civil service joint council, 29 Nov. 1919.

28 *Red Tape,* 9:100 (Jan. 1920).

29 WUMRC, MS 232, Association of Staff Clerks and Other Civil Servants, executive committee minutes, 20 Apr. 1920.

30 *Red Tape,* 9:104, May; Special Issue, 9 June; 9:107, Aug.,1920; WUMRC, MSS 415, Association of Assistant and Supervisory Clerks, 'Minutes of special council meeting 15 Apr. 1920'.

31 WUMRC, MS 232, Association of Executive Officers, 'Reorganisation committee 14 Oct. 1921'.

32 Ibid., MSS 415, Civil Service Clerical Association, 'Executive committee 27 Apr. and 19 June 1919'; Assistant Clerks' Association, 'Annual Report 1918'; *Red Tape,* 8:94, (July 1919).

33 Gallagher, 'Memoirs of a civil servant', pp. 43–4.

34 Institution of Professional Civil Servants (IPCS), council minutes, 25 Feb. 1920.

35 James E. Mortimer and Valerie A. Ellis, *A Professional Union: The Evolution of the Institution of Professional Civil Servants* (London, 1980), pp. 2–4.

36 IPCS, council minutes, 7 and 27 May, 8 and 17 June 1920.

37 Ibid., First Annual Report of Council, 1920–21, p. 1.

38 WUMRC, MSS 232, Association of Staff Clerks and Other Civil Servants, executive committee minutes, 16 Jan. 1919.
39 WUMRC, MSS 232, Association of Staff Clerks minute book, 4 Mar. 1918; 16 Jan. 1919.
40 Ibid., 4 April 1919.
41 Ibid., 15 Oct. 1918.
42 Ibid., 9 Jan., 12 Feb. 1920.
43 Ibid., 20 April, 6 May, 20 May, 28 June 1920; *Staff Clerks' Circular*, No. 1 (31 July 1920).
44 Ibid., 'Report of the executive committee 1920'.
45 NA, T1/12289, 'Unestablished civil servants Ireland, claim July–Nov. 1918'.
46 Gallagher, 'Memoirs of a civil servant', p. 15; Humphreys, *Clerical Unions*, pp. 47–54.
47 W.J. Brown, *So Far . . .* (London, 1943).
48 WUMRC, MS 48, Assistant Clerks' Association, annual reports, 1904–18.
49 Ibid.
50 Arthur Marsh and Victoria Ryan, *Historical Directory of Trade Unions, Volume 1 Non-manual Unions* (London, 1980).
51 Gallagher, 'Memoirs of a civil servant', pp. 1–6.
52 Irish Civil Service Alliance, *Civil Service Salaries: Basis of Re-assessment. Report by a sub-committee appointed by the Irish Civil Service Alliance January 1920* (Dublin, 1920).
53 Gallagher, 'Memoirs of a civil servant', pp. 35–40.
54 Ibid., p. 55; WUMRC, MSS 232, Assistant Clerks' Association, minutes AGM 26 Nov. 1919.
55 WUMRC, MSS 232, Assistant Clerks' Association, minutes AGM 28 Nov. 1918.
56 Irish Labour Party and Trade Union Congress (ILPTUC), *Annual Reports and Congress proceedings*, twenty-sixth annual meeting Aug. 1920, report.
57 *Irish Civil Servant*, 1:2 (Dec. 1920), p. 8.
58 WUMRC, MSS 232/SDA, 'Chairman's report for 1919'.
59 Ibid., MSS 232, Association of Executive Officers, 'Annual reports, 1905, 1906'.
60 Ibid., Association of Executive Officers, general purposes committee minutes, 8 Feb., 16 and 22 Mar., 7 and 14 Apr. 1921.
61 Ibid., Association of Executive Officers, finance and organisation sub-committee minutes, 7 Mar., 2 May 1921; reorganisation committee 14 Oct. 1921.
62 Gallagher, 'Memoirs of a civil servant', p. 67
63 *Irish Civil Servant*, 1:1 (Nov. 1920), p. 4.
64 Humphreys, *Clerical Unions*, pp. 46–7.
65 *News Sheet, Association of Executive Officers of the Civil Service*, No. 15 (Jan. 1922).
66 Ibid.; Humphreys, *Clerical Unions*, pp. 66–72, 91–2.
67 Humphreys, pp. 92–3.
68 WUMRC, Civil Service Alliance, annual report 1919–20.
69 *Red Tape*, 9:99 (Dec. 1919); *Irish Times* 19 Nov. 1919, 'Irish civil service demands'.
70 Gallagher, 'Memoirs of a civil servant'.
71 *Irish Civil Servant*, 1:2 (Dec. 1920), p. 10.

72 Ibid.
73 RIA, Dictionary of Irish Biography database, Earlsfort Terrace, Dublin 2.
74 NA, T1/12481, 'Case of Mr R.J.P. Mortished 1914–20'.
75 *Irish Civil Servant*, 1:1 (Nov.1 920), p. 3; 1:5 (Mar. 1921), p. 44.
76 Ibid., 1:2 (Dec. 1920), p. 3; 1:5 (Mar. 1920); 1:8 (June 1921), p. 44.
77 UCDAD, Cornelius J. (Conn) Murphy Family Papers, P141/12.
78 Humphreys, *Clerical Unions*, pp. 114–31.
79 Government of Ireland Act, 1920 [10 & 11 Geo. 5 c. 67].
80 *Red Tape*, 9:99 (Dec. 1919).
81 NA, CAB 27/69, memoranda of cabinet committee on Ireland (1919–20) (C.I. series), vol. II; WSRO, Long Papers, 947/147, 'Barlas to Long, 9 Oct. 1919'.
82 WSRO, Long Papers, 947/147, 'Barlas to Long, 8 Oct. 1919'.
83 10 & 11 Geo. 5, c. 67 (23 Dec. 1920). The relevant clauses are 54–9 and the Eighth Schedule; NA, CAB 27/69 & 70, memoranda of cabinet committee on Ireland (1919–20) (C.I. series) vols II and III; 'Supplementary Statement by the General Committee of Irish Civil Servants as to their position in view of further legislation affecting the government of Ireland' (10 Nov. 1919).
84 NA, CAB 27/69, C.I.36, 'Irish office, position of Irish civil servants under the new Government of Ireland Bill, 26 Nov. 1919'.
85 WSRO, Long Papers, 947/147, 'Worthington-Evans to Long, 28 May 1920'.
86 NA, CAB 27/70, 183, C.I.78, 'Government of Ireland Bill, notes on clauses 51–7'.
87 Ibid.
88 Trevor Wilson (ed.) *The Political Diaries of C.P. Scott 1911–1928* (London, 1970), pp. 382–3.
89 O'Halpin, *Sir Warren Fisher*, pp. 46–65.
90 Kenneth O. Morgan, *Consensus and Disunity: The Lloyd George Coalition 1918–22* (1979), pp. 125–6.
91 HLRO, Lloyd George Papers, F/16/7/24.
92 Periscope [G.C. Duggan], 'The Last Days of Dublin Castle', *Blackwood's Magazine*, 212:1,282 (Aug. 1922), pp. 137–190, 139.
93 Richard Murphy, 'Walter Long and the making of the Government of Ireland Act, 1919–20', *Irish Historical Studies*, 25:92 (May 1986), pp. 82–96; McBride, *The Greening of Dublin Castle*, p. 260.
94 O'Halpin, *Decline of the Union*, p. 138; UCDAD, LA24, Duggan, 'Life of a civil servant'.
95 NA, William Evelyn Wylie Papers, PRO 30/89/2, 'Wylie memoirs', pp. 45–50; Leon Ó'Broin, *W.E. Wylie and the Irish Revolution 1916–1921* (Dublin, 1989), pp. 43–5.
96 HLRO, Bonar Law Papers, 83/2/21, 97/3/31, 'Walter Long to Bonar Law, Feb.–Mar. 1918, 21 May 1919'.
97 UCDAD, LA24, Duggan, 'Life of a civil servant'.
98 Periscope, 'The Last Days of Dublin Castle', p. 140.
99 O'Halpin, *Sir Warren Fisher*, pp. 83–5.
100 O'Halpin, *Decline of the Union*, pp. 200–1.
101 General Sir Nevil Macready, *Annals of an Active Life* (2vols, London, 1925), vol. II, pp. 448–9.

102 Thomas Jones, *Whitehall Diary vol. III, Ireland 1918–1925*, ed. Keith Midlemas (London, 1971), pp. 16–18.

103 Headlam, *Irish Reminiscences*, p. 216.

104 O'Halpin, *Sir Warren Fisher*, p. 84.

105 McColgan, *British Policy and the Irish Administration*, p. 23.

106 HLRO, Bonar Law papers, 98/9/1–2, 'Lynn to BL, 1 and 2 Apr. 1920'.

107 HLRO, Lloyd George papers, F/31/1/32, 12 May 1920, fols 124–8.

108 Ibid., F/31/1/33, 'WF to PM, 15 May 1920'; O'Halpin, *Sir Warren Fisher*, pp. 87–8.

109 NA, CO 904/188, Anderson Papers, 'Sir John Anderson to the Chief Secretary, 20 July 1920'; Jones, *Whitehall Diary*, pp. 25–34.

110 NA, T1/12592, 'Sir John Taylor retirement compensation claim'.

111 NAI, CSORP, 1921–22, 2602/30.

112 O'Halpin, *Decline of the Union*, p. 209.

113 McColgan, *British Policy and the Irish Administration*, p. 132; McBride, *The Greening of Dublin Castle*, pp. 279–80; O'Halpin, *Decline of the Union*, pp. 207–13.

114 Periscope, 'The Last Days of Dublin Castle', p. 150.

115 Ibid., p. 151.

116 Mark Sturgis, *The Last Days of Dublin Castle: the Diaries of Mark Sturgis*, ed. Michael Hopkinson (Dublin, 1999); Brian P. Murphy, *The Origins and Organisation of British Propaganda in Ireland, 1920* (Cork, 2006).

117 Ó'Broin, *W.E. Wylie and the Irish Revolution*, p. 65.

118 McColgan, *British Policy and the Irish Administration*, pp. 12–13; Ó'Broin, *W.E. Wylie and the Irish Revolution*, pp. 63–7.

119 NA, T1/12592, 'Irish questions – urgency of treatment', 13 and 26 May 1920.

120 Parliamentary Papers, 1920, VI, public accounts committee, paras 5275–80; Parliamentary Papers, 1922, VI, public accounts committee, paras 1754–9; NA, T158/1, Treasury conference on special allowances 11 Sept. 1920.

121 Periscope, 'The Last Days of Dublin Castle', p. 149.

122 NAI, CSORP, 1921–22, 2964/24, Treasury circular no. 36/21, 25 Aug. 1921.

123 Robinson, *Memories: Wise and Otherwise*, pp. 292–4.

124 *Freeman's Journal*, 28 May 1920.

125 Sturgis, *Last Days of Dublin Castle*, p. 13; Jones, *Whitehall Diary*, pp. 25–32; Ó'Broin, *Wylie and the Irish Revolution*, pp. 81–102

126 NA, CO/904/188/449, Anderson Papers, 'Wylie to Anderson, 30 July 1920'.

127 HLRO, Lloyd George Papers, F/34/1/27, 'Long to PM, 18 June 1920', fols 91–4.

128 NA, CO/904/188/447, Anderson Papers, 'Note by Irish situation committee 8 July 1920'.

129 HLRO, Lloyd George Papers, F/36/2/14, 'Macready to Miss Stevenson, 25 May 1920'.

130 NA, CO/904/188/476, Anderson Papers, 'Warren Fisher to the PM, 2 Aug. 1920'.

131 Ibid., 'Wylie to Anderson, 3 Aug. 1920'.

132 Sturgis, *Last Days of Dublin Castle*, p. 17.

133 Periscope, 'The Last Days of Dublin Castle', p. 172.

134 Sturgis, *Last Days of Dublin Castle*, p. 11.

135 Eunan O'Halpin, 'Cope, Sir Alfred William (1877–1954)', *Oxford Dictionary of National Biography*.

136 Sturgis, *Last Days of Dublin Castle*, p. 100.

137 NA, T158/2, 'Draft note on financial powers of Sir John Anderson as under-secretary Ireland, 22 Dec. 1920'.

138 Fanning, *Department of Finance*, p. 12.

139 NAI, CSORP, 1921–22, 2964/22, 'Employment of ex-servicemen in the civil service'.

140 *Red Tape*, 11:124 (Jan. 1922); 12:141 (June 1923).

141 NAI, CSORP, 1921–22, 22192/20, 'Employment of ex-servicemen', 22 June 1920.

142 Jane Leonard, '"The twinge of memory": Armistice Day and Remembrance Sunday in Dublin since 1919' in English and Walker (eds) *Unionism in Modern Ireland* (London, 1996), pp. 99–114, 101.

143 NAI, Department of Agriculture, AG1/G3543/19, 'Memorandum from Association of Irish Civil Servants . . . 9 Apr. 1919'.

144 NA, T158/6, 'Assoc. of ex-service civil servants to Waterfield, 6 Dec. 1921'.

145 NA, CO/904/188/595, Anderson Papers, 'Macready to Anderson, 27 Sept. 1920'.

146 NAI, CSORP, 1921–22, 22192/20, 'Employment of ex-servicemen 22 June 1920'.

147 NAI, Department of Agriculture, AG1/G4034/21, 'Statement showing what has been done by department for ex-servicemen since Armistice'.

148 NA, T158/3, 'Waterfield to Phillips, 7 May 1921'.

149 Ibid., T158/5, 'Waterfield to Patterson' and 'Waterfield to Cope', 8 Nov. 1921; T158/6, 'Waterfield to Minnis, 20 Dec. 1921'.

150 *Red Tape*, special number (Feb. 1920).

151 Ibid., 9:103 (Apr. 1920).

152 Ibid., 9:105 (June 1920).

153 NA, T158/2, 'Waterfield to Lord Chancellor', Dec. 1920.

154 *Irish Civil Servant*, 1:2 (Dec. 1920).

155 NA, T1/12531, 'Establishment officers in government departments', 12 Apr. 1920.

156 Ibid., T192/24, 'Waterfield to Fraser HM Treasury, 28 Aug. 1920'.

157 Ibid., T158/1, 'Notes of a conference Dublin Castle, 13 Oct. 1920'.

158 Ibid., 'Waterfield to R.A. Johnson, 16 Dec. 1920'.

159 Ibid., T192/47, 'Position of Irish valuers, 5 Apr. 1921'.

160 Ibid., T192/39, 'Reorganisation of the Irish departments under Whitley scheme, Dec. 1920'.

161 Ibid., 'Waterfield to Butler NEB, 23 Mar. 1921'.

162 O'Halpin, *Sir Warren Fisher*, pp. 46–67.

163 NA, T158/5, 'Waterfield to Micks, CDB, 11 Oct. 1921'; WUMRC, MSS 232, Association of Executive Officers, reorganisation committee minutes, 14 Oct. 1921.

164 NA, T158/2, 'Waterfield to Heseltine, 10 Mar. 1921'.

165 Ibid., T158/1, 'Waterfield to Stevenson, Nov. 1920; T158/2, 'Waterfield to Stevenson, 28 Feb. 1921'.

166 Ibid., T158/2, 'Waterfield to Dilworth, 2 Feb. 1921'.

167 Ibid., 'Waterfield to Butler, 24 Feb., 23 Mar. 1921'.

168 Ibid., 'Waterfield to Atkinson, 9 Feb 1921'; WUMRC, MSS 232, Association of Executive Officers, reorganisation committee minutes, 8 Nov. 1921.
169 NA, T158/2, 'Waterfield to Beckett, 24 Feb. 1921'.
170 Ibid., 'Waterfield to Robinson, 28 Dec. 1920'; T158/3, 'Waterfield to Robinson, 5 Apr. 1921'; T158/4, 'Waterfield to Barlas', 29 June, 'to Robinson, 10 Oct.', 1921'.
171 Ibid., T158/5, 'Land Registry inspectorate, Oct. 1921'.
172 Ibid., T158/2, 'Waterfield to Craig, Treasury London, 23 Mar. 1921'; T158/3, 'Waterfield to Gallagher, 8 Apr. 1921'.
173 Ibid., T158/1, 'Waterfield to Cope, 21 Dec. 1920'; T158/2, 'Waterfield to Cope, 24 and 31 Jan. 1921'; T 158/5, 'Waterfield to Cope; 'to Wylie, 24 Sept. 1921'.
174 NAI, CSORP, 1921/2638/2, 'Reorganisation of the civil service, assimilation CSO, Nov. 1920'.
175 WUMRC, MSS 415, Clerical Officers' Association annual report 1920–21, Dublin branch annual report 1921.
176 *Irish Civil Servant*, 1:1 (Nov. 1920).
177 Ibid., 1:4 (Feb. 1921).
178 NA, T158/2, 'Waterfield to Scott, Dec. 1920'.
179 Ibid., 'Waterfield to Mulvin CSA, 31 Jan. 1921'.
180 Ibid., 'Waterfield to H.P. Boland, 7 Dec. 1920'.
181 Ibid., 'Waterfield to Mulvin ICSA, 31 Jan. 1921'.
182 Ibid., T158/4, 'Waterfield to Craig, Treasury Whitehall, 6 July 1921'; T158/5, 'Waterfield to Legge, Treasury Whitehall, 17 Sept. 1921'.
183 Ibid., T158/4, 'Waterfield to Craig, Treasury Whitehall, 6 and 7 July 1921'.
184 Ibid., T1/12481, 'Insurance commission Ireland, Feb. 1920'; T158/1, 'Waterfield to chairman NHIC, 16 Dec. 1920'; T158/2 'Waterfield to chairman NHIC, Jan. 1921'; Gallagher, 'Memoirs of a civil servant', pp. 51–2.
185 McColgan, *British Policy and the Irish Administration*, p. 76.
186 NAI, CSORP, 1921/2638/12, 'Treasury (Ireland) circular, 29 Mar. 1921'.
187 *Red Tape*, 10:116 (May 1921).
188 NAI, CSORP, 1921–22, 2964/24, 'Economy in staff organisation, circular 36/21, 25 Aug. 1921'.
189 *Red Tape*, 11:121 (Oct. 1921).
190 NA, T158/4, Waterfield to Craig, Treasury Whitehall, 7 July 1921'; T158/5, 'Waterfield to Greer, 3 Nov. 1921'; T158/6, 'Waterfield to Rowe-Dutton, 2 Dec. 1921'.
191 Ibid., T158/3, 'Waterfield to Upcott, Treasury London, 15 June 1921'.
192 Ibid., 'Waterfield to under-secretary Dublin Castle, 31 May 1921'.
193 *Irish Civil Servant*, 1:4 (Feb. 1921).
194 Gallagher, 'Memoirs of a civil servant', p. 51.
195 NA, T158/4, 'Waterfield to Weekes, civil service commission, 16 Nov. 1921'.
196 Ibid., 'Waterfield to Scott, Treasury London, 3 Aug. 1921'.
197 UCDAD, Hugh Kennedy Papers, P4/735, 'Saorstát Éireann return of staff in govt depts', March 1924.

3

The revolutionary State, partition and the civil service, 1920–21

Introduction

BY THE TIME OF THE JULY 1921 Truce between the republican and Crown forces there were three State authorities in Ireland: Northern Ireland, Dáil Éireann and the Dublin Castle regime. The 1920 Government of Ireland Act proposed to create two Home Rule parliaments in Ireland while retaining Westminster sovereignty. Only one of these, Northern Ireland, actually assembled in June 1921. Dáil Éireann continued to function despite being suppressed by the British authorities and maintained its claim to be the only legitimate State in Ireland. Dublin Castle continued to function but was paralysed both by the military forces of the Crown who displaced civilian rule, and by the IRA who assassinated its functionaries. Civil servants were recruited for the Dáil departments of the counter-State, which functioned with different degrees of effectiveness. It was clear that it would take more than the offer of Home Rule to bring Dáil Éireann to negotiate with the British government. For Irish civil servants in the Dublin Castle departments the priority was to secure the best possible protection for their interests in an unstable world. The leadership of the GCICS worked to ensure that the civil service clauses of the 1920 Act gave them what was to prove a staggering degree of security for the future. The leadership of the civil service trade unions meanwhile worked to prevent the enforced partition of the civil service to serve the new Belfast regime while secretly maintaining contact with the revolutionary forces in Dáil Éireann, just in case.

The revolutionary State: Dáil Éireann, 1919–21

On 16 January 1922 a Dáil Éireann delegation led by Michael Collins swept into the upper Castle yard and 'accepted the surrender of Dublin Castle' from Lord Fitzalan.[1] That moment brought to a victorious conclusion the revolution that began on 21 January 1919, precisely three years earlier, when the Sinn Féin members elected in the December 1918 general election assembled in Dublin as Dáil Éireann (the assembly of Ireland) and declared it to be the lawful government of the independent Irish State. In the December 1918 general election Britain had voted 'khaki' and for Lloyd George, but Ireland voted Sinn Féin and for secession from the United Kingdom. Historians have been reluctant to describe events in Ireland between the assembly of the first Dáil Éireann and the takeover of the Castle as 'revolution'. Euphemisms such as 'violence', 'struggle', 'troubles', 'takeover', 'rebellion' and 'war' have been used in order, it would seem, to avoid revolution.[2] Among the recently written histories Kostick and Fitzpatrick explicitly describe the period as revolutionary.[3] The historian of the Dáil administration also recognises the revolutionary nature of the assembly.[4] However, if we recognise that revolution in the twentieth century was a State-centred event – the violent seizure of State power with the intent to then use State power to transform society, putting the State rather than society at the centre of revolutionary developments – then there is no doubt that the takeover of Dublin Castle was as revolutionary an event as the storming of the Winter Palace.

The surrender of the Castle administration to the revolutionaries was not simply a consequence of the IRA military campaign. The IRA could survive but it could not topple a State. Explaining the Irish revolution in terms of the failure of the British State in Ireland rather than in terms of the actions and intents of the revolutionaries, would suggest that the crisis of the Castle administration was deeply rooted in the long-term failure of the British State to receive the complete consent of the Irish people (unionist as well as nationalist) since the emergence of the Home Rule issue, or arguably since the Union of 1801. This crisis of the State came to a final stage in the period 1919–22. However, the failure of the British State was not simply the failure of legitimacy brought about by the increasingly militarised response to Irish nationalist opinion. It was also a failure in effectiveness as the State apparatus became so saturated with politics it ceased to work and ground to a halt. The failure of the State created a vacuum of both legitimacy and effectiveness in which the revolutionary challenge of Dáil Éireann, that might have been a comic farce, succeeded in taking State power.

Sinn Féin was the first Irish party to explicitly give a State form to the historic demands of Irish nationalism for separation. Sinn Féin's strategy was not aimed at simply destroying British State power but rather at its displacement by a national State power. As a strategy it did not emerge from the traditional engine of revolutionary nationalism, agrarian discontent. Previous Irish social movements had sometimes developed beyond the agrarian issues that had given rise to them and had taken on functions that could be described as Statelike. The Land League, which began as a tenant agitation, began to behave as a proto-State and assume judicial, welfare and educational functions.[5] But, though the Land League and later the United Irish League both had the capacity to create a proto-State, neither progressed beyond local agrarian issues.[6] As movements they remained limited to expressing traditional tenant demands. The ability of the British State to respond to those demands had led to the assimilation and blunting of their revolutionary potential. The Ulster Unionist Council had threatened to form a provisional government for Ulster in the event of a Home Rule government being installed in 1914. The Unionist Provisional Government had made elaborate plans to support the UVF in the field and to maintain an Ulster government in defiance of a Home Rule executive in Dublin. The outbreak of world war meant that the Ulster Unionist counter-State strategy was never activated.

As a revolutionary strategy, conceived by an intellectual elite within Irish nationalism, essentially urban and middle class in its membership and ideology, Sinn Féin succeeded in creating the broadest alliance against the British State. Rather than aiming simply at the destruction of the State it aimed to construct a more legitimate and effective form of the State. In the minds of the revolutionaries taking over the Castle administration the transfer of State power was simply the first stage of a State-led transference of society from a British to a Gaelic way of life. Much has been written on the cultural aspects of Sinn Féin strategy.[7] Today there is a general tendency to treat this cultural aspect of the movement in an ironic tone, noting the enormous degree of abstraction and delusion it entailed about the Irish language, the working class, Irish women, unionism and rural Ireland.[8] While much of this criticism is accurate it misses the fact that Sinn Féin, despite the rhetoric of cultural nativism, was thoroughly modern in situating nationalism within an *Étatisme* that gave priority to the State, not the nation, in achieving progress and social justice. Sinn Féin was effective because it succeeded in using the cultural rhetoric of tradition as a form of broad mobilisation across Irish society and as a strategy to State power. Of the two forces that were engaged in the revolutionary struggle, the IRA and Dáil Éireann, it was the Dáil that came out on top. This is because it used the revolution as a State-building opportunity. It undermined the claim of the British State in Ireland to legitimacy by portraying the British State as alien, oppressive and exploitative and by successfully countering its status as a progressive and enlightened force in Irish society. By the time of the 'surrender' Dublin Castle was stained with 'Black and Tanism' and viewed with contempt while Dáil Éireann basked in the glow of the Dáil courts and police, a local government department that was pushing through reforms, and the appearance of an energetic programme of industrial development; all presented to the world by a thoroughly modern and effective propaganda department. The decision of the successful Sinn Féin candidates in the December 1918 general election to assemble in Dublin's Mansion House and to declare themselves, as Dáil Éireann, the legitimate government in Ireland was therefore in itself a revolutionary action. Resistance to the alien British State was to be expressed through a rival popular State.[9]

The civil service of Dáil Éireann

The emphasis on a State-centred revolutionary struggle necessarily focuses on the role of the civil service both in the British State and in the revolutionary counter-State. We now turn to the experience of those men and women who made the Dáil function as a government from the assembly of the first Dáil to the surrender of the Castle (see Appendix: Dáil Éireann civil service, Jan. 1919–Jan. 1922).

The constitution of Dáil Éireann, adopted provisionally at the opening session of 21 January, was the organisational basis of the Dáil government. Modified at the sessions of April 1919 it was composed of an inner circle of the president of the Dáil (príomh aire) and four ministers of finance, home affairs, foreign affairs and national defence with an outer circle of variously termed ministers and directors. On de Valera's departure for the USA Griffith, as acting prime minister, set out the realisation of the domestic and constructive side of the Sinn Féin programme as the work for the departments and directories of the Dáil.[10] The Dáil was determined to give real effect to its claim to be the legitimate government of the Irish State.

A government to function required a civil service. The Dáil had in the writings of Griffith some guidance on how a revolutionary counter-State should organise its civil service. Arthur Griffith, in his *The Resurrection of Hungary: A Parallel for Ireland*, proposed that the four to six thousand officials of the local government bodies would form the basis of a national civil service.[11] This was further developed in the pages of the *Sinn Féin Weekly* where he detailed how, once stripped of nepotistic and corrupt recruitment practices, a national civil service would have a profound impact on Irish education and would offer an attractive alternative to the British and imperial services for young Irish men.[12] Under this scheme of a single unified service comprising local and central government a clerk on Ballina Urban District Council could aspire to the secretaryship of a department of State.

In the session of 18 June 1919 the Dáil decreed 'the establishment of a National Civil Service embracing the employees of all public elective bodies, and that a sum of £500 be appropriated for the purpose of the Scheme'. A short debate, of which no record was kept, ensued. Griffith, in reply to the debate, said that 'the Ministry were not wedded to any particular scheme and that a consultative committee would be selected to go into the whole matter'.[13] In the session of 19 August Griffith's statement that the committee had not completed its deliberations but 'that it was for the Dáil or the Ministry to propose a scheme, or for the committee to proceed with the completion of a scheme' suggested that the question of who exactly controlled the recruitment and role of the civil service in the revolutionary State was not clarified. It might also suggest that not a lot of thought was being put into the question. At the session of 27 October the final report of the committee implied that the national civil service would in fact apply to local authorities only and not to the Dáil administration, though again the lack of a full debate report leaves the question open.[14]

The question as to whether the civil service of the State would be controlled by the Dáil or by the executive arose in June 1919 when the appointment of Gavan Duffy as secretary to the ministry led to a debate on whether the government ought to be allowed to make appointments without the sanction of the Dáil. Thomas Kelly pointed to the real question at issue, expressing a fear of the government appointing members of the Dáil to paid positions, presenting an opportunity for corruption and cronyism, the very vice of which the Castle was so often guilty. It was agreed that in future all appointments of members of the Dáil to paid positions would be sent to the Dáil for ratification.[15] However, the only civil service appointment that was in fact brought to the Dáil for sanction was that of Accountant-General, a post that went to George McGrath.[16] For this post Collins sought permission for the appointment of a professional auditor and accountant at £500 per annum to co-ordinate the system of accounting in the various departments, except defence, and to keep track of day-to-day spending.[17] McGrath visited the various departments and helped to set up proper accounting systems. He also carried out occasional internal audits, very much like a one-man committee of public accounts.[18] Though some thought it desirable that the elected representatives should have direct control of the developing civil service, the suppression of the Dáil made it impracticable. In practice the various ministers had the freedom to recruit their own staff as required. The only control was that exercised by Collins in finance who had to be notified of appointments and who provided the cash to pay their salaries, thus replicating the British system of Treasury control of staff.[19] Ministers notified Collins of the duties and salaries of the new appointees; these were then registered in the departmental schedules held by finance. Presumably Collins could also use his central control to ensure that all those employed were trustworthy. Dáil departments were instructed not to pay staff themselves. Staff was paid directly by Seán McGrath, the Department of Finance's 'walking bank', who sometimes carried thousands of pounds on his person as he walked with the weekly wages around the streets of Dublin.[20] It proved an efficient system of controlling payments and insuring a central control of numbers while also ensuring that staff was paid regularly.[21]

The recruitment of a civil service for the counter-State raised questions around issues of cost, control of recruitment and, linked to that question, proficiency in the Irish language. Initially, as most of the departments remained largely nominal, the civil service remained relatively small so the question of where control of the civil service lay was of little practical importance. In June

1919 £24 2s 4d was the total monthly bill for all seven staff of the Dáil; O'Hegarty, clerk of the Dáil; Lynch, the official translator; O'Siochain, a private secretary to Austin Stack; O'Donoghue, an accountant; Murphy, a clerical assistant; Miss Mason a typist; and Conlon, a messenger.[22] The Department of Agriculture sought permission to empower the National Land Commission, decreed by the Dáil, to appoint a registrar, secretary, assessors, valuers and 'such officers, clerks or employees as it deems necessary'. The Dáil agreed but, cautious of the political capital that the ability to make grants of land commanded, also decreed that no official of the proposed land commission could be elected to, or be a member of, the Dáil.[23]

However, successful departments inevitably expanded and this was especially the case with local government.[24] As the Dáil department sought to take over the role of the LGB the 'clean-break' decree was promulgated in September 1920, ordering all local authorities to cease contact with the British LGB and to accept the authority of the Dáil Éireann department. The minister, W. T. Cosgrave, sought sanction from the Dáil for a dramatic expansion of staff: four inspectors, ten clerks and nineteen auditors at an annual cost of £23,000. Collins immediately refused, saying that the money was not available. Collins was not going to diminish the priority of the IRA in the competition for finances. Seán MacEntee suggested that the local authorities should be made to finance the cost of the department by a levy but this was rejected by both Cosgrave and Collins as undermining the dominance of the Dáil. No department that supervised local authorities should depend on those authorities for finance. Collins finally agreed to find £5,000 to cover the expenses of the department to the end of 1920.[25] By the time of the Treaty the Dáil Department of Local Government had seventy-nine office staff, inspectors, auditors and stocktakers. Interestingly, in view of the later Free State attitude to female civil servants, the Dáil departments in general, and local government in particular, were good employers of women. Women were rarely detained or searched and so could be safely entrusted with the most sensitive documents.[26] Of the thirty-six office staff of the Department of Local Government, sixteen were women. In the more demanding and dangerous work of the inspectors and auditors there were seven women among the staff of forty-one.[27]

Cosgrave was a stickler for correct procedures and so far as possible he wanted recruitment by examination only to apply. For the recruitment of auditors this required an elaborate charade. Advertisements were placed in the newspapers inviting applications for the posts, detailing the requirements but without disclosing the name of the employer. Michael De Lacey, the officer in charge of the outdoor staff, set and conducted an examination for the qualified candidates in the offices of Dublin Corporation. The exact nature of the work and the employer were revealed only to the successful candidates. Frank Barnard, who was delighted to be told he had got first place, initially refused the post when its full nature was revealed to him.[28] James Kavanagh, secretary of the department, ran into trouble with Cosgrave on the issue of staff recruitment. When Cosgrave was under arrest in early 1920 Kavanagh, in need of extra staff, recruited Tom McArdle, a dismissed Castle civil servant. Cosgrave on his release refused to sanction the appointment. It took a great deal of pressure from Kavanagh to force Cosgrave's reluctant agreement.[29] McArdle went on later to become the first secretary of the Department of Health.[30] Cosgrave could not maintain such Spartan recruitment procedures and personal recommendation by the trusted was resorted to. Michael De Lacey personally recruited Nicholas O'Dwyer as an inspector. O'Dwyer in turn recruited James McLysaght. O'Dwyer had no recollection of there ever being an interview; the jobs were offered and accepted in personal conversations.[31]

However imperfectly it managed to recruit its own staff by open competition, one of the key functions of the Dáil Department of Local Government was to enforce fair and open competition in local posts. Whatever compromises were necessary to run the Dáil departments, appointments there were not, in the longer term, as significant as local appointments because it was intended that the post-revolutionary State would be staffed by a 'National Civil Service' recruited and trained locally and advancing by ability alone. The department closely watched the employment practices of the local authorities and refused to sanction any appointment of elected persons to paid posts. In Baltinglass in Co. Wicklow sanction was refused when the chairman of the local Rural District Council successfully applied for the post of clerk to the council. The appointment of an elected member of the Waterford Corporation as town clerk was raised in the Dáil as an example of the bad practices that a native government ought to eradicate.[32] In August 1920 the Dáil Department of Labour circularised local authorities with a proposed scheme of arbitration for settling salaries of employees and officials, implying a centralising of authority over local government by the Dáil.[33] This was strongly welcomed by the trade union of the local government officials the Irish Local Government Officers' Trade Union (ILGOU).

The ILGOU had its roots in the Dublin Municipal Officers' Association (DMOA). The DMOA was founded in 1901 to defend the Dublin municipal officers against a wage-cutting corporation. The DMOA was from the beginning sympathetic to the Sinn Féin ideal of a national civil service with open competitive entry and promotion in the whole of the local and State civil service. Henry Mangan, chairman of the DMOA in 1910, gave a critical but positive response to Griffith's original proposals for a single national civil service.[34] Mangan was later an advisor to Collins in the negotiations on the financial provisions of the Treaty. Among those executed in 1916 Éamonn Ceannt and John MacBride were both members of the DMOA. Ceannt served on the executive between 1907 and 1913. The founding energy of the ILGOU

came from a group of DMOA members, many of them IRB, who had participated in the 1916 Rising or were strongly sympathetic.

Thomas Gay, a corporation librarian, who was close to Collins and allowed
him the use of the Capel Street library as a meeting place, was a prominent
figure in the ILGOU. The driving force was Harry Nicholls, an engineer in the
corporation, unusual in his militant republicanism in that he was a Protestant.
He was an officer in the fourth battalion Volunteers, the same battalion as
Patrick Pearse, Cosgrave and Ceannt. Arrested as a member of the St Stephen's
Green garrison in the Easter Rising he was interned in Frongoch until his
release in December 1916. He immediately began organising the ILGOU as a
national union for all local government officers. There is every likelihood that
the ILGOU was conceived in Frongoch as an arm of the coming struggle.[35] The
ILGOU announced itself as a militant white-collar organisation by staging in
Dublin in June 1920 the first ever strike by public servants in either Britain or
Ireland.[36] At its first annual general meeting Nicholls committed the ILGOU to
supporting the Dáil department in its struggle against the LGB. The ILGOU
refused to represent officials, such as Henry Campbell and John Flood, dismissed for maintaining contact with the LGB despite the resolution of Dublin
Corporation. Instead the union gave full support to local authorities that threw
in their lot with the Dáil department. The reason that the local officers were
ready to support the revolutionary assembly was the promise of better pay and
conditions through the creation of a national standard salary scale, better promotional opportunities and an end to corruption in local appointments.[37]

Another issue which intruded into recruitment of the Dáil civil service was
that of competence in the Irish language. The general feeling was that, all else
being equal, the candidate with Irish was to be given preference over the one
without Irish. Collins as Minister for Finance had to abandon his search for
Irish-proficient clerks and accept monolingual but efficient candidates.[38] The
preference for Irish speakers was justified not on terms of efficiency – none of
Collins's departmental business was conducted in Irish – but as a cultural
measure that would counteract the view of the language as a mark of ignorance
and poverty and enhance its status. This was seen as especially vital in the Irish-
speaking areas where English was the passport to employment. If Irish could
be seen as securing well-paid and high status employment it would be a
significant cultural shift. However, there was defensiveness in the debate and a
repeated insistence that Irish competence was to be the final criterion and not
the first.[39]

The reality for the departments of the Dáil government was that it was more
important that staff be discreet, loyal to the republic and willing to face the
danger that loyalty entailed. The departments could not be too fussy about
procedures of recruitment and officials were recruited by any and every means.
J.D. O'Connell, a solicitor in Tralee, came under considerable pressure to 'lend'

his typist Mary Hogan to the Dáil secretariat. His response lacked the zeal of revolutionary commitment: 'I trust she will be well looked after in Dublin. She has not been out of home before and she is rather quiet in her disposition . . . She is only lent to you temporarily, as soon as she can be spared I would like to have her back again . . . Her people are quite elderly . . . if she does not like the city she must be allowed back again'.[40] Evidently the city suited Mary Hogan very well as she settled into her job at £3 per week. Seán McCluskey, caretaker of the Dáil offices at 76 Harcourt Street, and therefore privy to every secret of the counter-State, was recruited by Kathleen Brennan, a member of Cumann na mBan (the women's arm of the republican army). After a hurried interview by Michael Collins (one of the few instances of anything like an interview for applicants) he was given the job and moved into the basement flat of the Dáil premises.[41] The couriers who carried the correspondence between the Dáil departments and their covering addresses were all recruited from the Dublin brigade IRA and from the IRB.[42]

The Sinn Féin party was an obvious source for staff but one with constitutional difficulties. The 1917 party executive included several civil servants.[43] Collins and de Valera, who were to come to such fundamental disagreement, were at one on the necessity of separating the party from the State apparatus. Not only was it undemocratic to merge party and State, it was also recognised that the fundamental weakness of the Castle administration was its saturation in party politics. Collins objected to two of the staff of the local government department being elected to the second Dáil in May 1921. De Valera from the earliest days of Dáil Éireann worked to exclude members of the party from positions within the State apparatus.[44]

It was, however, impossible to ignore the potential offered by the party, though it would be truer to say that the State exploited the party rather than the party the State. In fact many of the Sinn Féin officials who migrated into the Dáil civil service assumed that the work of the party and the State were interchangeable. Seán Nunan, who was appointed the first clerk of the Dáil, was recruited from the Sinn Féin party, though he was also known both as a Volunteer and as an IRB man. He was then withdrawn from the Dáil to act as de Valera's secretary in the USA.[45] Much of the maintenance of the ledger records of the Dáil Éireann loan was done by Sinn Féin staff at the Sinn Féin offices or at home.[46] It was Sinn Féin members who did the hard graft of organising and running church-gate meetings to persuade the anti-conscription fund subscribers to allow the money to be diverted for the use of Dáil Éireann.[47] When James Kavanagh, who was the accountant in Sinn Féin, was invited by Kevin O'Higgins to take up the post of secretary to the Department of Local Government, Patrick O'Keeffe, secretary of Sinn Féin, strongly objected to the Dáil departments raiding his staff resources. However, Kavanagh was in no doubt that the work of the Dáil 'was of greater importance than that of a political organisation'.[48] Cathleen Napoli-McKenna thought that the Dáil department of propaganda and the production of the *Irish Bulletin* had always been run by Sinn Féin rather than the State.[49] Vera McDonnell was employed as a stenographer in Sinn Féin but also did the typing of ministerial memoranda for Michael Collins and Cosgrave, as well as encoding cablegrams on the Dáil Éireann loans for transmission to the USA.[50] She transferred to the republican side in the civil war and, at the request of de Valera, worked to keep the Sinn Féin office functioning. For her the Sinn Féin party, the Dáil counter-State, and the anti-Treaty republicans were a seamless organisation. After the November 1919 arrests, the gaps in the administration of local government were filled by transferring Frank Kelly (one of the London Irish who came over for 1916) and Miss Enie O'Hegarty (sister of Diarmuid) from Sinn Féin to the Dáil department.[51]

In choosing its civil service one further source available to the Dáil ministry was the dismissed and former civil servants of the British government. Former civil servants would be already well-versed in the intricacies of record-keeping and bureaucratic procedures. A properly indexed and ordered record system would be well able to bear the brunt of loss of officials through arrest and imprisonment. Former civil servants of the British regime who worked in the counter-State were F.X. Thunder, David O'Donoghue, Edward Cleary and Hugh Hehir from the Land Commission; Diarmuid O'Hegarty and Michael McDunphy from the DATI; Tom McArdle from the LGB; and Paddy Cremins with Eamon Duggan from the Post Office. Most of these had been dismissed for participating in the 1916 Rising or for refusing to take the oath of allegiance in 1918.[52]

Procedures in the Dáil departments were, of necessity, informal and non-hierarchical. The only employees with clearly defined positions were the typists, couriers, George McGrath the Accountant-General and James Kavanagh who described himself as secretary and accounting officer in the Dáil Department of Local Government. There was no apparent division of work into administrative and executive grade, nor was there clear grading of salaries or promotional posts.[53] Salaries were determined in an ad hoc manner by the cabinet and, if we take salary as reflecting grade and status, were not any higher than those of the clerical grades in the British civil service. The lowest paid were the couriers, despite the danger of their work, next the typists, above them the equivalent of the clerical assistants.[54] Ministers themselves acted as an administrative or first division rank. Just as in Dublin Castle, the Dáil civil service soon found that inflation was rapidly eroding the value of their salaries and a co-ordinated request for a general salary increase was met by the cabinet in June 1920.[55] Co-ordinating demands for salary increases has always proved a most potent source of organisation; however, the civil service of the Dáil did not last long enough to develop its own *corp d'esprit*. Any sense of comradeship was provided in the main by prior membership of Sinn Féin, the IRB, the Volunteers or Cumann na mBan. If there was one single organisation binding the Dáil civil service together it was the IRB. What bound the civil service to the Dáil was a shared and intense commitment to achieving an independent Ireland. That shared commitment blurred the distinction between politicians and civil servants. Tom McArdle describes the Department of Local Government as working with a 'generous spirit' with no distinctions of ranks and with ministers doing the work of drafting and typing that ordinarily would be done by officials and staff.[56] Informality can, however, also be a sign of incoherence and lack of direction. Where there was no clear division of responsibility and no presiding minister with energy and vision a department might never progress beyond a paper existence.

The Truce brought an opportunity to evaluate the performance of the Dáil departments and to address the question as to what extent the apparatus of the counter-State was capable of undertaking the task of replacing the existing Castle apparatus. The Truce gave equality to the counter-State and, in contrast to the fear and confusion that permeated the Castle apparatus, the counter-State was animated by a keen anticipation of power.[57] The executive was reorganised with six inner cabinet and seven minor non-cabinet ministries.

Liam de Roiste, TD (Teachta Dála, 'delegate to the assembly') for Cork City, closely questioned Collins on the numbers and salaries of the officials employed by the Dáil departments.[58] In fact the cabinet had already recognised that the informality in grading and recruitment of the underground administration was not sustainable in the circumstances of the Truce. The proposal to create a committee on the civil service that had first been mooted early in 1919 was resurrected, for a 'salaries board'. This board, acting in either an advisory or a supervisory capacity to the cabinet, would grade and determine salary levels across the administration, ensuring uniformity and equality of the different departments. In some ways this would cut across the work of the finance department's Accountant-General appointed by Collins who had in fact evolved into an 'establishments officer'. The names suggested for the salaries board were John Murphy of O'Loughlin, Boland and Murphy accountants; Richard Foley of the Underwood Typewriting Company, who had provided office space for Collins; Henry Dixon, the solicitor and Sinn Féin founder-member; David O'Donoghue of the Dáil Department of Finance; and Patrick O'Keeffe the Sinn Féin secretary.[59] Such a board would have been dominated by those with business and commercial traditions, rather than with the traditions of the public service.

There is no evidence that the proposed board was ever formed and recruitment continued on an ad hoc basis. The Dáil Department of Local Government was, again, the most energetic. Of the seventy-nine staff in the department at the time of the Treaty almost half, thirty-eight, were recruited in the months after the Truce.[60] Cosgrave was still intent on enforcing local government competitive recruitment and approached Professor Hayes of the National University of Ireland about setting up an external examination board for local government appointments.[61] Austin Stack fretted about the lack of supervision over the Dáil staff, suggesting that general regulations be enforced with office hours for all government departments from 9.30 a.m. to 5.30 p.m. with an hour for lunch and a half-day Saturday.[62]

During the Treaty debate much was made on the pro-Treaty side of the fact that the IRA had reached the limits of its operational capacity. However, prior to the Truce in early June, Collins was considering a shift in the fighting strategy, which suggests that the revolutionary counter-State had not run out of options. Collin's proposal was to shift the target of the struggle from the police and army towards the civil service of the Crown in Ireland. Citing as a precedent Benjamin Franklin's proclamation of October 1778 against loyalists in the United States, Collins wanted the Dáil to pass an Act declaring as illegal and a usurpation of lawful authority all practices that assisted the British government:

> My chief desire is not to single out any particular institution but to get at them all. No English connection should be tolerated, except a connection we could not get rid of, or that we would be unwilling to get rid of, for instance the P.O. is not doing us any particular harm and might be allowed to operate, or the Board of Education, in certain ways at any rate, might be allowed to operate. This is a matter that has been weighing heavily on me and I have been anxious to see you about it. To my mind we must widen the attack at the present moment. We are attacking with our weakest arm and are attacking their strongest arm.[63]

Collins was once again stressing the advantages that disorder and chaos in the British administration would bring to the revolutionary forces. In response Austin Stack drafted a memorandum for the cabinet detailing the new offensive against the Castle administration. The memorandum listed nine categories of officials of the British State in Ireland:

1. Dublin Castle officials including the Chief Secretary, the Under Secretary, the Attorney General and Solicitor General, Chief Crown Solicitor and their many subordinates.
2. The members of the Privy Council.
3. The Lord Chancellor and other judges of the 'Supreme Court of Judicature in Ireland'.
4. The officials of the 'Four Courts'.
5. Recorders and County Court Judges.
6. Clerks of the Crown and Peace, Crown Prosecutors, Crown Solicitors.
7. Sheriffs and Under Sheriffs, Baliffs and Process Servers.
8. Civil servants engaged in the imposition and collection of taxes, custom duties and the like.
9. Other civil servants.

Categories one to three were clearly directing and assisting in the application of martial law in Ireland and in the activities of the Auxiliaries and Black and Tans and therefore 'made themselves enemies of the Republic in time of war and are . . . called upon the leave their present offices; otherwise they themselves will be responsible for the consequences'. Civil servants in the categories four to seven were essential to the administration of British law. If they could be compelled to resign it would make it impossible for the writ of British law to run in any practical sense. Categories eight and nine, 'whilst not actually harmful in themselves', did form part of the enemy administration. If they also could be compelled to resign then British government in Ireland would be 'seriously handicapped if not entirely impotent'. Their fate, the memorandum concluded, could be left over for later decision.[64]

This new aggressive strategy was overtaken by the Truce but was unveiled to the post-Truce Dáil as a 'decree as to purported exercise of public functions'. The decree asked that the Minister for Home Affairs may 'impose penalties by fine, imprisonment, banishment from a particular area *or otherwise*' (my italics) on persons 'purporting to exercise judicial, administrative and legislative functions without the authority of the Republic'.[65] Launching an attack on the civil service was now being offered as a strategy held in reserve in the event of the Truce breaking down and war being resumed. Gavan Duffy entered an objection to the 'or otherwise' which, as Austin Stack made clear, meant execution. Gavan Duffy was not squeamish about the death penalty as such. In fact he suggested that barristers ought to be included on the list. But if the Dáil was to impose the death penalty then it should say so in plain and simple language and it should be imposed by judges and not by politicians. This view gained strong support from among the members of the Dáil, including later die-hard anti-Treatyites such as MacEntee. With Stack in danger of allowing the debate to be smothered in details on the right of appeal, Collins intervened to bring the argument back to the central issue saying, 'it was not a question of preventing those officials from functioning, but a question of not allowing the British government to carry on any functions at all in this State'.[66] From his sources Collins was aware of the panic that swept through Dublin Castle in the wake of the killing in March 1920 of Alan Bell, a civil servant who had been investigating the hiding places of the Dáil finances. The killing of a civil servant clearly had much greater impact on the administrative machine than that of a policeman or a soldier. In Bengal the assassination of officials of the Indian civil service had a devastating impact on recruitment and morale and fatally undermined the ability of the British to suppress Indian nationalist activists.[67] Perhaps it was just as well that the Castle civil servants themselves had no inkling of their probable fate in the event of a resumption of hostilities.

Partitioning the civil service

Waterfield, in reorganising the Irish civil service, was simply applying with local variations a policy that was also being applied in Great Britain. He could check with Whitehall at every stage and ensure that his schemes were in line with Treasury policy generally. Partition of the civil service was, however, uniquely Irish in its application and was also an unprecedented administrative act. Earlier Home Rule proposals provided that some of the Irish civil servants would be transferred to an Irish parliament and that some would remain under the control of the London government. The 1920 Government of Ireland Act divided the Irish administration in ways never previously proposed.[68] Originally the legislation proposed that the Irish departments would be divided north and south with sections that could not be partitioned allocated to the Council of Ireland, thus being shared between north and south. By the final stages of the bill, under pressure from the Ulster Unionists, a 'clean cut' between north and south was envisaged with the Council of Ireland acting as a potential vehicle for future unity.[69] Through the various drafts Westminster continued to retain most of the financial, revenue and customs departments. Of all these State and quasi-State administrations only two actually existed in reality, Dublin and London. Belfast had only a paper and the Council of Ireland a purely conceptual existence. Therefore the new civil service of north and south in Ireland would have to be carved out of the existing Irish administration through partition.

On the 'appointed day' for the operation of the new governments, the functions of existing departments would be transferred simultaneously to the Southern and Northern Ireland governments and with them their civil servants who were also transferred en bloc. For the purpose of partition the 1920 Act created two categories of Irish civil servant. Those civil servants who 'on the appointed day were concerned solely with the administration of public services' in Southern or Northern Ireland automatically became officers of that government. For all other civil servants the Civil Service Committee established by the Act, and on which the civil servants themselves had two representatives, would determine their allocation north or south. This was a further development of the Civil Service Committee established by the 1914 Act. The original committee had the power to determine the status and entitlements of Irish civil servants who opted to retire. Under the 1920 Act this committee was further empowered to determine the allocation of the civil service to north and south and, in doing so, was instructed to defer to the wishes of the individual officer so far as possible.[70] The success of the GCICS in getting representation on this committee was crucial to securing the confidence of the civil servants themselves in the new governments. Sam Sloan of the AEO and Michael Gallagher of the CSCA, the two most active representatives of the membership, were elected to the committee.[71]

Another class of civil servant whose welfare was being secured by Waterfield was Englishmen who happened to be posted in Ireland and who faced being allocated to either of the Irish governments on the appointed day. There was also evidence that some Irish civil servants in Britain were looking for transfer to Ireland in anticipation of native government. Waterfield established an informal transfer between the British and the Irish departments for those officers. His objective was to ensure so far as possible that the Irish governments would take over a civil service staffed by men who wished to serve in Ireland.[72] To his surprise the number of officials wishing to transfer out of Britain to Ireland far outnumbered officials wishing to transfer the other way. Generally civil servants of the higher executive grades wished to transfer out of Ireland, those of the lower clerical grades into Ireland. This reflects the anticipation of where the better future opportunities lay for the respective classes.[73]

However, the main preoccupation of the civil service associations, as we have seen, was reorganisation and re-grading. The threat, or promise, of Home Rule had been part of Irish administration for the lifetime of many of the Irish civil service and most had grown used to the waxing and waning of the issue and even regarded it with some indifference.[74] The GCICS was diligent in protecting the interests of the service and used each revision of Home Rule to extend previously won concessions. The mood within the Irish committee of the cabinet was abjectly conciliatory to the Irish civil service, perhaps in an unstated apologetic agreement with accusations of a breach of faith on the part of the State. The amendments sub-committee on the Government of Ireland Bill recommended that the Treasury should go out of its way to meet the inevitable 'hard cases' that partition of the civil service would throw up, meaning most probably those that neither north nor south wanted.[75]

As partition emerged as cabinet policy Anderson instructed the Irish departments to draw up a paper allocation of their work and a 'provisional list of officers available for transfer to the governments of Northern and Southern Ireland, or the Council of Ireland'.[76] However, the 1920 Act was so convoluted that it was confidently felt that partition would never actually happen and the whole work of preparing the Irish departments for the appointed day had an air of unreality to it.[77] For the civil service itself 'the nightmare of transfer to Belfast' as it was described in *Red Tape*, the civil service journal, seemed remote.[78] Such was the conviction within the civil service associations that partition would not happen or, if it did, would not work, that they several times repeated their determination that they would remain as all-Ireland associations.[79]

A civil service for Northern Ireland

Of the political forces then shaping Ireland the only one that saw virtue in the 1920 Act was the Ulster Unionists. The key figures in turning the 1920 Act to successful regime-building were James Craig and Ernest Clark. However, it is important to appreciate that Craig saw little virtue in the 1920 Act as such and simply used it as the means to the end of Ulster Unionist autonomy in a six-county Northern Ireland.[80] Craig was among the more 'State-minded' Irish politicians of his times. Close to Walter Long he deputised for him at times. He transformed the paramilitary UVF into an armed force of the northern State, the Special Constabulary, before the State itself came into existence. A skilled administrator and negotiator rather than an original thinker, the record shows that he had a keen appreciation of the importance of securing early control of administration. Even though he had no actual position in the Irish government it was assumed that Craig, as leader of the Ulster Unionist Council, was the future prime minister of Northern Ireland and he was consulted as such.

Sir Ernest Clark, like Anderson a civil servant from the Treasury departments, was appointed in September 1920 as Assistant Under-Secretary in the Irish Office with responsibility for the six counties that were to form Northern Ireland. The appointment of Clark prompted Wylie to draw up a memorandum on the Irish situation in which he described the appointment as a 'blunder leading to permanent partition'.[81] A former evangelical preacher, Clark retained throughout his life a sense of mission but was clearly overwhelmed by James Craig's towering presence and adroit flattery.[82] Although he was supposed to report to Anderson in Dublin Castle and remained a civil servant of the Crown, Clark was soon acting at the behest of Craig. The civil service staff representatives found him capable but ruthless in pursuing his ends. On his trips to Dublin to meet with the civil service representatives he mentioned more than once that he had 'set up' the South African government equipped with no more than an Act of Parliament, a table and a chair and that he would do the same in Northern Ireland.[83]

Months before the elections under the 1920 Act to establish the new Irish governments, Craig and Clark worked together to create an administrative apparatus for Belfast that would have written across it, as Craig urged Clark to write across his own chest, ULSTER! In an echo of the strategy of Sinn Féin they created an administration from the top down. First a framework for a cabinet of ministries was elaborated, then the existing departments were allocated to these ministries and finally a civil service to run these ministries was assembled. The shape of the cabinet was developed in discussion between Clark, Craig and Adam Duffin of the Belfast Chamber of Commerce between February and April 1921. Clark's suggestion for a cabinet of five ministries was countered by Duffin's suggestion of eight. Despite Clark's warning that, for a party that would have between thirty-two and forty seats in the northern parliament, to have one-quarter or one-fifth of them in cabinet would make a nonsense of parliamentary government, Craig plumped for seven ministries; six plus the prime minister.[84] Craig seems to have already sounded out his

Ulster Unionist colleagues as to prospective ministerial posts. The task then was to start staffing the ministries with a civil service. It was here that the Ulster Unionists ran into trouble with the Anderson team in Dublin Castle and with the civil service staff associations.

Relations between Craig and Clark and the Anderson team were fraught as Belfast became suspicious that Dublin was being obstructive and was preventing the smooth working of the Belfast administration. Most informed opinion was well aware that the Anderson team were sceptical of the 1920 Act and were working for a Dominion Home Rule settlement. Cope and Sturgis were hostile and Anderson became even more stiffly formal.[85] Anderson's position on Home Rule and partition has been described as 'enigmatic'.[86] The creation of the office of a Belfast Under-Secretary seems to have been his idea, yet he was less than enthusiastic about its operation. If we assume that Anderson's main objective was to ensure continuity and integrity in administration, then his actions appear more consistent. By insisting that the Belfast administration would not have a free hand in recruiting its civil servants he hoped to ensure that the State apparatus would not be tainted by the sort of politicisation that had brought the Castle regime into disrepute. Anderson reminded Clark that the assignment of the civil service was entirely in the hands of the Civil Service Committee, which could not come into existence until both the northern and the southern governments had been elected. The sequence therefore should be that the civil service heads of the Irish departments would make a putative division of the work of the department between northern and southern business. Staff would be discreetly sounded out as to their preference for future service, north or south. The heads of the departments would then, so far as possible, ensure that individual civil servants were assigned to the jurisdiction they preferred in advance of partition. In order to make partition of the staff as uncontentious as possible Anderson suggested that departmental Whitley Councils of staff and official sides could determine the preferences of each civil servant and prepare provisional allocations. On partition the Civil Service Committee would then find it simplest to assign the staff on the lines already worked out provisionally by the departmental Whitley Councils. The governments of north and south would then have to either accept or pension the staff assigned to them.[87] Anderson's confidence lay in the civil service loyalty to the State and to its *esprit de corps*, rather than in the putative governing parties, to ensure that there would be an essential continuity. The determination of Craig and Clark to push ahead with staffing the Belfast departments in advance of elections and the creation of the Civil Service Committee fatally undermined Anderson's strategy. In this determination Craig and Clark had the support of the Lloyd George cabinet.

In March Clark wrote to Sturgis asking for the list of the civil servants who had opted to go north. Clark was suspicious that the departments in Dublin

Castle were dividing up the staff in such a way as to transfer the 'duds' of the service to the north. Cope in his reply, denying that there was any such intent, told Clark that there was an equally strong suspicion on the staff side in Dublin Castle that the few plum jobs in the new administration were being earmarked for English civil servants.[88] Clark, who anticipated that the southern government would retain most of the experienced men, began looking to recruit pensioned civil servants as temporaries to set up the departments.[89] Anderson offered Clark further assurance that nothing was being withheld from him and the problem was that the men were unwilling to commit themselves either way in advance of the actual date of transfer. In fact, as we have seen, the civil service associations were fully occupied with reorganisation and re-grading. Also, with the future so uncertain, a sensible civil servant might reasonably fear that too enthusiastic a display of support for either government might jeopardise future prospects if he had the misfortune to end up under the other. Anderson suggested that the best course of action for Clark would be to pick men for the principal posts in the departments and let them work out schemes of organisation and staffing for their departments.[90] Anderson assumed that Clark would recruit the heads of the departments from the Irish service, as these were the men who best knew the requirements of the work and the calibre of the officers available. He also assumed that this would be a purely paper exercise until the Civil Service Committee could function and make allocations. In fact Craig and Clark were already filling the key posts with Ulstermen such as Sam Watt with his well-known anti-Catholic views, Gordon from the DATI, Dale and Litchfield from the British service, Magill and Duggan from Dublin and W.D. Scott from the Treasury.[91] In order to make Belfast an attractive posting Clark recommended that the staff scheme should have a 'liberal number of higher posts'.[92] He also offered considerably higher salaries to English officers as an inducement to transfer. Waterfield, conscious of the resentment this injustice would cause among the officers transferred from Dublin, later insisted on Treasury salary scales being applied evenly.[93] There was also an attempt to prevent the reorganisation grades being applied so far as the northern jurisdiction was concerned, leaving the Northern Ireland government free to offer better terms if necessary to attract the right men.[94] Clark staffed his own office first, recruiting officers from London such as Scott from the Treasury, but also choosing men of Ulster Protestant background like Captain Petherick, a war veteran who had served in the Iniskilling Fusiliers.[95] In this initial recruitment to the senior ranks of the nascent northern civil service preference was given to firstly, men of Ulster Protestant background, secondly Englishmen who were presumed to be sympathetic to an Ulster Protestant state and lastly, other Protestant Irishmen. The northern State-builders saw Northern Ireland primarily in sectarian rather than territorial terms; 'Ulster' meant 'Protestant'. This was now to apply to the lower ranks of the new civil service being assembled in Belfast. Protestant loyalism would bind the civil service to the new Northern Ireland State.

Relations with the Irish civil service, where there were growing suspicions about the recruitment of staff to the northern government, were also poor. Mortished, in his *Irish Civil Servant* journal, noted as early as April 1921 that allegations of patronage appointments in 'Carsonia' were circulating within the Irish service.[96] In May 1921, before the elections to establish the Belfast government, the AEO published its correspondence with Craig as the 'prospective head of government of Northern Ireland'. The AEO had written to Craig in April 1921 asking him to express support for recruitment by open competitive examination and for the principle of promotion by merit alone. Specifically the AEO asked him for assurances that appointments to the Northern Ireland civil service would be made through the Civil Service Committee established by the 1920 Act. On neither count would Craig offer any substantial assurance.[97] The creation of two governments and the partition of departments necessarily reduced the work and opportunities that each government offered as compared to an all-Ireland service. In much reduced administrations, which coincided with a large number of retirements, the competition for the few top posts would be even keener.[98]

The May elections and the establishment of the Northern Ireland government in June added another force to the partition of the civil service, the Belfast cabinet. The 1920 Act stated quite unambiguously that the allocation of staff north and south was exclusively a function of the Civil Service Committee. That could not happen until both governments were established and both could nominate their representatives to the committee. However, as Craig indicated to his cabinet, the northern government did not want to recruit the whole of its civil service from Dublin. He regarded the Dublin civil servants as undesirable and, in particular, was unhappy that the allocation of staff was under the control of the Whitley Councils of each department. This, the northern cabinet agreed, was in itself prejudicial to Northern Irish interests. Greenwood suggested to Craig that the problem could be addressed by the loan of temporary staff from Dublin. This, he assured the cabinet, would not lead to the northern administration acquiring too many civil servants, and therefore a demand for extensive pensioning of redundant staff, as Greenwood had also offered assurances that any surplus would be re-absorbed. Anderson does not seem to have been informed of these assurances.[99] Fortified by these assurances the northern government began recruiting a civil service by personal contact with individuals in the Dublin administration and by public advertisement inviting applications to a selection board. The mysterious migration northwards of certain officials was noted and condemned as 'wire-pulling' by the civil service associations. The Irish CSA sent a delegation on the issue to the new Minister for Finance Pollock, the first Irish minister they had met.

Refusing to accede to the delegation's demand that the hand-picking of men stop and that transfers only take place as the Civil Service Committee directed, Pollock lamely referred to the problem of finding housing or lodging for transferred officers from Dublin. It was clear to the civil service associations that with the northern government now a reality, and the Truce adding to uncertainty as to the future of Dublin government, a scramble for posts was going on behind the scenes and fatally undermining the safeguards that had been won. Those without influence in Belfast would end up with little choice.[100]

In fact the possible employment of Catholics was already exciting debate within the Northern Ireland cabinet. Complaints about the employment of Catholics in the civil service were being forwarded by the Orange Order and by the Ulster Ex-Service Association and were being treated with utmost seriousness by the cabinet. Clark might have dismissed as 'pure imagination' allegations of anti-Catholic bias but the *Freeman's Journal* was completely accurate in its reporting of a furore in cabinet around the employment of Coyle in the Ministry of Agriculture. Coyle was a Catholic transferred from the DATI who was an early target of Orange Order complaint.[101] The cabinet members regarded the selection board as the vehicle for their personal patronage and there was stout resistance to Clark's suggestion that recruitment would be entirely in the hands of the Ministry of Finance. Cabinet ministers arranged it so that the crucial selection board would in fact be simply a 'rubber stamp' on the employment of the individuals they recommended.[102] The pattern of Ulster Unionist Party and civil service relations was established in the short period of 1920–21 as intensely parochial, nepotistic and anti-Catholic.[103]

Mention of a selection board alarmed Dublin. Fairgrieve wrote to Clark reminding him that the only body competent to assign staff to the northern government was the Civil Service Committee mentioned in the 1920 Act and that a selection board was 'not on'. Clark assured him that the board was for purely temporary posts to ensure the operation of the administration and that as soon as the new officers were assigned to the northern government they could be dispensed with. A public notice was drafted and then redrafted to exclude references to an interview panel and preference being given to men of an 'Ulster' background.[104] By now allegations were flying around Dublin Castle of the northern government refusing to entertain any applications for transfer from Dublin by Catholics.[105]

Resisting partition of the civil service

The Truce of 11 July and the search for a basis for negotiation that took up the months that followed gave the priority to conciliation with Sinn Féin rather than to establishing the northern administration. The transfer of authority that was meant to follow the elections under the 1920 Act was delayed. The threat to impose Crown Colony government in the area of Southern Ireland was not followed through. In the aftermath of the Truce the establishment of the Civil Service Committee and the partition of the civil service became in effect a 'slow bicycle' race with all the contestants determined to go as slow as possible. The winner, it was felt, would be whoever was last in. For Sinn Féin it was vital in the period between the Truce and whatever agreement would emerge that the government of Southern Ireland should not be established.

While Craig was desperately anxious for the transfer of functions he was not at all anxious for the transfer of staff. He was confident that between local recruits and selected transfers from Dublin he had in fact a functioning civil service and did not particularly want or need an allocation of the existing civil service.[106] Yet he could not say this. The non-functioning of the administration disguised the degree of 'Stateness' it had already acquired through its security apparatus, the Special Constabulary. Therefore Pollock and Clark, who was now head of the Northern Ireland civil service, began to delay the question of transfers. Pollock asked for an inquiry by the Civil Service Committee, prior to allocation, into the staffing of the existing Irish departments, alleging that there was evidence that the staff levels were excessive. He argued that it was the responsibility of the British government to either absorb or pension excess staff and not place this burden on the Irish governments. Waterfield quickly quashed that line, insisting that his own reorganisation had dealt with the issue (which it had not) and there was no excess in the Irish service.[107] The long delay between the Truce and the actual start of negotiations on 11 October allowed the Belfast government further time to consolidate its security and administrative apparatus.

On 9 November, soon after the Treaty negotiations had started, the British government announced suddenly the transfer of services to Northern Ireland.[108] Over the next few days, in a rush of orders-in-council, the Dublin Castle departments were commanded to assign officers for temporary transfer to the north, even though the Civil Service Committee, which had the statutory function of distributing staff, had not yet formally met. Lord Chancellor Birkenhead and Lloyd George had been considering how it would be possible to transfer power to Northern Ireland without setting up crown colony government in Southern Ireland. The difficulty was that the 1920 Act could not be put into operation without the Joint Exchequer Board and the Civil Service Committee, on which there would be a representative of the government of Southern Ireland. Birkenhead suggested that the 1920 Act could be stretched to authorise the Lord Lieutenant to appoint the southern representative without having to dissolve the Southern Ireland parliament that had never met and declare Crown Colony government.[109] The place of the government of Southern Ireland on the Civil Service Committee, which remained unfilled, was allocated to MacMahon by order of the Lord Lieutenant.[110] At the same time the 'appointed days' for transfer of the departments of government were set out as 22 November, 1 December, 1 January and 1 February.[111]

While Craig sat on his rock of 'Ulster' the civil service sat on the rock of the Civil Service Committee. The associations were confident in their understanding that partition of the civil service could only be done by that committee and therefore, in the absence of a representative of the southern government, it could not be established. The civil service associations were confident that whatever would emerge from the London negotiations would be at least as good as existing terms and might be even better. The civil service had always done well in setting the terms in the discussions on Home Rule. In those circumstances it was better to wait. As the Treaty negotiations made progress Conn Murphy and Mortished of the CSA maintained contact with Sinn Féin and the Dáil and received assurances that the protection granted in the 1920 Act to civil servants would be continued into any new agreement.[112]

Every Home Rule proposal, from 1886 to 1920, had been based on some form of division between Ireland and Britain of the departments of State and therefore of the civil service. For instance customs and trade had been excluded in each and every Home Rule proposal thus implying that the civil service of the revenue and custom and excise departments would remain as they were. The Post Office, by far the largest of all government departments, was also excluded, as was the Ordnance Survey, which had its own service traditions that owed much to its military origins. This would in part explain the detached complacency with which many Irish civil servants regarded the Anglo-Irish negotiations, confident as they were that they at least would not be affected. The Treaty, to the amazement of the Irish civil servants, transferred all twenty thousand of them without exception to the new Irish Free State (Saorstát Éireann). Even the postal service which had been reserved to the imperial parliament in all the Home Rule bills, and which represented the vast majority of the Irish civil service, was to be transferred in its entirety to the Irish government. It was even possible that the Treaty could be interpreted as transferring authority over the Northern Ireland government to Dublin.

There was considerable disagreement within the civil service associations as to the correct response in the aftermath of the Treaty.[113] Despite his later avowal of anti-Treaty republicanism, which cost him his civil service job, Conn Murphy was initially an ardent supporter. On its announcement he addressed an impromptu audience from the steps of his departmental offices on Merrion Square on the momentous achievement.[114] Murphy as chairman of the CSA took the view that the 1920 Act, and all associated with it, had been swept away by the Treaty and that the civil service should throw in its lot with the elected government of the Irish people, Dáil Éireann. They should do nothing that would validate partition and in particular should not participate in the Civil Service Committee now summoned to meet. Gallagher and Sloan were loath to simply refuse to attend, not least because the committee could function without them. It was eventually decided that the CSA would enter a legal challenge to the validity of MacMahon's appointment in an effort to stop the committee in its tracks. Legal advice was sought from Hugh Kennedy, later legal advisor to the Irish government.

The Civil Service Committee first met on 8 December, two days after the Treaty had been signed and after the first two of the appointed days for transfer of services had actually passed.[115] The committee consisted of Sir Courtauld Thomson, chairman; A.P. Waterfield, Treasury (Ireland); R.A. Johnson, Treasury London; James MacMahon, the southern government; R.D. Megan (later replaced by Ernest Clark), the northern government; and Sam Sloan with Michael Gallagher representing the existing Irish officers. Sloan and Gallagher immediately challenged the appointment of MacMahon as not in accordance with the 1920 Act, and protested against the 'Civil Service Committee undertaking any functions or carrying out any duties until it has been duly constituted in accordance with provisions of the Act'. Having entered their protest Sloan and Gallagher then agreed that the committee could continue so long as the proceedings remained provisional and transfers were confined to volunteers. A paper allocation would be made and civil servants were to be asked (a) did they wish to be allocated to the northern government (b) were they willing to be allocated and (c) did they object to being allocated? All transfers were to be at existing ranks but promotions were the sole concern of the government employing the officers.[116]

At the second meeting Sloan and Gallagher returned to question once again the appointment of MacMahon. A letter from Anderson was read stating that the order-in-council was valid but, if it proved necessary, steps would be taken to put it beyond doubt by effective legislation. Sloan and Gallagher then withdrew from the meeting to consult with the CSA. The rest of the committee may not have accepted the position of Sloan and Gallagher but they were certainly willing to play for time and delay matters. When Ernest Clark, who had replaced Megan as the northern representative, began to name individual officers as having indicated a willingness to transfer north the committee determined that it would be necessary to have the personal signature of each officer consenting to transfer. Clark interpreted this as pure obstruction, but in fact the rest of the committee was more likely to have been afraid of the growing reaction within the civil service to the work of the committee.[117] At a mass meeting of the Dublin civil service on the 12 December it was resolved that no civil servant, whatever his personal opinion may be, should answer the questionnaire or any other document issued by the Civil Service Committee as at present constituted, but that in each Department the representative of each Association or the Chairman of the Staff Side of the Whitley Council or Committee should collect the blank forms issued and return them to the head of the department accompanied by copies of this resolution in explanation of the refusal of each officer to reply to the questions.[118]

As the 17 December meeting of the Civil Service Committee was drawing to a close a messenger arrived with a notice of proceedings by Conn Murphy acting on behalf of existing Irish officers seeking an injunction against those 'purporting to act as the Civil Service Committee' thus effectively ending the work of the committee.[119] The proceedings were heard by the Master of Rolls on 21 December, as the Treaty debate continued in the Dáil. Not surprisingly the courts rejected the case put by the CSA; however, it had served its main function of further delaying the process of partition until the provisional government took power.[120] The committee was finally halted by the decree of the Provisional Government of 16 January forbidding all movements of civil servants without the permission of that government. On the following day when Clark asked that the committee immediately allocate those civil servants who had declared a willingness to move north but had not yet done so, he found no support. Instead the committee, whether from fear of the Provisional Government or exasperation at Clark, adjourned indefinitely.[121]

The committee meetings worked by allocating staff for the departments and then trying to find sufficient volunteers to fill them. This involved a notional allocation of proportions of the work of the department as to north and south. When it came to actually filling the positions it was clear that though there were volunteers to go north, there were not enough of them. Service in Northern Ireland was not attractive to the majority of the civil service, especially as the prospects now looked more promising in the Free State. In Waterfield's own Treasury (Ireland) not one man volunteered to go north to the new Belfast Ministry of Finance. Besides, allocation north or south was a function of the Civil Service Committee, not the Treasury, so there could be no question of compulsion.[122] The Civil Service Committee, for its part, insisted that each civil servant allocated north indicate in writing that he was indeed a volunteer. In order to make up the numbers the committee decided to move outside the strict letter of the 1920 Act and invite applications from any civil servant serving in Ireland, whether in an Irish or an imperial department.

The number of staff actually allocated by the short-lived committee was 235.[123] It was calculated that the new northern administration required between six and seven hundred staff but by May 1922 only 280 were actually transferred officers from Dublin and London.[124] The only comprehensive list of transferred civil servants is that compiled from memory in 1978 by Frederick Falkiner of the Board of Works. He lists 185 transfers from Dublin.[125] Had the Civil Service Committee actually operated then about six out of ten civil servants in Northern Ireland would have been allocated by compulsion. Though Clark recorded a great deal of indignation at the obstruction he encountered from the committee, he was in fact probably happy enough with the result.

Along with the London transfers, officers who supported the Unionist regime formed a core staff of the civil service of Northern Ireland. The vacancies could be used to sate the feeding frenzy of applications that formed around every northern minister. The selection board filled 245 posts in the first five months of 1922. As early as March 1922 concerns were being expressed by senior Whitehall civil servants as to the narrow sectarian bias of the emerging northern government.[126] On the other hand the Free State acquired an unpartitioned and functioning civil service. As for the civil servants themselves they had prevented compulsory allocation to the north while preserving all the safeguards that had been won in the 1920 Act. All in all everybody could feel satisfied.

Notes

1 Michael Hopkinson, 'From Treaty to civil war, 1921–2' in J.R. Hill (ed.) *A New History of Ireland VII, Ireland, 1921–84* (Oxford, 2003), pp. 1–59, 13.
2 Charles Townshend, 'Historiography: telling the Irish revolution' in Joost Augusteijn (ed.) *The Irish Revolution, 1913–1923* (Manchester, 2002), pp. 1–17.
3 Conor Kostick, *Revolution in Ireland: Popular Militancy in Ireland 1917 to 1923* (London, 1996); David Fitzpatrick, *The Two Irelands 1912–1939* (Oxford, 1998).
4 Mitchell, *Revolutionary Government in Ireland.*
5 Philip Bull, *Land, Politics and Nationalism: A Study of the Irish Land Question* (Dublin,1996), pp. 116–42.
6 Charles Townshend, *Political Violence in Ireland: Government and Resistance since 1848* (Oxford, 1983), pp. 232–3.
7 E.g. John Hutchinson, *The Dynamics of Cultural Nationalism: The Gaelic Revival and the Creation of the Irish Nation State* (Dublin, 1987).
8 Michael Laffan, *The Resurrection of Ireland: The Sinn Féin Party, 1916–1923* (Cambridge, 1999), pp. 214–65.
9 Townshend, *Political Violence*, pp. 328–9.
10 *Dáil Éireann debates*, vol.1, 21 January, 1–10 Apr., 17–8 June 1919.
11 Arthur Griffith, *The Resurrection of Hungary: A Parallel for Ireland with appendices of Pitt's Policy and Sinn Féin* (Dublin, 1904).
12 Ibid., pp. 155–6; *Sinn Féin Weekly* 11 Feb. 1911, 'A national civil Service'; Richard Davis, *Arthur Griffith and Non-violent Sinn Féin* (Dublin, 1974), p. 133.
13 *Dáil Éireann debates*, vol. 1, 18 June 1919, p. 122.
14 Ibid., vol. 1, 19 Aug. 1919, p. 122, 27 Oct. 1919, p. 240.
15 Ibid., vol. 1, 18 June 1919.
16 NAI, BMH, ws 1728, Nicolás Ó'Nualláin.
17 *Dáil Éireann debates*, vol. 1, 29 June 1920, p. 180.
18 NAI, BMH, ws 548, Daithi O'Donnchadha [David O'Donoghue].
19 *Dáil Éireann debates*, vol. 1, 10 May 1921, p. 284; Andrew McCarthy, 'Michael Collins – Minister for Finance 1919–22' in Gabriel Doherty and Dermot Keogh (eds) *Michael Collins and the Making of the Irish State* (Cork, 1998), pp. 52–67.

20 NAI, DE5/72 [E114/4/28] 'MacGréil to Boland 16 Oct. 1929, old Dáil staff'; NAI, BMH, ws 548, David O'Donoghue.
21 NAI, DE5/48&49, 'General secretariat staff'.
22 *Dáil Éireann debates*, vol. 1, 18 June 1919, p. 124.
23 Ibid., vol. 1, 6 Aug. 1920, pp. 199–202.
24 Mary E. Daly, *The Buffer State: The Historical Roots of the Department of the Environment* (Dublin, 1997), pp. 47–92.
25 *Dáil Éireann debates*, vol. 1, 17 Sept. 1920, pp. 222–3.
26 Peter Hart (ed.) *British Intelligence in Ireland, 1920–21: The Final Reports* (Cork, 2002), p. 59.
27 NAI, BMH, ws 501, T.J. McArdle.
28 Ibid., ws 889, James Kavanagh.
29 Ibid., but see ws 548, David O'Donoghue for a different version of McArdle's recruitment.
30 Daly, *Buffer State*, p. 322.
31 NAI, BMH, ws 680, Nicholas O'Dwyer.
32 *Dáil Éireann debates*, vol. 1, 17 Sept. 1920, pp. 227–8.
33 NAI, DE2/1, 17 July 1920; UCDAD, Richard Mulcahy Papers, P24/14, 'Report of Dáil Éireann Dept of Labour 19 May 1921'.
34 *Sinn Féin*, 9 January 1909, 'The Dublin Corporation and the National Civil Service'.
35 Martin Maguire, *'Servants to the Public': A History of the Local Government and Public Services Union 1901–1990* (Dublin, 1998), pp. 8–10, 27–32.
36 Ibid., pp. 36–41.
37 Ibid., pp. 43–50.
38 NAI, DE1/2, minute 4 August 1920.
39 *Dáil Éireann debates*, vol. 2, cols 50–1, 17 Aug. 1921.
40 NAI, DE2/60, 'Dáil Éireann general secretariat July 1920'.
41 NAI, BMH, ws 512, Seán McCluskey.
42 Ibid., ws 817, Seán Saunders.
43 Laffan, *Resurrection of Ireland*, p. 193.
44 Ibid., p. 323.
45 NAI, BMH, ws 1744, Seán Nunan.
46 Ibid., ws 548, Daithi O'Donnchadha [David O'Donoghue].
47 Ibid., ws 548, Daithi O'Donnchadha [David O'Donoghue].
48 Ibid., ws 889, James Kavanagh; ws 1725, Padraigh O'Caoimh [Patrick O'Keeffe].
49 Ibid., ws 643, Cathleen Napoli-McKenna.
50 Ibid., ws 1050, Miss Vera McDonnell.
51 NAI, DE5/72, 'Kelly to O'Hegarty', 25 July 1928.
52 NAI, BMH, ws 683, Hugh Hehir; ws 460, Joseph Thunder.
53 Ibid., ws 449, W.T. Cosgrave.
54 NAI, DE1/1, 26 June; 5 Sept., 17 Oct. 1919; 27 Feb., 31 May 1920.
55 Ibid., 10 June 1920.
56 NAI, BMH, ws 501, T.J. McArdle.
57 Mitchell, *Revolutionary Government in Ireland*, p. 300.
58 *Dáil Éireann debates*, vol. 4, cols 66–7, 25 Aug. 1921.

59 NAI, DE2/491, 'Dáil Éireann secretariat, E. Price, 17 Oct. 1921'.

60 NAI, BMH, ws 501, T.J. McArdle.

61 NAI, DE1/3, 24 Nov. 1921.

62 NAI, DE4/11/20, 'Home Affairs to Dáil secretary', 24 Oct. 1921; DE1/3, 4 Nov. 1921.

63 NAI, DE2/296, 'Memorandum M. Collins [to Mulcahy?], intensification of attack on all British institutions', June 1921.

64 Ibid., 'Austin Staic to Runaidhhe na h-Aireachta', 4 July 1921.

65 *Dáil Éireann debates*, vol. 4, cols 75–9, 26 Aug. 1921.

66 Ibid.

67 Anthony Kirk-Greene, *Britain's Imperial Administrators, 1858–1966* (London, 2000), p. 241.

68 O'Day, *Irish Home Rule*, pp. 294–300.

69 NA, CAB 27/68, cabinet committee on Ireland (1919–20) (C.I. series) vol. I, fourth report, 24 Nov. 1919, pp. 39–78.

70 Government of Ireland Act, 1920 [10 & 11 Geo. 5 c. 4] section 59 (1 and 2).

71 *Red Tape*, 10:119 (Aug. 1921.)

72 NA, T158/3, 'Waterfield to Fraser, Treasury London, 15 June 1921'.

73 Ibid., T158/5, 'Waterfield to Craig, Treasury London, 8 Nov. 1921'; WUMRC, MSS 232, Association of Assistant and Supervisory Clerks, executive committee minutes, 6 Sept. 1921; *Red Tape*, 11:121 (Oct. 1921).

74 *Red Tape*, 10:115 (Apr. 1921).

75 NA, CAB 27/156, 'Amendments sub-committee, 12 May 1920'.

76 Public Record Office Northern Ireland (PRONI), FIN/18/1/142, 'CSO circular, 20 Jan. 1920'.

77 UCDAD, LA24, Duggan, 'Life of a civil servant'.

78 *Red Tape*, 10:115 (Apr. 1921), p. 8.

79 Ibid.; *Irish Civil Servant*, 1:3 (Jan. 1921); 1:6 (Apr. 1921).

80 Nicholas Mansergh, *The Unresolved Question: The Anglo-Irish Settlement and its Undoing 1912–72* (New Haven, 1991), pp. 153–4.

81 NA, Wylie Papers, PRO 30/89/3, 'Review of Irish situation, Sept. 1920'.

82 Bryan A. Follis, *A State Under Siege: The Establishment of Northern Ireland, 1920–25* (Oxford, 1995), pp. 7–8; Sturgis, *Last Days of Dublin Castle*, p. 53.

83 Gallagher, 'Memoirs of a civil servant', p. 65

84 PRONI, FIN18/1/109, 'Government of Northern Ireland dept. and staff schemes'; Follis, *State Under Siege*, p. 28.

85 McColgan, *British Policy and the Irish Administration*, pp. 56–8.

86 Ibid., p. 57.

87 PRONI, CAB/4/23, copy of Anderson memo on Irish civil servants under 1920 Act.

88 PRONI, FIN18/1/43, 'Cope to Clark, 27 Mar. 1921'.

89 Ibid., 18/1/112, 'Craig to Cuthbertson, 16 Feb. 1921'.

90 Ibid., 18/1/142, 'Anderson to Clark, 1 July 1921'.

91 Follis, *State Under Siege*, p. 34; McColgan, *British Policy and the Irish Administration*, p. 59.

92 PRONI, FIN18/1/107, 'Government of Northern Ireland dept. and staff schemes 23 Feb. 1921'.

93 NA, T158/6, 'Waterfield to Gill, 22 Nov. 1921'.

94 PRONI, FIN/18/1.235, 'Pollock to Craig, 26 Aug. 1921'.

95 Follis, *State under Siege*, pp. 11, 34–5; NA, T158/2, 'Waterfield to Cope, 27 Jan 1921'.

96 *Irish Civil Servant*, 1:6 (Apr. 1921).

97 Ibid., 1:7 (May 1921); PRONI, FIN/18/1/138, correspondence with AEO, Apr. 1921.

98 Gallagher, 'Memoirs of a civil servant', pp. 57–9.

99 PRONI, CAB/4/12, 9 Aug. 1921; CAB/4/14, 16 Aug. 1921; CAB/4/23, 27 Sept. 1921.

100 *Irish Civil Servant*, 1:9 (July-Aug. 1921); Gallagher, 'Memoirs of a civil servant', pp. 67–8.

101 PRONI, CAB/4/14, 16 Aug. 1921; FIN18/1/142, 'News cutting with Clark annotations'; *Freeman's Journal*, 5 Sept. 1921, 'No Catholics need apply'.

102 PRONI, CAB/4/26, 4 Nov. 1921.

103 Brian Barton, 'Northern Ireland, 1925–39' in Hill (ed.) *A New History of Ireland VII*, pp. 199–234, 200–1.

104 PRONI, FIN18/1/138, 'Fairgrieves to Clark, 10 Aug. 1921'.

105 *Freeman's Journal*, 5 Sept. 1921, 'No Catholics need apply'.

106 McColgan, *British Policy and the Irish Administration*, p. 64.

107 PRONI, FIN18/1/235, 'Clark to Waterfield, 25 July 1921', 'Pollock to Craig, 26 Aug. 1921'.

108 Periscope, 'The Last Days of Dublin Castle', pp. 186–7.

109 HLRO, Lloyd George Papers, F/4/7/32, 'Birkenhead to PM, 1 Nov. 1921'.

110 NAI, CSORP, 1921–22, 2429/156, 'Order-in-Council to create a temporary Civil Service Committee, 9 Nov. 1921'.

111 McColgan, *British Policy and the Irish Administration*, p. 69.

112 Gallagher, 'Memoirs of a civil servant', p. 72.

113 Ibid., pp. 73–4.

114 Ibid., p. 74.

115 McColgan, *British Policy and the Irish Administration*, p. 75.

116 PRONI, Ernest Clark Papers, D1022/2/18, Civil Service Committee meeting minutes, 8 Dec. 1921.

117 Ibid., minutes, 15 Dec. 1921; Gallagher, 'Memoirs of a civil servant', p. 74.

118 Copy in PRONI, Ernest Clark Papers, D1022/2/18, Civil Service Committee meeting minutes, 19 Dec. 1921; WUMRC, MSS 232/SDA, *News Sheet*, No. 15 (1 Jan. 1922).

119 PRONI, Ernest Clark Papers, D1022/2/18, Civil Service Committee meeting minutes, 17 Dec. 1921.

120 NAI, CSORP, 1921/3866/3, Civil Service Committee papers.

121 PRONI, Ernest Clark Papers, D1022/2/18, Civil Service Committee meeting minutes, 17 Jan. 1922.

122 NA, T158/6, 'Waterfield to Niemeyer, 10 Jan. 1922'.

123 PRONI, Ernest Clark Papers, D1022/2/18, Civil Service Committee meeting minutes, 19 Dec. 1921–17 Jan. 1922.
124 *Parliamentary Debates, Northern Ireland*, First Series, vol. 2, col. 471, 16 May 1922.
125 NLI, Leon Ó'Broin Papers, MS 31,664.
126 Michael Hopkinson, 'The Craig-Collins pact of 1922: two attempted reforms of the Northern Ireland government', *Irish Historical Studies*, 27:106 (Nov. 1990), pp. 145–58.

4

The Provisional Government and the civil service, 1922

Introduction

THE ANGLO-IRISH TREATY of December 1921 provided for the formation of an Irish Provisional Government to take control of the Dublin Castle administration and write a constitution for the Irish Free State (Saorstát Éireann). The government of the Irish Free State with executive and administrative responsibilities would come into being within one year of the Treaty. The stability of Irish democracy in the aftermath of revolution and civil war is sometimes explained by the new government retaining the State structures and especially the civil service inherited from the former regime. It is argued that because of its innate conservatism and its distance from the revolutionary State-building process the former civil service ensured stability and continuity.[1] This argument, that what happened to the Irish State could be characterised as evolutionary rather than revolutionary, was articulated as early as 1936 by the Brennan Commission. Brennan's report on the civil service concluded that

> The passing of the State services into the control of a native Government, however revolutionary it may have been as a step in the political development of the nation, entailed, broadly speaking, no immediate disturbance of any fundamental kind in the daily work of the average Civil Servant. Under changed masters the main tasks of administration continued to be performed by the same staffs on the same general lines of organisation and procedure.[2]

The question arises as to whether the Provisional Government did simply continue with the same civil service, given that every other institution of the British State in Ireland was changed – parliament, executive, judiciary, police and the military – to be replaced by native institutions. In the midst of so much change why retain the same civil service, especially as the revolutionary regime had built up a civil service of its own? If continuity was the case, why did the Provisional Government accept what was described as an anti-Irish, extravagant, corrupt and run-down apparatus? The accepted view is that the Irish civil service, notoriously inefficient, had been thoroughly overhauled and successfully rebuilt into a modern and efficient machine by Waterfield in the previous year and a half.[3] That transformation, were it true, would in itself be remarkable, though as we have seen, it had not in fact occurred. Waterfield had reassigned the civil servants to the new grading structures but had not even begun to address the dispersal of authority that many considered the fundamental problem in Castle government. He had succeeded in dressing mutton as lamb, but it remained mutton. The emphasis on continuity also begs the question as to the fate of the civil service of Dáil Éireann. Did the men and women who had loyally served the revolution allow themselves to be meekly absorbed into the inherited apparatus of the State they had fought to destroy?

The process by which the Provisional Government constructed the civil service of the Irish Free State was in fact one of immense complexity to which the anodyne assurance of continuity does not apply. We now turn to examine in turn the constitutional path that was laid down for that process and the deviations from that path which the emergence of anti-Treaty sentiment necessitated; the reactions of the civil service itself in the Castle administration as well as in the administration of Dáil Éireann to the formation of the new Irish Free State civil service and their attempts to shape it as it emerged; the emergence of the marginal pressure groups such as those civil servants who for whatever reason felt left out by the transformations in the State; and finally the practical problems of unifying the civil service of the Castle administration and that of the revolutionary Dáil.

Debating the Treaty in Dublin and London

The situation in which the Castle civil service found itself in January 1922 was one that was inconceivable in 1912. The Treaty proposed a constitutional relationship between Britain and Ireland far in advance of all previous Home Rule proposals, including the 1920 Act, a tribute to the negotiating skills of Griffith and Collins. Unlike all previous Home Rule bills, which limited the range of executive responsibilities of an Irish government, Article 1 of the Treaty stated that the Irish executive would be responsible only to the Irish parliament with no reference to any authority being retained in Westminster. The civil service was not to be divided between an imperial and an Irish service; the authority of the Irish parliament over the entire State apparatus was absolute. Also, looking no further than the title, *Articles of Agreement for a Treaty between Great Britain and Ireland – December 6, 1921*, it brought into question the very existence of Northern Ireland. It could be interpreted as implying that the Treaty had superseded the Government of Ireland Act of 1920 and that partition would be a purely temporary arrangement. Even if the Northern Ireland parliament were to continue it might well be as a subordinate authority to the Irish Free State.[4] Article 10 of the Treaty provided that civil servants dismissed or who wished to retire under the new government would receive compensation terms 'no less favourable' than those offered in the 1920 Act.

Article 17 of the Treaty provided a mechanism for transferring the administration of Ireland from British to Irish control via the interim Provisional Government. Precisely how this would work was, however, still unclear and the Treaty was marked by not only political but also institutional confusion.[5] For instance it was not at all clear at what point the Treaty could be said to have taken effect; was it when it was agreed by the Dáil cabinet or by the British cabinet, or by Dáil Éireann or by Westminster?[6] The only certainty was that the ratification of the Treaty by the Dáil would be immediately followed by the withdrawal of the 'military and auxiliary Forces of the Crown in Southern Ireland'.[7]

The Treaty required that the MPs elected for the constituencies of 'Southern Ireland' under the 1920 Government of Ireland Act should meet as such, ratify the Treaty and approve the formation of the Provisional Government.[8] The British government could therefore claim that the Provisional Government was a continuity of British authority in Dublin Castle. However, while the British government were determined to 'preserve unbroken the line of British statutory authority' and had allotted no role to the Dáil in establishing the Provisional Government, Collins and Griffith were equally determined to preserve the authority of the Dáil.[9] On both sides therefore, as the Treaty was being considered by parliament and Dáil, there was considerable thought being given to the practicalities of transferring authority over the State and the civil service.[10] Throughout the Treaty debate Collins and Griffith suggested proposals that were constitutionally ambiguous but were designed to prevent a resurgence of the British State in Ireland and to bring partition of the civil service to a halt. In a memorandum drafted on Christmas Day 1921 Griffith outlined a strategy whereby the Dáil Éireann administration would continue to function during the interregnum and then, after the passing of the new constitution, merge with the Free State; 'the Provisional Government would do nothing to consolidate the Castle system of administration by filling vacancies etc., but would on the contrary let that system wither and die and allow the Dáil system to grow and strengthen . . . [B]y the time the new constitution was in operation the Irish system of administration would have superseded the Castle system'.[11] The Provisional Government, which would take control of the existing civil service, would take over and isolate the inherited administrative machine in Dublin Castle. All business would be directed to the civil service under the control of the Dáil Éireann ministries. Tightening the grip of the Dáil on the departments would also make further partition difficult. The Dáil departments would continue to meet as a government under President de Valera while only the members of the Provisional Government would be required to declare allegiance to the Treaty. Collins and Griffith envisioned the

Provisional Government acting as a 'committee of public safety' under a united Dáil. The Dáil would continue in being ready to reassume full authority on completion of British withdrawal.[12] With both the Provisional Government and the Dáil functioning there would be in effect a dual government. It would be possible, whatever the British might legislate, to maintain that the Provisional Government was a creation of the Dáil as much as it was a creation of the British government.

However, this was too subtle for those opposed to the Treaty, and even for some of those who supported it. As Collins said 'hardly anyone, even those who support it, really understand it'.[13] The debate failed to get to grips with the mechanics of taking over the State and never got beyond an argument between those who saw the Dáil government in symbolic terms and those who saw it in functional terms. Indeed, those opposed to the Treaty insisted that the Provisional Government was as much a usurpation of the Dáil as of the Castle government that it replaced. Seán T. O'Kelly described it as the 'partitionist, provincial, provisional' government.[14] Piaras Béaslaí countered by insisting that the Treaty was popularly accepted and that 'the State is the people organised in a coherent from, and no matter whatever you call it a Republic or a Free State, my allegiance is to the people of Ireland and to the State which represents the national will. If we do not represent the national will, we [the Dáil] are a usurpation.'[15]

De Valera's counter-proposal to the Treaty, known as Document Number Two, made unnecessarily explicit what was implicit in the Treaty on the transfer of State power, but missed the key element of preserving the Dáil as a continuing and separate authority. In de Valera's proposal the Provisional Government of the Treaty became the 'transitional government to which the British Government and Dáil Éireann shall transfer the authority, powers and machinery requisite for the discharge of its duties'. The clear difference from the Treaty was that de Valera's transitional government derived its authority from the members of Dáil Éireann, not the members of the Southern Ireland constituencies and replaced the Dáil instead of acting as a sub-committee to it.[16] Document Number Two also reproduced precisely Article 10 of the Treaty on compensation for dismissed or retired civil servants.

De Valera's tactics during the Treaty debate suggest that initially he anticipated the Dáil would reject it, but that Collins, through his IRB centres, would ensure the IRA accepted it. His emotional outburst at the vote in favour of the Treaty also suggests this remained his hope up to the last moment and that he had no second line to retreat to. His resignation and offer of re-election were a desperate attempt to retrieve his position by continuing the Dáil as suggested by Collins, but now as an opposition to the Provisional Government. Even at this stage Collins was prepared to postpone the vote on the Treaty and offer once again the idea of a 'committee of public safety' to take over the Castle, to 'do all the dirty work' as Collins termed it, while preserving the Dáil as a united and separate authority.[17]

But the rancorous tone of de Valera's opposition and the transparency of his intent to use Collins's constitutionally ambiguous dual authority to undermine the Provisional Government at every turn meant that the offer was no longer on the table.[18] Liam de Roiste, in rejecting de Valera's offer, put it plainly when he said that the Provisional Government was simply the mechanism whereby the British could hand control of the 'abomination' of Dublin Castle administration over to the Irish. In the absence of the Provisional Government that abomination was retained.[19] Ernest Blythe also recognised that what de Valera was proposing differed significantly from the offer originally made by Collins. Under the original idea the Provisional Government, either informally or formally, would derive its authority from the Dáil. What de Valera proposed was two distinct and rival governments.[20] The reality was that de Valera had little experience of statecraft. Except for a brief period he had not participated in the Dáil between his arrest in March 1918 and his return from America in December 1920. Choosing to exercise his authority at the heady level of international diplomacy he had no experience of cabinet decision-making or the reality of running departments of State.

The strategy of constitutional ambiguity began to unravel with the resignation of de Valera and the election of Griffith as president of the Dáil. A new Dáil executive was elected with Collins as Minister for Finance, Gavan Duffy in Foreign Affairs, Eamon Duggan in Home Affairs, William Cosgrave in Local Government, Kevin O'Higgins in Economic Affairs and Richard Mulcahy in Defence. Collins, Duggan, Cosgrave and O'Higgins were also members of the Provisional Government, along with Patrick Hogan, Fionan Lynch, Joe McGrath and Eoin MacNeill. The shared membership of the Provisional and Dáil governments was an attempt to reconstruct a creative ambiguity around the authority of the State. Collins acted as chairman of the Provisional Government while retaining his post as Minister for Finance in the Dáil Éireann executive. Arthur Griffith's absence from the Provisional Government provided constitutional cover for the same persons in the same posts acting as distinctly different executives – that of the Provisional Government and that of the Dáil. When Collins was chairman it was the Provisional Government, when it was Griffith it was the Dáil ministry. In the end the steady undermining of the authority of the Dáil executive by the anti-Treaty deputies and its outright rejection by the anti-Treaty IRA undermined the constitutional ambiguity and exposed it to ridicule. The Dáil ministry was silently merged into the Provisional Government and by the end of April had ceased to exist as a separate body.[21] Whether dual government could be effective government was never actually tested, but the strategy of constitutional ambiguity did mean that during the crucial months of State-building the anti-Treaty forces were confined to an armed strategy and no attempt was made to establish a rival republican Dáil until October, by which time it was too late.[22]

The weakness of the strategy of constitutional ambiguity lay in the hesitancy of the Provisional Government in asserting its 'Stateness' by confronting the anti-Treaty forces and in the equally slow response of the British government that allowed the northern government time to consolidate its control. The British government interpreted the December vote in Westminster as merely approving and not ratifying the Treaty. Ratification could only occur later with the simultaneous ratification of the constitution of the Irish Free State, which would take some months. It was not until 13 March that the British parliament passed its own measure to enact the Treaty.[23] This delay created a three-month 'moment of ambiguity' in which the British source for the authority of the Provisional Government was missing.[24] Had the Dáil remained united this period of ambiguity would have been to its advantage and could have reinforced the Irish source for the authority of the Provisional Government.

Taking over Dublin Castle

On the British side it was generally expected that the takeover of the Castle departments would be a gradual process, with the inexperienced new government proceeding one department at a time. But the Provisional Government in fact moved with great speed and decisiveness to assume full control of the State. The takeover of Dublin Castle was a revolutionary event, but it was not a spectacle. At that time there was no precedent for British withdrawal from her colonies so there was none of the elaborate ceremonial to which a later generation became accustomed, with flags coming down and flags running up, accompanied by gun salutes. Instead, in the Privy Council chamber Collins handed Lord FitzAlan, the first Catholic viceroy since the seventeenth century and the last viceroy of all, a copy of the Treaty signed by the members of the Provisional Government. FitzAlan then congratulated the Provisional Government and, wishing them the best of luck, left.[25] The Provisional Government was then introduced to the few senior civil servants rounded up for the occasion, at least some of whom enjoyed the irony that men who just a few months before had a price on their heads or languished in Mountjoy Prison were now being introduced as the new government. For others there was a deep sense of betrayal and disgust at being invited to 'grasp hands red with the blood of government servants'.[26]

The Provisional Government then returned to the Mansion House and issued a press statement announcing that 'the members of Rialtas Sealadach Na hÉireann [Provisional Government of Ireland] received the surrender of Dublin Castle at 1:45 p.m. today. It is now in the hands of the Irish nation. . .' The reference to 'surrender' angered Sturgis, who hoped that Lloyd George would use the Honours List to signal some recognition of the achievement of the Anderson team.[27] Honours were indeed distributed but, apart from Anderson himself, their work in extricating Britain from Ireland was not the launch of a brilliant career for these civil servants and the members of Anderson's 'Junta' faded into obscurity. A new cohort of civil servants was assembled in Dublin to assist in the construction of the civil service of the Irish Free State, most notably William O'Brien from Inland Revenue, Joseph Brennan and Walter Doolin from the CSO, along with T.K. Bewley and C.J. Gregg on loan from Whitehall.[28]

The revolution that opened with the rhetoric of the Declaration of Independence, the Appeal to the Free Nations of the World and the Democratic Programme, announced its victory with its first directive:

> WE do hereby direct that all Law Courts, Corporations, Councils, Departments of State, Boards, Judges, Civil Servants, Officers of the Peace, and all Public Servants and functionaries hitherto under the authority of the British Government shall continue to carry out their functions unless and until otherwise ordered by us, pending the constitution of the Parliament and Government of Saorstát na hÉireann, and without prejudice to the full and free exercise by that Parliament and Government, when constituted, of all and every its powers and authorities in regard to them or any of them . . . Published at Dublin this 16th day of January, 1922.[29]

The Provisional Government also prohibited any action 'altering the status, rights, perquisites or stipends or the transfer, or dismissal of any officer, servant, employee or functionary of the State', or the removal of any records, documents or correspondence.[30] While these directives lack the rhetorical flourish that began the revolution they display a sober understanding of what revolution entails, the seizing of State power, and they are directed precisely at the apparatus of the State, the civil service. Though the country had been partitioned, due to the action of the civil servants themselves the entire State apparatus remained united, available and now firmly under the control of the Provisional Government.

Although the power of the Provisional Government was purely administrative and not legislative, and in that respect seemed limited, to the civil service that was the power that mattered.[31] The Provisional Government, by seizing control of the civil service, seized control of the entire existing machinery of the State. Thus, a revolutionary act was cloaked in a constitutional and parliamentary form. The new government shunned the Castle, establishing itself in the City Hall. As the British soldiers, Auxiliaries, Black and Tans, and RIC all departed the Castle fell silent. It was even suggested that the entire Castle complex should be demolished in a series of spectacular detonations to demonstrate the reality of the ending of British rule.[32]

The Provisional Government and the civil service

Collins, Duggan and O'Higgins travelled to London on Tuesday 17 January, the day after the takeover of Dublin Castle. Patrick McGilligan travelled as secretary, Kevin O'Sheil acted as liaison with the Dublin Castle departments.[33] As the Provisional Government began to implement the Treaty it was pressed by the British government to use the mechanisms created by the 1920 Act to facilitate the partition of the civil service. In particular the British government wanted to see the Joint Exchequer Board and the Civil Service Committee established by the 1920 Act constituted as part of the transfer of authority.[34] Waterfield administered a mild fright to the Provisional Government by reminding O'Brien that the Irish government would have to either employ or pension all the civil servants it would acquire on the setting up of the Free State and that it might be in its own interest to agree to some sort of civil service committee to facilitate transfers north immediately.[35] Waterfield reckoned that he could immediately identify about thirty officers still in Dublin, willing to transfer north, costing about £10,000 in salaries. He suggested that the Provisional Government could agree to allow, while refusing to compel, transfers north.[36]

Instead of facilitating partition, however, the Provisional Government ordered the Civil Service Committee, which had begun to allocate officers to Belfast, to cease.[37] Collins intended to use the control exercised by the Provisional Government over the civil service to prevent the northern government establishing itself. In a characteristically succinct note to Kennedy he asked for instructions as to 'what we are entitled to do and what we entitled to prevent the north-east government from doing'.[38] In February the Provisional Government instructed departments to accord no facilities for allocating staff to Northern Ireland.[39] At a London conference in late March Collins refused to hand over State documents until the boundary was settled.[40] This refusal to send staff north suited the heads and staff of the departments in Dublin because it is part of the culture of bureaucracy that size is equivalent to status and no head of a department will reduce staff unless compelled to do so. However, perhaps as part of the *rapprochement* leading to the second Craig-Collins pact, the Provisional Government did eventually allow the voluntary transfer north of thirty officers.[41]

In early February Anderson in a memorandum on the power of the Provisional Government attempted to create an administrative cordon sanitaire around the six counties, saying that the terms of the Treaty established that the British government could not transfer, and the Provisional Government could not exercise, 'any powers within or in respect of that area'. The administration of Northern Ireland would continue as if the Provisional Government had never been established. Following this, Treasury (Ireland) instructed that all payments of salaries to civil servants serving in the territory of Northern Ireland would cease as from 1 April and would become the responsibility of the Belfast government.[42] Kevin O'Sheil dismissed this as a far-fetched interpretation. In his view, which we may assume was also that of Collins, the only limitations on the Provisional Government's power were twofold: that all the members of it should have signed the Treaty and that it should cease to exist after twelve months. O'Sheil summarised his interpretation as 'briefly we are not obliged by the Treaty to assist the Belfast Parliament in any way'.[43]

Though the threat of immediate and compulsory transfer to the north had receded, the civil service would have been apprehensive had they known that even as the Provisional Government was taking over the Castle it was already discussing its replacement. At the meetings with the British government for establishing the Provisional Government and transferring responsibility for the administration, the Irish delegation had originally wanted the entire Irish civil service transferred on loan rather than permanently. This would have allowed the Free State to pick and choose, leaving the British government to deal with the rest. Not surprisingly the British rejected this suggestion.[44] Nevertheless there was an intense debate going on within the Provisional Government as to the future of the civil service. This debate was characterised by outright hostility to the Castle apparatus and a determination to replace it, reflecting the strategy outlined in Griffith's Christmas memorandum. Collins indicated that he looked forward to replacing the 'alien and cumbersome administration', scrapping the inherited civil servants and replacing them with fresh 'Gaelic' ones.[45] The leading Sinn Féin ideologue Aodh De Blacam called for the imposition of an 'iron Bismarckian phase' as a step on the road to the creation of a model corporate Catholic State and society.[46] J.J. (Ginger) O'Connell, Assistant Chief of Staff in the IRA at the time of the Treaty and a supporter of Collins, proposing a virtually militarised civil service, urged a purge of those civil servants 'with the wrong outlook', an immediate imposition of salary ceilings, big cuts in staffs and a government directive to 'bring all public servants under thorough discipline and prohibit and make criminal strikes by government employees'.[47] Meanwhile the IRB was being courted to support the Treaty with promises of civil service jobs.[48]

The most detailed, and realistic, analysis of the relationship between the Provisional Government and the Castle civil service is contained in a ten-page memorandum on Provisional Government policy toward the civil service prepared by Eoin MacNeill, the founder of the Gaelic League and Irish Volunteers and a member of the Provisional Government.[49] MacNeill sent the memorandum to Collins outlining a proposal to 'make the fact of the change of government penetrate every cell and fibre of the old governmental system'. At the heart of his scheme was a supervisory commission of a small number of the best men in the civil service, qualified by their 'sound national outlook', to act as a kind of watchdog over the senior civil servants.[50] The memorandum outlined a vital role for the civil service in consolidating Provisional Government control of the State. Listing the Dublin Castle offices it suggested that the Provisional Government select 'three or four existing Irish civil servants from each of these offices of sound national outlook' to act as the eyes and ears of the Minister for Finance, Collins, and the Minister for Home Affairs, Duggan. Those civil servants, with their understanding of the State apparatus, would have a vital role in preventing the northern government consolidating itself. They were to be joined by the best of the Dáil Éireann staff from the local government and secretariat departments. The next suggested step in taking control of the State was the appointment of an officer equivalent to Anderson in the Treasury and Clark in Belfast, a civil servant expert in Treasury matters to take control of staff and financial matters.

From the point of view of the civil service the most interesting proposal was one to establish an advisory committee of civil servants 'to take an immediate survey of the machinery required for finance and civil administration and to report to a small cabinet committee'. The memorandum stressed that 'it is of the highest importance for the Provisional Government to get in touch with and take the fullest advantage of the experience of the Irish civil service generally'. This advisory committee would assist in preparing a budget, keeping an eye on transfers of revenue from Whitehall, and in reshaping the departments of government and staffing in preparation of the assumption of power by a native government. It would also be vital in directing departments 'away from British and toward Irish considerations' and would have blanket powers of access to all departments and records.

The MacNeill memorandum also suggested that a cabinet secretariat could be drawn from the loyal elements of the existing civil service to 'give effect to cabinet decisions'. It also suggested a civil service commission to replace the Civil Service Committee established by the 1920 Act. This would consist of two members elected by the staff and two appointed by the Provisional Government, with a Dáil Éireann judge acting as chairman. It would therefore have no representative from either the British Treasury or the Belfast government. This commission would deal with all questions of 'retirement and discharge of civil servants owing to the recent change of government', and transfers of civil servants between Britain and Ireland, and would consider all applications for new appointments and make recommendations on 'Principles of Promotion'. The memorandum also strongly recommended that the Provisional Government should publicly adopt a 'self-denying ordinance' to give no undertakings and make no promises as to jobs or promotions. Finally, a full list of forty-six 'reliable and efficient' civil servants, who the Provisional Government could consult with confidence on the work of the departments, was attached. The 'reliable civil servants' included seven civil service trade union activists: E. Fahy, Conn Murphy, P.J. Troddyn, H. Bell, E.P. O'Toole, Thomas A. Murphy and Michael Smithwick.

The Conference of All Associations of Irish Civil Servants

In some of its suggestions the MacNeill memorandum reflected the position of the civil servants themselves, as is shown by an equally detailed memorandum presented by them to the Provisional Government. In fact it is possible that the MacNeill memorandum may have been partly written by Conn Murphy, who had several unofficial meetings with Collins, Griffith, and MacNeill.[51] As soon as the Treaty was approved Conn Murphy and Michael Gallagher wrote to the secretary of Dáil Éireann, Diarmuid O'Hegarty, introducing themselves as the staff side of the 'Irish Civil Service Joint Whitley Committee' but now representing the new 'Executive Committee of the Conference of All Associations of Irish Civil Servants', with whom 'any future Irish government may conduct such negotiations as may be deemed necessary'. They also forwarded a detailed fifteen-page memorandum on the current situation of the Irish civil service and its relationship with the Castle government, the Belfast regime and the Provisional Government.[52] Murphy knew O'Hegarty personally from the 1918 campaign against the oath of allegiance and addressed him on first name terms. The civil servants' memorandum was entirely positive and optimistic about the situation of the civil service. The memorandum initially explained that the staff side of the Whitley Committee represented the entire fifty-six organisations of the civil service. With the formation of the Provisional Government the official side of the council, appointed by the Chancellor of the Exchequer, had lapsed. The staff side now looked to the Provisional Government to form 'consultation and conciliation machinery of a kind more suitable to Irish conditions', which implied that they were not entirely happy with the Whitley scheme and were anxious for an opportunity to put their views on an alternative.

Although the civil servants' memorandum did not detail what they thought was 'more suitable' the expectation was that the machinery would be more than a mechanism for conveying Treasury decisions and would offer the civil service more real control over their conditions. It had been the experience of the civil service organisations that substantial gains had always been negotiated with politicians. For instance, all the safeguards and guarantees in the Home Rule proposals had been secured through dealing with the government. In contrast the experience of dealing with the Treasury in the Whitley Committees or in the person of Waterfield had produced mere consultation and not negotiation. However, the memorandum did recognise that the Treaty imposed no obligation on the new government beyond that of compensation to discharged or dismissed civil servants and that the Provisional Government was free to deal with the existing civil service as it thought fit.

The memorandum shows that the civil service was dominated by fear of the imposition of partition and responded to the Provisional Government's resistance to partition with encouragement and support. It also shows that the civil service hoped to use the transition to the Provisional Government to end the dominance of the Treasury in civil service negotiation. On partition the memorandum not only underlined the resistance of the civil service but also directed attention to the danger posed to the authority of the new government if the changes in train were allowed to continue unchecked.

On the handover of services such as education the memorandum warned that though this was not to be completed until the Council of Ireland had been set up, a number of services had already been transferred with consequent division of staffs, with more transfers due in February and March. The northern government was pushing for these transfers to be dated from 16 January, the day the Provisional Government took power. This was clearly a challenge to the authority of the Provisional Government. The memorandum urged that the government consider the validity of the transfers already made and whether it was prepared to agree to further transfers.

On the reserved services, such as the Post Office and police, the civil service view was that the Treaty clearly handed these over to the Provisional Government for the area of 'Southern Ireland' but equally clearly did not give the northern government any additional power over them. The question for the civil service, and for the Provisional Government, was whether these services and their staffs in the northern area would pass to the control of the Provisional Government or remain under the control of the British government. This was also the case with the excluded services, such as customs and excise and revenue, where the legislation was quite clear that the northern government had no authority whatsoever. Yet the actions of the northern authority indicated that it wanted to partition all the government departments in advance of the establishment of the Free State.

The memorandum also emphasised the hostility of the civil service to the Civil Service Committee created by the 1920 Act and the 'repugnance with which they, as a whole, viewed the liability of transfer to Belfast'. They asked that the Provisional Government support their resistance to compulsory transfer, even if it led to surplus staff in Dublin, and suggested that the government form a new Civil Service Committee composed of three staff side representatives, three Irish government representatives and a Dáil Éireann judge to act as chairman, almost replicating MacNeill's scheme. The staff side would sit opposite a politician, not a higher-ranking fellow civil servant. The committee would deal with all questions arising from retirements and discharges; make recommendations on inter-departmental transfers and new appointments; set up an open competitive recruitment scheme; act as a conciliation and arbitration board on salaries, hours, terms of service and conditions of employment; and, finally, prepare a superannuation scheme.[53]

The civil service memorandum also warned that there were strong grounds for objecting to a continuing role for Waterfield and warned that, if he was retained, 'means should be devised to ensure that the policy of the Provisional Government shall be observed . . . and that his work . . . should properly be directed from Dublin and not from London'.[54] The memorandum reinforced the distaste that the civil service felt for higher officials in its recommendation that the Provisional Government immediately appoint a minister corresponding to a secretary to the Treasury with whom the civil service could make representations. Although the memorandum complained of the distaste the civil service felt at making representations to the British Treasury now that there was a native government, the real difficulty lay with the higher officials.

The memorandum also conveyed the view of the civil service that it had ample talent to staff the new departments which the Provisional Government would have to create and asked that 'in no circumstances should English civil servants or outsiders be imported for these purposes'. Other issues of lesser, but still of some, importance, were the reorganisation of the existing departments, the imminent cut in the cost-of-living bonus, transfers of civil servants between Great Britain and Ireland, the liability for pensions and the principle of open competition. In order to address these issues Murphy pressed O'Hegarty for an immediate meeting.[55] Murphy and Gallagher were essentially offering to throw the full weight of civil service organisations behind the Provisional Government and any changes they might wish to make, so long as they could be assured that there would be no worsening of conditions and changes would be negotiated through the staff side, now known as the Executive Committee of the Conference of All Associations of Irish Civil Servants.[56] The draft rules of the new association included as its objects that of encouraging 'educational and social development among the members along Irish lines and in harmony with Irish interests'.[57] The relationship binding the civil service to the Provisional Government would, they expected, be based on a shared suspicion of Whitehall, joint resistance to partition and a united determination to create anew a native administration.

A delegation of the Irish branch of the Customs and Excise Federation (CEF), which had always expected to be retained as an imperial service, also met with the government to seek reassurances, while also indicating a general enthusiasm for serving the new government. Even the professional civil servants, who were now in a grading limbo, could summon up some degree of enthusiasm. The initial response of the IPCS to the establishing of the Provisional Government was a guarded optimism. At the annual general meeting in March 1922 the IPCS president spoke warmly about the 'new vista of usefulness that was gradually opening before the Institution'.[58]

There was, however, no reason to suppose that the Castle civil servants were irreplaceable. Almost all of them were lower-level clerical grades with few in the higher policy-developing levels. The signing of the Treaty unleashed a flood of job applications to the Dáil, most of them accompanied by a recommendation from a parish priest, a TD and the local IRA commander, with some of the applications in fact coming from the local IRA men themselves.[59] It ought to be noted that the Provisional Government decided that there would no toleration for canvassing by politicians or by ministers on behalf of any applicant for employment or promotion, a decision that was, with a few exceptions, rigidly obeyed.[60] There were also, to the surprise of Waterfield, a considerable number of applications by civil servants in Britain to transfer to the Provisional Government.[61]

A 'thoroughly Irish' civil service

The Provisional Government did not in fact simply take over the existing Castle administration. It drew its staff variously from the Sinn Féin party, Dublin Castle departments and the Dáil departments, while maintaining strict separation between the Dáil Éireann accounts and those of the Provisional Government.[62] Between January and April, that is between setting up the Provisional Government and the formal transfer of authority, the departments had a free hand in recruiting staff on a quasi-permanent, temporary or even casual basis.[63] Staff was recruited from the existing civil service in the Castle departments, from the civil service of the Dáil departments and from civil servants who had been dismissed since 1916 for disloyalty. The intent here was clearly to draw from all the potential officials to forge a completely new civil service. The Provisional Government took immediate steps to disperse the Castle civil service by reassigning men. The CSO staff was dispersed to the Ministry of Finance and the Ministry of Home Affairs with other individual civil servants sent to various separate departments.[64] The core Provisional Government Ministry of Finance was made up of civil servants recruited from the Treasury in London, the CSO, the NHIC, customs and excise, the LGB and the Dáil local government department, along with Collins's personal secretariat almost entirely consisting of the staff of the Dáil Department of Finance; Joe O'Reilly of the 'Squad' acted as Collins's personal bodyguard.[65] The CDB, which had played such a key role in making the State a positive force in transforming western Ireland, found itself dispersed among the departments of agriculture, fisheries and the Irish Land Commission.[66]

However, pouring the new wine of native government into the old skin of the Castle departments proved more difficult than had been anticipated. The clash of authority between Dáil and Castle civil servants was causing problems in the Department of Local Government. The Dáil Department of Local

Government was one of the successes of the revolutionary administration and by the time of the Treaty had already effected radical changes in the local administration of the country. Between the Truce and the Treaty the department had continued recruitment and maintained its authority as the *de facto* local government department. With the passing of the Treaty the old Custom House officials, transferred to Jury's Hotel after the burning of their departmental headquarters by the Dublin IRA, immediately began to undo the work of the Dáil department. Lorcan Robbins of the Dáil local government department demanded that the Provisional Government put the LGB under the control of sympathetic men or, if that was not possible, close it down.[67]

As the IRA split and opposition to the Treaty became militarised the pretence of a dual power was dropped and the Dáil ceased to meet from mid-April. In May Collins circulated a request to the members of the Provisional Government to provide a summary of the work of their departments with an outline of reforms, economies and improvements. Collins indicated that 'it was essential that each department should become thoroughly Irish, and that forms and circulars associated with the old administration should be altered to suit the new condition'.[68] This suggests that the Provisional Government was still planning major changes in the inherited civil service. However, that a shift in thinking was underway is indicated by the decision of the Provisional Government to invite civil servants from both Castle and Dáil to offer their names for inclusion in a pool of candidates for a selection board to the new higher clerical and junior executive grades that would be created in the new departments.[69] The outbreak of civil war in June prevented the sweeping changes that clearly were being planned for the Irish administration. From that point on the Provisional Government had to assert control over not only the Castle administration but also the remnants of the Dáil departments.

The split in the republican movement profoundly affected the Dáil Éireann civil service. The Dáil Éireann district court clerks had been replacing the dismissed petty session clerks, but as some took an anti-Treaty position and loyalties became uncertain the Dáil clerks found themselves put on probation, a status they still held ten years later.[70] The Dáil ministry was initially minded to facilitate the retirement of any of its civil servants who had a genuine objection to the Treaty and there was some discussion of compensation on resignation. Attitudes hardened as the rhetoric of the anti-Treaty forces became more extreme and militaristic. The Belfast Boycott staff, which initially had been offered compensation for loss of office, was threatened with summary dismissal. Thirteen of the staff forwarded a memorandum to the Dáil cabinet comparing their treatment as civil servants of the Dáil with that accorded by the Treaty to the 'British officials who worked against the Republic'.[71] The more political Cosgrave convinced his cabinet colleagues to offer three months' wages to buy off the boycott staff.[72]

Insubordination was noted in which some messengers refused to carry out orders, alleging that the authority of the Provisional Government officials was not valid.[73] Absences in either the Dáil or Provisional Government departments were noted and, in an echo of the response of the British government to suspected involvement in the Easter 1916 Rising, civil servants were compelled to give an account of their movements on the days after 27 June and the outbreak of the civil war.[74] It was instructed that women staff suspected of irregular sympathies were to be imprisoned if caught in the act of spying.[75] If a minister was not satisfied with the attitude of any member of staff toward the Provisional Government then the officer was to be suspended and prevented from entering government buildings.[76] Bolstered by the results of the June general election the Provisional Government now treated both the Dáil and the Castle civil service as equally under the control of the Provisional Government, not Dáil Éireann.[77]

An oath of fidelity to the Provisional Government was imposed on both the civil service of Dáil Éireann and the Castle departments.[78] Each civil servant was required to sign an undertaking stating that, 'I have not taken part with, or aided or abetted in any way whatsoever the forces in revolt against the Irish Provisional Government and I promise to be faithful to that government and to give no aid or support of any kind to those who are engaged in conflict against the authority of that government.'[79] A note from Collins accompanied each copy of the declaration emphasising that the irregulars were in opposition to the elected government of the people and denying that the declaration sought to prescribe the political opinions of civil servants. Rather than being directed against opinions it was directed against activities incompatible with public service, an echo of Nathan's attitude to civil service engagement with the Irish Volunteers.[80]

The judge of the Dáil land courts, Conor Maguire, it soon emerged, was actively working to draw the staff of the Land Resettlement Commission away from the Provisional Government. He was immediately suspended.[81] Conn Murphy was another victim. Despite his earlier enthusiasm for the Treaty, by the outbreak of the civil war he had changed sides. In September 1922, after writing to the newspapers complaining of the heavy-handed raids by the military on his home, he was immediately dismissed though he had not actually taken any active part in hostilities, but had merely signalled his opposition by his letter to the newspaper. His son Fearghus, who was an active anti-Treatyite, was interned in the Curragh. Perhaps because of the high profile enjoyed by Murphy as an organiser within the civil service trade union movement and his status on the National Whitley Committee and despite the key role he had played in preventing the partition of the civil service, the Provisional and Free State governments took a particularly hard line with him. He did not help his own case by writing a personal letter to Blythe reporting how his family had been terrorised by 'an organised murder gang, the members of which are at present employed and paid by the Provisional Government'.[82] He was refused permission to retire under the Treaty provisions as he had been dismissed already and was also denied his accumulated pension as a signal of government disapproval, despite the pleas of Áine Ceannt, widow of the 1916 leader, on his behalf.[83] Dismissed in October 1922 he was briefly reinstated in December 1927 by the government in order that he be formally discharged as redundant and awarded an inadequate pension.[84]

Assimilating the Dáil Éireann civil service

Plans to construct a completely new apparatus were abandoned and the civil service of the Dáil was assimilated into the old Castle administration rather than the other way round. The terms of the Treaty and the need for a speedy transfer of authority did not encourage any radical restructuring of the civil service. In the absence of such radical restructuring, for each department the process of assimilating the staff of the Dáil ministries to the Castle administration was simply a matter of assigning each member of the staff to a grade, based on an inspection of the work done. Curiously enough this was exactly the process that Waterfield had been laboriously doing in each department of the Castle administration. However, although the Castle civil service were reassigned and dispersed across the new departments, the Dáil civil service tended to move en bloc into the parallel department of the Provisional Government. It was decided that as a fundamental principle of assimilation the Truce would be the deciding line for allocating the staff of the Dáil ministry to permanent or temporary positions. This was in recognition of the special claim to permanent pensionable posts of the staff that had borne the risks of the pre-Truce service while, at the same time, being fair to the existing staff with years of efficient service. In effect this isolated the civil service of the pre-Truce Dáil as a special case. The staff of the Dáil civil service recruited after the Truce became temporary civil servants and would have to compete along with the rest of the civil service for any permanent posts that might become available. They were, however, assimilated at the same salary they had enjoyed under the Dáil departments, even though it was generally higher than a temporary civil servant usually enjoyed, subject to that salary being liable to any subsequent reductions due to the fall in the cost-of-living bonus.

Both the LGB and the Dáil Department of Local Government were now in disarray. Though it would have been preferable to decide on the future shape of the department and fit the two organisations into that model, it had proved impractical as a way of progressing.[85] The LGB was still in disarray due to the stand-off between Robinson and Waterfield on reorganisation. A further difficulty was that the Provisional Government had brought into its Ministry of Local Government departments other than the LGB. It was anticipated that these would become sections in a rationalised ministry run by a single minister rather than a collective board, with a consequent reallocation of staff, but that was yet to be arranged.[86] On the Dáil department side there was the difficulty that the Treaty split was undermining control over republican local authorities and testing departmental staff loyalties. The appointment of McCarron, a former auditor in the LGB, as acting departmental secretary tested the loyalty of the Dáil staff, with rumours that some were threatening mass resignations. The assimilation and grading of the Dáil staff was done by McCarron of the LGB and De Lacey of the Dáil department and sanctioned by Gregg in finance. Loyalties were further tested when the staff that had been given permanent status discovered that in many cases the scale of pay in the Provisional Government was lower than that of the Dáil ministry. There is, however, no evidence in the records for Blythe's claim that he had averted the threatened mutiny by random increases and decreases of salaries, thus fostering distrust in the ranks of the mutineers. The salary levels on assimilation were in every case those appropriate to the LGB staff on the same grade and were set by Gregg in finance. Gregg in fact resisted Blythe's suggestion that some staff should enter their scales at a higher level. The Provisional Government seems to have determined that service in Dáil Éireann would neither help nor hinder any member of staff. All staff were assimilated at the bottom of the scale, with, in the cases of some younger officers, the direction that they should 'mark time' until they had attained the age usually appropriate for their point on the scale.[87]

In agriculture assimilation of the Castle and Dáil departments was complicated by the ILC status as a reserved service. The staff of the ILC, like other reserved services, remained the employees of the British government, which acted as agent for the Provisional Government. The Dáil Department of Agriculture staff were the members of the Dáil Éireann Land Resettlement Commission, established to quell the rising unrest over land, and so therefore engaged in much the same sort of work of inspection and adjudication as the ILC.[88] From the point of view of assimilation, however, this made the task a straightforward one. Following a practice that was being elevated to a principle it was decided that the staff of the Dáil land commission would be assimilated to similar grades and scales as the ILC staff.

Civil servants who had served the Dáil felt badly treated by the favour, as they saw it, with which the old regime's civil service were treated. Years later, in evidence to the Brennan Commission, the Association of Dáil Civil Servants and Dismissed British Civil Servants claimed to represent 120 members. Most were clerical officers, with some from higher posts. Their main complaint was that on assimilation 'due regard was not paid to the nature of the duties on which they had been engaged previously'. It was their contention that the duties on which a Dáil Éireann officer had been engaged ought to have determined their grade and not the duties to which they were assigned in the Provisional and Free State governments. The informal and unstructured Dáil departments had, rightly or wrongly, given them a greater sense of status than that attached to their new Provisional Government grades. The implication clearly was that they felt that'people who had suffered in support of the national cause' had undergone loss of status. It was also their view that the civil servants who had been dismissed under the British regime had suffered loss of promotion and that 'it is a distinct loss to have been patriotic in the civil service'.[89]

That was not true for at least some of the Dáil civil servants. One group of Dáil civil servants that did do well in the change of government was drawn from those dismissed by the British for disloyalty. Alexander J. Connolly, interned in Frongoch after 1916, was reinstated in the Department of Industry and Commerce and ended his civil service career as private secretary to Lemass. Michael Cremen, another 1916 veteran, became private secretary to Patrick Little in Posts and Telegraphs, then to Gerald Boland in Justice, as well as being appointed secretary to the Military Pensions Board. Patrick J. Daly emerged from the Dáil Éireann local government department to finish as assistant secretary to the Department of Local Government. Michael De Lacey was another civil servant interned after 1916 who entered the Dáil Éireann local government department. He ended his career as assistant secretary in the department. Michael Heavey transferred from the Land Resettlement Commission to the Irish Land Commission as senior commissioner. Thomas McArdle, who had served in the Dáil Éireann local government department, went on to become the first secretary of the Department of Health. James J. McElligott, interned after 1916, returned to become the dominant figure in the Department of Finance. His case underlines the fact that participation in revolution does not preclude an intense conservatism. George McGrath transferred to the Free State as Auditor-General from the equivalent post of Accountant-General in Dáil Éireann. Michael McDunphy, dismissed by the British government for refusing to take an oath, ended his career as secretary to the president of Ireland. Maurice O'Connor, dismissed during the War of Independence, was reinstated and retired as assistant principal in the Department of Education. Henry O'Friel, another civil servant dismissed for refusing to take the oath in 1918, ended his career as secretary of the Department of Justice. P.S. O'Hegarty, dismissed for refusing the oath in 1918, was a long serving secretary to the Department of Posts and Telegraphs. Diarmuid O'Hegarty, dismissed in 1918, served the Dáil cabinet and the Provisional Government as secretary, ending his career as chairman of the Office of Public Works (OPW).[90]

However, these cases perhaps served to underline the poor treatment meted out to others who felt themselves as well qualified on grounds of commitment to the national cause and ability. Diarmuid Fawcett had served Sinn Féin and the Dáil as a member of Cork Industrial Development Association, as

Consul-General in the USA and as technical advisor to both the Dáil and the Provisional Government on economic affairs. Then in September he was told that he was to act as assistant to the secretary of the Department of Industry and Commerce, Gordon Campbell, former Castle civil servant and son of the chairman of Seanad Éireann, Lord Glenavy, but without a right of access to the minister. In a bitter letter of complaint at this demotion he detailed the service he had freely given 'when to serve Dáil Éireann was not the secure and pleasant office that comparatively speaking it is today. Moreover I rendered this service at a time when those many others who professed to be possessed of technical and administrative knowledge elected to serve under an entrenched despotic alien government than under a popularly-elected national administration in the adolescent stage'.[91] Joe O'Reilly, who as a member of 'The Squad' had killed several British intelligence agents, found the transition from gunman to civil servant particularly difficult. When he remarked that it was his opinion that there would be 'more than a few irregulars [anti-Treaty republicans] to be cleared out' in the government departments, he was sharply reminded by O'Brien that 'whatever his qualities as a soldier he had better understand his position as a clerk'.[92]

T.H. Nally and Leon Ó'Broin, who had resisted Conor Maguire's attempts to alienate their loyalty to the Provisional Government, were shocked to discover that they would have to suffer a reduction of salary on assimilation. Nally took the high view that his salary had been negotiated with the minister personally and was therefore not subject to finance controls. Neither got very far in their challenge to the emerging power of the Department of Finance.[93]

In the Ministry of Home Affairs P.J. Crump got a particularly raw deal. As the Treaty split began to undermine the Dáil departments Crump was appointed to the legal staff in February 1922 to replace an official who was taking an increasingly anti-Treaty line. Crump abandoned a good post in a solicitor's practice on the assurance that he would get a permanent post and also because he was pressed by Eamon Duggan to do his duty by the country. However, because he was recruited after the Truce the Department of Finance refused to make his post permanent, despite the pleas of Duggan and the protests of Crump that he had been duped. Regardless of the difficulties that it might cause for ministers, finance was demonstrating its unwavering determination to achieve sole control of establishments. Although this can be seen as an early expression of the dominance of the finance mandarins, it was in fact as much a reflection of the mind of Collins as the official mind of finance. Of all the ministers of the Provisional Government it was Collins who best understood that though control of the IRA was vital, no less vital to the success of the Provisional Government was control of the civil service of both the Dáil and the Castle.[94]

Whether because of the speed of their assimilation, or the short period in which they had functioned as a corps, the civil service of the former Dáil did not manage to form any organisation to fight their interests.[95] Where the Dáil staff did manage to combine to make a protest about reduced salaries, as happened in the Department of Local Government in November 1922, they succeeded in winning some concessions but Gregg in finance refused to allow Blythe to make any offer that would be 'embarrassing for us vis-à-vis the civil service generally'. The Provisional Government was learning to think of itself as a cohesive if isolated collective that had to stand united against all claims, even those of loyal supporters.[96] The only organised pressure group to emerge was the 'Irish Republican Soldiers 1916–1921 and Prisoners of War Association' that acted as a not very effective conduit for pleas for employment for the ex-IRA men and the relatives of the fallen.[97] The final 'clean break' with the Dáil came on 14 December 1922 when a directive ordered McGrath to cease making payment from the Dáil funds and to transfer all the staff and payments to the Provisional Government.[98] All those employed by the Dáil and transferring to the Provisional Government were required to sign the declaration of fidelity to the government.[99] Finally, Article 10 of the Treaty (and Article 77 of the constitution of the Free State) gave a constitutional standing to the vested interests of the former Castle civil service, guaranteeing their status, tenure, salaries and conditions. On the other hand the staff of the Dáil Éireann departments were not offered any constitutional or indeed any legal status at all.

Ending the Whitley Councils

In the cabinet the correspondence from the civil service associations in Dublin Castle welcoming the Provisional Government and asking for a meeting was noted but ignored. Conn Murphy had some unofficial meetings with Collins, Griffith, and MacNeill, but nothing concrete emerged from these meetings.[100] Although the official break with Whitleyism was not announced until December 1924, and although departmental councils continued to meet, the decision to do away with it was in fact made early in the term of the Provisional Government.[101] Discussing a memorandum on the Whitley Councils prepared by James MacMahon, which included Conn Murphy's observations, the Provisional Government decided that they posed an unacceptable limitation to the power of the executive, were un-Irish, and ordered that they should immediately cease working.[102] As the Treaty split began to edge toward crisis Collins agreed to meet a deputation from the civil service associations. The CEF submitted a memorandum detailing the points that the deputation wanted to discuss: the status and continuity of service and salaries, the establishment of a new Civil Service Committee, the setting up of a new Irish Civil Service National Council in which government and civil servants would negotiate a future relationship, and retirements and pensions.[103]

On the first point the deputation was assured that the government, while not being in a position to give a guarantee (as they could not bind their successors), had no desire to interfere with the existing rights and privileges of civil servants. The specific assurance offered was that the government 'would try to ensure that future conditions will be no worse than hitherto and had no intention to deprive civil servants of any rights held under the former government'. The question of a Civil Service Committee was being addressed by what emerged as the Wylie committee. On the question of retirements and pensions Collins directed the deputation to Article 10 of the Treaty. On the request for an Irish Civil Service National Council Collins was wary and it was clear to the deputation that the Provisional Government was opposed to the idea. Instead it offered a special commission to find out 'whether the object of an Irish National Council could not be effected in a different manner'. Until the question was decided a temporary consultative committee was offered.[104]

Waterfield and the Provisional Government

As the Dáil debated the Treaty, Waterfield's main concern was those departments that he had never re-graded, such as the Post Office, on the assumption that they would remain part of the reserved civil service. The Treaty, to his surprise, proposed to transfer the entire civil service to the new Free State. Waterfield spent Christmas and New Year hurrying through a series of notional reorganisations with immediate effect while moving a few key men from Dublin Castle to Whitehall.[105] The proclamation of 16 January put an immediate stop to all changes. To those civil servants who disagreed with their new grading Waterfield could only offer the view that they were lucky to have been re-graded at all. To the civil servants still waiting a new grading he could only offer the advice to wait until the new Provisional Government had found its feet before opening the question.[106]

It was made clear to Waterfield that the Treasury in Whitehall would be co-operating with the Provisional Government in giving effect to the proclamation. Cope's assurance that the proclamation was for appearance only and that the prohibitions might not be applied as rigidly as might appear at first sight did not reassure Waterfield. He feared that a close scrutiny of the re-gradings he had already completed might lead in some cases to their rejection by the Provisional Government.[107] There is no doubt that Waterfield was pessimistic as to the future prospects of the civil service in the Irish Free State and was burdened by a deep sense of obligation to those civil servants left out of his re-grading who, he feared, would be ejected on to the street on inadequate pensions. On 23 January he sent a detailed memorandum to the Provisional Government on the outstanding problems in reorganisation that had been brought to a halt by the proclamation. These included cases where the Treasury had sanctioned appointments but the formalities had not been completed before the proclamation, cases where individuals had passed the civil service examinations but had not been actually appointed and cases where persons had not qualified for permanent appointment but were eligible to compete in the civil service examinations for pending permanent appointments. Waterfield pressed all of these as requiring decisions one way or the other. A month later he was still waiting a reply.[108] All through January and February he attempted to secure a personal interview with the Provisional Government while assuring the civil service associations that outstanding re-gradings might yet go through.[109] Waterfield's own feeling was that the Provisional Government was convinced that the Castle was over-staffed and in need of severe cutbacks. Besides, they would want to keep any vacancies to satisfy the demands of their own supporters.[110] What finally enabled Waterfield to get his foot in the door was the question of salary cuts for the civil service.

In order to compensate for wartime inflation the government had introduced the 'bonus' as a multiplier on basic salary. This multiplier was based on a cost-of-living index figure calculated every six months. It was expressly declared that the bonus would be temporary. With post-war deflation this figure began to fall. Civil servants, having got used to thinking of their combined basic and 'bonus' as their real salaries, now faced what was in effect a cut in pay. As the Provisional Government came into office the British government had already made a decision that the civil service would face a significant reduction in pay. The post-war euphoria had evaporated in Britain. The conservative newspapers, the *Morning Post* and the *Daily Mail*, ran a populist campaign against the expanded civil service. The root of the emerging economic problems they confidently asserted lay in 'squandermania' and those mythical civil servants 'Dilly and Dally'.

In reaction to this campaign the British government instituted the Geddes investigation into the cost of the civil service. Geddes, one of the allegedly efficient businessmen brought into the war cabinet by Lloyd George, had been personally responsible for the creation of the enormous Department of Transport. In February 1922, following the recommendations of his investigation, the British government imposed the 'Geddes Supercut' of between 10 and 50 per cent on civil service salaries along with an overall maximum total remuneration of £2,000.[111] Waterfield wrote to O'Hegarty to ask whether the Provisional Government 'concurred' in the cut.[112] At this stage the authority of the Provisional Government was being eroded by anti-Treatyite propaganda and it seemed that actual State authority lay in Portobello barracks, headquarters of the Irish army, rather than in the Merrion Street offices of the government. In Cork the civil servants in the Ministry of Labour went on a three-day strike when the reduction was first announced. It seemed probable that strikes would spread when the cut was actually imposed. Waterfield would actually have been happier of the government had ignored his letter as they had ignored earlier ones. Once the transfer date of 1 April was reached responsibility would pass from his hands and it would be up to the Provisional Government and not Treasury (Ireland) to impose economies. However, his acute sense of professional propriety and responsibility to both staff and Provisional Government would not allow him to delay the question.[113]

Waterfield was called immediately to a meeting where he could elaborate his concerns on reorganisation, as well as on the cuts. Within a few weeks he felt sufficiently confident of his position to offer a mild reprimand for excessive government expenditure, asking whether the Provisional Government could not have secured less expensive accommodation for the constitution committee than the Shelbourne hotel and refusing to sanction the purchase of calculating machines for the Department of Finance.[114] Waterfield established a good working relationship with Cosgrave, similar to that of any Treasury official and a politician, and together they ironed out some of the difficulties that were pressing. It ought to be noted that compared to the problems facing the Provisional Government, Waterfield's anxieties about the accounting officers of the LGB or temporary ex-servicemen would have seemed absurdly trivial.[115] In fact while Waterfield's concern for the rank and file of the Irish service shows a commendable decency, it was Cope who managed the delicate task of discreetly moving staff out from the Castle into the departments of the Provisional Government and ensuring that those formerly engaged in security work found safe niches.[116]

The postal workers strike, 1922

In contrast to the British Post Office, which was profitable, the Irish Post Office ran at a massive loss due to the density of its service in a thinly populated country. When the Provisional Government decided to impose the 'Geddes' cut, only the postal workers signalled resistance. The postal workers had not won any revision of their grades or scales since 1870. Great hopes had been placed in the Whitley reorganisation but in Ireland Waterfield had ignored the postal grades, expecting they would be included in the general British reorganisation. When the Treaty clarified that the entire postal staff would in fact be transferred Waterfield worked up a hasty reorganisation in some of the managerial sections that was only completed the day before the transfer of the administration. It was in any case rejected by them as an 'utterly worthless proposal'.[117] The Provisional Government decided that the best policy was to follow the line it took over the departments as they found them and that the reductions would be allowed take effect.[118] The postal workers, organised in three unions – the Irish Postal Union (IPU), the Irish Postal Workers' Union (IPWU) and the Irish Post Office Engineers' Union (IPOEU) – threatened to go on a co-ordinated strike if the cuts were imposed. A request by J.J. Walsh to the British Postmaster General to provide strike-breakers got a positive response. The British government was anxious about the impact on their own civil service of any successful agitation in Ireland against cuts at a time when the two civil services were still closely linked.[119] The British civil service unions were in fact following the course of this first confrontation between the new government and its civil service with great interest.[120] But the Dáil and Collins repudiated this 'scab' tactic.[121]

Collins was in fact very worried by the complications that labour troubles would add to the developing Treaty split and wanted a settlement. He asked James Douglas to chair a commission to consider wages, salaries, organisation of work and conditions generally in the Post Office. Apart from Douglas as chairman the commission consisted of Grattan Esmonde TD and Henry Friel of the Department of Finance as the Provisional Government nominees with T.J. O'Connell of the Teachers' Union and L.J. Duffy of the Distributive Workers' Union as Labour Party nominees.[122] The Department of Finance was hesitant about this, the first commission of inquiry within the early weeks of native government in Ireland, which in their view set an unhealthy precedent. Gregg wanted to establish as a governing principle of civil service pay that no higher basic wage would be paid in the Free State than was paid by the British government to similar grades. Walsh argued that such a principle was wrong in itself as, firstly, wages should be determined solely by local conditions, and, secondly, it implied that not paying more also meant not paying less.[123]

Douglas settled the threatened strike by securing a temporary rise in the basic salary, rather than a reduction in bonus, and promising to effect a reorganisation of the Post Office. It was also agreed that the government would calculate an Irish cost of living figure rather than rely on the British figure.[124] Part of the opposition to the cut had been that the cost of living in Ireland was higher than in Britain and that in justice the British figure could not be used to cut wages. The Ministry of Economic Affairs of Dáil Éireann was given the task of calculating an Irish figure based on the cost of rent and basic foodstuffs. The secretary to the committee was Michael Gallagher.[125] Five thousand forms were sent to national schoolteachers in every school in the country asking for details of local rents and prices. Three hundred and eight were returned, from 112 towns.[126] The dramatic gains that had been won by the threat of strike did not go unnoticed by other civil service associations. When Walsh refused to meet the AEO branch in the PO accountant-general's office, they pointed out that staff had always been consulted on reorganisation and expressed the hope that his decision to meet the humble postmen, which contrasted with his refusal to meet the accountancy staff, was not because of their threat to strike.[127]

In September the next cost-of-living calculation, based on the new Irish figure, was due. In Britain the figure was calculated at eighty-five, that is the cost of living was 85 per cent above that of August 1914. In Ireland, based on the local cost-of-living figure, it was ninety. This meant that the civil service still faced a cut in salaries, though not as severe as in Great Britain. The reduction amounted to 3/26ths, or between 11 and 12 per cent, on the bonus element of salary. Departments were instructed to apply the reduction from 1 September.[128] O'Hegarty was sanguine, predicting that the postal workers would contest the cuts but would use the Labour party in the Dáil to make complaints rather than take direct action. The government offered to phase in the reductions, so long as the principle of reductions was accepted. The postal unions shifted position by arguing that basic wages were too low to bear any cuts in the bonus and asked that the cuts be withdrawn and their claim for an increase in basic pay be submitted to arbitration. Negotiations broke down and a strike was declared.[129]

By now the civil war was entering its darkest phase in the weeks after the killing of Michael Collins. Faced with a strike by the Post Office workers the government responded as if the strike was inspired by 'Irregulars' rather than by discontent on pay. The Provisional Government recruited pensioners and the unemployed to act as strike-breakers and issued a statement that 'the government does not recognise the right of Civil Servants to strike. In the event of a cessation of work by any section of the Postal Service picketing such as is permitted in connection with industrial disputes will not be allowed.'[130] Few civil servants would have conceived of ever going on strike, but to be told that the right to strike was expressly denied them by their employer was a shock, especially since that same government had left the Whitley Councils in suspension, the only institutional forum for addressing grievances in the civil service. Nor had it been forgotten that the same politicians had applauded strikes by civil servants in support of Irish political prisoners in April 1920.

In the Dáil it was implied that the strikers were motivated by hostility to the government and sympathy for the irregulars and that they were out to subvert the government. It was also alleged that a clique of Dublin postmen, who used intimidation to enforce their will, drove the strike.[131] The army broke up the attempted pickets of the Dublin telephone exchange by firing volleys over their heads. Pickets in Dundalk were arrested by military patrols. Eventually the defeated postal workers returned to work, their return negotiated by Thomas Johnson of the ILPTUC. They accepted the government's offer to impose the cuts in phased reductions over three months, an offer that had been made before the strike but rejected.[132] As the strike leaders told the IPU conference, 'the power of the government was derived from the circumstances of the time, and because of civil war. The government did not care at any time if the whole place fell down about them.'[133] The other civil service organisations, which had accepted the cuts, remained aloof from the strike but the assertion that they had no right to strike made a deep impression and was often referred to as an example of the autocratic attitude of the government.

The near hysterical atmosphere in the Provisional Government, which treated any opposition as treason, can be sensed in the memoirs of the then secretary to the Department of Posts and Telegraphs, P.S. O'Hegarty.[134] O'Hegarty was in fact urging the government to break the unions completely by adopting an aggressively intransigent attitude. O'Hegarty, it ought to be noted, was just as aggressive as any trade unionist in preventing a reduction in his own salary as secretary to the Post Office.[135] It was only fear of a general strike, as the railway men began to threaten sympathetic action, that persuaded the government to resubmit the original offer.[136] The only member of the government who objected to Walsh's handling of the strike was Joe McGrath, an IRB man and director of Intelligence in the army, but even he toed the line.

The Irish Free State constitution and the civil service

The postal workers' September strike coincided with the first meeting of the Third Dáil, elected in June 1922 to debate and pass the constitution and so allow the Irish Free State come into official existence on 6 December, the anniversary of the Treaty.[137] The debate on the status of the transferred civil servants was brief and uncontroversial.[138] All of the 21,035 officials transferred had, under the Treaty, a right to compensation if they resigned as a consequence of the transfer of government or were dismissed. In fact, however, the majority of this apparently vast bureaucracy was the now thoroughly humiliated postal staff. The civil service proper, of administrative, executive, clerical and professional grades, were 6,403.[139] Article 77 of the constitution provided that 'every such existing officer who was transferred from the British Government by virtue of any transfer of services to the Provisional Government shall be entitled to the benefit of Article 10 of the Scheduled Treaty'. Article 10 of the Treaty stated that 'the government of the Irish Free State agrees to pay fair compensation on terms not less favourable than those accorded by the Act of 1920 to judges, officials, members of police forces and other public servants who are discharged by it or who retire in consequence of the change of government'. The inclusion of this assurance in the Treaty, in effect a constitutional guarantee of their status, seemed to assure a fair deal in future negotiations and was initially of great relief to the civil service.[140] The 1920 Act set out in considerable detail the compensation and pension entitlements of civil servants dismissed, permitted to retire, or who chose to retire. However, the Treaty Article 10 differed in significant ways from the guarantees contained in the 1920 Act. The IPCS immediately noted that though Article 10 offered guarantees to those civil servants who were dismissed or chose to retire, it offered no guarantees in terms of status or conditions to those who chose to remain in the service of the Irish Free State. The relationship between the State and the civil service in the new Irish Free State remained to be negotiated.[141]

It was also noted that under the 1920 Act the British government had the security of the Irish share of reserved taxes to ensure compensation was paid to any discharged or retired civil servant. If necessary the British government could make the payment and recover it by deduction from the reserved funds. Under the Treaty all payment would be made by the Irish Free State and if that government decided that, for whatever reason, the compensation was unreasonable or excessive and would not be paid, then there was nothing the British government could do about it. The retired civil servant would go penniless.[142]

Also, under the 1920 Act transferred 'Irish officers' were only those civil servants working in the transferred government departments. A great number of civil servants would have remained servants of the Crown and part of the British service though serving in Ireland. Under the Treaty all civil servants serving in Ireland were transferred, even those in the War Office who were busy evacuating the British military from Ireland![143] From the point of view of the staff of those departments reserved under the 1920 Act such as the Land Commission, Registry of Deeds or the Post Office, the Treaty offered them positive guarantees as to status and pension that they would forgo if they opted to serve in the north, where these departments remained reserved.[144]

The last days of Treasury (Ireland)

In contrast to Cope, who continued to enjoy a close relationship with Collins, and Anderson, who was a member of the British cabinet committee on Ireland, Waterfield found himself increasingly marginalised during the administration of the Provisional Government. It was only after Waterfield repeatedly pressed O'Brien for a decision that the Provisional Government decided to retain Treasury (Ireland) staff on loan for a further six months after the 1 April handover of responsibility. Waterfield was under some pressure from Whitehall to return, or at least to allow some of his principal officers to return. For his part he was anxious that the Provisional Government and the civil service should both feel that he had not allowed either to be badly treated. His main anxiety was the dual role he had to play as a representative of the imperial government running the few remaining all-Ireland departments and defending the interests of the Whitehall Treasury, while also advising the Provisional Government on Treasury matters. In fact, however, the Provisional Government never sought his advice and he was allowed a free hand to run down the British administration. Acting as O'Brien's subordinate Waterfield was primarily engaged in a 'sunset' department, tidying up the withdrawal of British government from Dublin Castle.[145]

The LGB was the department that continued to cause Waterfield most difficulty. Despite Waterfield pointing out that his department had done well on reorganisation, Robinson continued to demand more higher-grade posts for his department right up to 1 April. Waterfield was aware of the difficulty that though the Provisional Government had ambitious plans for local government, it had a department of its own. The combined staff, in his view, was too big and therefore the LGB, the only department for which he was responsible, had to be reduced.[146] Waterfield was acutely embarrassed to discover after 1 April, when the departmental records were handed over, that Robinson had been using the soldiers and sailors housing scheme in Killester in north Dublin as a sort of works scheme under his personal patronage with over-employment, high specification and slow completion. The financial allocation was almost all spent but the scheme remained unfinished. He had also run up enormous legal bills of over thirteen thousand pounds in two years with a single senior counsel, presumably a friend of his, in pursuit of mandamus claims by staff against local authorities.[147]

Waterfield was also deeply involved in arranging for the transfer of staff between Ireland and Britain.[148] The scheme that was agreed provided for a head for head transfer between the British and the Irish administrations of officers at the same class and grade, with the agreement of the heads of the departments concerned.[149] Each government agreed to accept full liability for the pensions of the officers that they received. What this meant was that transfers could in reality occur only where there were officers closely matched in terms of years of service, class and grade, and were thus actually very few.[150] Some heads of departments were not satisfied that the officer being transferred to Dublin was of the same calibre as the officer transferred to London and as a result refused permission. A further inhibition on transfers was the requirement that the officer transferring into Ireland sign an undertaking that he was not covered by Article 10 of the Treaty. When the scheme was finally wound up in July 1931, 271 civil servants had transferred into the Free State and 88 had transferred out. Of those transferred only 139 were on a head for head basis.[151] One task that Waterfield was happy to hand over to the Provisional Government was that of meeting delegations of the staff associations anxious as to their position. Waterfield refused to meet Michael Smithwick of the AEO, redirecting him to O'Brien.[152]

The main task that occupied Waterfield in the last days of Castle rule was the establishment of a committee to deal with those civil servants who would be discharged, or who would resign, as a consequence of the change of government.[153] The Civil Service Committee set up by the 1920 Act, which was seen by the Provisional Government and the civil service alike as a partition committee, had of course stopped functioning by order of the Provisional Government. But, under the 1920 Act, this same committee also had the task of determining the status and the compensation of discharged and retiring civil servants. The Provisional Government was not going to operate any committee established by the 1920 Act, which it regarded as superseded by the Treaty.

In the absence of the committee established by the legislation it was clear that some equally acceptable forum had to be established to deal with the task of retirements and compensation.

Section 7 of the order-in-council of 1 April dealt with the transfer of the civil service from British to Irish authority. It provided that 'Where an officer is transferred to the Provisional Government under this order, he shall hold office by a tenure corresponding to his previous tenure and if he is discharged by the Provisional Government, or if he retires in consequence of the change of government, he shall be entitled to receive compensation from the Provisional Government on terms no less favourable than provided by the 1920 Act.'[154] The order-in-council deliberately omitted any reference to a civil service committee, thus putting the onus on the Provisional Government to either use the 1920 committee or set up by its own authority a committee to fulfil the same functions.[155] The original committee had the widest discretion to determine the question of status and the terms of compensation free of either Treasury or political influence. Now, with that committee defunct, if any officer protested that the terms of compensation offered by the Provisional Government were less favourable than those offered in the 1920 Act it would be impossible to determine what the committee might have decided. As was to become apparent, Waterfield was far-sighted in his prediction that this question had endless possibilities for disputation between the awarding body and the staff. Waterfield had also been anxious since the publication of the terms of the Treaty about the phrase 'in consequence of the change of government'. This phrase was not in the 1920 Act and again was one that invited litigation.[156]

Waterfield decided to press ahead with the original committee accepting that the Provisional Government would not attend. It was therefore concerned only with the Northern Ireland civil service. The last meeting of the committee was held in London on 16 May 1922. MacMahon refused to attend and sent a note questioning the legality of the meeting.[157] Sam Sloan, who had transferred to Belfast, was regarded as the staff representative of the committee. The Irish civil service associations immediately revoked his appointment but Sloan had already decided to be unavoidably detained and arrived late to the meetings. With a quorum sufficient to do its business the committee was able to wrap up the allocation of the staff to Northern Ireland and tidy up that part of its remit.[158]

The only departments that continued to present difficulty were the reserved departments of the ILC and the Registry of Deeds where the staff, many of them highly skilled, refused to be transferred north, even those that had been working in the transferred Ulster counties. Though this may have been distaste at working under the Unionist government it was also prompted by the fact that in the Free State they had rights under Article 10, rights which disappeared if they transferred north where the ILC remained a reserved service. As none were 'rabid Ulstermen' Waterfield could only suggest that the Belfast government bribe them with promises of promotion.[159]

Once the question of the allocation of staff to the north had been dealt with, the Provisional Government committee working on the financial aspects of the Treaty put in a claim for compensation for the amount of pension liability in excess of that which would have fallen on the Free State if there had been 'a complete and equitable allocation of all-Ireland staff based on the separation of work as contemplated by the Government of Ireland Act'.[160] Though Waterfield took the view that that was entirely the fault of the Provisional Government, which had torpedoed the transfers north, it was recognised that the Dublin government had incurred a much heavier liability for pensions than had Belfast, where most staff were newly recruited.[161] The Irish and British sides were agreed that though the civil servants 'should not be left in the lurch' the Provisional Government should not be trapped by Article 10 for more than a just portion of the civil service.[162]

By November Waterfield was winding up eight centuries of Dublin Castle rule. A departmental circular and newspaper advertisement advised that 'the office of Treasury Remembrancer and Treasury Assistant Secretary in Ireland will be closed and the post abolished in consequence of the change of government, as from 1st November next'. The notices in the newspapers, at advertisement rates, were to prevent anybody 'making malicious political capital' from the notice.[163] Waterfield's last official act was to agree compensation for the destruction of O'Neill's Irish House in Tipperary by Crown forces.[164] The last word may be left to an anonymous colleague of Waterfield who contributed a piece to *Red Tape* on his experiences as a 'Temporary Irishman'. Despite the lurid accounts of irregular activity in the English newspapers the last months in Dublin were, he wrote, characterised by a 'delightful lack of formality and stiffness' along with 'a staggering degree of responsibility' though unfortunately without any extra pay for assuming it. The months spent working for the Provisional Government were ones he would 'always remember with fond nostalgia'.[165] One group that could not conceal their delight at the winding up of Treasury (Ireland) was the Public Accounts Committee of the House of Commons. Again and again they asked Sturgis and Waterfield to confirm that department after department of Dublin Castle had been transferred to the Free State and that the demands of the Irish government on the exchequer were indeed at an end.[166]

The Wylie committee

The Dáil civil service was purged by demands of loyalty to the Provisional Government. But the old Castle administration was also purged, not by the usual firing squads of revolutionary regimes, but through the operation of the Wylie committee on Article 10 of the Treaty. In order to deal with its obligations under Article 10 of the Treaty the Provisional Government established its own advisory committee on compensation for discharged and retired civil servants. Collins asked Justice Wylie to act as chairman of the committee, emphasising that it would be advisory only and also that its work would not include the allocation of staff north and south.[167] Chaired by Wylie, the committee had an official side of two senior officers nominated by the Department of Finance and a staff side of two representatives drawn from the CSF. Gregg and Hugh Kennedy proposed alternative terms of reference for the advisory committee, with Gregg laying down a more restricted brief. Despite the reputed dominance of the finance department it was Kennedy's terms that were adopted: 'to enquire into and advise as to the compensation and all matters consequent thereon which should be paid under Article 10 of the Treaty to any civil servant or other public servant or officer of the Irish government who may be discharged or may retire in consequence of the change of government'. Wylie was told that, though his committee was purely advisory, the government could offer a commitment that his advice would be accepted and followed in every case, so long as the compensation was not more generous than it would have been under the 1920 Act.[168]

Gregg and Gordon Campbell were both so worried at the government's failure to restrict the Wylie committee's latitude in rewarding compensation that they asked for specific instruction a week before the public announcement of the committee's establishment. The case of those civil servants that the government wished to dismiss was straightforward. They would be got rid of and Wylie would award them the pension they were due. It was the civil servants who chose to retire that worried them. Under the 1920 Act civil servants could opt to retire and be granted seven extra years on their pensionable service. The only restriction on such civil servants was that they could not exercise their right to retire for a period of six months. The heads of departments at their meeting on the committee had expressed the view that the government should not allow civil servants to retire on enhanced pensions if it could be avoided as the future liability was unknowable and the departments were in danger of losing a cohort of experienced officers. They argued that the words in Article 10 'in consequence of the change of government' imposed a new condition that was not in the 1920 Act and that an applicant for retirement should be made to explain what exactly there was in the change of government that justified him asking to go out on pension. The memorandum concluded that it ought to be made mandatory for the Wylie committee to actually establish, rather than simply accept, that the retirement 'is in consequence of the change of government'. If the applicant could not establish such, then they went out on ordinary terms and not the terms of the 1920 Act. But as this raised the question of an interpretation of an article of the Treaty the senior civil servants wanted a direction from the politicians.[169]

The Provisional Government was unwilling to grasp this particular nettle. Cosgrave circulated the memorandum among his colleagues, but only Walsh actually penned a response. It may have been that the ministers felt that Gregg and Campbell were exaggerating the danger, or that it was inspired by pique after rejection of Gregg's advice. It was also the case that the Provisional Government was fighting for its survival in the depths of civil war and after the death of Collins and Griffith. Walsh, predictably, supported the memorandum and urged that the Wylie committee should be instructed to make it as difficult as possible for civil servants to resign.[170] When Gregg brought this issue to the initial meeting of the Wylie committee the staff side strongly maintained that the Treaty carried forward unaltered the rights they had won in the 1920 Act and they would not allow any questioning of motives nor the implication that an applicant entertained 'traditional prejudice against a native government' which had to be then proved.[171] Wylie used his casting vote to engineer a compromise; he agreed that the phrase 'in consequence of the change of government' implied a new condition. He therefore proposed that the form of application for retirement would require that the applicant be asked 'On what basis is compensation claimed?' and 'If retirement, state is retirement in consequence of the change of Government?' What Wylie would not do was grill each individual applicant as if he were the defendant in a court of law. Gregg and Campbell asked that Cosgrave himself should meet with the heads of department and impress upon them the government's view as to the importance of the key phrase, instructing them to brief, in utter confidence, the official side to the Wylie committee on 'the merits of the individual applicants by reference to the new condition'.[172]

What exactly Gregg meant by individual merits is not clarified in the written memorandum. Based on Walsh's response and the original memorandum what seems to have been envisaged was that if the applicant was someone the department was happy to be rid of, then the application would not be contested. If it was an experienced officer that the department wanted to retain then, unless he was a rabid unionist, Protestant, and had always expressed extreme loyalist views, it would be contested. It was therefore up to the heads of the departments to supply the material for the official side on the committee to make a case that the application was not 'in consequence of the change of government' but due to some other cause, such as a desire to retire on pension with seven years of unearned increments and bonus added. Gregg, Campbell and the departmental heads were aware that the treatment of the postal workers and the hostility toward the civil service that the dispute had revealed had created a great deal of resentment within the service. There were already signs that civil servants were intent on a mass exodus on the generous terms available under Article 10, rather than suffer what was clearly going to be a hardening of conditions under the new government. The operation of the

Civil Service Committee (Compensation) was announced to the service by a Department of Finance circular and began operation on 12 October.[173] Smyth, Fitzgibbon and Smithwick of the CSF represented the staff side.[174] The civil service associations had their own concerns about the Wylie committee. Firstly, it would only deal with those civil servants who were leaving the service and thus would have nothing to say on those who remained and, secondly, it would be *advising* the Minister of Finance on compensation rather than making a firm determination. A minister is always free to reject advice.

Under the terms of the 1920 Act there were three categories of applicant to the Wylie committee: those discharged by the Irish government, those seeking permission to retire and those opting to retire under the statutory conditions provided by Act. The precise details of qualification and compensation were laid out in the eighth schedule to the Act. The initial intent of the Provisional Government was to use the Wylie committee to purge the administration of the more obnoxious of the Castle civil servants. There were some departments that the government simply cleared out. The Marlborough Street Teacher Training College was closed down and the entire staff of fifty-three discharged, from professors to charwomen.[175] The Catholic and Church of Ireland authorities had rejected Marlborough Street, as a non-denominational training college, and most of its graduates were from, and were employed in, the area of Northern Ireland.[176] The departments where the number of discharges was highest were the legal and judicial departments and the LGB. All thirty-six resident magistrates were also discharged, as were the petty session clerks and staff of the Supreme Court. In the LGB thirty of the senior staff were discharged, including Barlas who had led the negotiations that had won the eighth schedule. In other departments the government's intent was simply to get rid of the more awkward senior staff: two in the CDB, three in the DATI, and none at all in many other departments.[177] MacMahon, who had smoothed the waters for the transfer of authority, was given two weeks to clear out of the Under-Secretary's lodge in the Phoenix Park.[178]

But the government did intend that the Wylie committee would be simply a prelude to a thorough reorganisation of the civil service of the Irish Free State. This bloodless purge of the civil service was preparation for the installation of the new administration. Professor Henry Kennedy was asked to study recruitment in the civil service generally and to suggest a system of recruitment for the Irish public services. He studied the British, American and Commonwealth systems. He suggested a simplified organisation for a single local and central civil service and that recruitment and control of the civil service should lie with a single Public Service Commission. This was very much in the Sinn Féin tradition. This reasonable suggestion was rubbished by the Department of Finance civil servants who dismissed the report as uninformed, mistaken and even unconstitutional in its suggestions. The best system in the world, as they suggested and as Walsh agreed, was the British system where the Treasury reigned supreme on establishment matters. That this was a recent doctrine in Whitehall and one that was still contested was not admitted. Kennedy's report, holed below the waterline, sank without trace.[179]

As a purge of the senior ranks the Wylie committee was clean and effective and the civil service of the new State was comparatively free of the 'silverbacks' of the old administration, especially in the legal and local government departments. The Free State began with new men in new positions in most departments. But the quiet revolution in administration that was effected by the Wylie committee was not as contained and clean as the government had intended. What the government was not prepared for, though Gregg and Gordon Campbell had warned them, was the flood of applications for voluntary retirements from all ranks which soon overwhelmed the comparatively few cases of discharged officials. In the DATI there were 23 retirements, as compared with only 3 discharges. In the National Education Office, where there were no discharges, there were 13 retirements. In the OPW, where again there were no discharges, there were 15 retirements. In the vital revenue department there was only 1 discharge, but 21 retirements. The DMP had only 2 dismissals but had 578 resignations and the policing of Dublin seemed close to collapse. For many of the DMP it was not only the attraction of a pension but also a real distaste at serving under men responsible for the death of comrades. The postal services suffered 644 retirements but only 2 dismissals. It was the revenge of the postal workers on the government that smashed the strike.[180] Blythe was later to express regret that the government had not dismissed the postal workers, or allowed them to stay out on strike and so dismiss themselves.[181]

In every department the number of voluntarily retired civil servants far exceeded the number of discharged, running at the ratio of five to one.[182] What had been intended as a relatively swift and surgical purge of the senior figures was in danger of turning into an administrative rout. Wylie refused to summon applicants for cross-examination, as Gregg wanted; instead the committee simply agreed the correct calculation of benefits and recorded a decision with the applicant never actually having to attend, leaving it to the associations on the staff side to guard their interests. The civil service soon came to regard the eighth schedule of the 1920 Act, along with Article 10 of the Treaty, as their Magna Carta and even to sing the praises of their predecessors, men such as Barlas, who had won it for them.[183] If the government of the Irish Free State was not going to negotiate a new relationship binding the civil service and the State then the civil servants would rely on the contractual relationship and associated rights already won in the Treaty.

The loss of civil servants due to Article 10 retirements and discharges, especially from the upper ranks, opened up the civil service to vistas of opportunity and promotion that it had never seen before. There had been no examination for the executive and administrative classes since before the First World War so there was no cohort of candidates ready to fill the gaps. In April 1922 the Provisional Government invited heads of departments to make recommendations, and higher clerical and executive officers to offer themselves, for consideration by a promotional pool to fill the rapidly widening gaps in the departments. The board, made up of senior civil servants (rather than politicians as was happening in Northern Ireland at the same time), P.S. O'Hegarty, Pierce Kent and H.J. Smith, chose to interview all applicants rather than just those recommended by the departmental heads. Fifty-nine higher-grade officers were interviewed. Seven were identified as exceptional including Arthur Codling and E.P. McCarron. Fifteen were classed as very good and to be promoted; this group included some of those who rose to senior rank in the Department of Finance, which seemed to have first pick, such as J.T. Lennon, J.L. Lynd and T.S.C. Dagg. A further thirteen were classed as good and to be promoted as soon as the class above was exhausted. In the meantime they could be redeployed in more useful posts. Twenty-two were classed as adequately placed in the grade and department in which they were employed.

The board also interviewed 150 clerical officers and classified thirty-one as 'fit for promotion'; thirty-two as 'very promising'; thirteen as 'promising'; twenty-four as 'good' and fifty as 'to remain at present grade'. Included in those recommended for promotion were many of the leaders in the civil service associations such as Gallagher, Mortished (though in fact he took an Article 10 retirement), Smithwick and Mulvin. The interviews, necessarily short, valued evidence of initiative and energy. Knowledge of Irish was noted, but does not seem to have been as important as knowledge of book-keeping and accountancy.[184] A brief survey of the key staff in the Department of Finance in 1925, just three years after its establishment, illustrates the point: G.P. Fagan, thirty-one years of age, with eleven years of service, and J.L. Lynd, forty-one years of age, with sixteen years of service, had both progressed in three years from clerk class 1 to assistant principal; J.E. Hanna, thirty-six years of age, with seventeen years of service, progressed in three years from junior executive to assistant principal; T.S.C. Dagg, forty-nine years of age, with twenty-eight years of service, had progressed in three years from staff clerk to assistant principal; M.J. Beary, thirty-three years of age, after fourteen years of service, progressed in three years from higher executive to assistant principal. E. O'Neill, forty-eight years of age, with twenty-eight years of service, progressed from first class clerk to junior administrative officer. John Leydon, thirty years of age, after ten years of service, transferred from London and progressed from higher executive to assistant principal and then later went on to become departmental secretary.[185]

The civil service associations, doubtful of the idea of a board that decided promotions, were hesitant in their reactions. The CSF, recognising that a pool board was an improvement on former nepotistic practices, was prepared to allow it time and await judgement.[186] Of the associations the AEO was the one most uneasy at the pool board and also the one most open to a completely new civil service organisation based on the old Sinn Féin ideal of a single national service with a single grade and a simplified class structure to reflect ability and responsibility. The 'one-grade' service remained an ideal but as promotions were used to fill the gaps in the existing structure it was an ideal that looked less and less realisable.[187]

'Eight young men in the City Hall'

In most countries that have emerged into independence through a revolutionary struggle, the army of liberation has served as the main stabilising force. But in Ireland as the IRA split on the issue of the Treaty, the liberation army became in fact the main source of instability. As the Dáil, Sinn Féin and the IRA all split, some of the staff of the old Dáil departments, many of them also members of Sinn Féin and of the IRA, were seen as no longer reliable. The legitimacy of the Provisional Government was challenged and there were instances of insubordination and refusals to obey instructions. In contrast, whatever the private sentiments of individual civil servants, the entire Castle apparatus without exception accepted the legitimacy of the Provisional Government as the State authority. The Provisional Government became isolated from its roots in the Sinn Féin party and in the Dáil, and soon lost contact with any popular base. The Castle bureaucracy on the other hand had long learned to remain aloof from the political struggles in civil society and demonstrate its readiness to work with whatever authority it found. A besieged Provisional Government soon shared the barely concealed contempt with which many in the Irish civil service had long regarded the political classes.[188] It was these circumstances of civil war that enabled the Castle civil service to get a foot in the door of the independent State and establish itself as a stabilising force. However, the view that some senior civil servants later encouraged, that in the absence of political interference they quickly dominated their departments and were able to construct the State administrative machine without the politicians, is to be taken with a grain of salt.[189] To return to O'Higgins's cry about the eight young men in City Hall, not only were there the foundations of the old administration in ruins, the foundations of the new were still to be laid. The Castle civil service was viewed with suspicion. It was dispersed across the new departments and a close watch was maintained. The Treaty split then led to the Dáil civil service also coming under suspicion. The relationship between the new State and the civil service was therefore characterised by suspicion and fear.

The immediate task facing the fledgling State was waging war, the most State-defining activity of all. As the Provisional Government concentrated on the growing military threat of the anti-Treaty IRA its control of civil government weakened. Thoughts of building a completely new and national civil service were set aside. Collins, McGrath, O'Higgins, O'Hegarty and Lynch were transferred from civil government to the army and the Provisional Government seemed to exist only as a facade for the military. The survival of the new State depended on the army, not civil government. Gavan Duffy emphasised to Mulcahy the danger that lay in creating the impression that the 'men who matter have gone to Portobello leaving only a feeble residue in Merrion Street'.[190] In an echo of the fears expressed by Wylie, Cope and Anderson in 1920, there was a real danger that the military alone would become the expression of State authority in the Free State.[191] The Dáil civil service was further weakened by the formation of a Volunteer Reserve of the National Army from the civil service. A great many of the former Dáil civil servants enlisted, whether in the hope of bettering their status or simply to escape the tedium of administration.[192] With the death of Griffith and of Collins the Provisional Government lost its visionaries.

In October 1922 the anti-Treaty IRA, belatedly recognising the need to cloak their anti-Treaty war with a State form, nominated a government of the republic. De Valera issued a circular directed to all State employees asking that they sever their connection with the Provisional Government and recognise the government of the republicans.[193] The logical decision, which flowed from the formation of a republican government, was to target members of the 'illegal' Provisional Government that sanctioned the execution of republican 'irregulars'. The IRA murder of the TD Sean Hales on 7 December 1922 led in turn to the wholly unlawful executions of McKelvey, Barrett, Mellows and O'Connor at dawn on the following day. No challenge to the authority of the State was tolerated. Even the September postal strike against wage cuts was treated as subversion and ruthlessly crushed. This strike led the government to outline a view of an almost authoritarian relationship binding the State and the civil service that was far removed from the informality and casualness of the old regime.

The establishment of the new State was not an uninterrupted continuity with the old, as suggested by Joseph Brennan and accepted by later historians. Rather than being a smooth transfer of a functioning apparatus the Provisional Government operated in a country where the existence of any central government as a functioning reality could be questioned.[194] Kevin O'Higgins's picture of anarchy and smoking ruins got it right. The civil service that the Provisional Government took over remained in a state of organisational confusion. It is as well to remind ourselves that Waterfield's 'reorganisation' was in fact a regrading and entailed no more than assigning so many administrative, executive or clerical posts to each department and slotting the existing civil servants into these new grades. Although it was treated by Brennan, and by later historians, as having been delivered from a burning bush Waterfield's reorganisation was in fact purely imaginary in some departments and never existed in most.[195]

Waterfield had taken the model as agreed in Britain as a norm and attempted to apply it to the Irish departments, disregarding the very different function, structure and relative autonomy of the State in Ireland. Reorganisation did not begin with an analysis of the objective of each department followed by an assessment of its success or failure to achieve that objective. Assuming that Whitehall was best he stubbornly forced the Irish bureaucratic horse between the shafts of a London cart. In departments where there was an allocation of significant numbers of higher posts, individual clerical and executive officers could anticipate promotion, but the Irish administration as a whole retained what was regarded as its notorious low status, fragmentation and incoherence. This fragmentation was in fact simply the structures that had evolved through British government intervention in Irish society.[196]

The Provisional Government missed an opportunity to create completely new structures for the civil service of an independent Irish State. While many of the senior civil servants were fearful of the pace and revolutionary nature of the changes, the rank and file of the service enthusiastically anticipated the possibilities opening up before them. None of the civil service associations were enamoured of the Waterfield reorganisation, which was largely a paper reorganisation in any case, and all were prepared to negotiate something new. The only conditions they expressed were that change should be negotiated and that the civil service should be assured that they would suffer no worsening of conditions. Apart from that, anything was possible. The clerical and executive grades would have agreed to a much more streamlined and flattened civil service, the so-called 'one-grade' service. The professional civil servants were hopeful that the more senior administrative posts would be opened to their grade. Because of its quasi-colonial status Ireland had no administrative class to speak of. The leadership of the associations were nationalist to some degree, and some to a greater degree than others. They would have made great efforts to carry the membership with them in changes, even revolutionary changes. But the government, challenged by the republicans as to its legitimacy, responded with an aggressive display of effectiveness. The postal workers and the civil service generally were unfortunate in that they provided the opportunity for the government to show that it was in charge. The government deliberately used the postal strike in September to rally public opinion behind a government that was showing a determination to prevail over all opposition.[197]

Under the Provisional Government the failure to remember that it was a revolution that created the State meant also a failure to recognise the potential of the State to redirect Irish society. The Treaty that was meant to be a beginning, a stepping stone, became an end. This failure was not without resistance within the Cumann na nGaedheal party, where it was identified with the remnants of the old regime in the Department of Finance.[198] However, the positive aspect of this failure was that the State escaped the fate of many decolonised regimes where the bureaucracy becomes an instrument of the ruling party.[199] Hardly any of the revolutionaries inserted themselves into the civil service. It is very striking that the revolutionaries who remained in politics almost all chose the path of engagement in the uncertain world of electoral politics. Only two, P.S. O'Hegarty and Diarmuid O'Hegarty, chose what must have been the tempting option of a permanent career in the emerging bureaucracy.[200] The creation of a relatively incorruptible and professional civil service must rank as a major achievement of the Provisional Government and not the former British regime under whom Dublin Castle was a byword for nepotism. Despite the lingering doubts of the civil service associations about other matters, the independent State was well on the way to finally achieving what had been the rhetoric of civil service reform for over sixty years: meritocratic entry, promotion by ability and an apolitical culture of service to the State.[201]

However, the expectation of the Provisional Government that the civil service could be kept at a distance from the changes in the State were not only unrealistic but also counter-productive. The civil service was ready to embrace revolutionary changes with only the barest safeguards. Nationalists uncritically accepted the denigration of the pre-independence civil service, not reflecting that, among many achievements, it had successfully transferred the land to the tenants, democratised local government, set up a local health service through the dispensary system, transformed the western areas of greatest poverty and overseen the construction of one of the densest railway networks of Europe. The success of the local, centrally financed, autonomous boards, despite the problems of nepotism and cronyism in recruitment and promotion, was forgotten. The Irish administration had a great number of able and energetic civil servants who saw themselves as agents of State-driven social transformation. The opportunity passed and instead of building up a civil service suited to the needs of an independent Irish State – less hierarchical, decentralised, an agent of economic change, focused on development rather than administration – the government allowed a Whitehall to emerge with all the faults of the metropolitan original but of provincial dimensions.

The year 1922 was a deeply hazardous rite of passage for Irish democracy.[202] Much of the anarchy of the year of Provisional Government could be put down to the weakness of the State itself, a legacy of inherited neglect, failed reform and the Anglo-Irish war. For two years, at least, civil government had been overshadowed by military rule, either by republicans or by Crown forces. The ruthless and often illegal suppression of the anti-Treaty forces did ensure that the elected representatives and civil service of the new State could do their work and build the civil administration of the State in safety. Winning the civil war was the result not of a more coherent ideology but rather of a greater determination to use the conflict to consolidate control of the State. However, filled perhaps with an awful consciousness of the consequences of failure, the

Provisional Government in its determination to win became filled with a high-handed arrogance. The civil service was, initially, fired with a sense of mission and a determination to serve the new State fully and faithfully. Though there were instances of sympathy to the anti-Treaty irregulars the mood was one of enthusiasm, in which change would have been possible and perhaps even welcomed. The first issue of *Iris*, the journal of the Civil Service Federation, noted that at the time of the Treaty the civil service had been enthusiastic at the opening up of brighter prospects of an efficient service and had hoped that the camaraderie which had pervaded the Gaelic League in the old days would infuse the nation and its civil service once again. Most civil servants anticipated that national independence would mean a civil service in which patronage and nepotism would be a thing of the past, entrance would be by a 'ruthlessly just' competitive system and industry, integrity and intelligence in the service of the State would prove the only passports to promotion. However, one year later the mood was one of foreboding. National freedom meant an attack on workers, on trade unions and on the civil service.[203] The opportunity had passed. The Provisional Government squandered the goodwill of its civil service and as 1923 dawned and the Irish Free State came into office the attitude of the civil service was one of suspicion and defensiveness. For many civil servants the State was failing to embody the bright ideals and generous ambitions of the national struggle.

Notes

1 Fanning, *Department of Finance*, pp. 56–8; and again in Ronan Fanning, *Independent Ireland* (Dublin, 1983), p. 60.
2 Saorstát Éireann, R.54/3, *The Commission of Inquiry Into the Civil* Service, vol. 1, paras 8–12.
3 Fanning, *Department of Finance*, pp. 8–10.
4 Saorstát Eireann, Number 1 of 1922 *An Act to enact a Constitution for the Irish Free State (Saorstát Éireann) and for implementing the Treaty between Great Britain and Ireland signed at London on the 6th day of December, 1921*, second schedule.
5 Hopkinson, 'From Treaty to civil war, 1921–2' in Hill (ed.) *A New History of Ireland VII*, p. 12.
6 HLRO, Lloyd George Papers, F/10/2/42, 'Curtis to PM, 5 Feb. 1922'.
7 NAI, Department of the Taoiseach, S.21, 'Lloyd George to Arthur Griffith', 13 Dec. 1921.
8 NAI, Department of the Taoiseach, S.11, 'Anglo-Irish Treaty conferences', copy of 'Heads of working arrangements for implementing the Treaty'.
9 Mansergh, *The Unresolved Question*, p. 194.
10 Oxford, Bodleian Library, Lionel Curtis Papers, MS 89, fols 67–70.
11 NAI, Department of the Taoiseach, S.26.
12 *Dáil Éireann debates*, vol. 3, col. 32, 19 Dec. 1921.

13 Ibid.

14 Ibid., vol. 3, col. 136, 22 Dec. 1921.

15 Ibid., vol. 3, cols 179–80, 3 Jan. 1922.

16 Dorothy McArdle, *The Irish Republic* (Dublin, 1937, facsimile edition New York, 1999), pp. 959–61, 961.

17 *Dáil Éireann debates*, vol. 3, col. 349, 9 Jan. 1922.

18 Ibid., vol. 3, cols 352–3, 9 Jan. 1922.

19 Ibid., vol. 3, col. 363, 9 Jan. 1922.

20 Ibid., vol. 3, col. 367, 9 Jan. 1922.

21 Fanning, *Independent Ireland*, p. 9.

22 Michael Hopkinson, *Green Against Green: The Irish Civil War* (Dublin, 1988), p. 56.

23 12 Geo. 5, c. 4, An act to give force of law to certain Articles of Agreement for a Treaty between great Britain and Ireland, and to enable effect to be given thereto, and for the purposes incidental thereto or consequential thereto, 13 Mar. 1922.

24 Mansergh, *The Unresolved Question*, p. 194.

25 NAI, G1/1, minutes of the Provisional Government, 16 Jan. 1922; HLRO, Lloyd George Papers, F/20/2/1, telegram from Fitzalan, 16 Jan. 1922.

26 *Irish Times*, 17 Jan. 1922; Duggan, 'The Last Days of Dublin Castle'; Robinson, *Memories: Wise and Otherwise*, pp. 324–5.

27 Sturgis, *Last Days of Dublin Castle*, p. 227.

28 Fanning, *Department of Finance*, pp. 40–3.

29 NAI, Department of the Taoiseach, S.1, 'Transfer of services hitherto administered by the British government in Ireland', 16 Jan. 1922.

30 NAI, CSORP, 1921/3864/2, 'Provisional Government arrangements pending transfer of powers of existing departments'; NAI, G1/1, minutes of the Provisional Government, 16 Jan. 1922; NAI, Department of the Taoiseach, S.1, 16 Jan. 1922.

31 Fanning, *Department of Finance*, pp. 30–1.

32 NAI, Department of the Taoiseach, S.36, 'Civil service general position', 1922.

33 NAI, G1/1, minutes of the Provisional Government, 17 and 25 Jan. 1922.

34 NAI, Department of the Taoiseach, S.11, 'Conference with British government'; NAI, FIN1/17a, Feb.–Mar. 1922; NAI, G1/1, minutes of the Provisional Government, 25 Jan. 1922.

35 NA, T158/7, 'Waterfield to O'Brien, 23 Feb.', 'to Clark, 28 Feb.' 1922.

36 Ibid., 'Waterfield to O'Brien, 7 Mar. 1922'.

37 NAI, G1/1, minutes of the Provisional Government, 17 and 20 Jan. 1922.

38 NAI, FIN1/536, 'Administration of the Council of Ireland services'.

39 NAI, G1/1, minutes of the Provisional Government, 18 Feb. 1922.

40 NA, CAB 43/5, 'Conference 29 Mar. 1922 transfer of documents and officials'.

41 NA, T158/8, 'Waterfield to heads of departments, 9 Mar. 1922'.

42 NAI, Department of Finance, 'early E files', E20/2, 'Officials serving in Northern Ireland, Mar.–Apr. 1922'.

43 NAI, FIN1/223, 'Provisional Government, position of existing departments in relation to Northern Ireland'.

44 NAI, G1/1, minutes of the Provisional Government, 20 and 24 Mar. 1922.

45 Michael Collins, *The Path to Freedom* (Cork, 1968), p. 27.
46 Aodh De Blacam, *What Sinn Féin Stands For: the Irish republican movement Its history, aims and Ideals examined as to their significance to the world* (Dublin, 1921) pp. xvi, 132–48.
47 NLI, J.J. O'Connell Papers, MS 22,142, 'Memorandum on reform of civil service'.
48 Hopkinson, *Green Against Green*, p. 46.
49 NAI, Department of the Taoiseach, S.36, 'Memo on the Irish Public services as affected by the Treaty and the setting up of the Provisional Government', 28 Jan. 1922.
50 Ibid., 'Civil service general position', 1922.
51 NAI, DE4/11/40; UCDAD, Desmond Fitzgerald Papers, P80/899, 'Letter Conn Murphy, 25 Feb 1925'.
52 NAI, Department of the Taoiseach, S.36/22, 'Memorandum submitted by staff side, Irish civil service joint council acting as executive committee to the associations of civil servants in Ireland as set out hereunder', Jan. 1922.
53 Ibid., annex 3.
54 Ibid., Memorandum, p. 6.
55 Ibid., 'Murphy to O'Hegarty', 25, 26, 28 Jan. 1922.
56 See letter by Conn Murphy in UCDAD, Fitzgerald Papers, P80/899.
57 Customs and Excise Federation, minute book, 22 Mar., 25 May 1922.
58 IPCS, council minutes, 31 Mar. 1922.
59 NAI, DE4/10/1–69, 79–116; DE5/80; NAI, Department of Finance, 'early E files', E71/5–10. [These boxes are one example that is replicated in the papers of every department and member of the Provisional Government.]
60 NAI, G1/2, minutes of the Provisional Government, 20 July 1922; NLI, Brennan Papers, MS 26,205, notes on finance circular E.35, 18 Dec. 1922, reference civil servants canvassing politicians for preferment; UCDAD, Kennedy Papers, P4/617(1); /1563, 'Kennedy to Cosgrave, May 1924' for Cosgrave's response to Kennedy's recommendation for Thomas O'Connor 'who had done good work on behalf of the movement'. Cosgrave suggested that O'Connor enter by exam like everybody else.
61 NA, T158/8, 'Waterfield to secretary clerical officers union, 22 Mar. 1922'.
62 NAI, Department of the Taoiseach, S.490, 'PG payment of staff'; S.1249, 'Transfer of staff from DÉ to PG'.
63 NAI, Department of Finance, 'early E files', E/135, 'Secretariat staff at Merrion Street', 1 Apr. 1922.
64 Ibid., E1/8, 'CSO staff arrangements', 22 Apr. 1922.
65 Ibid., E50/11, 'Ministry of Finance staff at Merrion Street', Apr. 1922.
66 UCDAD, Kennedy Papers, P4/529(a), 'Drennan to Kennedy, 26 Oct. 1923'.
67 NAI, DE4/11/60, memorial assistant minister for local government, 17 Feb. 1922.
68 NAI, G1/2, minutes of the Provisional Government, 15 May 1922.
69 NAI, Department of Finance, 'early E files', E75/15–21, Apr. 1922.
70 NAI, Brennan Commission, BC/5, evidence of F.J. Gearty, 15 June 1934.
71 UCDAD, P24/26, Belfast Boycott committee staff.
72 NAI, DE1/4, minutes of Dáil Éireann cabinet, 11, 16, 24, 27 Jan., 3, 17, 24 Feb. 1922.

73 NAI, Department of Finance, E135/5, 'Refusals to carry out instructions'.
74 NAI, G1/2, minutes of the Provisional Government, 7 July 1922.
75 Ibid., 30 June 1922.
76 Ibid., 13 July 1922.
77 Ibid., 27 June 1922; NAI, DE5/96, 'Dáil Éireann departmental files and estimates', correspondence concerning ministers and civil servants, 1922–23.
78 NAI, G1/2, minutes of the Provisional Government, 26 July, 8 Aug. 1922.
79 NAI, Department of Finance, 'early E files', E 326/1, copy of finance circular E 365/5, 22 Aug. 1922.
80 NLI, Brennan Papers, MS 26,205, Ministry of Finance circular 354/5 file.
81 NAI, DE5/96, 'Provisional Government to McGrath, 25 July 1922'; NAI, Department of Finance, 'early E files', E40/1, 'Assimilation of Dáil staff Dept of Agriculture'.
82 UCDAD, Ernest Blythe Papers, P24/86, 'Murphy to Blythe, 7 Sept. 1922'.
83 NAI, Department of Finance, 'early E files', E131/20, 'Dr Conn Murphy retirement under article 10'.
84 NAI, CAB 1/2, 23 Dec. 1927; UCDAD, Fitzgerald Papers, P80/899.
85 Daly, *Buffer State*, pp. 95–105.
86 NAI, Department of Finance, 'early E files', E43/8, 'Amalgamation of the DELG and LGB staff', July- Sept. 1922.
87 On the DELG 'mutiny' see Daly, *Buffer State*, pp. 102–3; on the assimilation of the staff see the bulky and somewhat tattered 'early E file' E43/8, 'Amalgamation of DELG and LGB staff'.
88 Daly, *The First Department*, pp. 70–2.
89 NAI, Brennan Commission evidence, BC/3, 22 Feb. 1934.
90 All details from the RIA, Dictionary Irish Biography database.
91 UCDAD, Mulcahy Papers, P7/B/250.
92 NAI, Department of Finance, 'early E files', E50/32, 'Ministry of Finance staff on military service'.
93 Ibid., E40/1, 'Assimilation of Dáil staff Dept of Agriculture'.
94 Ibid., E137/10, 'Assimilation of Dáil staff Home Affairs'.
95 'The Association of Dáil Civil Servants and Dismissed British Civil Servants' emerged in later years and operated more as a pressure group formed to present evidence to the Brennan Commission.
96 NAI, Department of Finance, 'early E files', E43/8, exchange of letters between McCarron, Blythe and Gregg, Nov. 1922–Jan. 1923.
97 Ibid., E71/11, 'Employment of "Irish Republican Soldiers"'.
98 Ibid., E117/2, 'Cessation of payment from Dáil funds', 14 Dec. 1912.
99 UCDAD, Kennedy Papers, P4/221.
100 NAI, DE4/11/40; UCDAD, Fitzgerald Papers, P80/899, 'Letter Conn Murphy, 25 Feb. 1925'.
101 NA, 158/8, 'Waterfield to Ingrams, Ministry of Transport (Ireland), 29 Apr. 1922'.
102 NAI, G1/1, minutes of the Provisional Government, 20 Jan. 1922.
103 WUMRC, Customs and Excise Federation, executive committee minutes, 25 May 1922.

104 Ibid.

105 NA, T158/7, Waterfield to various departments, 13–18 Jan. 1922.

106 Ibid., 'Waterfield to McClintock; to Herbert, Forestry Commission; to Craig, Treasury Whitehall; to Harrison, Inland Revenue, 18 Jan. 1922'.

107 Ibid., 'Waterfield to Craig, Treasury Whitehall, 19 Jan. 1922'.

108 NAI, Department of the Taoiseach, S.36, 'Civil service general position 1922'; NA, T158/7, 'Waterfield to O'Brien Dublin Castle, 16 Feb. 1922'.

109 NA, T158/7, 'Waterfield to under-secretary Dublin Castle, 21 Jan.', 'to Clerical Officers Association, 26 Jan.', 'to Sir Percy Thompson, 8 Feb.', 'to O'Brien, Dublin Castle, 16 Feb.' 1922.

110 Ibid., 'Waterfield to Minnis 27 Jan.', 'to Leadbetter, Treasury Whitehall, 7 Feb.' 1922.

111 A.J.P. Taylor, *English History 1914–1945* (London, 1965, revised edition 1975), pp. 240–1.

112 NA, T158/7, 'Waterfield to the secretary Provisional Government, 17 Feb. 1922'.

113 Ibid., 'Waterfield to Fraser Treasury Whitehall, 17 Feb. 1922'.

114 Ibid., 'Waterfield to O'Brien, 23 Feb. 1922'; T158/8, 'Waterfield to secretary, Ministry of Finance, 30 Mar. 1922'.

115 Ibid., 'Waterfield to Anderson, 7 Mar. 1922'.

116 NAI, Department of Finance, 'early E Files' E1/8, 'Cope to Gregg', 20 Apr. 1922.

117 Ibid., E94/20, 'Reorganisation of the accountants' office PO', AEO letter June 1922.

118 NAI, G1/1, minutes of the Provisional Government, 1 Feb. 1922.

119 NAI, CSORP, 2638/21, 'Reorganisation of the civil service'.

120 *Red Tape*, 11:126–130 (Mar.–July 1922); *Civilian*, 101 (16 Sept.–15 Nov. 1922).

121 NAI, G1/1, minutes of the Provisional Government, 27 Feb. 1922; *Dáil Éireann debates*, vol. 1, cols 142–3, 1 Mar. 1922.

122 NAI, G1/1, minutes of the Provisional Government, 22 Mar. 1922; James G. Douglas, *Memoirs of Senator James G. Douglas (1887–1954) concerned citizen*, ed. J. Anthony Gaughan (Dublin, 1998), p. 87.

123 NAI, Department of Finance, 'early E files', E82/18, '"Douglas Commission", Finance to PMG, 26 Mar. 1923'.

124 NAI, G1/1, minutes of the Provisional Government, 1, 27 Feb.; 3, 6 and 22 Mar. 1922.

125 Gallagher, 'Memoirs of a civil servant', pp. 78–82.

126 NLI, Brennan Papers, MS 26,209.

127 NAI, Department of Finance, 'early E files', E94/20, 'AEO correspondence, reorganisation accts dept PO', June 1922.

128 NLI, Brennan Papers, MS 26,205.

129 NAI, Department of Finance, 'early E files', E94/38, 'Strike of postal employees', Sept. 1922.

130 NAI, G1/3, minutes of the Provisional Government, 4–28 Sept. 1922; *Dáil Éireann debates*, vol. 1, cols 108–30, 11 Sept. 1922.

131 *Dáil Éireann debates*, vol. 1, cols 42–50, 9 Sept., cols 230–54, 13 Sept., cols 294–317, 14 Sept. 1922.

132 NAI, Department of Finance, 'early E files', E94/38, 'Strike of postal employees', Sept. 1922.

133 *An Díon*, 1:1 (June 1923).
134 P.S. O'Hegarty, *The Victory of Sinn Féin* (Dublin, 1924, reprint edition 1998), pp. 128–9. Had any other serving civil servant criticised government policies in a publication, or referred to members of the government with such contempt, he would have been instantly dismissed.
135 NAI, Department of Finance, 'early E files', E14/, 'salary of secretary PO, 7 Mar. 1922'.
136 Ibid., E94/38, 'Strike by postal employees', P.S.O'H memorandum, 11 May 1922.
137 Oxford, Bodleian Library, Curtis Papers, MS 90, fols 64–74.
138 *Dáil Éireann debates* vol. 1, cols 1448–51, 11 Oct. 1922.
139 UCDAD, Kennedy Papers, P4/735(2), 'Return of staff in government departments'.
140 Gallagher, 'Memoirs of a civil servant', p. 62.
141 IPCS, executive council minutes, 18 Jan., 2 Feb. 1922.
142 NA, T158/6, 'Transfer of staff consequent to Treaty', 10 Jan. 1922.
143 Ibid., T158/7, 'Waterfield to Fleming, War Office, 23 Jan. 1922'.
144 Ibid., T158/9, 'Waterfield to Niemeyer, 16 Oct. 1922'.
145 Ibid., T158/7, 'Waterfield to Rae, 6 and 25 Mar.', 'to O'Brien, 11 Mar.' 1922.
146 Ibid., T158/8, 'Waterfield to O'Brien, 18 Mar.'; 'to Robinson, 31 Mar.' 1922.
147 Ibid., 'Waterfield to Anderson, 4 Apr. 1922'.
148 *Civilian*, 101:2759 (7 Oct. 1922).
149 NAI, Department of Finance, E116/1/33, 'Transfers of staff between GB and IFS'.
150 NA, T158/8, 'Waterfield to Anderson, 29 Apr.', 'to Viscount Cross, 11 May', 'to heads of departments, 2 Sept.' 1922.
151 NAI, Department of Finance, E116/1/33, 'Finance circular 19/31, returns on transfers Tables ii and iv'.
152 NA, T158/9, 'Waterfield to Smithwick, 23 June 1922'.
153 Ibid., 'Waterfield to Whiskard, 30 Sept. 1922'.
154 UCDAD, Kennedy Papers, P4/197 (52).
155 NA, T158/8, 'Waterfield to Anderson, 6 Apr. 1922'.
156 Ibid., 'Waterfield to secretary, Ministry of Finance, 27 Apr.'; 'to Gregg, 24 May' 1922.
157 PRONI, Ernest Clark Papers, D1022/2/18, civil service committee meeting minutes, addendum to meeting of 17 Jan. 1922.
158 Ibid.; NA, T158/9, Waterfield to Clark, 6 May and 12 June'; 'to Rae, 9 May', 'to Gregg, 26 June' 1922.
159 Ibid., 'Memorandum on transfer of reserved services', Oct. 1922.
160 Ibid., 'Waterfield to Fraser, Treasury Whitehall, 26 Sept. 1922'.
161 Ibid.
162 UCDAD, Kennedy Papers, P4/204(1), copy of minutes of technical sub-committee of the cabinet committee on Irish affairs, 9 Nov. 1922; NLI, Brennan Papers, MS 26,203(2), 'Cabinet committee on Irish affairs 18th meeting', 9 Nov. 1922.
163 NA, T192/85, 'Winding up of Treasury Remembrancer', 26 Oct. 1922.
164 Ibid., T158/9, 'Circular to secretary Ministry of Finance, O'Neill's Irish House Compensation', 31 Oct. 1922.

165 *Red Tape*, 12:142 (July 1923).

166 *Public Accounts Committee* para. 3477–3502, Parliamentary Papers 1923, IV.

167 NA, Wylie Papers, PRO 30/89/3, Collins to Wylie, 6 June 1922.

168 UCDAD, Kennedy Papers, P4/221; NAI, G1/3, minutes of the Provisional Government, 5, 23 and 28 Sept. 1922; NAI, Department of Finance, 'early E files', [S.1716] 'Wylie committee on civil service retirement under article X'; *Dáil Éireann debates*, vol. 1, cols 1027–8, 3 Oct. 1922.

169 NAI, Department of Finance, 'early E files', [S.1716] 'Wylie committee on article X', Gregg and Gordon Campbell memorandum to Minister of Finance, 6 Oct. 1922.

170 Ibid., 'Walsh to Cosgrave', 27 Nov. 1922.

171 *Iris Seirbhise An Stáit (The Civil Service Journal) Official Organ of the Civil Service Federation (Iris)*, 1:1 (Jan. 1923), p. 4.

172 NAI, Department of Finance, 'early E files', [S.1716] 'Wylie committee on article X', Gregg and Campbell to Minister of Finance, 11 Oct. 1922, form of application for compensation under Article 10 of the treaty; *Iris*, 1:1 (Jan. 1923).

173 NAI, Department of Finance, 'early E files', [S.1716] 'Wylie committee on article X, Ministry of Finance to heads of departments', 12 Oct. 1922.

174 *Iris*, 1:1 (Jan. 1923).

175 NAI, Department of Finance, 'early E files', register of the civil service committee (compensation). [This register is in a box marked 'Finance early files/misc.' in the 'early E files' boxes. Entries are colour-coded, red ink is for discharged and black ink is for retired.]

176 E. Brian Titley, *Church, State and the Control of Schooling in Ireland 1900–1944* (Dublin, 1983), p. 101.

177 The individual files for each applicant are in the 'early E files', E83/432–1052 [DMP and LGB]; E131/1–289 [Prison services, legal and judicial services]; E186/9 [RMs]. These are the files relating to each individual appeal to the Wylie committee on compensation and cover all government departments.

178 NAI, Department of Finance, 'early E files', E131/262, 'Article 10 compensation, Rt. Hon. James MacMahon'.

179 Ibid., E18/1, 'Recruitment for the public service, report', Jan. 1923.

180 Ibid., register of the civil service committee (compensation).

181 *Dáil Éireann debates*, vol. 5, cols 878–80, 15 Nov. 1923.

182 NAI, Department of Finance, 'early E files', register of the civil service committee (compensation).

183 *Iris*, 1:1 (Jan. 1923), p. 3.

184 NAI, Department of Finance, 'early E files', E75/15, 'Pool selection board (Executive) report and correspondence'; E75/27, 'Pool selection board (clerical) report and correspondence'.

185 NLI, Brennan Papers, MS 26,013, 'Finance internal memo', Dec. 1924.

186 *Iris*, 1:1 (Jan. 1923).

187 *Iris*, 1:3 (Mar. 1923), AEO [cumann feidhmanach seirbhis an stait] notes.

188 John M. Regan, *The Irish Counter-Revolution 1921–1936* (Dublin, 1999), pp. 96–100.

189 McElligott, quoted in Fanning, *Department of Finance*, pp. 98–9.

190 UCDAD, Mulcahy Papers, P7/B/100.

191 Hopkinson, *Green Against Green*, pp. 140–2.

192 NAI, Department of Finance, 'early E files', E50/32, 'Staff on military service'.

193 UCDAD, Dr James Ryan Papers, P88/82, circular of 22 Nov. 1922.

194 Hopkinson, *Green Against Green*, p. 89.

195 For an interesting early statement of this view see the evidence of P.S. O'Hegarty to the Brennan Commission, 11 Oct. 1932, NAI, BC/4.

196 See NA T158/9, 'Gilbert to secretary Ministry of Finance', May 1922, for a long detailed list of the anomalies that had arisen in Waterfield's attempts to maintain the same lines in Ireland as in England as regards reorganisation.

197 UCAD, Blythe Papers, P24/68.

198 Maryann Gialanella Valiulis, 'After the revolution: the formative years of Cumann na nGaedheal' in Audrey S. Eyler and Robert F. Garratt (eds) *The Uses of the Past: Essays on Irish Culture* (Dublin, 1988), pp. 131–43.

199 John M. Regan, 'The politics of Utopia: party organisation, executive autonomy and the new administration' in Mike Cronin and John M. Regan (eds) *Ireland: The Politics of Independence, 1922–49* (London, 2000), pp. 32–66.

200 UCDAD, Blythe Papers, P24/376(3).

201 Eunan O'Halpin, 'Politics and the State, 1922–32' in Hill (ed.) *A New History of Ireland VII*, pp. 86–127, 110.

202 Tom Garvin, *1922: The Birth of Irish Democracy* (Dublin,1996).

203 *Iris*, 1:1 (Jan. 1923).

5

Cumann na nGaedheal and the civil service, 1923–32

Introduction

L ATE IN 1922 THE Provisional Government and pro-Treaty members of Sinn Féin regrouped in a new political party, Cumann na nGaedheal [Society of the Gael].[1] On 6 December 1922, one year after the Treaty was signed, the Provisional Government came to an end and the first Executive Council of the Irish Free State was approved by Dáil Éireann. In August 1923 the 'Constituent' third Dáil dissolved and the general election returned the Cumann na nGaedheal party to government, led by W.T. Cosgrave. Although the immediate threat from the anti-Treaty forces was defeated the Cumann na nGaedheal governments remained deeply influenced by the crisis of legitimation that continued to surround the State in Ireland. They were in fact all minority administrations empowered by the abstention of republican TDs.[2] The opposition was composed of small groups made up of the Labour Party, Farmers' Party, Businessmen's Party (mainly ex-Unionists) and other individuals. Most of the opposition, apart from the Labour Party, were to the right of Cumann na nGaedheal. These were also governments that were too fond of Public Safety Acts which curtailed civil liberties, an unwelcome continuance of the British tradition of ruling Ireland by coercion. Republicanism, crushed as an armed force, survived in the remnants of the anti-Treaty Sinn Féin and IRA. When it later reorganised as the political party Fianna Fáil [Soldiers of Destiny] under the leadership of Éamon de Valera republicanism proved both popular and resilient, despite denying the legitimacy of the Irish Free State.

Reinstating dismissed civil servants

The fourth Dáil, which continued until June 1927, laid down the foundations for the relationship between the Irish Free State and the civil service free of any constraints. The government could, if they wished, give whatever shape it liked to the civil service. Also, for the first time, the Department of Finance was no longer shared with any other office and the minister Ernest Blythe was free to concentrate on finance affairs exclusively. The government was more concerned initially with regularising the few civil servants that had been carried over from the Dáil administration than with the civil service inherited from the Castle administration. In July 1923, in the last days of the third Dáil, a superannuation and pensions bill to grant them civil service pensions was enacted.[3] The government also responded to pressure to reinstate those civil servants that had been dismissed by the British government because of nationalist sympathies or activities in the period from the 1916 Rising to the Truce. These civil servants were well organised in the Association of Victimised Civil Servants in Ireland and vocal in their demand for reinstatement and compensation for lost income.[4] Following a cabinet decision that these men and women were entitled to re-employment, if the dismissal was indeed for nationalist activities, a committee of senior civil servants chaired by P.S. O'Hegarty reinstated about 200 of the 400 original claimants. Pension entitlements were restored as if there had been no break in service but without compensation for loss of earnings.[5] The actual number of reinstated civil servants is an elusive figure due to the rapid political changes. For instance, Seán O'Ceallacháin was dismissed after participating in the 1916 Rising. He was reinstated in 1922, but was then dismissed again in 1923 for anti-Treaty activity. He was then once again reinstated in 1928, but on a lower clerical officer scale as a form of discipline. With the return of the Fianna Fáil government in 1932 he was promoted to the grade that he would ordinarily have reached after his years of service.[6] The Cumann na nGaedheal government reinstated in total 129 civil servants who had lost their post due to disloyalty to the British regime.[7] A further issue relating to the civil service, which came up at most, if not all, cabinet meetings, was that of identifying sympathisers of the republican irregulars and dismissing them if already appointed or excluding them from civil service examinations.

Legislating for the civil service of the Irish Free State

The Civil Service (Regulation) Act, 1924 and the Ministers and Secretaries Act, 1924 offer an insight into how the Cumann na nGaedheal government intended to build new State organisations and how the new State would relate to its civil service. Under the British regime the various boards and commissions in Dublin Castle enjoyed considerable autonomy, worked to a budget and recruited and paid their own staff. The Irish government's Civil Service (Regulation) Act of 1924 swept aside all of these boards and brought their staffs into a single civil service under the control of the Minister of Finance. Yet, surprisingly, the bill was also described as continuing 'the system with which we are familiar'.[8] Rupture was denied and continuity of the State was now portrayed as a virtue by the former revolutionaries. The Provisional Government and the first Executive Council of the Free State had recruited many temporary civil servants to handle the volume of work associated with the changeover from the British administration and to process the many claims for compensation for war damage and Land Act transfers, but no permanent civil servants had been recruited. The Civil Service (Regulation) Act of 1924 established the Civil Service Commission to recruit future civil servants by open competitive examinations. The Act also empowered the Minister of Finance to make, change or revoke regulations for establishing the classification, remuneration, conditions and terms of service of the civil servants. Thus while the Civil Service Commission controlled recruitment the minister would remain solely responsible for management of the civil service. In line with the general expectation for a minimal State apparatus Blythe expected that the commission would have very little work to do and the commissioners would be very much part-time positions.[9] The first commissioners were the Ceann Comhairle [chairman] of the Dáil and the secretaries of finance and of education, the two departments most directly involved. Civil servants were aghast at the appointment of the Ceann Comhairle to chair the commission as his was a political position.[10]

The opposition, while approving of the commission, proposed that it ought to report to the Dáil rather than to the Minister for Finance and that control of the civil service ought to lie ultimately with the Dáil as the legislative assembly rather than with the executive. The intent was to make the management of the civil service of the new State subject to a detailed code enshrined in legislation rather than to ministerial prerogative. Although this was rejected as unpractical it does underline the extent to which the question of recruitment and control of the civil service was still under debate.[11] During the debate Blythe expressed an 'ultra-montane' view of the relationship between the State and the civil service, essentially denying any contract. It was his view that the executive could brook no interference in dealing with civil service organisations. The debate was actually threatening to become an interesting and sophisticated analysis of executive and democratic control of the State apparatus in which the hopeless position of the civil service under minister Blythe began to win sympathetic consideration. Blythe relented in so far as he agreed to lay any regulations on the table of the House for scrutiny by TDs.[12] Johnson, the Labour leader, unfortunately rather late in the day, hit the nail on the head when he pointed out that Blythe wanted to import into his ministry the customary authority of the Crown over the civil service in Great Britain. However, unlike in Britain, where civil servants were entirely 'at the pleasure of the Crown', the Irish civil servants had secured certain statutory rights and not merely personal rights. Their conditions were not variable at the whim of the minister.[13] The Executive Council strongly supported Blythe's resistance to attempts by the Dáil or Senate to interfere in his control of the civil service.[14]

In 1925 the Senate rejected an amendment to the regulations that proposed to allow the Civil Service Commission to restrict admission to certain examinations to men only. This was one of the few legislative acts subject to the suspensory power of the Senate, preventing its enactment for 270 days.[15] This had arisen out of attempts by Blythe to restrict candidates for the first recruitment of the administrative class, out of which future departmental heads would arise, to men only.[16] Blythe made it obvious that he disliked having women in the civil service and used his power to direct that female civil servants were to retire on marriage. The first examinations for the clerical class were confined to men with army service. The standard was deliberately kept low to accommodate men who had been a great many years out of school. Nevertheless the failure rate was high: 571 from a field of 1,244.[17] Thus, at a time when the demobilisation of the army was causing great difficulties leading to the so-called 'army mutiny', the civil service was to provide a useful avenue to siphon off discontent, while retaining competitive entry.[18] In the pursuit of economy Blythe also used his powers to cut the salary scales for new entrants to the service.

The Ministers and Secretaries Act centralised the departments of government in an executive of twelve ministers. The ministries were conceived as essentially administrative or executive. The governing Executive Council was made up of the executive ministers only.[19] Cosgrave described the bill as second only to the constitution in importance in laying down the foundations of the State.[20] He also saw the bill as rationalising the inheritance of two former governments – one that was young and inexperienced but enjoyed popular support and the other unpopular and disorganised but handed over with certain Treaty rights.[21] The broad principle of the bill was to take the multiplicity of boards and commissions of the inherited administration, and reorganise them into a few ministries under ministers described as 'corporation sole'; in other words the minister *was* the department and all acts of the civil servants of that department were done as if directly ordered by the minister. For many civil servants this represented a loss of the personal autonomy that marked the more casual and decentralised Castle administration.[22] The key department was that of finance, which took charge of the administration and business of public finances and to which was assigned the Civil Service Commission. Although each department continued to appoint its own civil servants each appointment required the express permission of the Minister of Finance. The former departmental autonomy of the old British regime had truly passed beyond recall.[23]

The Dáil debate on the key section of the bill referring to the role of parliamentary secretaries reveals the lingering suspicion within the Executive Council about the reliability of the inherited civil service and doubts about its willingness to embrace the revolution that had swept over it.[24] Taunted by the contradictions between his calls for national economy and his plans for an extra layer of paid 'assistant ministers', Blythe was quite frank in expressing his doubts about the willingness of the civil service, 'which was not created as a Civil Service for an Irish State', to accept ministerial control.[25] Within the Cumann na nGaedheal party Milroy voiced a general suspicion about the 'rump of officialdom of the old regime' which was still in power in the civil service.[26] In what was becoming a predictable contribution to any debate on the civil service the Farmers' Party used the bill to demand cuts in civil service pay.[27] It is also clear that it was generally accepted that the State would seek to reduce its presence in Irish society and that, after the initial pressure of reconstructing the State was complete, the Oireachtas [Irish Parliament] would have little to do and might meet at most for three or four weeks in two or three sessions a year.[28] The only relief offered to the civil servants was by the eccentric Darrell Figgis who suggested that the State required fewer politicians and more civil servants.[29]

One further piece of legislation of 1925 illustrates the developing attitude of the Cumann na nGaedheal government to the civil service. The Treasonable and Seditious Offences Bill included a paragraph decreeing that 'every person who incites any person in the civil service (other than a police force) of the Government of Saorstát Éireann to refuse, neglect, or omit to perform his duty or to commit any other act in dereliction of his duty, shall be guilty of felony.'[30] The constitution guaranteed the right to join unions and organise. The postal workers' and clerical officers' trade unions were both affiliated to the ITUC and to the Labour Party. But the 1925 Treasonable Offences Act, the 1927 Trade Union Act and the Department of Finance circular 14/1927 'Civil service (approved associations) regulations' were designed to suppress any public display of civil service discontent, including withholding labour, which would almost certainly lead to dismissal.[31] Denying the right to organise a strike was simply the logical extension of the denial of the right to strike. It was only by overcoming its deference and inherent conservatism that the civil service could make full use of its labour affiliation.[32]

H.P. Boland, head of the establishment division in the Department of Finance, transferred from Whitehall in September 1924. Boland came from the same mould as Waterfield. Within the Whitehall tradition senior civil servants' status was measured by their closeness to the minister. In his meetings with the civil service representatives, and in his advice to his minister, Boland treated the idea of personal meetings between them as a personal affront. Neither did he bother to conceal his contempt for the lower grades of the civil service.[33] Hostile to the 'one-grade' idealism of the lower grades, Boland was devoted to hierarchy. Some years later, during the currency commission hearings, Boland in one of his many personal letters to Brennan wrote of another reason why finance control of the civil service was so important. Boland warned Brennan that this reason was one that could not be quoted as it might 'do us more harm than good'. He wrote, 'the position that our department occupies in the mind of the service generally and the respect they show for our minister's authority must obviously be very largely affected by the feeling that ours is the minister and the department who in so large a sense can control and determine the fortunes of individual civil servants. I need not enlarge on this point.'[34] For Boland, and for Brennan, finance dominance was more a matter of power and prestige than one of efficiency. That is why Boland insisted that civil service organisations could not have non-service general secretaries to represent them on the representative council; 'such outsiders would be at liberty to express opinions and adopt an attitude not open to a civil servant'.[35] Boland, along with McElligott, had a very high estimate of Whitehall procedures in dealing with the civil service. They both assiduously sought and retained copies of British Treasury organisational forms and booklets. Years later, their successors in finance Twamley and Feeney, when they stumbled on this horde of documentation, were mystified as to where they had come from and, sceptical as to their usefulness, ordered they be dumped.[36]

Dáil debates reveal a depth of unthinking hostility to the civil service which never abated and which all parties indulged in to a greater or lesser degree.[37] Even the Labour Party joined in on occasion. William Davin TD and Richard Corish TD, in the July 1924 debate on the estimates, attacked the civil service as an unreformed and domineering 'Castle' apparatus that needed to be 'cleared out bag and baggage'. In the same debate the government TD Grattan Esmonde suggested replacing 'the old regime' of inherited civil servants in finance with a panel of experts. [38] Even from within the Executive Council support for the civil service was conditional and qualified.[39] Assailing civil servants fast became a regular ritual of the Dáil debates and the failings of the civil service a cliché of political discourse in independent Ireland.

The underlying assumption of these pronouncements was that the civil service of the Irish Free State ought to be a minimalist one and certainly would be smaller than that handed over by the Treaty. However, the tradition of a large section of the civil service in Ireland was 'maximalist'. Under the British regime, outside the confines of the Castle departments, there had developed a large and decentralised corps of non-political experts whose objective was the transformation of Irish society and economy through government action. In the last decades of the British regime many civil servants were recruited to run the autonomous institutions being developed as a solution to the problems of Irish society, especially its chronic poverty and under-development. Inheriting pre-independence nationalist suspicion of the Castle apparatus as an alien intrusion, government policy was to reshape the civil service into a smaller, centralised administrative rather than executive bureaucracy. The civil service of the newly independent State was viewed as an essentially administrative machine that dealt with simple repetitive tasks rather than as a source of expertise and advice. The resentment of the political classes toward the civil service was a revival of the pre-independence attitude of nationalist opinion to the Castle regime. In that, the Cumann na nGaedheal party was the inheritor of Redmond and the Irish Parliamentary Party rather than Griffith and Sinn Féin.

Civil service trade union reorganisation

In response to the establishment of the Irish Free State the civil service was experiencing a drive to organise in every grade and section, ready to meet the new State in negotiation. In February 1923 a conference of Irish civil service organisations formally recognised the Irish Civil Service Federation (CSF), which had been formed early in 1922, to act as a single voice in negotiation with the government. The Federation was an alliance of various staff federations that grew out of the ad hoc 'Executive Committee of the Conference of All Associations of Irish Civil Servants' that had met with Collins. Thus the Federation in its structures sought to act as an umbrella organisation for the many autonomous and diverse civil service organisations.[40] The IPCS and the Post Office Workers' Union (POWU) remained outside the Federation.[41] The CSF was therefore dominated by the ordinary rank-and-file civil servants of the clerical grades, most of them nationalist and many of them Gaelic League members. It was expected that the Federation would be successful in establishing a new basis for civil service and State relations based on a shared commitment to making an 'Irish-Ireland' of the newly independent nation. At its height the Federation organised sixteen associations representing just over 1,500 civil servants.[42] This poor level of saturation in a potential membership of approximately 6,000 requires explanation. The low level of support reflects the loss of leadership due to retirements and promotions, the reorganisation of the government departments which were the organisational base, the concentration on the rights of retiring officials, but especially the failure to achieve a replacement for the powerful Whitley Councils.

The pre-war leadership of the Irish civil service associations continued into the time of the Provisional Government but was then reduced by retirements and by promotions.[43] Despite their trade unionism the calibre of these civil servants was recognised and awarded. Michael Smithwick, secretary to the executive grade association, was promoted and transferred to act as secretary to the Dáil Éireann Courts (Winding Up) Commission, from which he was transferred to the Revenue Commissioners. Thomas A. Murphy was promoted first as secretary to the Douglas Commission on the postal service, then to the secretaryship of the Civil Service Commission (despite the protests of Gregg at favour being shown to a 'prominent trade unionist'[44]). W.F. Nally became a principal officer in the Department of Finance. Mortished served on the constitution committee and then took Article 10 retirement and began a successful career in labour organisation outside of the civil service.[45] Sam Sloan went to Belfast and Michael Gallagher was promoted to the executive grade.[46] The only pre-independence leader of the associations not to enjoy success was Conn Murphy. However, the associations had sufficiently deep roots to generate a new cadre of leadership with relatively little difficulty. The experiences of the First World War and independence struggle also encouraged a more aggressive and less deferential style of leadership. This was in fact a general European phenomenon as white-collar trade unions and professional associations of the middle classes gave the lead in post-war industrial unrest.

In the absence of formal negotiation machinery the civil service associations began to develop contacts in the Oireachtas and to revive the practice of political lobbying. For lobbying purposes the IPCS generally favoured former Unionists. However, although the IPCS may have been instinctively Unionist it was also a strong supporter of trade union principles of solidarity. Thus in the Dáil by-election in Dublin South in February 1926 the IPCS placed advertisements in the daily papers urging support for William Norton the successful Labour Party candidate and leader of the POWU.[47] Norton then proved a staunch defender of the civil service in the Dáil chamber. The CSF in its journal *Iris Seirbhise An Stáit*[Journal of the State Service], maintained a close watch on political changes and was not afraid to publicise its grievances.[48] In Dáil debates Major Bryan Cooper (ex-Unionist), Thomas Johnson (Labour) and T.J. O'Connell (Labour) often reflected the Federation viewpoint. O'Connell was the invited guest speaker at the annual general meeting of the CSCA in May 1925.[49] With the election of Norton as a Labour TD the POWU had a powerful voice in the Dáil.

Following the split in the Sinn Féin movement, and facing a hostile government in Cumann na nGaedheal, the civil service associations came to identify with and support the Irish Labour Party. The clerical officers had been members of the ILPTUC since 1920 and their first full-time general-secretary, Archie Heron, was a son-in-law of the executed 1916 leader James Connolly, a former IRB man and a prominent Labour Party activist. The POWU had, of course, William Norton the later leader of the Labour Party, as its first full-time general-secretary. Given that there were significant differences in the status and labour power of civil servants and the working class the links between them were surprisingly strong and the civil service union motions for debate at Congress were generally supported.[50] The Irish Federation also affiliated to the international organisation of civil service trade unions, the International Federation of Public Officials.[51]

However, although the energy that the civil service displayed in organisation is impressive, the form of that organisation can be questioned. The failure of the

Cumann na nGaedheal government to escape from the British State model was mirrored by the failure of the civil service to escape the model of organisation inherited from the British associations. The Irish departments and grades were too small to accommodate the complex organisational structures of the British service. Deference to British norms and habit reproduced the British model of organisation but the total membership of the Irish association was often less than that of a single branch of its sister organisation in Britain. In 1932, when the civil service had experienced eight years of retrenchment and a ban on promotions, the total number of administrative, executive, clerical, secretarial, professional and technical civil servants was 6,403. Yet this small service had sixteen representative associations.[52]

These civil service unions faced the task of mobilising membership on two opposed fronts. On the one hand they had to fight to defend the interests of recently appointed civil servants and civil servants who opted to remain with the Free State while on the other hand fighting for the best terms possible for those who wished to retire under the Treaty provisions. As could be expected any concentration on the rights of those who were 'deserting the ship' led to tensions and disagreements with those who remained on board.[53]

'Economy' and cuts in civil service pay

Justifiably proud of its success in stabilising the State and enacting the constitution, the Cumann na nGaedheal government increasingly relied on its ability to prudently manage the meagre State finances to assert its legitimacy as a government to the electorate. Relentless economic retrenchment became a form of ideological compensation for the retreat from the inspirational policies that had led the national revolution. Also, despite the efforts of the Labour Party to mount an active opposition to these policies, the more significant opposition influence on the government came in fact from the right-wing farmer and business parties that pressed for even greater cuts.[54] In May 1923, as an investigation into the financial position of the Irish Free State revealed a deficit of £1.2 million for the current year, the departmental heads were instructed to find economies.[55] In pursuit of a balanced budget, and fearful of the hyperinflation that was sweeping Germany, the Cosgrave government cut old-age pensions, blind pensions and teacher salaries.[56] In this pursuit of an aridly conservative economic strategy the civil service was an obvious target for reductions in expenditure.[57]

The Department of Finance's review of the budget position late in 1923 identified the civil service as being ripe for 'economy'. The review identified a two-pronged approach to lower costs by, firstly, scrapping inessential services and ending the 'unnecessary multiplication of departments as an obvious source of waste' and, secondly, by cutting the cost of the services then remaining. The objective of the review was to ensure that the costs of the public services would reflect the diminution of work that was necessarily consequent on the 'exclusion of the six-counties'.[58] As economy in the public service emerged as an insistent theme of government it was linked to the cost of compensation for civil servants dismissed or resigned under Article 10 of the Treaty.[59] The Labour Party suggested withholding superannuation payments from the retired officials of the former British administration, saving money that would be better spent on social needs.[60]

In 1924, as part of its economy drive and also to assert control over the civil service, the government substantially reduced the basic salary scales and annual leave for new entrants to the clerical and executive classes. It also introduced a new differentiated scale between married and unmarried civil servants, with an additional children's allowance.[61] This was a pet project of Blythe's.[62] Blythe's marriage differential was carefully designed so that a single woman would not reach the maximum of the scale before forty years of service, that is retirement age. The unmarried man would begin to notice the differential at about the age of twenty-three to twenty-five, the age when he ought to thinking of marriage.[63] It would thus operate as a social engineering mechanism, encouraging marriage in young men while using women to replace single men as cheaper labour. A complicated scheme, it required departmental heads to keep track of their officers' marital status and procreation. For fear of established officers going out under Article 10 it was applied to new recruits only.[64] P.S. O'Hegarty, never lost for an opinion, strongly supported Blythe and denounced 'the modern women's movement, disguised as a movement for equality, [which] is a movement to shirk wifehood and motherhood because independence looked more pleasant'.[65]

With the enforcement of the differential there were in fact two completely different salary schemes in the civil service. For the transferred civil servants protected by Article 10 there was a continuance of the old scales, with the new lower scales being applied to the new entrants. However, the government imposed a ban on promotion and, after 1926, introduced university graduate entry (male only) for the top administrative grades.[66] For civil servants tied to definite salary scales the only avenue to prosperity was promotion. Without promotion the lower grades became dead ends. These changes, introduced without any negotiation, tended to drive experienced officers out from the service protected as they were by Article 10 of the Treaty and to create resentment between the old and the new civil servants.[67] The AEO picked holes in the scheme in a series of carefully crafted questions which included whether the child allowance was equal for each child and was it paid from the date of birth and whether a civil servant on the maximum of his scale would be promoted to the next scale on receipt of an allowance for an extra child that brought him into that grades' pay range.[68]

A civil service representative council

As we have seen, in May 1922 Collins had assured a delegation of the civil service that though he could not commit any future government to acceptance of the Whitley Councils he did accept the need for some consultative body to establish the relationship between the new State and the civil service. The Whitley Joint Committee was abolished but the departmental councils were allowed continue and an ad hoc consultative council of official and staff sides was established for the transition period. The consultative council had six staff side and six official side representatives. All matters that ordinarily came before the Whitley Committee were to be dealt with by the consultative council. It met first on 20 September 1922 and monthly thereafter.[69] While the staff representatives saw this arrangement as a temporary substitute for some future form of reinstated Whitleyism, Collins and the Provisional Government saw this as a purely temporary arrangement to facilitate the transition from British to Irish rule. Though the CSF was willing to work the consultative council the POWU and IPCS were suspicious as it was clear that as a purely ad hoc and temporary body it was no substitute for the Whitley Committee.[70] The CSF continued to hope for a Whitley-like body on which 'representatives of official and staff sides meet, not for mere ventilation of grievances but to give both sides co-equal interest and power . . . a body for action not talk, fostering and developing in the staff that spirit of co-operative responsibility which was the guiding principle in the Irish-Ireland movement'.[71] Thus the civil service was still thinking of the relationship between it and the State as different to that with the former Castle regime and one that would be bound by a shared and equal commitment to national renewal. The government would recognise and value the cohort of expertise and commitment that the civil service represented and would invite it to engage in addressing the problems that faced the new State.

A year later, with the transition period complete and the Civil Service (Regulation) Act in force, the civil service associations continued to demand the reinstatement of something like the departmental Whitley Councils. In the Dáil, deputies Bryan Cooper's and Johnson's repeated questioning of Cosgrave and Blythe on the Whitley Councils got vague and non-committal replies. Within cabinet, however, and eventually in a statement to the Dáil, Cosgrave took the view that sole power to determine pay and conditions within the civil service lay with the government and therefore only a consultative body could be allowed.[72] However, early in 1924, the Whitley Committee was formally abolished with the government offering, at a meeting with civil service representatives, nothing more than a promise to establish new machinery 'more suited to Saorstát Éireann conditions'.[73] This rhetorical flourish might have seemed promising to the more nationalist members of the civil service, but few were convinced and most of the associations continued to press for a restoration of a Whitley-type committee. Ideally the service would have preferred that a panel of ministers and other politicians, along with a non-governmental representative but with no senior civil servant, would constitute an official panel.[74]

In December 1924 Blythe issued without discussion or consultation a scheme for a purely consultative representative council for the civil service made up of official and staff sides, composed of civil servants, with no political representative. The chairman of the council was to be a nominee of the minister but with no vice-chair nominated by the staff side, as had been the case with the Whitley Committee. The chairman had full control of the agenda and also the report of the proceedings to the minister. The minister also forbade any non-service members, thus thwarting the recent decision of the POWU and the CSCA to appoint full-time general secretaries and professionalise their representation. In every aspect the ministerial proposal was a rejection of the Whitley system and its implied equality between State and civil servant.[75]

At this point the civil service was organised in three main blocs: the CSF, the POWU and the IPCS. Unhappy at the retreat from the Whitley Councils, a meeting with the Minister of Finance was requested. Initially the joint approach worked well. When the minister, predictably, refused to meet them it was pointed out to the government that it had already broken a pledge to consult the service and that any scheme drafted and put into operation by one side only lacked the first element of conciliation, agreement by both sides.[76] Within a few weeks however the unity of the service associations was broken. The CSF, assured by the minister that the council's mechanisms could be revised to remedy any defects that might emerge once it was working, agreed to give it a trial. In fact the Federation, as the largest and most nationalist organisation in the civil service, had come under considerable pressure to work the government scheme. The CSCA, after a divisive debate, agreed to work the scheme but only under protest.[77] The POWU and the IPCS decided to stick with the decision that the scheme was completely unacceptable and both protested at the Federation's decision to break ranks with the rest of the service. Confident that the other associations would eventually have to come on board the government pressed ahead and the Civil Service Representative Council (CSRC), without either the POWU or the IPCS, held its first meeting on 15 March 1926. The fragmentation of the civil service organisation is evident in the range of associations on the CSRC. The only general service classes represented were the executive officers (AEO) and the clerical officers (CSCA). The rest of the staff side was made up of fourteen associations, many with less than a hundred members.[78] The POWU description of the scheme as 'utterly worthless' proved correct. While the civil servants might have continued to refer to it as a 'conciliation' council the minister, correctly, referred to it as a 'representative' council. From the beginning the CSRC proved unsatisfactory and the 'recognised' associations within the CSF unanimously pressed an unconvinced minister to accept that the constitution had to be revised.[79]

The civil service search for a united front

The year 1927 was crucial in stabilising the Free State as the republican Fianna Fáil party entered Dáil Éireann to form a constitutional opposition. To the civil service associations Fianna Fáil seemed to be more sympathetic to their complaints and with the government facing two elections in 1927 they tried once again to build up a single service voice. In February 1927 the Federation called for a conference between civil service associations to rebuild cross-service unity.[80] The IPCS and the POWU proved equally dismissive. In truth neither the POWU nor the IPCS were interested in joining what was clearly a sinking ship.[81] By the end of the year the clerical officers had seceded from both the CSF and the CSRC and so therefore, as the Federation broke up, the so-called 'Representative Council' now represented a minority of civil servants.[82]

It has to be admitted that the efforts of the various civil service associations to unite and defend the interests of those civil servants who chose to remain in the civil service of the Irish Free State bore little fruit. The expectation that a shared nationalism and a shared enthusiasm for the possibilities of independence would be sufficient to establish a new relationship between the State and the civil service had failed. In terms of influence and solid gain the most effective organisation that the Irish civil service had ever generated was the pre-independence GCICS. That committee had recognised that the civil service of the State had, despite departmentalisation and complex grading, a single employer with unique power to shape their working conditions. It followed that the civil service ought to be associated in a single organisation to speak as one in dealing with the State. It was when the civil service turned to defend the gains won by the GCICS that it discovered the unity and success that previously had eluded them. In defending the contractual rights of those civil servants who chose to retire under Article 10 of the Treaty the civil service unions built and maintained cross-service unity and achieved a defeat of the government that re-opened the whole Treaty debate and brought into question national sovereignty. Described by Thomas Johnson as 'the turning point in the whole constitutional relationships between Great Britain, the Irish Free State and the British Dominions', this was the Wigg-Cochrane case.[83]

The Wigg-Cochrane case

The IPCS were dissatisfied at its lack of representation on the Wylie committee and continued to demand a right to represent members during its deliberations.[84] Unhappy at many rulings of the committee, the IPCS council began looking for legal advice on challenging it in the courts. The main question centred on how the 'bonus' was being included when calculating the pension.[85] Originally, thinking that the wartime inflation was a temporary difficulty only, the British Treasury in introducing the bonus in 1916 explicitly stated that it would not count for pension or gratuity payments under the Superannuation Acts. As the war bonus became in fact a regular part of the pay of civil servants pensions emerged as anomalous and unfair. In April 1919 this was temporarily addressed in a memorandum of agreement between the Treasury and the civil service associations. Under this agreement subsequent pension awards would include a bonus-related supplementary pension. In the post-war period as the bonus, though temporary and fluctuating, had become in reality part of the pay of civil servants the National Whitley Council for the civil service turned its attention to the continuing problem of pensions. The council agreed that in addition to the normal calculation of pension there would be added three-quarters of the bonus paid at the time of retirement and that in calculating the lump sum gratuity the bonus would be added on. The Treasury, without agreement or legislation, then decided that the part of a pension of retiring civil servants that was based on the bonus would, just like the bonus itself, be subject to periodic quarterly adjustment based on the cost-of-living calculation, and would be subject to an over-riding maximum. This Treasury minute introduced a notional maximum for the bonus element that would allow the bonus to fluctuate downwards but prevent it fluctuating upwards beyond a certain percentage. The notion of a 'maximum' was introduced to prevent the total annual sum payable in pensions exceeding the statutory proportion of the total salary on which civil servants pensions were calculated because, it was conceivable, the bonus element of the pension might in time rise to exceed the actual basic salary paid to a civil servant on retirement.

The legality of an Act of Parliament, the Superannuation Acts, being altered by an order of the Treasury ought to have been queried, but it wasn't. These changes were effected by a Treasury minute dated 20 March 1922, that is in the period between the Provisional Government taking over Dublin Castle on 16 January, when Collins forbade any alterations in personnel or conditions, and 1 April 1922 when the civil service in Ireland was formally transferred. Justice Wylie, at the first sitting of the compensation committee, indicated that he intended to allow this Treasury minute to govern the compensation payable under the Treaty, that is to say to take the view that the transfer of the civil service had occurred on 1 April 1922.[86] Curiously enough the Civil Service Committee set up under the 1920 Act, which had been blocked in its operation by the civil service associations and by the Provisional Government, had agreed that the compensation payable under the 1920 Act would be subject to a variable element related to the current rate of bonus on the salaries of serving civil servants. This was intended to act as a disincentive to voluntary retirement because of the danger of a diminishing pension in the future. Had the Provisional Government allowed the committee to function it may never have faced the difficulties it was about to encounter.[87]

By early January 1923 the IPCS council, dissatisfied with some of its decisions, decided that it would have to fight the Wylie committee in the courts and instructed the member associations to forward to the council a list of the cases past and pending in the committee. These were then carefully monitored.[88] Meanwhile a 'Treaty Pensioners' Association' was formed to act as the organisation of the civil servants affected. This association, funded by the civil servants in the IPCS who remained in service, travelled to London to lobby the British government on the issue of compensation and pensions.[89] At their request the House of Lords attempted to insert into the 'consequential provisions' an explicit guarantee that the British government would undertake responsibility for the pensions under Article 10 if the Irish government reneged, but this was rejected by the Commons.[90]

It is ironic that the 1920 Civil Service Committee, had it functioned, would have had an absolute authority to determine 'fair compensation' and so therefore would not have been amenable to judicial review. The Provisional Government, determined to assert its sovereignty, made the Wylie committee a purely advisory committee. As an advisory committee its decisions, though accepted by the government, were neither final nor conclusive in any way. Advice can of course be rejected, by either side. By autumn two cases had emerged as promising vehicles to challenge the compensation committee: that of John Howard Wigg and that of Robert Oliver Cochrane, both of them members of the IPCS.

Wigg was assistant architect in the OPW in Dublin on a salary of £430 plus bonus of £232 3s 0d, which, by his date of retirement, had reduced to £119 giving him a salary of £549 on retirement. Wigg had, on 1 April 1922, seventeen years of service. The pension awarded to Wigg was £200 on his basic salary plus a supplementary bonus of £103 0s 9d subject to a maximum of £88 6s 5d. This gave him a pension of £288 6s 5d. Cochrane was a chief executive officer in the OPW on £415 plus bonus of £194 5s 6d with twenty-six years' service on 1 April 1922 giving him a final salary of £609 5s 6d. Robert Cochrane had actually served on the executive of the 1893 civil service committee that had drafted the code on civil service compensation rights. Cochrane was awarded £206 5s 0d basic pension plus a supplementary bonus £106 5s 2d subject to maximum of £91 1s 7d giving him a final pension of £297 6s 7d. In both cases the pensions were calculated in the normal manner, taking account of years of service and added years. However, following the Treasury minute of March 1922, the awards carried the conditions that the supplemental pension would be subject to quarterly reassessment based on the cost-of-living figure and that at no time would the supplemental pension exceed its prescribed amount at the date of retirement, the 'over-riding maximum'. Had the 1920 terms been applied the basic salary and bonus would have been considered together as 'pay', the pension would have had no periodic reassessment and the over-riding maximum would not have applied.

On 15 November 1923 Wigg-Cochrane issued a writ in the High Court. In their writ Wigg-Cochrane asked that the High Court declare that the compensation awarded them was not 'fair compensation' inasmuch as part of the compensation was put on a sliding scale, the quarterly cost-of-living reassessment, which would not have been the case under the 1920 Act. The central argument hung on the words of Article 10 of the Treaty, 'the government of the Irish Free State agrees to pay fair compensation on terms not less favourable than those accorded by the Act of 1920 . . . to public servants who are discharged by it or who retire in consequence of the change of government'. Wigg-Cochrane argued that terms less favourable than those accorded by the 1920 Act were in fact being imposed by the Irish government because in 1920 there was no 'maximum' and no adjustment of the bonus element of the pension. What they wanted was the courts to declare that the 'bonus was part of the salary formerly enjoyed and that in calculating the superannuation allowance a fixed award should be made, and that no part of such allowance should be put on a sliding scale'.[91] They also asked for a declaration that the Treasury minute of 20 March 1922 did not apply because they were at that moment under the authority of the Provisional Government, not the Treasury. The three-month gap between the handing over of the Castle to the Provisional Government, when Collins ordered that there should be no alteration in conditions, and the transfer of authority on 1 April opened up the question of where the authority of the State lay for that period. If the Irish government argued that the Treasury minute did apply then they argued that the Provisional Government was not a State, it was only an administration empowered by the British and the talk about the 'surrender of the Castle' was no more than empty rhetoric.

As the question was contested far bigger issues began to emerge from the dreary arguments about dates and definitions. Looming behind the molehill of pensions was a mountain of constitutional confrontation with implications for the entire British Commonwealth of Nations. The government defence was that the Minister of Finance of the Irish Free State had inherited the authority of the former British Treasury. Under that authority civil servants were employed at pleasure and had no legal *right* to a pension. The decision as to the amount of any pension, which lay formerly with the Treasury, lay now with the Minister of Finance. Therefore the action of Wigg-Cochrane was not sustainable and ought to be dismissed. In the High Court, however, the judgement, delivered on 18 July 1924 by Mr Justice Meredith, former president of the 1920 Dáil Éireann Supreme Court, found not only that the pensions of Wigg-Cochrane ought to be calculated under the 1920 Act as they argued but, more importantly, that their pensions, and by implication those of all transferred civil servants established or temporary, were guaranteed by the constitutional incorporation of the Treaty. What was at issue was not pension entitlements but constitutional guarantees. Rights that were secured in the constitution could not be governed or qualified by a Treasury minute, or by a decision of the Minister of Finance, or even an Act of the Oireachtas. The pensions of dismissed or retiring transferred officers were not a gift of the Minister of Finance but a constitutional right and therefore enforceable in the courts whose task it was to defend the constitution.[92]

The State immediately appealed to the Supreme Court. Meanwhile Wylie, once his authority was questioned, resigned from the committee to take up a position as judge of the High Court. Initially the government was not unhappy at these developments and may well have welcomed them, confident that their interpretation of the rights of the transferred civil servants would stand. The official side at the Wylie committee had been taking a much more aggressive line and had circulated a letter to all applicants demanding an explanation as to *why* and not merely a statement *that* he was 'retiring in consequence of the change of government'. They would no longer simply accept the statements but would forcefully interrogate all applicants on the basis of their stated reasons for retirement.[93]

The decision to abolish the Whitley Councils and the stubborn refusal to establish any replacement arbitration scheme made civil servants uneasy and more willing to take the money on offer and resign. The Free State government had immediately discharged 454 civil servants. But, in July 1924 just before the High Court delivered its judgement, Blythe revealed that a further 864 civil servants had resigned 'in consequence of the change of government' costing a lump sum of £208,870 and an annual pension of £124,666, and there were still many hundreds of applications in the pipeline. These payments to dismissed and retired civil servants were being made against the background of cuts in old-age pensions and teacher salaries.[94] By the end of 1925 the cost of compensation under Article 10 was running at £254,785 per annum in payments to 1,851 former civil servants with a further 2,139 still pending.[95] Even before the High Court case Blythe described Article 10 as 'the worst article in the Treaty'.[96] The High Court decision and the resignation of Wylie allowed the government to suspend all the pending cases and halt the flow of resignations. Civil servants who wished to retire were now in a limbo as the government refused to process any claims until the courts clarified the position.[97]

For the civil service associations the purpose of the Wigg-Cochrane case was not to enforce the rights of retired former civil servants, but to compel the government to reinstate some form of the Whitley Councils, to determine pensions in the first instance but ultimately to re-establish arbitration as a permanent part of the transferred civil service industrial relations and compel the government to treat the civil service with some respect.[98] The civil service made a direct connection between the rush of resignations, 600 in six months, and the aggressive attitude of the government, saying 'it will not do to tell us we have no right to strike and deny us at the same time adequate conciliation and arbitration machinery for the settlement of legitimate grievances'.[99]

The initial hope was that with the High Court decision in the associations' favour the government would not appeal but would look to establishing what was the true objective of the litigation, a properly constituted statutory arbitration scheme. When the government did decide to appeal the decision of Meredith to the Supreme Court, and the case made its slow progress toward that appeal, it was noted with anxiety that the government was not bothering to replace Wylie and was refusing to name a date for the reconstitution of the compensation committee.[100] The financial implications for the civil service associations of a further appeal were a worry, but unavoidable, once the government decided to go to the Supreme Court.[101]

Early in 1925, as it became clear that the government was going to pursue the case of Wigg-Cochrane all the way to the Supreme Court, the civil service associations combined to form the Transferred Officers' Protection Association (TOPA).[102] The object of TOPA was to 'safeguard the rights of members under articles 77 and 78 of the Constitution of Saorstát Éireann and Article 10 of the Treaty'.[103] The driving force behind TOPA was William Norton, general-secretary of the POWU and later leader of the Labour Party. It was Norton who drew up the initial memorandum detailing the decline in service conditions under the Free State government and inviting the other associations to join forces.[104] The twelve-member executive of TOPA was made up of four appointed by the POWU, four by the CSF and four by the IPCS.[105] Thus TOPA was a much more unified organisation of the civil service than the Federation and, as most civil servants in the Free State were 'transferred officers', might well have proved a base to build cross-service unity but, as we shall see, it never became more than an organisation to fight the Wigg-Cochrane case. Nevertheless, as such, it was an undoubted success. It is therefore ironic that the civil service unions and associations that had failed to build a unified platform to negotiate on behalf of those civil servants staying in the Free State came together to fight the cause of those who were retiring.

Civil servants who were going to stay in the civil service of the Free State, or recently recruited civil servants, were understandably reluctant to finance a court case that would benefit those who were retiring and create hostility to those who remained. It was alleged that TOPA was solely concerned with those civil servants who intended to retire under Article 10 but had not got a chance to go because the Wylie committee was hamstrung since the court case and the resignation of the chairman. It was also alleged that TOPA was being run by people whose sympathies were British rather than Irish and that TOPA was motivated by a desire among 'the usual garland of Poppies sustained by Freemason wires' to humiliate the native government.[106]

In the Supreme Court the government won and so it might have seemed that that was the end of the case.[107] The decision of the majority of the court was that, bluntly, a civil servant under the Treaty had no pension *rights* as such which are enforceable by law and that the Minister of Finance was the sole authority to determine matters between the State and the civil service. Consequently a civil servant must accept whatever the minister offered and had no right of action against the minister whatever. This was consistent with the British tradition under which all civil servants were employed 'at pleasure' and had no rights, properly speaking. But, in a dissenting judgement, one of the three judges raised the question as to the status of the Treaty and the other legislation establishing the new government. While the other two judges, O'Connor and Fitzgibbon (a former leading Dublin Unionist) accepted the government argument for continuity of authority, and therefore superannuation and compensation powers, the third, Justice Johnston, dissented. He argued that the Treaty had completely displaced the Act of 1920 and had 'brought to an end the whole existing administrative, executive and judicial machinery of the country and made suitable provision for the substitution of something different'.[108] In his view the case of Wigg-Cochrane was not about the power to determine superannuation but about fundamental constitutional rights as guaranteed by the Treaty agreed with Great Britain by Dáil Éireann and the constitution that it subsequently enacted. If the government, he argued, could disregard Article 10 of the Treaty then it could equally disregard any other article of the Treaty, the constitution and the orders transferring authority to the Free State, making them no more than so much waste paper. In a paradoxical reversal therefore the government of the Free State was now arguing that what had taken place was not a revolution whereas the civil servants were arguing that it was. Breaking through the question of pension rights was the status of the Treaty itself.[109]

The appeal to the Judicial Committee of the Privy Council

Even before the High Court judgement the civil service associations had discussed the possibility of invoking a controversial and contentious avenue of appeal if the decision went against Wigg-Cochrane. This was an appeal to the Judicial Committee of the Privy Council in the British House of Lords.[110] The appeal to the Judicial Committee of the Privy Council was not mentioned in the Treaty, but had been included in the Irish Free State Constitution (article 66) at the insistence of the British government.[111] Article 66 of the constitution implied wrongly that there was an existing right of appeal; there wasn't, but it was decided that it would not be wise to reveal that error and to allow the article to stand as first written.[112] The British government viewed the appeal to the Privy Council as a vital expression of Commonwealth unity and British judicial supremacy within the Dominions.[113] It derived from the Judicial Committee Act of 1844, which gave statutory validity to the right of the Crown to hear appeals from any colonial court.[114] The British government wanted the Privy Council to be seen, and act, as the supreme court of the empire and dominions. Collins and Griffith had objected to the appeals procedure on the grounds that three of the judges of the Privy Council were vehemently unionist and opposed to Irish self-determination: Lords Carson, Sumner and Cave. Judges who already expressed strong views on the Irish constitution might be invited to interpret that constitution. The British government had offered an assurance that in any controversy of a political nature on Irish appeals these judges would be considered as disqualified and stand aside.[115] A further assurance was offered that in an Irish case the procedures would follow the more restrictive South African rather than Canadian precedent; that is an appeal to proceed would require that it be permitted by the Irish Supreme Court and would be only in cases that affected a great number of people.[116] Around the time that TOPA was being formed the judicial committee had already breached these understandings by hearing the case of *Lynham* v. *Butler*, which dealt with the powers of the Irish land commissioners.[117] At the 1926 Imperial Conference the appeal to the Privy Council came under fire from both Canada and the Free State.[118] The existence of such an appeal, and its exercise, was considered an insult to the Irish Supreme Court and the competency of the Irish judiciary. By appealing the Supreme Court decision to the Judicial Committee of the Privy Council the civil service of the Irish Free State was asking a British court to overturn the Irish Supreme Court's interpretation of Article 10 of the Treaty, thereby undermining the Irish Supreme Court and Irish national sovereignty.

The appeal to the Privy Council, heard by Lord Cave (despite the assurances offered in June 1922) along with Lords Haldane, Dunedin and Shaw (all three of them Liberals) and the Scottish Unionist Finlay, went even better for the civil service than could have been imagined. The Privy Council decision, delivered 3 May 1927, overturned the Supreme Court decision and gave Wigg-Cochrane the compensation and pensions they had demanded by agreeing that the rights of the transferred officers were constitutional rights. The claims of the civil servants rested on the Treaty, the Transfer of Functions Order of 1922 and the Constitution of the Irish Free State, and not on any superannuation Act. In response to the government argument that the Civil Service Committee had never been established and therefore the power of the committee reverted to the Minister of Finance, the judges found that the powers in fact reverted to the courts, which were the proper authority to determine constitutional rights. The judges also found that the Treasury minute of March 1922 was not binding as the civil service had been transferred to the Provisional Government by that date. As a *coup de grâce* the judges also found that the over-riding maximum was unfair as it allowed a pension to fluctuate downwards but limited its upward movement.[119]

This judgement sent shock waves through the governments in Dublin and in London. Under the British administration civil servants were by law employed 'at the pleasure of His Majesty' and status and pensions were by gift rather than by right. It was also the British view that the Irish Free State was not the creation of revolution but was a devolved government, created by Westminster legislation, continuous with the former administration. The Privy Council decision implied that the Irish Free State was in fact a break with the former British administration. Far more seriously, from a financial point of view, the decision also meant there was now a group of civil servants within the British and Irish system whose status and security were far superior to their colleagues' and were in fact under-pinned by constitutional guarantees. The Law Lords had determined that transferred civil servants now benefited from a status far better than any they would have enjoyed had there never been a Treaty and were now entitled to more favourable treatment than they would have received had they remained under the British administration or had they been recently recruited in the civil service of the Free State. The British associations were themselves intrigued by civil servants successfully suing the State and extracting explicit legal guarantees as to their rights.[120]

For the Dublin government the decision of the Privy Council was the last straw. The Wigg-Cochrane decision was now far more than a dispute about pensions. In fact most of the civil servants that had applied to retire under Article 10 had accepted the decision of the committee and there were only about 400 disputed cases outstanding.[121] The right to resign as a consequence of the change of government had a seven-year limit and would run out in December 1929. There was a reasonable fear that the civil service might now see a rapid collapse over the next year as officials seized upon the Wigg-Cochrane decision to retire on what were extraordinarily favourable terms.

But the main objection to the Wigg-Cochrane decision was on constitutional grounds. The Irish government had already objected at the Commonwealth conferences to the claims of the Privy Council to act as an imperial supreme court. By the Wigg-Cochrane decision the Privy Council, dominated in the eyes of the Free State government by the most reactionary of the Tory legal establishment, now claimed an authority to interpret the Treaty itself against the Irish Supreme Court. The government's argument that the Treaty, in the words of Michael Collins, gave the 'freedom to achieve freedom' now rang hollow. Even before the decision of the judicial committee Blythe announced that the government had no intention of complying with the decisions of a 'bad, useless and unnecessary court' while other deputies attacked the 'disloyal, unpatriotic and rapacious civil servants'.[122]

However, constitutionally eccentric as the decision may have been, neither the British nor the Irish governments could simply ignore it. Blythe's response was uncharacteristically terse: 'The judgement in the Wigg-Cochrane appeal raises not merely financial but constitutional questions, and I think a quick decision is not to be looked for.'[123] While the Irish government was primarily engaged on the constitutional aspects of the decision the British government was itself quite alarmed at the Privy Council decision that some civil servants would be better treated and have definite rights as a result of the Treaty. Clearly it was to the advantage of both governments to come to an understanding on the way of retreat from the decision. Both governments were also trying to ignore the fact that the compensation terms of Article 10 of the Treaty and the eighth schedule of the 1920 Act were not in any sense part of the superannuation code, which of course remained the responsibility of the Treasury or Minister of Finance, but were part of the Treaty.

The Irish civil service, through TOPA and the CSF, looked for assistance from the British civil service organisations, though it might have preferred that the British Confederation did not express its support with such an enthusiastically imperialistic resolution:

That this meeting of the executive Committee of the Civil Service Confederation accords its full support to those ex-British Civil Servants who are resisting the action of the Irish Free State Government and the British Government in seeking to avoid the consequences of the Privy Council judgment in the Wigg-Cochrane case. It is of the opinion that such action raises the following vital issues:

(1) The effect of such legislation on the constitutional legal fabric of the British Empire.
(2) The question whether the parliament should usurp the power of the Courts in interpreting Statutes.
(3) The denial of justice to those who adopt the ordinary legal procedure of the Empire.
(4) The refusal of the rights under the Treaty to Civil Servants; and that for these reasons the contemplated action should not be proceeded with by the respective governments.[124]

On 22 February 1928 Blythe announced to the Dáil that the government's response to the decision of the Privy Council was to reconstitute the Wylie committee as a statutory rather than an advisory committee, to apply the controversial Treasury minute and to make its decision absolute.[125] In short the government would ignore the decision of the Privy Council. The next day Leopold Amery, Secretary of State for the Dominions, in a statement that precisely echoed that of Blythe's, told the House of Commons that it was clearly inequitable that the transferred civil servants of the Irish Free State should receive more favourable treatment than if they had remained in the British civil service and, as the decision of the Privy Council did not reflect the intention of those who made the Treaty, it would co-operate with the Irish government's intent to change the law so that the decision of the Privy Council would be avoided. This was an extraordinary statement as the interpretation of statute law (the Treaty was statute law) lay with the courts and not parliament. The British civil service associations continued to take a keen interest in the struggle between the courts and the government, touching as it did on the authority of the Treasury over the salaries and conditions of the civil service.[126] The CSF took up the Wigg-Cochrane case with the British Labour Party, which was actually rather wary of the issue and would go no further than saying that the Irish civil service must be no worse off as a result of the Treaty, which was precisely the view of the Irish government.[127]

At this point the Irish government, instead of pressing ahead with this agreed strategy, allowed itself to be drawn into a farcical pantomime the point of which was to allow the British government to escape the consequences of defying the Privy Council decision. Carson, the former Ulster Unionist leader, took up the cause of the civil servants. What offended him was that the two governments were clearly conspiring to alter the terms of compensation without consulting the aggrieved party, the civil servants themselves. In April, in an acrimonious debate in the House of Lords on the decision, with sharp exchanges between Carson and the Law Lords, Lord Birkenhead (F.E. Smith, one of the British signatories of the Treaty) solemnly announced that the recently deceased Lord Cave, who had delivered the controversial judgement, had summoned the prime minister to his deathbed and confessed to him that the judgement in the Wigg-Cochrane case was wrong in law and that his conscience could not allow him to die without discharging the painful duty of admitting his error. The Marquess of Reading then rose to suggest that the Privy Council be asked to reconsider the opinion expressed earlier and thus allow the error to be corrected without the necessity of legislation and debate.[128] Cave had indeed been troubled about the Wigg-Cochrane case, not because it was wrong but because a draftsman had made an error in the written judgement referring to the question of the mode of calculating the bonus and the date on which the civil service had actually been transferred. On the essential point of the rightness of Meredith's judgement, Cave had signalled no doubts whatever. But, having died in late March, he was not there to contradict Birkenhead.[129] Rather than insisting that the law in the Irish Free State is that of its Supreme Court the Irish government allowed itself to be persuaded to return once again to plead in a court it had already rejected as bad, useless and an infringement of national sovereignty. Once again the Privy Council heard the case and once again, contrary to the naive expectations of both governments, it found for Wigg-Cochrane and against the Irish executive.[130]

The first revision to the Treaty

The government might fulminate that the civil servants were not going to get a farthing more than they were entitled to under the Supreme Court decision but clearly the pension entitlements of transferred officers needed to be taken out of the courts and dealt with by legislation. Any legislation would have to be agreed between the Irish government, the British government (because any new law on Article 10 would be a renegotiation of the Treaty) and the transferred Irish civil servants (to persuade them to abandon further litigation). Finally, reluctantly and with bad grace the Irish government sat down to negotiate with, rather than bully, the civil service.[131]

Complex negotiations began between the Irish government and TOPA and between the Irish government and the British government.[132] The result of these negotiations was the Civil Servants (Transferred Officers) Compensation Act, 1929. This act was paralleled by the British Irish Free State (Confirmation of Agreement) Act, 1929 [20 Geo. 5, c. 4]. These two Acts were, in constitutional terms, a renegotiation of Article 10 of the Treaty by the British and Irish governments by which the Irish government conceded the better terms won by the Wigg-Cochrane case and the British government agreed to repay to the Irish government the additional moneys involved.[133] This little-known case was in fact the first revision of the hitherto sacrosanct Treaty.

Under the 1929 Act a statutory committee of a judge, representatives of the Minister of Finance and representatives of the transferred officers, was established with sole jurisdiction to determine compensation under Article 10. Written into the Act were the retirement conditions of the 1920 Act, thus securing the better terms of the 1920 Act for civil servants. Picking up the cost of these higher awards was the British government who agreed to compensate the Irish government for the 'excess'.[134] Thus honour was saved and the Irish, if not the British, public purse left no lighter after nearly ten years of litigation and frustration. Finally a definite resolution had emerged to the whole vexed issue of civil service pensions but it left a residue of hostility to the civil service within the Dáil and public opinion.[135]

The Wigg-Cochrane case spurred on the government to mount a consistent attack at the Commonwealth conference on the Judicial Committee of the Privy Council as a court 'obnoxious because it is an extra-State institution exercising judicial control over the internal affairs of the State without any form of democratic sanction'.[136] During the debate on the Civil Service (Transferred Officers) Compensation Act Blythe had argued that the bad decision in the Wigg-Cochrane appeal illustrated the anti-Irish bias on the English bench and that it 'has become more and more clear every day that this appeal to the Privy Council is an anomaly'.[137] The British government refused to yield to demands to abolish the appeal to the Privy Council, the last institution that made the

Commonwealth a legal rather than simply a diplomatic unit and it was a
Fianna Fáil government that finally abolished the right to appeal in 1933.[138]

The compensation panel finally assembled in early January 1930 under Judge
Cahir Davitt, the son of the Land League founder and a judge in the revolutionary courts of the 1919–22 period. The tribunal expected to deal with about
1,600 cases, many of them of civil servants who had retired but whose compensation and pensions had been delayed by the Wigg-Cochrane case.[139] Blythe
appointed Messrs Boland, Doolin, Redmond and Leydon to represent the
Department of Finance. A panel of twenty-five nominees represented the civil
service trade unions and organisations.[140] In dealing with any case the court was
limited to five members, two each for the department and the civil service along
with Davitt the chairman. The very first case was the high profile Drennan, the
secretary of the Land Commission. Judge Davitt treated his case with great
courtesy and care. However, as the months dragged on and the cases of the lower
ranks of the civil service were being dealt with, the tone of Judge Davitt became
more caustic and sneering. As he was a government appointee there is no reason
to doubt that in this he was faithfully reflecting the official mind.[141] Lowly
postmen and junior civil servants, many of them women, had to endure
sarcasm and heckling from Judge Davitt. He rubbished the logical argument
that as the Fianna Fáil party were committed to destroying the Treaty, and as
they were likely to form the next government, it was reasonable to assume that
the guarantees contained in Article 10 would not long survive such a change of
government.[142] Davitt was particularly sneering when dealing with the stock
claim made by nearly all applicants (who echoed mantra-like the phrase of
Article 10) that their wish to retire was 'in consequence of the change of government'. The national and provincial press picked up and echoed his hostility.
The *Clare Champion* editorialised against the 'lickspittle British-backed civil
servants' as offering gratuitous insults to the elected representatives of the
'unfortunate people who will have to pay out to them money that has not been
earned'.[143] It was true most of the applicants simply wanted to seize an opportunity that few would let pass, to retire early on a decent pension and enjoy a
life of leisure. However, there was also a general feeling that the service had
become degraded, supervision stricter (if not bullying), hours longer and pay
shorter under the Free State with every sign that the future under Fianna Fáil
would be worse. As one inarticulate woman telegraphist, who simply wanted
out, put it 'it is atmospheric conditions'.[144] Davitt was ruthless in interpreting
the terms under which retirement was claimed and the civil service unions, who
had bought in, could not opt out. By the end of March the court had heard 461
cases and allowed only 250, rejecting 160 with 51 withdrawn. Thus nearly one
half of all cases ended up either withdrawn or rejected.[145]

The complaints of the civil servants at the Davitt court reflect the transformation of the Irish civil service from an informal, casual and poorly supervised

collection of boards to a centralised and ruthlessly driven State machine. The nostalgia that many felt for the old days of the British regime was, however, misplaced for those days had long passed in Britain as well. The Whitley Councils were far less successful than the Irish civil service liked to imagine. Meetings were either chilly gatherings of the mute or red hot rows due to official side resistance to the whole concept of negotiation.[146] Nor was the gain of a civil service arbitration board any more useful than the Whitley Councils. In 1922 the 'Geddes Axe' that aimed to secure cuts in government costs simply and unilaterally abolished the arbitration board.[147] It was restored in 1925 after a political campaign by the civil service unions, but without official side appro- bation it proved ineffective.[148]

The time and effort of the Wigg-Cochrane case had the effect of identifying the civil service organisations with those civil servants who were retiring and making them seem of little relevance to the vast majority that were staying on. The CSCA, which was the largest organisation of the lower grades, virtually ignored the judgement. Civil service organisations had won the battle on the rights of retiring civil servants, but lost the war on the rights of those who con- tinued to serve. As soon as the case was won the pillar upon which civil service unity had been built collapsed, undermined by the extent of its success. The Privy Council awarded the civil servants all of the costs incurred in fighting the case. The Irish Treaty Pensioners' Association, which had initiated and first put up funding for the struggle, accused TOPA of pocketing the award of costs and allowing the Pensioners' Association share to 'go west'. The IPCS in turn sneeringly described the Pensioners' Association as a bankrupt organisation dependent on the 'serving service' to find the money to establish its right to jump ship and retire on pension.[149]

Notes

1 Laffan, *The Resurrection of Ireland*, pp. 420–2.
2 Of the 153 seats in Dáil Éireann Cumann na nGaedheal won 63 in 1923, 47 in June 1927 and 62 in September 1927.
3 *Dáil Éireann debates*, vol. 4, col. 1168, 20 July 1923.
4 NAI, G1/1, minutes of the Provisional Government, 20 Jan. 1922.
5 NAI, G1/2 and 3, minutes of the Provisional Government, 21 Apr., 26 Oct. 1922; *Dáil Éireann debates*, vol. 2, cols 1654–5, 23 Feb. 1923; vol. 3, col. 2455, 26 June 1923; NAI, Department of Finance, E109/43/32 and E114/1/29, 'Victimised civil servants'.
6 NAI, Department of Finance, E109/43/32.
7 NAI, Department of Finance, 'early E files', E85/116(iii), 'Reinstated civil servants', circular 54/23, 18 Dec. 1923.
8 *Dáil Éireann debates*, vol. 5, col. 1743, 14 Nov. 1923.
9 Ibid., vol. 5, col. 1218, 23 Nov. 1923.

10 NAI, G2/2, executive council minutes, 8 May 1923; *Iris*, 1:6 (June 1923).
11 *Dáil Éireann debates*, vol. 4, cols 1507–10, 26 July 1923.
12 Ibid, vol. 5, cols 1233–48, 23 Nov. 1923.
13 Ibid., vol. 6, col. 1464, 27 Feb. 1924.
14 NAI, G2/3, executive council minutes, 9 Jan. 1924.
15 Donal O'Sullivan, *The Irish Free State and Its Senate: A Study in Contemporary Politics* (London, 1940), pp. 208–9.
16 *Dáil Éireann debates*, vol. 10, cols 194–5, 13 Feb. 1925.
17 UCDAD, Fitzgerald Papers, P80/1057.
18 NAI, G2/3, executive council minutes, 21 Jan. 1924.
19 *Dáil Éireann debates*, vol. 5, col. 1500, 6 Dec. 1923.
20 Ibid., vol. 5, col. 919, 16 Nov. 1923.
21 Ibid., vol. 5, col. 1021, 21 Nov. 1923.
22 *Seanad Éireann debates*, vol. 2, cols 1096–103, 19 Mar. 1924.
23 *Dáil Éireann debates*, vol. 5, col. 1389, 5 Dec. 1923; *Seanad Éireann debates*, vol. 2, col. 1100, 19 Mar. 1924.
24 *Dáil Éireann debates*, vol. 5, cols 1634–64, 11 Dec. 1923.
25 Ibid., vol. 5, col. 1661, 11 Dec. 1923.
26 Regan, *Counter-revolution*, p. 200.
27 *Dáil Éireann debates*, vol. 5, col. 1525, 6 Dec. 1923.
28 Ibid., vol. 5, col. 1649, 11 Dec. 1923.
29 Ibid., vol. 5, col. 1651, 11 Dec. 1923.
30 Treasonable Offences Act, 1925, section 3, sub-section (1) (f).
31 NAI, Department of Finance, E125/13/27.
32 J. Anthony Gaughan, *Thomas Johnson 1872–1963* (Dublin, 1980), p. 225.
33 NAI, Brennan Commission, BC/1, '3 Nov. 1932'.
34 NLI, Brennan Papers, MS 26,313.
35 UCDAD, Patrick McGilligan Papers, P35a/31.
36 NAI, Department of Finance, E109/30/46 [2002/57/155], 'Notes on British government publications', Aug. 1946.
37 *Dáil Éireann debates*, vol. 5, cols 1233–48, 23 Nov. 1923; vol. 13, col. 244, 12 Nov., cols 503–43, 18 Nov., cols 859–902, 25 Nov. 1925.
38 Ibid., vol. 8, cols 1401–47, 16 July 1924, committee on finance, estimates.
39 Ibid., vol. 12, cols 1382–1410, 19 July 1925, for Blythe's comments on the civil servants in finance during the estimates debate.
40 Sweeney, *In Public Service*, p. 33.
41 IPCS, executive council minutes, 13 and 17 Feb., 21 and 27 Apr., 8 Aug., 6 Oct. 1922.
42 *Iris*, 2:4 (April 1924).
43 *Iris*, most editions through 1923 and 1924 record the loss of an officer in the leadership of an association.
44 NAI, Department of Finance, 'early E files', E18/7, 'Gregg to President', Apr. 1923.
45 UCDAD, Kennedy Papers, P4/238(1); NAI, Department of Finance, 'early E files', Wylie committee register.
46 NAI, Department of Finance, 'early E files', E2/58; E18/21; Gallagher, 'Memoirs of a civil servant', pp. 84–5.

47 IPCS, council minutes, 10 Feb. 1926.
48 E.g. *Iris*, 2:4 (Apr. 1924), 'Statement for the information of members of the Oireachtas'; 2:6 (June 1924), 'Circular to members of Dáil Éireann'.
49 *Iris*, 3:6 (June 1925).
50 Irish Labour History Museum and Archive (ILHS), ILPTUC, annual report and conference, 1920–27; WUMRC, Customs and Excise Federation, executive committee minutes, 19 Jan. 1922.
51 *Iris* (June–July 1925).
52 NAI, Department of Taoiseach, S.6247/FO/1, 'Memo on civil service by Department of Finance', Apr. 1932.
53 John Campbell, *'A loosely Shackled Fellowship': The History of Comhaltas Cána* (Dublin, 1980), pp. 126, 141.
54 Mary E. Daly, *Industrial development and Irish National Identity, 1922–1939* (New York, 1992), p. 14.
55 NAI, G2/2, executive council minutes, 12 May 1923.
56 NAI, G2/3, executive council minutes, 27 Oct. 1923.
57 NAI, FIN1/826/2, reply to circular F4/PMG.
58 Ibid., FIN1/826/5–6, financial statements, 5 Oct., 2 Nov. 1923.
59 *Dáil Éireann debates*, vol. 1, col. 1367, 6 Oct. 1922.
60 Arthur Mitchell, *Labour in Irish Politics 1890–1930: The Irish Labour Movement in an Age of Revolution* (Dublin, 1974), pp. 181–2.
61 NAI, G2/3 and 4, cabinet minutes, 15 May, 10 Oct. 1924.
62 NAI, Brennan Commission, BC/1, 'Evidence of H.P. Boland', 24 Nov. 1932, p. 9.
63 NAI, Department of Finance, E101/7/25.
64 UCDAD, Blythe Papers, P24/376, 'Differential in pay of women in the civil service'.
65 NAI, Department of Finance, E101/7/25, 'PSO'H to HPB', 30 May 1925.
66 NAI, Department of Finance, E100/3/26.
67 Civil Service Federation, *Statement Concerning Proposed Alterations in the Regulations Governing the Employment of Saorstát Civil Servants* (1924).
68 NAI, Department of Finance, E101/7/25.
69 WUMRC, Customs and Excise Federation, executive committee minutes, 25–6 Oct. 1922.
70 *Iris*, 1:4 (Apr. 1923); IPCS, council minutes, 23 Feb., 23 Mar., 12 Apr., 2 and 14 May, 23 June 1923.
71 *Iris*, 1:4 (Apr. 1923).
72 *Dáil Éireann debates*, vol. 8, cols 1028–9, 10 July 1924, cols 1540–2200, 17 July 1924.
73 NAI, Department of the Taoiseach, S.6247/FO/1.
74 *Iris*, 2:1 (Jan. 1924).
75 NAI, Department of Finance, circular 48/24; *Iris*, 3:1 (Jan. 1925); UCDAD, McGilligan Papers, P35a/31.
76 *Iris*, 3:2 (Feb. 1925); Civic and Public Services Union (CPSU), CSCA, executive committee minutes, 23 Jan. 1925; IPCS, council minutes, 3 and 17 Feb., 23 Mar. 1925.

77 CPSU, CSCA, executive committee minutes, 5 June 1925.
78 NAI, Department of Finance, E107/12/25, 'Circular no.10/26'.
79 *Iris*, 3:5 (May 1925); IPCS, council minutes, 23 June 1925, minutes of 6ᵗʰ AGM, 20 Apr. 1926; Sweeney, *In Public Service*, pp. 45–8.
80 CPSU, CSCA, executive council minutes, 4 Mar. 1927.
81 Ibid., 15 July, 12 Dec. 1927; IPCS council minutes, 7 Jan., 14 Feb., 4 Apr. 1927; Sweeney, *In Public Service*, pp. 46–8; NAI, Department of the Taoiseach, S.6247/FO/1.
82 NAI, Department of Finance, E107/12/25; NAI, Brennan Commission, BC/1, 'Finance memorandum section vi', 20 Jan. 1933.
83 *Seanad Éireann debates*, vol.13, col 27, 20 Nov. 1929.
84 IPCS, council minutes, 6 and 25 Oct. 1922.
85 Ibid., 6 Dec. 1922; 17 Jan. 1923.
86 *Iris*, 1:1 (Jan. 1923); *Wigg and Another* v. *Attorney-General of the Irish Free State*, No. 29 of 1926 in the Privy Council, pp. 46–102.
87 NA, T158/7, 'Waterfield to Cole, Whitehall, 20 Jan. 1922'.
88 IPCS, council minutes, 22 Jan., 23 Mar. 1923.
89 Ibid., 11 Jan., 4 Oct. 1923.
90 Irish Treaty Pensioners' Association, *Pensions and Compensation Guarantee of the British Government* (Dublin, n.d. 1923?).
91 *Wigg and Another*, writ of summons, 16 Nov. 1923.
92 Ibid.; *Iris*, 2:8 (Aug. 1924), 'AEO notes'.
93 *Iris*, 2:8 (Aug. 1924), 'Compensation committee notes'.
94 *Dáil Éireann debates*, vol. 8, cols 1249–50, 15 July 1924.
95 NAI, Department of Finance, E109/13/26, 'Superannuation payable under article 10 as at 1 Dec. 1925'.
96 *Dáil Éireann debates*, vol. 5, cols 877–8, 15 Nov. 1923.
97 Ibid., vol. 11, 14 May 1925, Questions.
98 IPCS, council minutes, 4 Oct., 5 Nov. 1923.
99 *Iris*, 1:7 (July 1923).
100 IPCS, council minutes, 3 Oct. 1924; 17 Feb. 1925; *Dáil Éireann debates*, vol. 9, cols 642, 1394, 4 and 21 Nov. 1924; vol. 11, 14 May 1925, Questions; vol.12, cols1390, 1403, 19 June 1925.
101 IPCS, council minutes, 25 Nov. 1924.
102 ILHS, MS 10/TOPA/1–3 [TOPA records are part of the deposition of the Communications Workers' Union]; IPCS, council minutes, 17 Feb., 23 Mar., 9 Apr. 1925.
103 ILHS, MS 10/TOPA/1; *Iris*, 3:5 (May 1925).
104 ILHS, William Norton Papers, 'Rough drafts of a constitution and circulars for a treaty officers association'.
105 ILHS, MS 10/TOPA/1.
106 *Iris*, 3:11 (Nov. 1925).
107 Niamh Brennan, 'Compensating southern Irish loyalists after the Anglo-Irish Treaty, 1922–32', Ph.D UCD1994, chapter 4.
108 Wigg-Cochrane, judgement of Mr Justice Johnston, 1 Apr. 1925.

109 ILHS, MS 10/ TOPA/, 'Opinion of counsel A. Alfred Dickie'; *Iris*, 3:6 (June 1925), 'Article 10 of the Treaty'.

110 IPCS, council minutes, 14 June 1924; CPSU, CSCA, executive council minutes, 10 July 1925; *Iris*, 3:8 (Aug. 1925), 'CSCA notes'.

111 NA, CAB 43/1, S.F. (B) 30th conclusions; 'Conclusions of a meeting of the British signatories to the treaty . . . 15 Jun. 1922'.

112 HLRO, Bonar Law Papers, 114/1/43, 'Memo on IFS constitution'.

113 NA, CAB 23/30, 'Cabinet 31(22) 1 June 1922, Irish situation'.

114 D.W. Harkness, *The Restless Dominion: The Irish Free State and the British Commonwealth of Nations 1921–31* (London, 1969), p. 9.

115 NA, CAB 23/30, cabinet conclusion 32(22) 2 June 1922; CAB 43/1, 'Conclusions of a meeting of British signatories, 10 Oct. 1922'.

116 Oxford, Bodleian Library, Curtis Papers, MS 90, fols 24–8.

117 Douglas, *Memoirs of James G. Douglas*, pp. 123–4.

118 Harkness, *Restless Dominion*, p. 81.

119 *Times Law Reports*, 1926–27, vol. XLIII, pp. 457–60.

120 WUMRC, MSS 232, Civil Service Confederation, annual reports, 1927–28, 1928–29.

121 *Dáil Éireann debates*, vol. 18, cols 727–8, 23 Feb. 1927, Questions.

122 Ibid., vol. 18, col. 385, 8 Feb. 1927.

123 Ibid., vol. 19, 20 May 1927, private notice questions.

124 WUMRC, MSS 232, Civil Service Confederation, seventh annual report 1927–28.

125 *Dáil Éireann debates*, vol. 22, col. 109, 22 Feb. 1928.

126 *Red Tape*, 17:199 (Apr. 1928).

127 WUMRC, MSS 232, Civil Service Confederation, half-yearly report 1928.

128 *Parliamentary Debates* (Lords), 70:25, cols 808–55, 25 Apr. 1928.

129 R.V.F. Heuston, *Lives of the Lord Chancellors 1885–1940* (London, 1964), pp. 440–3.

130 *Irish Law Times and Solicitor's Journal*, 62 (16 Feb. 1929), pp. 109–15; WUMRC, MSS 232, Civil Service Confederation, eighth annual report 1928–29; *Irish Times*, 14 Nov. 1928.

131 *Seanad Éireann debates*, vol. 13, cols 26–35, 20 Nov. 1929 for Senator Johnson's caustic and ironic history of the government's actions.

132 WUMRC, MSS 232, Civil Service Confederation, eighth annual report 1928–29; IPCS, council minutes, 9 Mar., 11 Dec. 1928; 12 Apr., 17 June 1929.

133 *Parliamentary Debates* (Commons), vol. 229, no.11, cols 1218–24, 11 July 1929; *Dáil Éireann debates*, vol. 31, cols 928–33, 11 July 1929; NAI, Department of the Taoiseach, S.5459; NAI, CAB 1/2, 26 Mar. 1928, Wigg-Cochrane case.

134 ILHS, MS 10/TOPA/1–3; *Parliamentary debates* (Commons), vol. 229, no. 11, cols 1218–24, 11 July 1929.

135 NLI, Thomas Johnson Papers, MS 17,171, 'Irish civil servants compensation 1928'.

136 Harkness, *Restless Dominion*, pp. 178–9.

137 *Dáil Éireann debates*, vol. 13, cols 45–7, 20 Nov. 1929.

138 Deirdre McMahon, *Republicans and Imperialists: Anglo-Irish Relations in the 1930s* (New Haven, 1984), pp. 128–35.

139 UCDAD, Kennedy Papers, P4/1228(1).
140 UCDAD, Fitzgerald Papers, P80/963; *Irish Times*, 7 Jan. 1930.
141 *Irishman*, 1 Mar. 1930.
142 *Irish Times*, 28 Feb. 1930.
143 ILHS, TOPA files, newscuttings, *Clare Champion*, 15 Mar. 1930.
144 *Irish Independent*, 21 Feb. 1930.
145 Ibid., 29 Mar. 1930.
146 WUMRC, MSS 296, National Whitley Council (staff side) minutes 18th meeting, 25 June 1923.
147 NA, CAB 23/29, 'Cabinet conclusion civil service arbitration board, 20 Jan. 1922'.
148 Mortimer and Ellis, *A Professional Union*, pp. 26–33.
149 ILHS, MS 10/TOPA/1–3, letters between Scales of the ITPA and Irvine of the IPCS, 11 May 1928–12 Jan. 1929.

6

Fianna Fáil and the civil service, 1932–38

Introduction

FIANNA FÁIL OFFERED the Irish electorate a synthesis of radical economic, social and constitutional change. It came to power as a republican party with a mandate to dismantle the Treaty as the constitutional basis of the Irish Free State, advance the gaelicisation of Irish society and secure the national economy through an autarchic policy of national self-sufficiency. In what was now in fact a two-party system Fianna Fáil was also seen as less hidebound than the Cumann na nGaedheal party and more ready to take radical action against the poverty and economic decline that was undermining public morale. The civil service had particular reason to welcome a Fianna Fáil government as the party deliberately courted its support with promises of an arbitration system to address its grievances. The promise of dynamic State action also signalled a central role for the civil service under a Fianna Fáil government. At the very least the Fianna Fáil party did not indulge in the anti-civil service rhetoric of the Cumann na nGaedheal government. The civil service could reasonably hope for a new, less confrontational relationship binding it to the Irish State.

The renewed campaign on pay

The year 1931 was one of reinvigorated organisation and protest in the Irish civil service. The renewal of campaigning was a response to economic depression, the example of successful agitation by British civil servants and the prospect of a general election in which the pay and conditions of civil servants would be an issue. In 1931 the economic situation in Ireland was bleak. The 1929 Wall Street crash had become a global depression cutting off emigration, then running at 33,000 a year, thereby raising unemployment. A bad harvest, stagnation in trade and a decline in tax revenues led to fears of a budgetary crisis. The Department of Finance urged reductions in pensions and in the pay of teachers, civil guards and the army both as a step toward a balanced budget and as a signal to employers to reduce pay and salaries in the private sector.[1]

In Britain, in response to civil service agitation, the Labour minority government elected in 1929 set up the Tomlin Royal Commission to inquire into and report on the structure and organisation of the civil service, its recruitment and remuneration; on differential rates of pay for men and for women; on arbitration machinery; and on conditions of retirement from the civil service. While the Tomlin committee investigation continued the Chancellor of the Exchequer agreed to postpone the reduction in bonus due when the British cost-of-living figure fell from sixty-five to sixty. Many of the Irish civil servants still looked to the British service, from which they had been severed for less than ten years, as the standard for comparisons in conditions and the model for organisation. Hence the Tomlin Commission was followed closely and its conclusions examined.[2] Tomlin's report, published in the summer of 1931, to the bitter disappointment of the British civil service, rejected almost all of their claims. However, on the issue of the war bonus Tomlin accepted that analogous employments outside the civil service did not have their salaries fluctuating in accordance with changes in the cost of living and that there was no good reason for continuing to fix the wages of the civil service on a basis different to that generally adopted in other employments. He recommended that the bonus system should be abolished and the bonus and basic pay be consolidated into a single salary. For civil servants in Ireland watching the British agitation this in itself was a significant advance and one they were determined to achieve for themselves.

The renewed agitation within the Irish civil service was driven by William Norton of the POWU, Archie Heron of the CSCA and T.J. Hughes of the CSF, who all jointly led the cross-service Cost-of-Living Bonus Joint Committee. More than anything else it was the campaign for a fairer bonus that forged unity and fighting spirit across the civil service. Archie Heron, a northern Protestant, republican veteran of 1916 and a Labour Party activist married to James Connolly's daughter Ina, was appointed the full-time general-secretary of the CSCA in December 1928.[3] The appointment of Heron was in response to the subtle, and less than subtle, intimidation visited on the CSCA executive by H.P. Boland. It was felt that a permanent general-secretary would be free to talk as an equal with the senior civil servants. The CSCA also decided to publish a monthly journal as a vehicle for information and to heighten its profile.[4] The journal, *An Peann*, was a quality production with regular reports on branches, executive council meetings, and meetings with officials, coverage of Dáil reports, updates on the fortunes of civil service in other countries, pieces in Gaelic and regular reports of civil service sports activity.

Together Norton, Hughes and Heron adopted a more confrontational and public campaign against the government. They organised a mass demonstration by the civil service in opposition to the government cuts in the cost-of-living bonus.[5] In December 1929 Norton invited Heron and Hughes, along with the IPCS, to join together in a new permanent Joint Council of Civil Service Organisations.[6] The emergence of Norton and Heron as leaders marks a new strategy for civil service agitation. In the absence of an arbitration forum they decided that the issue of the cost-of-living bonus would be politicised by lobbying TDs to support the single demand for a new calculation of the bonus figure. Blythe was to be harassed by the constant questioning of sympathetic, well-briefed Labour and other deputies. *An Peann* urged all civil servants to question candidates in the next general election on their attitudes and policies on civil service pay, an action that was censured by the cabinet as overtly political.[7] At the same time a publicity campaign on civil service pay and conditions was launched aimed at the newspapers to educate public opinion. The Department of Finance was sufficiently alarmed at this very public washing of dirty linen to caution the civil service representatives not to write to the press on official matters. This clumsy attempt at censorship was immediately published in the civil service journal *Iris*.[8]

In August 1930 a cross-party deputation of TDs and senators met the Minister for Finance to urge that he meet the cross-service Joint Committee. The delegation included Peadar Doyle and T.P. Hennessy from Cumann na nGaedheal, Sean Lemass and Gerry Boland from Fianna Fáil, and T.J. O'Connell and Senator Johnson of the Labour Party.[9] Blythe, while indicating a willingness to discuss these issues with the civil service, stuck by his refusal to meet any representative of the civil service who was not himself a civil servant. The problem was that Archie Heron and William Norton were both full-time union organisers, and not civil servants. Blythe maintained that as non-civil servants they would have access to confidential information but would not be bound by the rules of secrecy and disclosure that ordinarily covered public servants. The more pressing reason was that, as was becoming evident, both Heron and Norton were gifted organisers and skilled negotiators.[10] H.P. Boland, who clearly had a fetish about controlling access to the minister, had suggested that the service representation might be recast on the model of Northern Ireland. There the departments directly elected their delegates, emasculating the associations.[11]

The campaigns around which the civil service was successfully building a new cross-service unity concerned, firstly, the operation of the 'war bonus' and, secondly, the demand for an arbitration board. When the bonus had been first determined in 1920 it stood at 130, that is the purchasing power of £100 in 1914 was represented by £230 in 1920. However, only the lower civil service salaries were fully compensated for this inflation by a bonus of 130 per cent. As part of the contribution of the civil service to restoring the national economy, higher officers had their bonus reduced therefore forgoing full compensation. Only the first £91 5s 0d of a civil servant's salary attracted the full 130 per cent bonus; the next £108 15s 0d received 60 per cent and the next £300 0s 0d received 45 per cent. These rates had been further cut by the 'supercut' of September 1921. The bonus had risen initially but with the onset of the post-war depression, and especially as prices collapsed after the Wall Street crash, the bonus had fallen. A civil servant on a basic salary of £300 had, in July 1920, an inclusive salary of £537 because of the application of the war bonus. By July 1925 that had fallen to an inclusive salary of £467. A civil servant on a basic salary of £500 in July 1920 got an inclusive salary of £831. By July 1925 this had fallen to £733. Thus civil servants' actual income had declined year on year since the foundation of the State. This decline had initially been most severe for those on higher salaries because of the 'supercut' of 1921 but since then the application of periodic percentage cuts, rather than lump sum cuts, had particularly hit the lower paid. In addition the civil service, since the foundation of the State, had to accept the general increase in income taxation and longer hours of work with shorter holidays.[12] An extraordinary innovation was introduced in 1925 when the government imposed a differential scale for married and unmarried civil servants whereby single men and women were paid less than married men, who also got an additional allowance for any children.[13]

In March 1931 the Labour deputies Richard Sidney Anthony of Cork Borough and William Davin of Leix-Offaly brought to the Dáil a motion 'that in view of the discontent prevalent amongst the lower grades in the Civil Service, the Dáil is of the opinion that the Executive Council should set up a Commission of Enquiry to investigate and report on the present method of computation of the cost-of-living bonus and its application to civil servants' salaries and wages'.[14] Fianna Fáil had straddled the fence in the populist anti-civil servant campaigns being driven by provincial newspapers, farmer organisations, chambers of commerce and some local authorities, by combining attacks on the pay of higher civil servants with sympathy for the lowly pay of the clerical staff under them. In February 1929 the party newspaper the *Nation*, while insisting on the absolute necessity of reductions in the size and cost of the public service, using 1914 as the datum line for numbers and salaries, was sure that cuts of a general application were more welcome than 'the dismissal of some poor struggling, perhaps temporary, officials'.[15] In the Dáil debate on the Anthony and Davin motion it was the Fianna Fáil speakers who made the best speeches. Anthony tended to ramble off the subject and be repetitive in his speech though he did manage to make the point that the fundamental problem was the absence of any acceptable form of conciliation and arbitration within the civil service. MacEntee and Lemass spoke on the Fianna Fáil side in speeches that were sharply focused and well researched. MacEntee made the point that an inequitable method for calculating the government's cost-of-living figures had an impact on the industrial relations between all employers and employees throughout the country and not just within the State service. He then went on to discuss the historic roots of the cost-of-living figure to show that it never had any scientific or defensible method for its calculation, that it was based on the household accounts of a few unrepresentative working-class families, that a representative budget from the household of a civil servant had not been attempted and that the demand that it be re-examined was therefore eminently reasonable. Lemass in turn attacked the fact that the minister, by refusing to deal with the service in a reasonable manner and create acceptable forms of arbitration, had forced the civil service into public agitation and allowed the question to be politicised. Both Fianna Fáil speakers drew a distinction between what MacEntee called the 'privates and corporals in the cuff and collar brigade' and the higher civil servants. Lemass, pointing out thatthough the lower grades were being shabbily treated many of the higher civil servants were being paid far too much, explicitly gave it as party policy that the party would seek to level out salaries. Blythe and McGilligan, the Minister for Industry and Commerce, spoke for the government. Blythe, perhaps still smarting from the Wigg-Cochrane case, insisted that the cost-of-living bonus was part of the inherited conditions of the transferred officers and that any attempt to change it would simply unravel the whole issue of their Treaty rights; good or bad they were stuck with it. That the Whitley Councils and the arbitration board were also inherited conditions was ignored. The government ministers both drove home the point that the civil servants' real objective was the restoration of the Whitley Councils or some equivalent empowering body and this they were not going to get. The motion was defeated but the grievances of the civil service got a good airing and Fianna Fáil gave every sign that a better deal could be expected from them.[16] The civil service demand for an investigation into the cost-of-living bonus and for an arbitration board had received a degree of notice in the national newspapers.[17] What the debate had failed to clarify was that the objection of the civil service was not to the method of calculating the bonus but rather to its application. In particular they objected to the diminution in the upper end of salary scales by the reduction in the proportion of salary entitled to full compensation.

The civil service joint committee decided to step up the campaign against the bonus cut through well-publicised mass meetings of the civil service.[18] With the end of the seven-year transition period the Treaty right to retire 'as a consequence of the change of government' had ended. The threat of mass resignation, however unlikely it might have been in reality, was no longer available. The contractual relationship between the State and the civil service that was enshrined in the Treaty was approaching the end of its useful life. If the civil service was to achieve some control in laying a foundation for the relationship binding it to the State in the future it would have to create a united campaign to make it a political issue. This was despite a consciousness of the danger that political campaigns would pose to civil service traditions. The only basis for such a campaign was pay. Pay, it was hoped, would open the door to reconstituting an arbitration board, restoring some measure of power over their conditions to the civil service. With the Labour Party being supportive and with the Fianna Fáil party not being hostile, it seemed achievable.

The plan for the agitation included high profile public meetings of the impoverished wives and families of civil servants with advertisements in the press, placards, sandwich men and handbills. With a further cut in the bonus due at the beginning of September a mass meeting of civil servants was called at the Metropolitan Hall in Abbey Street, Dublin. The meeting, addressed by Norton, Hughes and Heron passed the motion that, 'having regard to the hardship involved, especially in the case of the lower-paid classes, calls for the suspension of the impending reduction in the cost-of-living bonus and an immediate inquiry into the cost-of-living index figure and its application to the Civil Service'. The meeting also proposed that 'steps should be taken to institute suitable conciliation and arbitration machinery for the Service'.[19] The journal of the CSCA, *An Peann*, maintained the campaign, carrying articles and letters critical of the government record on pay and promotions and urging members to come out in support of the Labour Party in the next general election. The campaign focused on the demand for an inquiry into the war bonus and the method of its calculation. It would have wiser, as we shall see, to have concentrated on the application of the bonus, rather than its calculation.

Fianna Fáil in power

In November 1931 Blythe proposed to meet a projected deficit of £900,000 by a combination of increased taxes and cuts in the salaries of the public service. Before the cuts could be implemented the government dissolved the Dáil and called a general election. The combined civil service associations sent a letter to all the Dáil candidates asking whether, if elected, they would support arbitration for the civil service subject to the over-riding authority of the Oireachtas. The governing Cumann na nGaedheal party campaigned on a shrill law and order platform. Fianna Fáil on the other hand campaigned on economic development, an end to emigration and full employment. As part of this strategy of concentrating on economic problems, Fianna Fáil introduced the threatened cuts in civil service pay as an election issue.[20] In a speech in Rathmines in Dublin South, a middle-class suburban constituency where many civil servants lived and where Sean Lemass was the party candidate, de Valera promised that though public service pay would have to be examined, civil service salaries below £300 or £400 a year would not be cut. Furthermore he stated it as his belief that 'it is only right that there should be an Arbitration Board for the Civil Service to deal with matters between the Service and Executive. We would be prepared to agree that an Arbitration Board be set up and would assent to an inquiry into the basis on which the cost-of-living bonus was calculated.'[21] Fianna Fáil's courting of the public service was in part a reassuring gesture toward civil service fears (fears that were shared with the army and the police) that if elected it would be a target for attack by the former anti-Treaty republicans. But it was primarily a shrewd attempt to win the support of the massed lower ranks of an increasingly disgruntled civil service. The threatened cuts in salaries, the generally sympathetic attitude of Fianna Fáil, along with the promise of an arbitration board meant that most civil servants welcomed the change of government in February 1932, especially as the minority Fianna Fáil government depended on the support of the Labour Party, now led by William Norton of the POWU who was elected in Dublin.[22]

Speaking in the Dáil, Sean Lemass once described Fianna Fáil as the 'slightly constitutional' party.[23] Entry to power was quickly to prove that it was also only slightly a revolutionary party. Initially de Valera moved to assure the senior civil servants that he had no intention of dismissing any of them and that Fianna Fáil were not about to introduce a spoils system into public service employment. De Valera was at the time under intense pressure from the IRA to purge the civil service of the old regime.[24] However, unlike the Cumann na nGaedheal government, Fianna Fáil shared with the civil service associations a dislike of the senior civil servants in the Department of Finance – men described by MacEntee as 'intensely hostile to Fianna Fáil . . . unalterably and fanatically attached to the English interest'.[25] In Tod Andrews' more colourful description they were seen as 'a crowd of Free State bastards'.[26] De Valera was himself afraid that the civil service would not co-operate with a Fianna Fáil government and had prepared a list of former students of Blackrock and Rockwell Colleges, now in the civil service, on whom he felt he could rely.[27] John Moynihan, assistant editor of the *Irish Press* and not a civil servant, was brought in to head the president's department.[28] But in fact the only civil servant dismissed by Fianna Fáil was E.P. McCarron, secretary of the Department of Local Government. But that was not until late in 1936 and reflected personal difficulties with his minister rather than with the government.[29]

Fianna Fáil did move quickly to placate one group, the dismissed civil servants of the civil war period. After the most cursory examination of their case a committee reinstated those civil servants of republican sympathies who had been dismissed or had resigned from the British government, or from Dáil Éireann, the Provisional Government or the Irish Free State.[30] The declaration of allegiance to the State that had been demanded of civil servants was dropped. Also the preference that had been accorded to ex-members of the army in public service employment was discontinued.[31] Many civil servants welcomed indications of the end of the dominance that the Department of Finance previously enjoyed.[32] The May 1932 budget, far from retrenching, promised increases in road-building, housing, unemployment benefit and pensions.

The Johnson and Brennan inquiries

The Fianna Fáil government moved to meet their commitments to the civil service on the bonus and on an arbitration board. Already it seemed that a more egalitarian and open relationship between civil service and State was being created. Two inquiries were announced, a committee to inquire into the principles and methods of the calculation of the cost-of-living index figure under Senator Thomas Johnson, the former Labour Party leader, and a commission to inquire into 'the method by which arbitration can best be applied for the settlement of questions relating to pay and conditions of service' under Joseph Brennan, former secretary of the Department of Finance.[33] The Department of Finance had tried to limit the brief of the Brennan Commission to 'the machinery for discussion and settlement of questions relating to pay and other conditions of service' so the explicit reference to arbitration seemed to signal a victory for the staff over the department.[34]

The promise, as it seemed, of a new era of State-civil service relations galvanised the civil service associations. The CSCA now dominated the organisation of the lower grades. The POWU had of course their own general-secretary Norton elected to the Dáil. The IPCS April 1932 annual general meeting saw earnest speeches on the valuable contribution made by civil servants to the State and a long discussion on the future policy of the Institution. Membership numbers began to climb again with new members joining from across the service.[35] The IPCS met with the CSF to compare their proposals for an arbitration scheme and bring them both into line so as to ensure the maximum of cross-service unanimity in meetings with the Brennan Commission. At the same time the IPCS executive circularised the membership to obtain data on family budgets and increased costs since 1922 for submission to the Johnson committee.[36]

Neither of these commissions lived up to the hopes of the civil service. There was disappointment that the Johnson inquiry had a narrow brief that precluded examining the application of the cost-of-living bonus rather than simply its calculation. Any examination of its application would have to look at the injustice of the reductions in bonus at the higher salaries. The campaign by the civil service associations failed to make this distinction clear. Instead their campaign seemed to suggest that they suffered because the index was based on a working-class rather than middle-class budget with the attendant extras of insurance, higher rents and the cost of maidservants.[37]

At the Brennan Commission hearings Boland worked to keep the discussion confined to the abstract principle of determining responsibility within the State for the civil service. He was quite prepared to admit that what he termed 'the fleshpots of Whitleyism' were of great value to the civil servant, but he was also absolutely sure that it was bad for the State. The ability to make decisions ought to be reserved to the highest circles of the State (which now included higher civil servants such as himself) and it would be unacceptable that lower staff should have a hand in that process. The making of policy was a higher function, its execution a lower function. It was in this light also that Boland chose to explain the objection to a non-civil servant acting as a representative of the civil service; he would be free to speak above his station. Boland also suggested, without being explicit, that Whitleyism was a relic of the former British regime and that the demand for it was primarily from transferred officers who pined for the old days.

Boland was prepared to talk at length about the problems that might arise, but it was clear that the main problem was there was no mechanism by which a non-civil servant could be controlled by the State. To admit a right to the civil service to decision-making, or to choosing its own representative, would be a surrender of the absolute control of the civil service enjoyed by the State.[38] Gordon Campbell, secretary of the Department of Industry and Commerce, was dismissive of this abstract argument and was quite clear that the problem was the civil service having no access to the minister, mainly because of Boland. Boland was exceptionally autocratic in his attitude and dealings with the civil service. This may have been a result of his First World War experience in Whitehall when the Treasury had let control slip away with disastrous results, as he saw it. William O'Brien, the doyen of the service, tended to agree with Campbell and cited the view of the customs staff that the reports of the CSRC were always treated with silent contempt by Boland in finance. O'Brien, who had run a department under the old regime, felt that the administration of the Free State had become utterly centralised under finance and matters that would have been decided at departmental level before were now entirely in the hands of finance.[39]

The staff side representatives, on the other hand, kept their contributions focused on concrete issues of salary levels and their determination. They scotched Boland's assertion that the civil service was well paid compared with other similar employments, as well as the 'article of faith' that civil service conditions were inherited from the British regime and preserved by Article 10 of the Treaty and any interference would be unconstitutional. The view of the association representatives was that the State ought to be a model employer. The main problem so far as they were concerned was the dominance of the Department of Finance on staff matters, which never looked beyond cost. Their recommendation was a specialised department of the State should take over but that the pay and conditions of the civil service should not be in the hands of elected politicians. The model for arbitration that was available was the Wylie compensation committee, which in their view worked efficiently and to the satisfaction of staff and State.[40]

The civil service associations were thrown by the line of questioning that they met at the hearings of the Brennan Commission. The terms of reference of the commission clearly implied that the principle of arbitration had been conceded and that the job of the inquiry was simply to arrive at how arbitration would best operate. Instead the civil service representatives found themselves being compelled to argue the case for arbitration in principle. Brennan in particular repeatedly threw in the point that under the constitution the Executive Council bore responsibility to the Dáil for the administration of the public service, a responsibility that could not be taken away, and therefore any arbitration tribunal that bound the Executive Council to any payment without the approval of the Dáil would be unconstitutional. In particular the responsibility of the Minister for Finance for the budget would be compromised. In fact the Brennan Commission had been thoroughly 'stitched up' by Brennan and Boland. Brennan's own correspondence shows that he and Boland were in complete agreement that any form of arbitration would fatally undermine the control that the department had over the civil service. By preparing and rehearsing questions before the daily sittings of the commission Boland and Brennan between them developed the strategy of the constitutional block and used it ruthlessly to destroy the principle of arbitration, despite the promises of the Fianna Fáil government.[41] The commission hearings thus turned into a pantomime with Brennan and Boland having cosy chats on why arbitration was constitutionally impossible and Brennan then aggressively accusing the civil service representatives of attempting to make the Executive Council act in an unconstitutional manner.[42] It is worth noting that the cabinet agreed to pay Boland a gratuity of £450 for his services to the Brennan Commission, which suggests that the cabinet was not unhappy at his success in undermining a government pledge.[43] The IPCS soon recognised the futility of the effort and decided early in the proceedings to make no further statement to the commission.[44]

The Johnson committee proved as disappointing. Limited to the operation of the cost-of-living figure Johnson was convinced by the argument of the civil servants that the figure was based on a cost of living of a working-class rather than a middle-class family. However, such a figure would not in fact alter the final result of the calculation, the general tendency to fall was simply confirmed via a different route. He recommended that a middle-class figure might be usefully compiled as a reassurance to the civil service and that alcoholic drink ought to be added to the basket of goods used in reckoning the cost of living. The Department of Finance was relieved at these findings. The real weakness of the figure was that it was based on a countrywide computation that made no allowance for the very significant difference between Dublin and the rest of the country in, for instance, rent. The fear that Johnson might recommend a separate figure for Dublin from that of the rest of the country was not borne out. The department could delay on establishing the middle-class cost-of-living figure in the expectation that the basic plus bonus salaries of the civil service would probably be consolidated into a single figure within ten years. Effort could now concentrate on ensuring that consolidation occurred at the lowest figure possible.[45]

'No man is worth more than £1000'

The civil service associations did get their face-to-face meeting with the minister, but in circumstances they had not expected. A decision by the government to impose salary cuts created an unprecedented unity across the entire civil service, embracing even their former nemesis Boland. The Irish land annuities were repayments by Irish peasants of the loans made by the British exchequer under the 1903 Land Act to facilitate tenants buying out their landlords. Under a secret agreement at the margins of the 1921 Treaty settlement the Irish Free State had agreed to continue collecting the annuities and to transfer the money to London. Fianna Fáil continued to collect the money but then retained it in the Irish exchequer. The British government retaliated by imposing a tariff on Irish cattle exported to Britain. This launched the 'Economic War' of tariff and counter-tariff that threatened an immediate financial crisis.[46] A cabinet committee recommended cuts in public service pay ranging from 2 per cent on a salary of £200 to a staggering 20 per cent on a salary of £1,500.[47] These cuts were not simply reductions in the bonus but cuts in the basic salaries, which had hitherto been sacrosanct. They cuts were not designed to deliver any substantial savings to the exchequer, nor could they.[48] Instead they should be seen as an implementation of the long-standing Fianna Fáil axiom of cheap government, frugal comfort and egalitarian poverty as the basis for national revival. In the Dáil de Valera had threatened to 'cut off the top hats' and his belief that 'no man is worth more than £1000' was confirmed by the experience of office. His first act as president of the executive was to reduce his own and his ministers' salaries.[49] De Valera was a man who liked sacrifice. The civil service would join the politicians as inspirational examples of frugality in the national interest. The cuts in public service pay which the Cumann na nGaedheal government had proposed as an economic measure were revived by Fianna Fáil but now as a social measure designed to effect a general levelling of incomes across Irish society.[50] All branches of the State service were to experience reductions in pay. Those civil servants protected by Article 10 along with the judiciary were to offer voluntary reductions.[51]

Not surprisingly the proposed cuts, contradicting as they did the whole tenor of the election campaign and the promise of the Brennan and Johnson inquiries, met with an implacable opposition from the civil service. Those opposed included the most senior departmental heads in the civil service who now found themselves on the receiving end of the rhetoric they had been delivering to their staff.[52] The national school teachers, the police and the army all rejected the cuts and the chances of the judiciary volunteering to accept salary cuts were immediately discounted.

In June MacEntee indicated to the civil service organisations that he would be available to the CSRC to discuss staff reaction to the cuts if the POWU, CSCA and the IPCS would rejoin the representative council.[53] The three organisations met to co-ordinate a response. The IPCS was very reluctant to re-enter a representative council that they had already rejected as an inadequate forum but because the issue of cuts was one that affected the whole service and was therefore one on which a united cross-service fight was possible the decision was made to rejoin. The CSCA were tempted if only because the minister had raised no objection to Archie Heron being their delegate. The POWU, led by William Norton, was now the only civil service association that still refused to rejoin the CSRC. But with Norton now in the Dáil and with Fianna Fáil needing the support of Labour, it may have seemed to the POWU that it had the better forum for negotiation.[54]

Predictably the minister was unable to attend, although the presence of McElligott, not Boland, in the chair did signal that the meeting was being treated seriously. Hughes, Heron and Brunicardi objected that they had returned to the CSRC and prepared statements on the assumption that the minister would be present to hear them. Despite the soothing promises of McElligott, Heron and the clerical officers' delegation immediately left the meeting but the IPCS delegation, while expressing their disappointment that the minister was not present, decided to stay. Hughes of the Federation led the attack on the proposed cuts. Sceptical of the assurances that the cuts would be for one year only, he underlined the inconsistency of the government initiating two inquiries into the pay and conditions of the civil service while prejudicing any conclusion they might reach by imposing a salary cut. Brunicardi dealt more briefly on the low rates of pay that the professional civil servants received when compared to those in private practice, pointing out that the only advantage that the State offered in return was certainty of income. With the government now proposing to cut salaries this single assurance was now worthless. What was perhaps surprising to the staff side representatives was the vehemence with which the official side agreed with them in attacking the cuts, although this was hardly unexpected as the official side was composed of the most senior and highly paid civil servants in the government departments. Henry O'Friel, who had refused to take an oath of allegiance to the Crown in 1918 and had been an active Sinn Féin judge and leader in Dublin County Council, predicted that it would lead to a loss of the senior civil servants under Article 10 retirements due to a worsening of conditions. Even Boland joined in the attack. Boland was, however, still very nervous of the consequences of the minister meeting the staff side and that the CSCA, an 'aggressive' association, would succeed in its attempts to coerce the minister into future attendance.[55]

At the next meeting of the representative council the staff representatives finally got to meet the minister. With the minister in attendance the meeting had representatives of the full spectrum of the civil service associations, including Heron of the CSCA. The implication of the submission by the associations was there would not be agreement for a voluntary cut and an imposed cut would damage the public service and certainly lead to a large number of resignations under Article 10. Again, despite the presence of the minister, the staff side senior civil servants (including Boland) weighed in with substantial reasons why the proposed cuts were unjust, unwise and would prove damaging in the longer term. For his part MacEntee insisted that there would have to be some cuts, 'intensely distasteful' as they might be.[56]

Faced with a wall of resistance the government shelved the cuts and established another committee, essentially to gain time, charged with inquiring into 'the facts and circumstances regarding the pay of each of the services . . . with a view to definite recommendations being made to government as to what reductions could be made' to achieve a reduction of £250,000 in the current year.[57] The O'Connell 'Cuts' Committee, as it became known, included a cattle dealer and two farmers, as well as a chartered accountant, Donal O'Connor, and the chairman Philip O'Connell, director of the Agricultural Credit Corporation. The civil service associations on the CSRC urged that the O'Connell committee should meet in public and hear oral testimony from the civil service.[58] This was denied and the O'Connell committee met in private, though it did invite submission. The O'Connell committee failed to agree on the extent to which the civil service salaries ought to be cut. The farmer representatives recommended that the basic salary as well as bonus be cut. In fact they recommended that discontented civil servants be sent to spend 'some time in the beet fields of Leinster, the cow pastures of the Kerry hills or the turf banks of the Bog of Allen for £1 a week' to bring them to their senses.[59] The other members of the committee reported that the civil servants' basic salary was already so low that it should not be cut but that the variable bonus could bear a further cut. So far as the minister was concerned neither report was useful as neither recommended the level of cuts already signalled. When the 'cuts' committee invited written submissions from the associations it was decided not to bother. The associations also asked that the bonus cut due in January 1933 should be postponed until the Johnson committee could make its report.[60] The government agreed that pending the report of the Johnson committee 50 per cent of the drop in bonus due to begin in January 1933 should be suspended on basic salaries below £2 per week.[61]

A Fianna Fáil majority government

By late 1932 the Fianna Fáil government was coming under increasing pressure. The anger of the larger farmers hit by the Economic War allied with frustration within the Cumann na nGaedheal party led to the creation of the fascistic Army Comrades' Association or 'Blueshirts'. Street fights between the Blueshirts and released IRA men created a fear of social disintegration. The government's attempts to restore control of the budget were being frustrated by the civil service and teacher resistance. When Norton warned in late December that his party would not support the public service pay cuts de Valera dissolved the Dáil during the Christmas recess. In the shortest possible election campaign, exploiting the disunity in the opposition, Fianna Fáil won a clear majority of one seat.[62]

The cabinet returned immediately to considering the cuts in public service pay. Despite the senior civil servants in the Department of Finance, Boland most prominently, reminding the minister of the cuts already imposed on the civil service the cabinet decided to impose percentage cuts on all public service salaries above £320 per annum ranging from 1 per cent to 10 per cent, to last for one year only.[63] The bill to implement the cuts, the Public Services (Temporary Economies) Bill was brought before the Dáil on 24 March. Deductions from civil service salaries began to be applied from 1 April, before the bill had completed its passage into legislation. The civil service associations co-ordinated a joint strategy of refusing to discuss or bargain, only offering an emphatic 'no' to the bill at the representative council, and insisting that it be brought to arbitration.[64] The IPCS invited the CSF and the CSCA to investigate the possibility of mounting a legal challenge to the cuts. Neither Heron nor Hughes, however, were interested in legal action, and the IPCS was not interested in any renewed public agitation. Probably Heron and Hughes were right. As Dickie, the legal opinion sought by the IPCS, reminded them civil service regulations gave the minister full authority to set pay and conditions for the civil service as he saw fit. In the absence of any other strategy the civil service associations all returned to pursuing the minister from within the CSRC while forwarding amendments to the Dáil and Seanad to weaken the bill.[65]

In May the Johnson committee reported on the cost-of-living calculation, recommending, as we have seen, that a middle-class budget more representative of the lifestyle of the civil service should be compiled. The CSRC seized upon this finding (although Boland already knew that it would have no effect on the final figure) and asked the minister to suspend the cut due in June. Boland warned MacEntee that the civil service representative associations were trying to draw him into a situation in which, by constant delay and reductions in the cost-of-living cuts, the whole system of the bonus would be undermined and consolidation achieved at a higher rate than was correct or justified.[66] The associations had already achieved a split in the cost-of-living cut in January 1933 when salaries below £2 enjoyed a lower rate of bonus reduction. At the CSRC meeting the civil service staff side spoke briefly and to some effect on the uncertainty that the cuts – 1 January, 1 April and now impending on 1 July – were having on civil service morale and suggested that a delay on imposing the July cut would go a long way to allay discontent. Despite Boland's memorandum MacEntee agreed to defer any further cuts for six weeks to allow the staff associations to consider the Johnson committee report. He did, however, firmly indicate that all discussions on civil service issues must remain within the CSRC and that the government had banned the public meetings that the Federation had planned to protest against the economies bill.[67] The civil service associations accepted this as it seemed that the door giving access to the minister was now opening to them.

The Lisney case and 'worsening of conditions'

It was at this point that Article 10 once again came to the rescue of the civil service. TOPA had been kept in being as the organisation to supply the staff side to the compensation committee. The right of civil servants to voluntary retirement had lapsed after seven years. But the right of civil servants to retire due to worsening of conditions had been retained in the 1929 Act. This form of discharge, equivalent to today's 'constructive dismissal', was rarely cited; the compensation board had decided only five cases since its original establishment. The compensation terms were the same as for ordinary discharge and therefore better than for voluntary retirement due to the change of government. In November 1933 TOPA successfully argued that in the case of Harry Lisney of the Valuation Office the cut in basic salary, not just the bonus, was a worsening of conditions. Lisney, who was fifty years of age with thirty years of service, was entitled to an added ten years of actual service. Lisney, on receiving the court's judgement, which under the legislation was not contestable by either side, went immediately to his office and handed in his resignation. He went on to employ his skills as a valuer in establishing a very successful auctioneering and valuation business that continues to this day. The result of the Lisney judgement was an immediate rush of 132 applications of which 109 succeeded. Most of these were from senior officers, forty-six of them from the Department of Finance, which was the department to suffer the greatest loss of senior officers. Neither claimant nor State could contest the decisions of the compensation board. The final cost was an annual pension charge of £29,645 and a lump sum payment of £48,675.[68] The result of the government's determination to assert its authority over the civil service was a considerable addition to the pensions bill of the State.[69] The gains of the temporary economies were wiped out and the cuts were restored the next year.[70]

When the Brennan Commission report raised doubts as to whether an arbitration scheme for the public service was constitutional, the CSF asked that the government call a special conference of the service representatives to finalise their own scheme of arbitration. The government replied suggesting that the Federation raise the Brennan report at the CSRC, ignoring the fact that

Brennan had in fact no acceptable proposal for an arbitration board. The Federation then withdrew from the CSRC, leaving the IPCS as now the only substantial service association on the council.[71] Without any formal decision the government allowed the CSRC to decline by extending the time between meetings, or simply failing to hold or call any meetings.[72] When the associations wrote to a minister asking to discuss some contentious problem the stock reply was always that the issue was one that properly ought to be dealt with by the representative council, which of course had ceased to have any real existence beyond the imagination of the establishment division in the Department of Finance.

The civil service associations had therefore to rely on the Labour Party and Norton in particular to make the case for less oppressive relationship between the State and the civil service. In January 1937 the government demanded that the civil service associations accept the arbitration scheme proposed by the Minister for Finance and agree to work it. In the absence of such an undertaking no arbitration scheme would be produced and the existing system would continue. The government scheme merely formalised the complete authority of the Minister for Finance over the civil service. The minister would have authority to appoint the chairman of an arbitration tribunal, determine what may be discussed at the tribunal, exercise a veto on the delegates of the associations, prevent publication of any recommendation and retain the right to reject any recommendation without explanation. The government proposal was a rejection of the fundamental requirements of the civil service associations – an agreed chairman, no restriction on the right of the civil service to employ professional representation, and some role for the Oireachtas in determining the relationship binding the State and the civil service. The government proposal was in effect an official muzzle on the associations. In the Dáil debates Norton concentrated on the breach of faith by the Fianna Fáil government, which was now prepared to abandon earlier promises made when in opposition. John A. Costello, speaking for Fine Gael, delivered a more historical and constitutional analysis of the relationship between the Irish State and its civil service. The political classes in Ireland, unlike in Britain where they were bred for power, were inexperienced with no expectation of a political career. They had been propelled to power in a revolution. Such a government required a highly efficient, adequately paid and secure civil service to compensate for its inexperience. This required also that the civil service should not fear the minister. The apparently vindictive dismissal of Edward McCarron in November 1936, the secretary of the Department of Local Government, had unnerved the civil service. What the State required, argued Costello, was an independent and expert civil service, not a cowed bureaucracy that was a machine in the hands of the minister. MacEntee did not even reply to the debate.[73]

Bunreacht na hÉireann

In 1937 a referendum approved *Bunreacht na hÉireann,* the new Irish constitution drafted by de Valera. This constitution was the last stage in the dismantling of the Treaty settlement. It described Ireland as the entire island but stated that pending the integration of the national territory the laws passed would apply only to the territory of the former Irish Free State. It stated that all power derived from the people and created an elected presidency as head of State.

Hoping to use the constitutional referendum as a springboard for electoral success the Fianna Fáil government dissolved the Dáil and called a general election for 1 July 1937. The result was the return of a reduced Fianna Fáil now once again dependent on Labour support to form a government. Included in the Labour TDs were Norton, general-secretary of the POWU and and Archie Heron the former general-secretary of the CSCA. The scenes of jubilant celebration by supposedly non-political civil servants in government departments brought a rebuke from finance at such a breakdown.[74] The civil service was now confident that with Labour pressure the government would have to concede an arbitration and conciliation scheme. A motion directing the government to establish arbitration machinery of the civil service was introduced by Norton and supported by the Fine Gael party. In the debate Costello dealt with the question as to what extent the civil service of the Irish State was in fact a continuation of the former Castle regime. He saw continuity in preservation of the worst aspects of Treasury attitudes and authority in the senior figures of the finance department. These attitudes had in fact been long abandoned, he argued, in Britain where the Whitley system of arbitration had empowered the civil service. In Costello's view an independent civil service was the best guardian of democracy and the public interest against corrupt and vindictive politicians. MacEntee was forced to reply. His defence of his proposed arbitration tribunal and of the record of Fianna Fáil dealings with the civil service was ineffectual. The Labour Party motion instructing the government to enter negotiations with the civil service for a conciliation and arbitration system was carried by one vote on 28 April 1938. Rather than concede to the Dáil motion de Valera dissolved the government and forced an election.[75] Fianna Fáil returned with a secure majority of sixteen and now even more determined not to concede anything to the civil service demand for arbitration.

The final case under Article 10

Article 10 had one last and rather shabby outing in 1938, in the aftermath of the passing of the new constitution. During the debate on the constitution the civil service associations had expressed their unease that their rights under the Treaty and under the Irish Free State constitution would be abolished. This would mean that the only protection was that provided by the 1929 Civil Servants (Transferred Officers) Compensation Act. As this was legislative and not constitutional protection a government would be perfectly able to alter or abolish it. Peter Hegarty, an assistant inspector of National Health Insurance, represented by TOPA, brought a claim to the compensation board on the basis that the new constitution of Ireland discharged him from the service of the Irish Free State and that he was entitled to compensation under his retained rights. At the hearing John A. Costello, representing Hegarty, argued that the constitution was a revolution in as much as it ended one State and initiated another. The government found itself having to argue, contrary to its rhetoric during the constitutional debate, that the constitution introduced no innovation and that Hegarty had the same employer before and after the passing of the constitution. On 17 August the board found that though Hegarty was not discharged by the National Health Insurance he was discharged by the government of the Irish Free State as one State had been replaced by another State and therefore he was entitled to his compensation claim.[76] The judgement of the board could be read as implying that the entire civil service had been discharged and therefore might be entitled to compensation. The government immediately issued an official circular to all civil servants stating that the government would not pay compensation and would introduce legislation to remedy the situation.[77] The circular indicated that these measures would not affect any claim which was lodged within six months after the coming into operation of the constitution, that is before 29 June, some forty-two days before the Hegarty judgement was made public. When the Dáil reassembled the government moved the Public Services (Continuity of Service) Bill, 1938. Section 5 of the bill set 26 October 1938, and not 29 June, as the final date on which the board could have heard and determined compensation. Norton closely questioned MacEntee as to how that date was arrived at and MacEntee was clearly uncomfortable and evasive.[78] At the heart of the question of the effective date was the only other case that had been agreed as a consequence of the Hegarty decision – that of T.J. Hughes of the AEO and secretary of the CSF.

The decision to go to the courts in the Hegarty case was controversial within the civil service associations. The IPCS objected to TOPA undertaking what might prove a costly claim without fully consulting the membership.[79] On the other hand the Cork engineering branch of the POWU was very enthusiastic after the successful hearing and urged Norton to use it to full effect in Dáil debates. The Cork branch was nearly moribund and it was hoped that the publicity would attract new members.[80] The British Whitley Council staff side offered to help TOPA in whatever way they could, suggesting it might bring up with the British government the question of the Treaty being unilaterally altered.[81] However, the British government had already signalled to the Irish government that it had no interest in the issue.[82] TOPA was in fact quite in the dark on the Hegarty case. Although it had been usual for the executive of the association to be kept updated on the progress of cases, the Hegarty hearings had been kept confidential. The compensation board held closed hearings in June and early August, a practice that was previously unknown to TOPA. When, on the insistence of the IPCS, a meeting was held Hughes, who represented the staff side of the compensation board, refused to attend or to divulge the likely result of the Hegarty hearing. This was despite the momentous impact it would have on the transferred officers. It was when the reward was announced that the reason for Hughes's reticence became apparent. Hughes had made an application to the compensation board himself for permissive retirement terms, along with another forty officers. When the likely result of the Hegarty decision became apparent but before it became public, with the permission of the board and the Minister for Finance, he withdrew his application for permissive retirement and reapplied for retirement on the same grounds as Hegarty, confident now that he would win. He had been a civil servant since 1913. He went out with twenty-five years' service and ten years added, giving him a pension based on thirty-five years' service plus a lump sum. It was clear a sordid bargain had been made. Hughes kept the rest of the civil service in the dark on the likely positive outcome of the hearing and in return was allowed resubmit his own application.[83] Changing the cut-off date was to facilitate his application. That is why there were only two civil servants who succeeded in taking advantage of the last judgements under Article 10: Hegarty and Hughes. Hughes had in fact applied for and been appointed to the post of general-secretary of the British Institution of Professional Civil Servants, worth £750–900 a year. He left the Irish service with a generous pension and moved to London to take up his new post. It ought to be recorded that he was not a success in the new post and his contract was terminated in 1943.[84]

Hughes, secretary of the AEO and of the CSF, was a central figure in civil service trade unionism since the establishment of the Free State and was clearly wearying of the struggle. In his evidence to the Brennan Commission he suggested strongly that it would be in the public interest, and not only that of his members, if the power of the Department of Finance over the civil service was transferred to another department of State such as Industry and Commerce where the ability of the civil servant would be recognised. He also felt that the salary cuts being pursued by the Fianna Fail government had little to do with economics but had a lot to do with the view that it 'would be a desirable thing that people in this country generally should adopt a simpler standard of living'.[85] Hughes had decided that a more useful and less frugal future lay elsewhere. As secretary of the staff side of the CSRC he had overseen a decade and a half of siege warfare. The only significant ground gained by the civil service unions had been through the courts and not the representative council, using a weapon forged by the pre-independence organisation. It was perhaps appropriate that he should have been the last to wield it.

The civil service and the state-sponsored sector

The courts had been used effectively by the civil service to gain legal protection for hard won rights, especially those covered by Article 10 of the Treaty. However, no progress in actually empowering the civil service to negotiate a new relationship with the State had been made. This is not surprising. Since its foundation Fianna Fáil had been focused on the need for the Irish government to assert the sovereignty of the independent State. Dismantling the Treaty, redefining Dominion status, the 1937 constitution had all been impelled by a drive toward a strong sovereign State. As a political movement that saw itself as the true inheritors of the revolutionary State Fianna Fáil would inevitably view the civil service as a remnant of the former Castle regime. The civil service was blindly optimistic in believing that the government would surrender any of its power to another authority. The very public use of its network of support in the Labour Party to advance its demands simply confirmed Fianna Fáil suspicions concerning the good faith of the civil service. It made good political sense to keep them firmly and visibly under the control of the State. Although the civil service had to wait another generation for arbitration and conciliation and thus some control over their conditions, their relationship with the State was actually changing as a more dynamic Fianna Fáil replaced the passive Cumann na nGaedheal. In fact de Valera consistently defended the civil service against the demands from within the party and the IRA leadership for a purge of senior officials.[86] Under Fianna Fáil the State, in the absence of an entrepreneurial class, undertook the role of developing the national economy. Unlike in Great Britain, where existing enterprises had been nationalised, the Irish State had to create an industrial sector from the ground up. This ideology of a strong State driving national development gave a central role to an expanding civil service.[87] The civil service found the channels of promotion that had been closed under the previous government were being opened up in new and unexpected directions. Departments were instructed not to block mobility and to allow civil servants to move to 'whatever posts their services are most likely to be of the highest value to the State'.[88] The pace of activity in the departments accelerated and soon there were complaints that the civil service was failing to keep pace with the demands of policy initiatives.[89] A consequence of the opening up of mobility was greater opportunity of promotion. The Irish civil service had very few university graduates recruited directly into the higher administrative class, the equivalent of the former first division, and higher posts were generally filled through competitive examinations in the lower executive grade. Civil servants of the clerical and executive classes crowded into the Bachelor of Commerce degree at Trinity College

Dublin, which was timetabled to cater for their working day. The number of civil servants rose under Fianna Fáil and opportunity opened up in the new State-owned companies where the civil service provided the primary leadership of these innovations in State-directed development. Dr J.H. Hinchcliff was seconded from the Department of Agriculture to take up the chairmanship of the Irish Sugar Company, raising his annual salary from £950 to £2,000. P.J. Dempsey, a junior executive officer on £313 was seconded to become the secretary of the state-owned Electricity Supply Board on £750 per annum. The chairman of the ESB on £1,700 annual salary, R.J. Browne, was formerly an inspector of taxes on £850.[90] The leading department in this expansion of the State was Industry and Commerce under Sean Lemass.[91] John Leydon, whose substantive appointment was secretary-general of the Department of Industry and Commerce, was appointed chairman of Aer Lingus, Irish Shipping, the Insurance Corporation of Ireland and later of the National Bank.[92] Not only did these civil servants enjoy enhanced salaries, they also gained considerable autonomy and freedom in running these State-sponsored businesses. Lemass took the view that civil servants running these enterprises would require wide discretionary powers and would report directly to himself as minister. H.P. Boland was initially complacent at this new role of the civil servant, taking it as natural that the civil service was the most likely source of administrative and commercial expertise.[93] However, as the scale of the State-sponsored sector grew he became very alarmed at the chaotic state of grading and salaries that it provoked. Even Doolin, his companion in finance, was now amused at Boland's predictable railings against change.[94] Thus the Irish civil service, apparently in an unplanned way, achieved the open path to the higher classes and grades that had been the ideal for the lower ranks and for the old Griffithite Sinn Féin.[95]

These new State-owned industries were essentially a reinvention of the unjustly despised boards of the old regime though now on a much more ambitious scale. This developmental leadership also brought the civil service back to a role that reflected its own view of itself as an executive rather than merely administrative arm of the State. This new form of State power necessitated a new image of the civil servant as professional and technocratic and the shedding of the old image of a colonial remnant of routine administrators. It also represented a reconnection with the traditions of the pre-independence era when the State viewed the civil service as an engine of social change, to be used to reshape the Irish society and economy. In this, curiously enough, Fianna Fáil was the inheritor not only of Griffith but also of the Balfours.

Notes

1 Fanning, *Department of Finance*, pp. 211–13.
2 *Iris*, 9:9 (Sept. 1931).

3 CPSU, CSCA, executive council minutes, Jan.–Feb., Oct. 1928; *An Peann*, 2:4 (Dec. 1928).
4 Ibid., 1:1 (Sept. 1927).
5 Ibid., 3:3 (Nov. 1929).
6 CPSU, CSCA, executive council minutes, 19 Dec. 1929.
7 NAI, CAB 1/3, 30 July 1931.
8 CPSU, CSRC, minutes 28 Mar. 1930; *Iris*, 8:5 (May 1930).
9 CPSU, CSRC, minutes 29 Aug. 1930.
10 NAI, CAB 1/3, 31 Dec. 1930.
11 NAI, Department of Finance, E107/12/25, 'HPB memorandum on CSRC', 17 May 1932.
12 *Iris*, 9:7 (July 1931).
13 NAI, Department of Finance, E109/13/26, 'Civil service staffs memorandum on numbers, pay and allowances for travelling and subsistence'.
14 *Dáil Éireann debates*, vol. 37, col. 978, 4 Mar. 1931.
15 *Nation*, 5 Feb. 1929, quoted in *Iris*, 7:2 (Feb. 1929).
16 *Dáil Éireann debates*, vol. 37, cols 979–89, 4 Mar. 1931; vol. 39, cols 388–421, 1 June, cols 144–60, 10 June, cols 288–321, 11 June, cols 338–55, 12 June 1931.
17 *Iris*, 9:7 (July 1931).
18 CPSU, CSCA, special delegate conference minutes, 5 Dec. 1930; *An Peann*, 3:12 (Aug. 1930).
19 *Iris*, 9:9 (Sept. 1931).
20 T.J. O'Connell, *100 Years of Progress: The Story of the Irish National Teachers' Organisation 1868–1968* (Dublin, 1968), pp. 265–6.
21 *Irish Press*, 2 Feb. 1932.
22 NAI, CAB 1/3, 30 July 1931; Regan, *Counter-Revolution*, pp. 295–6.
23 *Dáil Éireann debates*, vol. 22, col. 1615, 21 Mar. 1928.
24 MacMahon, *Republicans and Imperialists*, pp. 23–7.
25 UCDAD, Sean MacEntee Papers, P67/101.
26 C.S. Andrews, *Man of No Property* (Dublin, 1982), p. 119.
27 Leon Ó'Broin, . . . *Just Like Yesterday . . . an autobiography* (Dublin, 1985), p. 98.
28 McMahon (ed.) *The Moynihan Brothers*, pp. 174–5.
29 Daly, *Buffer State*, pp. 163–7.
30 NAI, CAB 1/4, 5 July 1932; NAI, Department of the Taoiseach, S.3406 H, 'Committee of inquiry into resigned or dismissed civil servants'.
31 NAI, CAB 1/4, 12 Mar., 5 July 1932.
32 Fanning, *Department of Finance*, pp. 216–18.
33 NAI, CAB 1/4, 12 Apr., 2 and 13 May 1932.
34 Ibid., 12 Apr., 13 May 1932.
35 IPCS, council minutes, AGM, 28 Apr. 1932; 13 May, 3, 24, 26 June 1932.
36 Ibid., 24 June, 26 July, 14 Sept. 1932.
37 NAI, Brennan Commission, BC/4, 2 Aug. 1934, for Brunicardi's discussion of his household budget.
38 Ibid., BC/1, 20 and 26 Jan. 1933.
39 Ibid., BC/2, 9 Mar. 1933.

40 Ibid., BC/2, 21 Dec. 1933; 2, 9, 10, 16 Feb. 1934; the CSCA closely monitored the evidence being presented at the hearings and prepared rebuttals where appropriate, see CPSU, CSCA minute book 1933 and 1934.
41 NLI, Brennan Papers, MSS 26,025–42; 26,279; Stephen Lalor, 'Policy-making in the Irish civil service: propriety and practice', Ph.D. University of Dublin, Trinity College, 1991, pp. 132–75.
42 Compare Boland 20 Jan. 1933 and Brunicardi 3 Mar. 1933 in NAI, Brennan Commission, BC/2.
43 NAI, CAB 1/5, 2 June 1933.
44 IPCS, council minutes, 23 Mar. 1933.
45 NAI, Department of Finance, E121/12/33.
46 Cormac Ó'Gráda, *Ireland: A New Economic History 1780–1939* (Oxford, 1994), pp. 411–16.
47 NAI, CAB 1/4, 5 and 7 May 1932.
48 NAI, Department of Finance, E121/12/33.
49 *Dáil Éireann debates*, vol. 25, col. 498, 13 July 1928; *Irish Press*, 2 Feb. 1932.
50 Fanning, *Department of Finance*, pp. 225–37.
51 NAI, CAB 1/4 23 and 24 May 1932.
52 Fanning, *Department of Finance*, pp. 224–5.
53 NAI, CAB 1/4, 3 June 1932; CPSU, CSCA, executive council minutes, 1 June 1932.
54 CPSU, CSCA, executive council minutes, June 1932. [Despite almost daily meetings the executive found it difficulty to co-ordinate a strategy.]
55 CSRC, minutes of the twenty-eighth meeting, 16 June 1932. [The minutes of the CSRC can be found at NAI, Department of Finance, establishment files E/107/12/25–6; and in various issues of *Iris*, the journal of the CSF.]
56 Ibid., minutes of the twenty-ninth meeting, 21 June 1932.
57 Quoted in Fanning, *Department of Finance*, p. 228.
58 CSRC, minutes of thirty-first meeting, 30 Sept. 1932.
59 Fanning, *Department of Finance*, p. 234.
60 IPCS, council minutes, 28 Sept., 13 Oct., 12 Dec. 1932; NAI, CAB 1/4, 23 Dec. 1932.
61 NAI, Department of Finance, E121/12/33.
62 Fanning, *Department of Finance*, p. 237; Dermot Keogh, *Twentieth-Century Ireland: Nation and State* (Dublin, 1994), pp. 75–7.
63 Fanning, *Department of Finance*, pp. 237–9.
64 IPCS, council minutes, 7 Apr. 1933; CSRC, minutes of the thirty-fifth meeting, 28 June 1933.
65 IPCS, council minutes, AGM, 10 Apr., 17 and 24 May, 9 June 1933.
66 NAI, Department of Finance, E121/12/33.
67 Ibid.; NAI, CAB 1/5, 30 June, 7 July 1933; CSRC, minutes of the thirty-sixth meeting, 30 June 1933; IPCS, council minutes, 4 and 17 July 1933.
68 *Dáil Éireann debates*, vol. 73, cols 199–200, 2 Nov. 1938, Questions.
69 NLI, Brennan Papers, MS 26,316, 'Retirements under article 10, 1922–34'.
70 ILHS, MS 10 TOPA/3, 'Notes re Lisney case'; *Irish Independent*; *Irish Times*; *Irish Press*, 8 Nov. 1933.
71 *Iris*, 12:10 (October 1934); IPCS, council minutes, 5 Oct. 1934.

72 IPCS, council minutes, 24 Jan. 1935.
73 *Dáil Éireann debates*, vol. 65, cols 1733–816, 11 Mar. 1937; vol. 66, cols 1894–917, 28 Apr. 1937, for Deputy Norton's motion on arbitration and Costello's contribution.
74 NAI, Department of Finance, E109/43/37, 'Civil servants and election', July 1937.
75 *Dáil Éireann debates*, vol. 70, cols 1196–225, 30 Mar., cols 1593–623, 6 Apr., cols 1815–53, 8 Apr. 1938; vol. 71, cols 1830–69, 25 May 1938.
76 ILHS, MS 10/TOPA/3; ILHS, Norton Papers, 'Correspondence 1938'; *Dáil Éireann debates*, vol. 73, cols 282–304, 2 Nov. 1938.
77 NAI, Department of Finance, circular 19/38, 'Notice to transferred officers'; ILHS, MS 10/TOPA/3.
78 *Dáil Éireann debates.*, vol. 73, col. 392, 9 Nov. 1938.
79 ILHS, MS 10/TOPA/3, 'IPCS, executive committee to Norton', 19 Jan. 1938.
80 ILHS, Norton Papers, J. Mahony to W. Norton, 28 Oct. 1938.
81 ILHS, MS 10/TOPA/3, 'Simpson to TOPA', 6 Oct. 1938.
82 *Dáil Éireann debates*, vol. 73, col. 284, 2 Nov. 1938.
83 Ibid.; ILHS, MS 10/TOPA/3, 'Hegarty case'.
84 Mortimer and Ellis, *A Professional Union*, pp. 99–100, 128.
85 NAI, Brennan Commission, BC/1, 6 Feb. 1933, BC/3, 13 Apr. 1934.
86 Thomas M. Feeney, 'Fianna Fáil and the civil service 1927–1937' MA UCD 1999; MacMahon, *Republicans and Imperialists*, pp.126–7.
87 D.S. Johnson and Liam Kennedy, 'The two economies in Ireland in the twentieth century' in Hill (ed.) *A New History of Ireland VII*, pp. 452–86, 467.
88 NAI, CAB 1/6, 17 Feb., 3 May 1935.
89 Feeney, 'Fianna Fáil and the civil service', pp. 31–2.
90 NAI, Department of Finance, E62/12/33, 'Appt of Dr Hinchcliff', 1933.
91 NAI, Department of Industry and Commerce, E13/1/4, 'State-sponsored bodies information'.
92 Michael Kevin O'Doherty, 'Working for Sean Lemass, 1944–46: reflections of a Private Secretary', paper delivered at the Research Seminar in Contemporary Irish History, University of Dublin, Trinity College, 15 Oct. 2003.
93 NAI, Department of Finance, E68/1/33, 'Dept of Industry and Commerce peat scheme staff'.
94 Ibid., E72/10/36, 'Remuneration of civil servants on Industrial Alcohol Board', 1936–39.
95 Daly, 'The formation of an Irish nationalist elite?', pp. 281–301.

Conclusion: the civil service, the State and the Irish revolution

CHANGES IN THE State in Ireland provide the point of departure for understanding continuity and change in the civil service and assessing its response to, and its place in, the process of revolutionary State-formation. The third Home Rule crisis and the emergence of proposals to partition the country, the outbreak of the First World War and then the 1916 Rising, were all State-transforming moments that questioned the relationship between the civil service and the State in Ireland. The established British tradition by which a non-political civil service gave an undivided loyalty to the State in return for permanence was broken. In response to what the civil service saw as a breach of good faith it began to fight to establish a contractual basis for its relation to the State. This sustained political campaign by a united civil service organisation succeeded in transforming their sectional interests into constitutional rights. The Irish civil service displayed a precocious ability to organise. The Home Rule proposals transformed organisation, firstly by permitting cross-class and -grade combination in a unified Irish civil service association, and secondly by tolerating intensive political lobbying by that association. It was adept at cultivating political support from both Nationalist and Unionist in Ireland to counter the dominance of the Treasury in London. This level of organisation and political activism would, in any other context, have been considered subversive of the State and been suppressed. The civil service used each opportunity presented by political division to protect its interests in advance of changes in the State. The objective was to ensure that any government that might emerge out of the struggle for control of the State would find it difficult and expensive to make significant unilateral alterations in the conditions of the civil service. This organisation was shaped by a growing consciousness of their essentially colonial and therefore dispensable status, a status that facilitated unity across departments and classes.

The 1916 Rising revealed the extent to which some civil servants were disloyal though it has been noted that the response of the State was surprisingly muted. Meanwhile the demands of world war created different influences within the civil service in Ireland. The marginality of Ireland to the war effort, the pressure on civil servants to enlist, the recrudescence of sectarianism in the higher reaches of the Castle that accompanied the growing power of the Unionists in government, all served to further weaken the British State in Ireland. The period 1919–22 saw the final phase of the development of Irish Statehood that involved the creation of two different Irish States through partitioning the former State, while a rival counter-State waged a war against it. It has been argued that the success of the revolutionary forces had more to do with the now chronic weakness of the British State in Ireland than with the actions of the IRA.

Historians of the process of British decolonisation have written with warm congratulation on the legacy of sound administrative foundations laid down during the colonial period and the care with which the departing power had guarded the security of the public servants left behind.[1] The terms of transfer of the public service in the colonies were modelled on the Irish experience, the first such transfer. However, the security for salaries, pensions and conditions, which was to prove beneficial to public servants from Ireland to Ceylon, was the result not of the warm generosity of the departing power but of the sustained struggle of the Irish civil servants themselves. Security was not granted, it was won.

During the immediate period after the ending of the First World War the Irish civil service got swept up in the wave of organisation mobilising the British civil service into trade unions. That meant importing into the relatively small Irish service the organisationally sophisticated structures of classes and grades of the very much bigger and more complex British service. Whether this was an example of 'colonial cringe' or simply the force of habit, it was a mistake that weakened the civil service as a whole in the new independent State. The newly independent State retained the hierarchical structures of the former power. Hierarchy was the simplest way to subordinate the inherited bureaucracy to the new executive. However, it was not the best or the most appropriate relationship between the civil service and the government of the newly independent State. Still carrying the pre-independence nationalist contempt for the Castle bureaucracy, and acquiring the post-war Whitehall view of the necessity of Treasury dictatorship in dealing with rank-and-file civil servants, the Cosgrave government failed to recognise the civil service as an agent of modernity.

The final transformation of the independent State was the accession to power in 1932 of Fianna Fáil. The party that formerly had denied the legitimacy of the State enacted a new constitution in 1937 that established the Irish State as the expressed will of the Irish nation and not the British parliament. Under Fianna Fáil the civil service was reinvented as the State institution that transformed the political aspirations of the governing party into economic and social outcomes. If the State was to develop the nation then it had to turn to the civil service because there was no other institution capable of such a task. The achievement of a self-sufficient and sovereign Ireland, which was the goal of the Fianna Fáil party, would be the achievement of the civil service and would integrate the civil service into the national revolution.

The question of the survival of the civil service in an era of revolutionary State change has been addressed. Revisionist histories of the formation of the Irish independent State emphasise the emergence under British rule of the modern State institutions that ensured success for the new government. These histories argue that Irish democracy was secured by revolutionaries embracing institutions moulded and nurtured by the British and abandoning notions of revolutionary transformation. The government of the newly independent State is therefore, according to these histories, to be congratulated for embracing the inheritance of an incorruptible and dedicated civil service derived from the finest British State traditions. The belief that the new State simply inherited a thoroughly modernised and reformed civil service, a belief that is based on a favourable assessment of Waterfield's reform of the Castle, can be refuted. Waterfield's attempt to fit the Irish civil service to the Whitehall mould created more turmoil than order. The view that saw more of continuity than revolution and that sought to detach the civil service from the revolution has also been challenged. The revolution established a new kind of State and therefore required a new kind of civil service. The executive, legislature, army and police force of the new State were all newly formed out of the revolutionary forces. Contrary to statements of anodyne continuity there was in fact a rapid purge of the personnel of the senior ranks in the civil service, paralleled by an even greater exodus through voluntary retirements. New men were brought rapidly to the fore in a short-lived blossoming of promotions. The civil service was also reorganised into a centralised and hierarchical structure of departments under finance control and answerable to politicians. This was the sort of structure that the British had tried and failed to achieve in Ireland. Whether that model was appropriate for the new State was not considered by the new government.

It may be asked whether Article 10 of the Treaty and its attendant enactments, which created constitutional rights out of the vested interests of civil servants, operated to block desirable reforms. The answer is a conditional 'yes', with the caveat that the reforms pursued by Cumann na nGaedheal were not the reforms that were desirable. Instead of seizing the opportunity to create a civil service more suited to the revolutionary conditions (less hierarchical, more dynamic) the government attempted to create a cheaper version of the Whitehall model. This was not the sort of reform that the civil service anticipated or that the revolution had signalled, nor was it even desirable. The Irish civil service was confident of its ability to deliver on radical policies and was in fact characterised more by enthusiasm and ambition than by fear or hostility to the new State. An opportunity to engage in truly revolutionary State transformation was lost.

What did the civil service want from the revolution? The demand that was voiced was actually a modestly negative 'no worsening of conditions'. The difficulty with the Irish civil service under the old regime was the persistence of nepotism and sectarian recruitment patterns, a difficulty that persisted in Northern Ireland. The leadership of the Irish civil service associations had become thoroughly nationalist, mainly through the influence of competitive recruitment and membership of the cultural movements. Their hope was that these movements would act as the training ground for a new administrative elite of an 'Irish-Ireland' complexion. For them the British model clearly embodied social and cultural principles that were anathemas. The more complex the civil service structures, the more hierarchical they are. The Irish civil service was prepared to embrace a more simplified and therefore more egalitarian structure. Locked out of the process of decision-making the civil service adopted a *non possumus* attitude. The relationship between the State and the civil service became a matter not of negotiation but of constitutional law, fought out in the Wigg-Cochrane case that led to the first revision of the Treaty. However, the hostility of the political classes to the civil service was purely reflexive and not the result of any coherent alternative vision, after all they had no difficulty steering their children into the civil service for careers and employment.

The ability of the State to conceive, plan and execute policies of social and economic transformation depended on the ability of politicians to shed the persistent view that the civil service was simply a legacy of British domination. The despised boards of the British regime, 'enough to make a coffin for Ireland', were in fact effective agents of social and economic transformation. Irish civil servants could deliver a modernising Ireland, what they could not do was make British government accepted in nationalist Ireland. Nor could the civil service of the Irish Free State deliver cheap administration. The Cumann na nGaedheal campaign to cut salaries and worsen conditions, running the State as if it were a corner shop, merely antagonised the civil service and drove a significant number to choose early retirement. However, the Cumann na nGaedheal governments did resist party pressure to use the civil service as an instrument of political patronage and avoided party penetration of the State apparatus and the evil of cronyism that has infected many decolonised States.

Fianna Fáil was able to re-imagine the civil service as an agent of State-driven change and so begin to reinvent, through the semi-State corporations, the boards of the British State. Under the Fianna Fáil government, especially in the Department of Industry and Commerce under Sean Lemass, the civil service was given the task in which the native entrepreneurial classes had failed, the development of the nation. This is perhaps best illustrated by the most significant plan for State-directed economic change in independent Ireland being popularly known by the name of the civil servant who drafted it, T.K. Whitaker.

Note

1 E.g., Sir Charles Jeffries, *Ceylon the path to independence* (London, 1962), pp. 122–30; Hugh Foot, *A Start in Freedom* (London, 1964), pp. 237–41.

Appendix: Dáil Éireann civil service, January 1919 to January 1922

Dáil Éireann secretariat

Byrne, P.
Harling, Seán.
Hogan, Mary.
McDunphy, Michael.
O'Hegarty, Diarmuid.
Price, Eamon.
Ryan, Mollie.

Department of Finance

Brennan, Miss L.
Farrelly, R.
Fleming, Eamon.
Hoey, Michael.
Keavey, Sean.
Kinnane, Sean.
Lawless, Eileen.
Lynch, Michael.
Lyons, Alice.
Lyons, Miss E.
McCluskey, Mrs.
McCluskey, Seán.
McGrath, George (Accounting Officer).
McGrath, Seán (Banc ar siúil).
Mason, Jenny (later married Tom Derrig).
Mason, M. Miss.
Murphy, Fintan.
O'Donoghue, David [O'Donnchadha, Daithi].
O'Donovan, Dan.

O'Mara, Miss N.
O'Reilly, J.K.
O'Toole, Kate.
Sheehan, Patrick.
Slattery, Joe.
Staines, Miss M.
Thunder, Frank.
Toal, Miss.
Tobin, Miss S.
Wheatley, Thomas.

Department of Publicity

Gallagher, Frank.
Kelly, Annie (née Fitzsimons).
Madden, P.
Napoli-McKenna, Cathleen.

Department of Foreign Affairs

Austin, Miss.
Bhriain, Maire ni.
Bolger, J.
Carty, J.
Duffy, George Gavan.
Dunnes, J.
Grattan Esmonde, T.
Homan, G.
McGilligan, K.
McWhite, M.
Moore, Wilfred.
Murphy, J.
Murphy, Miss S.
Nolan, P.
O'Brien, Art.
O'Byrne, Count.
O'Byrne, Miss E.
O'Donovan, C.
O'Reilly, Count G.
Power, Miss N.
Walsh, J.P.

Department of Defence

Kennedy, Miss K.
O'Dwyer, Miss K.
Sheppard, Kevin.
Sloan, Miss.

Department of Agriculture [Land Resettlement Commission]

Byrne, J.
Collins, John.
Flanaghan, Matthew.
Geoghegan, Bernard.
Gould, Sean.
Heavey, M.J.
Maguire, Conor.
O'Broin, Leon.
O'Broin, Sean.
O'Connor, N.
O'Sheil, Kevin.
Quinn, Leo.
Shaughnessy, Miss.

Department of Education [Irish language]

Davitt, Miss.
Joyce, J.
O'Shea, T.
Sugrue, J.
Sugrue, M.

Department of Fisheries

King, R.F.

Department of Local Government

Office staff

Archer, Miss E.
Bevan, Kathleen.
Carraghamhna, Maire ní.
Carron, Mary.
Cearnaigh, Eilis ní.

Chonghaile, Eilis ní.
Clancy, Miss.
Clare, William.
Connolly, Elis.
Crosby, Kathleen.
Dowling, Kathleen.
Giles, Miss A.
Kavanagh, Seumas.
Kearney, Elis.
Kearney, Miss.
Kelly, D.L.
Kelly, Frank.
Kenny, Miss C.
Kenny, Denis.
McArdle, Thomas J.
McCann, Tom.
McCarthy, Daniel.
McLoughlin, Miss Mary.
Meghen, P.J.
Merriman, Edward.
Moore, Andrew.
Murray, Miss M.
Neligan, Miss.
O'Brien, Peader.
O'Farrell, Seán.
O'Flanaghan, Miss L.
O'Flynn, Myra.
O'Grady, Miss.
O'Hegarty, Enie.
O'Kavanagh, J.
O'Mahony, Taghd.
O'Reilly, Miss B.
O'Reilly, Miss M.
O'Reilly, P.
O'Shannon, Maire.
Parker, Augustus.
Redden, Miss K.
Robbins, Lorcan.
Saunders, Seán.
Shannon, Maire C.
Shortall, William.
Skinnider, Miss.

Inspectors

Barrett, Dr Boyd.
Conkling, P.
Connaughton, Daniel.
Coogan, Eamon.
Crofts, Mrs.
De Lacy, Michael.
Dunne, Thomas.
Dwyer, Dr W.
Geraghty, James.
Gleeson, S.
Hernon, Patrick J.
Lister, Miss E.
McGrath, Seán.
McGuinness, Mr.
McLysaght, James [Seamus].
Meagher, Francis G.
Moynihan, Simon J.
O'Carroll, Eamon.
O'Donovan, David J.
O'Dwyer, Nicholas B.E.
O'Kelly, Dr D.L.
O'Kelly, Patrick.
O'Loughlin, Mr G.
O'Muchadha, Seamus.
O'Rourke, Patrick.
O'Sullivan, Miss.
Raftery, Patrick.
Ryan, Michael B.E.
Stack, Seán [De Staic, Seán].

Auditors

Barnard, Frank.
Barry, John.
Brady, Beatrice.
Browner, Anna.
Browner, May.
Crowe, Luke.
Foley, Edward H.
Healy, J.J.
McGinley, Eamon.
Moran, Seán.

O'Farrell, Una.
O'Keeffe, David.

Stocktakers

Keegan, E.
O'Leary, S.

Registry Office

Killeen, Maurice.
Merriman, Ned.

Department of Labour

Cotter, Dick.
Mee, J. (ex-RIC).
Riain, Eilis ní.

Directory of Trade and Commerce

Byrne, Miss M.B.
Chartres, John.
de Paor, Miss.
Dillon, J.
Duggan, Edward [Eamon].
Figgis, Darrell.
O'Donovan, Colman.
Wrafter, Miss M.J.

Department of Home Affairs

Browne, Daniel J.
Clifford, Madge.
Connolly, Miss Bridget.
Crilly, Miss Edith.
Crump, P.J.
Davitt, Judge Cahir.
Kelly, P.
McKeown, Owen.
MacNicholls, George.
Markey, M.H.
Meredith, Judge James Creed.
Murphy, T.
Nunan, Seán .
O'Siochain.
O'Toole, Sean.

Couriers

Burke, Alec.
Byrne, P.
Caffrey, Seán.
Conlon, Bob.
Craig, Leo.
Harling, Seán.
Jordan, Joe.
Markey, Mick.
Murphy, M.
O'Connor, Jimmie.
O'Hanrahan, Paddy.
O'Mara, Paddy.
O'Neill, Martin.
O'Reilly, Joe.
Redmond, Seamus.
Saunders Liam.

Department of Dáil Éireann not identified

Cleary, Edward.
Cremen, Michael.
Cremins, Francis Thomas.
Cremins, Richard J.
Hehir, Hugh.

Source: NAI, BMH, witness statements, 501 T.J. McArdle, 817 Seán Saunders, 375 Diarmuid O'Sullivan, 1728 Nicolas O Nuaillain, 643 Cathleen Napoli-McKenna, 1725 Padraig O'Keeffe, 512 Seán McCluskey, 548 Daithi O'Donoghue, 889 James Kavanagh, 1050 Vera McDonnell, 683 Hugh Hehir, 460 Joseph Thunder, 680 Nicolas O'Dwyer; DE 5/72; Department of Finance, 'early E files', E1/8, E40/1, E43/8, E50/47, E50/11, E86/116(ii) and 118, E108/1, E108/4/24, E117/2, E137/10, E231/9; establishment files, E115/50/33.

Select bibliography

Primary sources

State and local government archives

National Archives Ireland
Brennan Commission records.
Bureau of Military History witness statements.
Cabinet minutes.
Chief Secretary's Office.
Dáil Éireann records 1919–22.
Department of Agriculture.
Department of Finance.
Department of Industry and Commerce.
Department of the Taoiseach.
Executive minutes.
Provisional Government records 1922–23.

Public Record Office Northern Ireland
Cabinet conclusions and memoranda.
Department of Finance.
Sir Ernest Clark Papers.

National Archives United Kingdom, Kew
Cabinet minutes and papers.
Colonial Office, Anderson Papers.
Home Office.
Ministry of Pensions.
Ministry of Transport.
Treasury and Treasury (Ireland).
War Office.
William Evelyn Wylie Papers.

Wiltshire and Swindon Record Office
Walter Hume Long Papers.

Library and university archives

National Library Ireland
Joseph Brennan Papers.
Bryce Papers.
George Gavan Duffy Papers.
Irish National Aid Association and Volunteers' Dependents Fund Papers.
Thomas Johnson Papers.
Leon Ó'Broin Papers.
J.J. O'Connell Papers.

Trinity College Dublin Library
John Dillon Papers.
Sir David Harrel, 'Recollections and reflections'.

University College Dublin Archives Department
Ernest Blythe Papers.
J.R. Clark memoir.
George Chester Duggan memoir.
Desmond and Mabel Fitzgerald Papers.
Michael Hayes Papers.
Hugh Kennedy Papers.
Sean MacEntee Papers.
Patrick McGilligan Papers.
Patrick Moylett memoir.
Seán and Maurice Moynihan Papers.
Richard Mulcahy Papers.
Cornelius J.(Conn) Murphy Family Papers.
Diarmuid O'Hegarty Papers.
Dr James Ryan Papers.
Eamon de Valera Papers.

Irish Labour History Archive and Museum
William Norton Papers.
Transferred Officers' Protection Association (TOPA).

House of Lords Record Office
Bonar Law Papers.
Lloyd George Papers.

Warwick University Modern Records Centre
Assistant Clerks' Association.
Association of Assistant and Supervisory Clerks (Civil Service).
Association of Clerks of the Second Division.

Association of Executive Officers of the Civil Service.
Association of Staff Clerks and Other Civil Servants.
Association of Writing Assistants.
Civil Service Alliance.
Civil Service Clerical Association.
Civil Service Clerical Union.
Civil Service Confederation.
Clerical Officers' Association.
Customs and Excise Federation.
National Whitley Council (Staff Side).
Society of Civil Servants.

Bodleian Library, Oxford
Lionel Curtis Papers.
Andrew Philip Magill memoir.
Matthew Nathan Papers.

Private collections

Comhaltas Reachtairí Dleachta agus Cánach/Customs and Excise Federation, minute book and rules 1922–23. PSEU, Merrion Square, Dublin 2.
Cumann na Stáit-Chléireach/Civil Service Clerical Association, minute book 1923–36. CPSU, Adelaide Road, Dublin 2.
Gallagher, M.J. 'Memoirs of a civil servant 1895–1974' (typescript in the possession of his son Rev. Colm Gallagher, Arklow, Co. Wicklow).
Institution of Professional Civil Servants (IPCS), minute book, IMPACT Union, Gardiner Street, Dublin 1.
O'Doherty, Michael Kevin. 'Working for Sean Lemass, 1944–46: reflections of a Private Secretary', paper delivered at the Research Seminar in Contemporary Irish History, University of Dublin, Trinity College (15 Oct. 2003).

Printed primary sources

Trade Union journals and publications
An Díon, Organ of the Post Office Workers' Union.
An Peann Irisleabhar Chumainn na Stáit-Chléireach, Official Organ of the Civil Service Clerical Association.
Civilian, The Accredited Organ of the Civil Service.
Civil Service Clerical Alliance, *The Organisation and Policy of the Alliance, with Special reference to the Control of the Civil Service* (Dublin, 1918).
Civil Service Federation, *Statement Concerning Proposed Alterations in the Regulations Governing the Employment of Saorstát Civil Servants* (Dublin, 1924).
Civil Service Gazette.
Civil Service News, The Journal of the Association of Established Civil Servants In Northern Ireland.

Gazette, Official Organ of the Northern Ireland Post Office Clerks' Association.

Irish Civil Servant.

Irish Civil Service Alliance, *Civil Service Salaries: Basis of Re-assessment. Report by a sub-committee appointed by the Irish Civil Service Alliance January 1920* (Dublin, 1920).

Irish Labour Party and Trade Union Congress, *Annual Reports and Congress proceedings.*

Irish Treaty Pensioners' Association, *Pensions and Compensation Guarantee of the British Government, 1921–1922 – Rt. Hon. D. Lloyd George. M.P. Prime Minister; 1922–1923 – Rt. Hon. A. Bonar Law, M.P. Prime Minister* (Dublin, n.d. 1923?).

Irisleabhar, Journal of the Customs and Excise Federation.

Iris Seirbhíse An Stáit (The Civil Service Journal), Official Organ of the Civil Service Federation.

News Sheet, Association of Executive Officers of the Civil Service.

Red Tape, A Civil Service Magazine.

Staff Clerks' Circular.

British Parliamentary Papers

Interim report of the national provisional joint committee on the application of the Whitley report to the administrative departments of the civil service, HC 1919, XII [Cmd. 198], 239 (Ramsay and Stuart-Bunning).

Irish Free State: Headings of working arrangements for implementing the Treaty, HC 1923, XVII [1911], 123.

Parliamentary Debates Official Report.

Report on the application of the Whitley report to the administrative departments of the civil service, HC 1919, XI [Cmd. 9], 227 (Heath).

Report of the machinery of government committee of the Ministry of Reconstruction, HC 1918, XII [Cd. 9230] (Haldane Committee).

Report of the proceedings of the Irish Convention, HC 1918, XII [9230].

Royal commission on the civil service, second appendix to the fourth report of the commissioners, minutes of evidence 9 Jan. 1913–20 June 1913 with appendices, HC 1914, XVI [Cd.7340], 363 (MacDonnell Commission).

Royal commission on the rebellion in Ireland, report of the commission, minutes of evidence, HC 1916, XI [Cd. 8279], 171; [8311], 185.

Second report of the committee of the Ministry of Reconstruction on the relations of employers and employed on Joint Standing Industrial Councils, HC 1918, X [Cd. 9002], 659 (Whitley Committee).

Government of Irish Free State Reports and Publications

Dáil Éireann debates.

Iris Oifigiúil.

Saorstát Éireann R.54/3, *The Commission of Inquiry Into the Civil Service* (3 vols, 1932–35) (Brennan Commission).

Saorstát Éireann 1933, R.46/1, *Cost of Living Index Figure, committee report P. 992.*

Seanad Éireann debates.

Government of Northern Ireland Parliamentary Papers
Government of Northern Ireland Command Papers, cmd. 66 (1926) *Report of Sir R.R. Scott, K.C.B., C.S.I. on the civil service of Northern Ireland.*
Government of Northern Ireland Command Papers, cmd. 116 (1930) *Report of the departmental committee on civil service re-grading.*
Government of Northern Ireland Statutory Rules and Orders, No. 118 (1928) *The civil service (approved associations) regulations (Northern Ireland).*
Parliamentary Debates, Northern Ireland.

Newspapers
Freeman's Journal.
Irish Bulletin.
Irish Independent.
Irish Law Times and Solicitor's Journal.
Irishman.
Irish Press.
Irish Times.
Nation.
Sinn Féin Weekly.
The Times.
Times Law Reports.

Edited collections of diaries and papers, memoirs, contemporary writings
Andrews, C.S. *Dublin Made Me* (Dublin, 1979).
——. *Man of No Property* (Dublin, 1982).
Barry-O'Brien, R. *Dublin Castle and the Irish People* (London, 1909).
De Blacam, Aodh. *What Sinn Féin Stands For: the Irish republican movement Its history, aims and Ideals examined as to their significance to the world* (Dublin, 1921).
Collins, Michael. *The Path to Freedom* (Cork, 1968).
Comerford, Maire. *The First Dáil* (Dublin, 1969).
Connolly, Joseph. *Memoirs of Senator Joseph Connolly (1885–1961): A founder of modern Ireland*, ed. J. Anthony Gaughan (Dublin, 1996).
Douglas, James G. *Memoirs of Senator James G. Douglas (1887–1954) concerned citizen*, ed. J. Anthony Gaughan (Dublin, 1998).
Griffith, Arthur. *The Resurrection of Hungary: A Parallel for Ireland with appendices on Pitt's Policy and Sinn Féin* (Dublin, 1904).
Hart, Peter (ed.) *British Intelligence in Ireland, 1920–21: the final reports* (Cork, 2002).
Headlam, Maurice. *Irish Reminiscences* (London, 1947).
Hobson, Bulmer. *Ireland Yesterday and Tomorrow* (Tralee, 1968).
Jones, Thomas. *Whitehall Diary Vol. III, Ireland 1918–1925*, ed. Keith Midlemas (London, 1971).
Lord MacDonnell of Swinford. 'Irish Administration under Home Rule' in Morgan (ed.) *The New Irish Constitution*, pp. 50–80.
Macready, General Sir Nevil. *Annals of an Active Life* (2 vols, London, 1925).

Magill, Charles W. (ed.) *From Dublin Castle to Stormont: the memoirs of Andrew Philip Magill, 1913–1925* (Cork, 2003).

Micks, W.L. *An Account of the Constitution, Administration and Dissolution of the Congested Districts Board for Ireland from 1891 to 1923* (Dublin, 1925).

Morgan, J.H. (ed.) *The New Irish Constitution: an exposition and some arguments* (London, 1912).

Mulcahy, Risteárd. *Richard Mulcahy (1886–1971) A Family Memoir* (Dublin, 1999).

Norway, Mary Louise and Arthur Hamilton. *The Sinn Féin Rebellion As They Saw It*, ed. Keith Jeffrey (Dublin, 1916, reprint edition 1999).

Ó'Broin, León. . . . *Just Like Yesterday . . . An autobiography* (Dublin, 1985).

——. *W.E. Wylie and the Irish Revolution 1916–1921* (Dublin, 1989).

O'Hegarty, P.S. *The Victory of Sinn Féin* (Dublin, 1924, reprint edition 1998).

'Periscope' [G.C. Duggan]. 'The Last Days of Dublin Castle', *Blackwood's Magazine*, 212:1,282 (Aug. 1922).

Redmond, John. *Ireland's Financial Relations with England: The Case Stated* (Dublin, 1905).

Robinson, Henry. *Memories: Wise and Otherwise* (London, 1923).

I.O. [Major C.J.C. Street], *The Administration of Ireland, 1920*, edited with a review of his other writings by Brendan Clifford (Belfast, 2001).

Sturgis, Mark. *The Last Days of Dublin Castle the Diaries of Mark Sturgis*, ed. Michael Hopkinson (Dublin, 1999).

Wilson, Trevor (ed.) *The Political Diaries of C.P. Scott 1911–1928* (London, 1970).

Secondary sources

Books and collected essays

Adams, R.J.Q. and Philip P. Poirer. *The Conscription Controversy in Great Britain, 1900–18* (London, 1987).

Augusteijn, Joost (ed.) *The Irish Revolution 1913–1923* (Manchester, 2002).

Barton, Brian. 'Northern Ireland, 1920–25' and 'Northern Ireland, 1925–39' in Hill (ed.) *A New History of Ireland VII*, pp. 161–98; 199–234.

Boyce, David George and Alan O'Day (eds) *Defenders of the Union: A Survey of British and Irish Unionism since 1801* (London, 2001).

Brown, Judith M. (ed.) *The Oxford History of the British Empire Volume IV, The Twentieth Century* (Oxford, 1999).

Brown, W.J. *The Civil Service Clerical Association: Its History, its Achievements and its Plans for the Future* (London, 1925).

——. *So Far . . .* (London, 1943).

Bull, Philip. *Land, Politics and Nationalism: A Study of the Irish Land Question* (Dublin, 1996).

Burk, Kathleen (ed.) *War and the State the Transformation of British Government, 1914–1919* (London, 1982).

Campbell, John. 'A Loosely Shackled Fellowship': The History of Comhaltas Cána* (Dublin, 1980).

——. *An Association to Declare a History of the Preventative Staff Association* (Dublin, 1996).

Chapman, Richard A. and J.R. Greenaway. *The Dynamics of Administrative Reform* (London, 1980).

——. *Ethics in the British Civil Service* (London, 1988).

Colum, Padraic. *Arthur Griffith* (Dublin, 1959).

Comerford, R.V. *Inventing the Nation: Ireland* (London, 2003).

Connolly, S.J. (ed.) *Kingdoms United? Great Britain and Ireland Since 1500: Integration and Diversity* (Dublin, 1999).

Cronin, Mike and John M. Regan (eds) *Ireland: The Politics of Independence, 1922–49* (London, 2000).

Crossman, Virginia. *Politics, Law and Order in Nineteenth-Century Ireland* (Dublin, 1996).

Curran, Joseph M. *The Birth of the Irish Free State* (Alabama, 1980).

Daly, Mary E. *Industrial Development and Irish National Identity, 1922–1939* (New York, 1992).

——. *The Buffer State: The Historical Roots of the Department of the Environment* (Dublin, 1997).

——. *The First Department: A History of the Department of Agriculture* (Dublin, 2002).

——. 'The state in independent Ireland' in English and Townshend (eds) *The State*, pp. 66–94.

Davis, Richard. *Arthur Griffith and Non-violent Sinn Féin* (Dublin, 1974).

Dix, Bernard and Stephen Williams. *Serving the Public-Building the Union: The History of the National Union of Public Employees, Vol. One: The Forerunners 1889–1928* (London, 1987).

Doherty, Gabriel and Dermot Keogh (eds) *Michael Collins and the Making of the Irish State* (Cork, 1998).

Dunphy, Richard. 'The enigma of Fianna Fáil: party strategy, social classes and the politics of hegemony' in Cronin and Regan (eds) *Ireland: The Politics of Independence*, pp. 67–83.

English, Richard and Graham Walker (eds) *Unionism in Modern Ireland: New Perspectives on Politics and Culture* (London, 1996).

English, Richard and Charles Townshend (eds) *The State: Historical and Political Dimensions* (London, 1999).

Eyler, Audrey S. and Robert F. Garratt (eds) *The Uses of the Past: Essays on Irish Culture* (Dublin, 1988).

Fanning, Ronan. *The Irish Department of Finance 1922–58* (Dublin, 1978).

——. *Independent Ireland* (Dublin, 1983).

Fitzpatrick, David. *Politics and Irish Life 1913–1921: Provincial Experiences of War and Revolution* (Cork, 1977).

——. *The Two Irelands 1912–1939* (Oxford, 1998).

——. 'Ireland and the Empire' in Porter (ed.) *The Oxford History of the British Empire Volume III, The Nineteenth Century*, pp. 494–521.

Follis, Bryan A. *A State Under Siege: The Establishment of Northern Ireland, 1920–25* (Oxford, 1995).

Garvin, Tom. *The Evolution of Irish Nationalist Politics* (Dublin, 1981).

——. *1922: The Birth of Irish Democracy* (Dublin, 1996).

Gaughan, J. Anthony. *Thomas Johnson 1872–1963* (Dublin, 1980).

Green, S.J.D. and R.C. Whiting (eds) *The Boundaries of the State in Modern Britain* (Cambridge, 1996).

Harkness, D.W. *The Restless Dominion: The Irish Free State and the British Commonwealth of Nations, 1921–31* (London, 1969).

——. 'Ireland' in Winks (ed.) *Historiography*, pp. 114–33.

Hennessy, Peter. *Whitehall* (London, 1989).

Hill, J.R. (ed.) *A New History of Ireland VII, Ireland, 1921–84* (Oxford, 2003).

Hopkinson, Michael. *Green Against Green the Irish Civil War* (Dublin, 1988).

——. *The Irish War of Independence* (Dublin, 2002).

——. 'From Treaty to civil war, 1921–2' and 'Civil War and Aftermath, 1922–4' in Hill (ed.) *A New History of Ireland VII*, pp. 1–59.

Humphreys, B.V. *Clerical Unions in the Civil Service* (Oxford, 1958).

Hutchinson, John. *The Dynamics of Cultural Nationalism: The Gaelic Revival and the Creation of the Irish Nation State* (Dublin, 1987).

Jackson, Alvin. *Home Rule: An Irish History 1800–2000* (London, 2003).

Jenkins, Brian. 'The Chief Secretary' in Boyce and O'Day (eds) *Defenders of the Union*, pp. 39–64.

Johnson, D.S. and Liam Kennedy. 'The two economies in Ireland in the twentieth century' in Hill (ed.) *A New History of Ireland VII*, pp. 452–86.

Kendle, John. *Ireland and the Federal Solution: The Debate over the United Kingdom Constitution 1870–1921* (Kingstown and Montreal, 1989).

Kenny, Kevin (ed.) *Oxford History of the British Empire Companion Series, Ireland and the British Empire* (Oxford, 2004).

Kissane, Bill. *Explaining Irish Democracy* (Dublin, 2002).

Kostick, Conor. *Revolution in Ireland: Popular Militancy in Ireland 1917 to 1923* (London, 1996).

Kotosonouris, Mary. *Retreat from Revolution: The Dáil Courts 1920–24* (Dublin, 1994).

——. *The Winding Up of the Dáil Courts 1922–1925: An Obvious Duty* (Dublin, 2004).

Laffan, Michael. *The Resurrection of Ireland: The Sinn Féin Party, 1916–1923* (Cambridge, 1999).

Leonard, Jane. ' "The Twinge of Memory": Armistice Day and Remembrance Sunday in Dublin since 1919' in English and Walker (eds) *Unionism in Modern Ireland*, pp. 99–114.

McArdle, Dorothy. *The Irish Republic* (Dublin, 1937, facsimile edition New York, 1999).

McBride, Laurence W. *The Greening of Dublin Castle: The Transformation of Bureaucratic and Judicial Personnel in Ireland 1892–1922* (Washington D.C., 1991).

McCarthy, Andrew. 'Michael Collins: Minister for Finance 1919–22' in Doherty and Keogh (eds) *Michael Collins*, pp. 52–67.

McColgan, John. *British Policy and the Irish Administration 1920–22* (London, 1983).

McDowell, R.B. *The Irish Administration 1801–1914* (London, 1964).

——. *The Irish Convention 1917–18* (London, 1970).

——. 'Administration and the public services' in Vaughan (ed.) *A New History of Ireland VI, Ireland Under the Union*, pp. 571–605.

McElroy, Gerald. 'Employment of Catholics in the public service in Ireland, 1859–1921: a broad view' in O'Day (ed.) *Government and Institutions in the Post-1832 United Kingdom*, pp. 305–56.

McLeod, Roy (ed.) *Government and Expertise: Specialists, Administrators and Professionals, 1860–1919* (London, 1988).

McMahon, Deirdre. *Republicans and Imperialists: Anglo-Irish Relations in the 1930s* (New Haven, 1984).

——. 'Ireland and the Empire-Commonwealth, 1900–1948' in Brown (ed.) *The Oxford History of the British Empire Volume IV, The Twentieth Century*, pp. 138–62.

——. 'Ireland, the Empire, and the Commonwealth' in Kenny (ed.) *Ireland and the British Empire*, pp. 182–219.

—— (ed.) *The Moynihan Brothers in Peace and War 1909–1918: Their New Ireland* (Dublin, 2004).

Maguire, Martin. *'Servants to the Public': A History of the Local Government and Public Services Union 1901–1990* (Dublin, 1998).

Mansergh, Nicholas. *The Unresolved Question: The Anglo-Irish Settlement and its Undoing 1912–72* (New Haven, 1991).

Mitchell, Arthur. *Labour in Irish Politics 1890–1930: The Irish Labour Movement in an Age of Revolution* (Dublin, 1974).

——. *Revolutionary Government in Ireland: Dáil Éireann 1919–22* (Dublin, 1995).

Mortimer, James E. and Valerie A. Ellis. *A Professional Union: The Evolution of the Institution of Professional Civil Servants* (London, 1980).

Murphy, Brian P. *The Origins and Organisation of British Propaganda in Ireland, 1920* (Cork, 2006).

Murray, Patrick. *'Oracles of God': The Roman Catholic Church and Irish Politics, 1922–37* (Dublin, 2000).

Ó'Broin, Leon. *Dublin Castle and the 1916 Rising* (London, 1966).

——. *No Man's Man: A Biographical Memoir of Joseph Brennan Civil Servant and First Governor of the Central Bank* (Dublin, 1982).

O'Day, Alan (ed.) *Government and Institutions in the Post-1832 United Kingdom.* Studies in British History volume 34 (Manchester, 1995).

——. *Irish Home Rule 1867–1921* (Manchester, 1998).

O'Halpin, Eunan. *The Decline of the Union: British Government in Ireland 1892–1920* (Dublin, 1987).

——. *The Head of the Civil Service: A Study of Sir Warren Fisher* (London, 1989).

——. 'Politics and the State, 1922–32' in Hill (ed.) *A New History of Ireland VII*, pp. 86–127.

——. 'The politics of governance in the four countries of the United Kingdom, 1922–22' in Connolly (ed.) *Kingdoms United?*, pp. 239–48.

O'Sullivan, Donal. *The Irish Free State and Its Senate: A Study in Contemporary Politics* (London, 1940).

O'Toole, Barry. *Private Gain and Public Service: The Association of First Division Civil Servants* (London, 1989).

Parris, Henry. *Staff Relations in the Civil Service: Fifty Years of Whitleyism* (London, 1973).

Paseta, Senia. *Before the Revolution: Nationalism, Social Change and Ireland's Catholic Elite 1879–1922* (Cork, 1999).

Peden, G.C. *The Treasury and British Public Policy, 1906–1959* (London, 2000).

Pellew, Jill. *The Home Office 1848–1914: From Clerks to Bureaucrats* (Liverpool, 1982).

Perkin, Harold. *The Rise of Professional Society in England since 1880* (London, 1985).

Porter, Andrew (ed.) *The Oxford History of the British Empire Volume III, The Nineteenth Century* (Oxford, 1999).

Pugh, Martin. *State and Society: British Political and Social History 1870–1992* (London, 1994).

Regan, John M. *The Irish Counter-Revolution 1921–1936* (Dublin, 1999).

——. 'The politics of Utopia: party organisation, executive autonomy and the new administration' in Cronin and Regan (eds) *Ireland: The Politics of Independence*, pp. 32–66.

Roseveare, Henry. *The Treasury: The Evolution of a British Institution* (Oxford, 1969).

Schreuder, D.M. 'Ireland and the expertise of imperial administration' in McLeod (ed.) *Government and Expertise*, pp. 145–65.

Shannon, Catherine B. *Arthur J. Balfour and Ireland 1874–1922* (Washington D.C., 1988).

Sutherland, Gillian (ed.) *Studies in the Growth of Nineteenth-Century Government* (London, 1972).

Sweeney, Garry. *In Public Service: A History of the Public Services Executive Union 1890–1990* (Dublin, 1990).

Taylor, A.J.P. *English History 1914–1945* (London, 1965, revised edition 1975).

Tierney, Michael. *Eoin MacNeill Scholar and Man of Action 1867–1945*, ed. F.X. Martin (Dublin, 1980).

Titley, E.Brian. *Church, State and the Control of Schooling in Ireland 1900–1944* (Dublin, 1983).

Townshend, Charles. *Political Violence in Ireland: Government and Resistance since 1848* (Oxford, 1983).

——. 'A state of siege? The state and political violence' in Green and Whiting (eds) *The Boundaries of the State*, pp. 278–98.

——. 'Historiography: Telling the Irish Revolution' in Augusteijn (ed.) *The Irish Revolution 1913–1923*, pp. 1–17.

Valiulis, Maryann Gialanella. 'After the revolution: the formative years of Cumann na nGaedheal' in Eyler and Garratt (eds) *The Uses of the Past*, pp. 131–43.

Vaughan, W.E. (ed.) *A New History of Ireland VI, Ireland Under the Union, ii, 1870–1921* (Oxford, 1996).

Wheeler-Bennett, John W. *John Anderson Viscount Waverley* (London, 1962).

White, Terence de Vere. *Kevin O'Higgins* (Tralee, 1966).

Wigham, Eric. *From Humble Petition to Militant Action: A History of the Civil and Public Services Association 1903–1978* (London, 1980).

Winks, Robin W. (ed.) *The Oxford History of the British Empire Volume V, Historiography* (Oxford, 1999).

Wright, Maurice. *Treasury Control of the Civil Service 1854–1874* (Oxford, 1969).

Zimmeck, Meta. 'The "New Woman" in the machinery of government: a spanner in the works?' in McLeod (ed.) *Government and Expertise*, pp. 185–202.

Journal articles

Cooney, Rev. D.A. Levistone. 'An Englishman in Ireland: Arthur Dean Codling', *Dublin Historical Record*, 47:1 (Spring 1994), pp. 5–23.

Daly, Mary E. 'The formation of an Irish nationalist elite? Recruitment to the Irish civil service in the decades prior to independence 1870–1920', *Paedogogica Historica* (Belgium), 30:1 (1994), pp. 281–301.

Donnelly, Edna. 'The struggle for Whitleyism in the Northern Ireland civil service', *Saothar*, 10, pp. 12–18.

Hopkinson, Michael. 'The Craig-Collins pact of 1922: two attempted reforms of the Northern Ireland government', *Irish Historical Studies*, 27:106 (Nov. 1990), pp. 145–58.

Jalland, Patricia. 'Irish Home Rule finance: a neglected dimension of the Irish question, 1910–14', *Irish Historical Studies*, 23:91 (1983), pp. 233–53.

McColgan, John. 'Implementing the 1921 Treaty: Lionel Curtis and constitutional procedure', *Irish Historical Studies*, 20:79 (Mar. 1977), pp. 312–33.

Murphy, Richard. 'Walter Long and the making of the Government of Ireland Act, 1919–20', *Irish Historical Studies*, 25:92 (May 1986), pp. 82–96.

'Periscope' [G.C. Duggan]. 'The Last Days of Dublin Castle', *Blackwood's Magazine*, 212:1, 282 (Aug. 1922), pp. 137–90.

Seedorf, Martin F. 'Defending Reprisals: Sir Hamar Greenwood and the "Troubles", 1920–21', *Éire-Ireland*, 25:4 (Winter 1990), pp. 77–92.

Townshend, Charles. 'The meaning of Irish freedom: constitutionalism in the Irish Free State', *Transactions of the Royal Historical Society*, Sixth series, 8, pp. 45–70.

Reference works

Connolly, S.J. (ed.) *The Oxford Companion to Irish History* (Oxford, 1998).

Ford, P. and G. *Select List of Reports of Inquiries of the Irish Dáil and Senate 1922–72* (Dublin, 1974).

Fraser, W. Hamish. *A History of British Trade Unionism 1700–1998* (London, 1999).

Heuston, R.V.F. *Lives of the Lord Chancellors 1885–1940* (London, 1964).

Maltby, Arthur. *The Government of Northern Ireland 1922–1972: A Catalogue and Breviate of Parliamentary Papers* (Dublin, 1974).

Marsh, Arthur and Victoria Ryan. *Historical Directory of Trade Unions, Volume 1 Non-manual Unions* (London, 1980).

Matthew, H.C.G. and Brian Harrison (eds) *Oxford Dictionary of National Biography From the Earliest Times to the Year 2000* (Oxford, 2004).

Quekett, Sir Arthur S. *The Constitution of Northern Ireland: Part III: A Review of Operations Under the Government of Ireland Act, 1920* (Belfast, 1946).

RIA, Dictionary of Irish Biography database, Earlsfort Terrace, Dublin 2.

Thom's Directory.

Vaughan, W.E. and A.J. Fitzpatrick (eds) *Irish Historical Statistics: Population 1821–1971* (Dublin, 1978).

Walker, Brian M. (ed.) *Parliamentary Election Results in Ireland, 1801–1922* (Dublin, 1978).
—— (ed.) *Parliamentary Election Results in Ireland, 1918–92* (Dublin, 1992).
Ward-Perkins, Sarah (ed.) *Select Guide to Trade Union Records in Dublin, with Details of Unions Operating in Ireland to 1970* (Dublin, 1996).

Unpublished dissertations

Brennan, Niamh. 'Compensating southern Irish loyalists after the Anglo-Irish Treaty 1922–32' Ph.D. UCD, 1994.
Cumisky, Mark. 'An analysis of the Commission of Inquiry into the civil service 1932–35' M.A. UCD, 1989.
Feeney, Thomas M. 'Fianna Fáil and the civil service 1927–1937' M.A. UCD, 1999.
Flanagan, Kieran. 'The rise and fall of the Celtic Ineligible: competitive examinations for the Irish and Indian civil services in relation to the educational and occupational structure of Ireland 1853–1921' D.Phil. University of Sussex, 1997.
Lalor, Stephen. 'Policy-making in the Irish civil service: propriety and practice' Ph.D. University of Dublin, Trinity College, 1991.
Maguire, Martin. 'The civil service, the State and the Irish Revolution, 1886–1938' Ph.D. University of Dublin, Trinity College, 2005.

Index